Adobe® Camera Raw FOR
Digital Photographers ONLY

Rob Sheppard

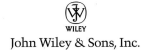

WILEY

John Wiley & Sons, Inc.

Adobe® Camera Raw for Digital Photographers Only

Published by
Wiley Publishing, Inc.
111 River Street

Hoboken, N.J. 07030
www.wiley.com

Copyright © 2005 by Wiley Publishing, Inc., Indianapolis, Indiana

Published by Wiley Publishing, Inc., Indianapolis, Indiana

Published simultaneously in Canada

Library of Congress Control Number: 2005926041

ISBN-13: 978-0-7645-9683-4

ISBN-10: 0-7645-9683-7

Manufactured in the United States of America

10 9 8 7 6 5 4 3 2 1

1K/SR/QZ/QV/IN

about the author

Rob Sheppard has had a long-time and nationally recognized commitment to helping photographers connect with digital imaging technology. He was one of the small group of people who started PCPhoto magazine nearly eight years ago to bring the digital world to photographers on their terms. He is the editor of PCPhoto as well as Outdoor Photographer magazines (second only to Popular Photography in circulation) and group editorial director of all Werner Publication photo magazines (PCPhoto, Outdoor Photographer and Digital Photo Pro).

He also writes a column in Outdoor Photographer called Digital Horizons and is the author of ten books related to photography. He teaches around the country, including workshops for the Palm Beach Photographic Centre, Santa Fe Photography and Digital Workshops, Digital Landscape Workshop Series and the Great American Photography Workshop group.

As a photographer, Rob worked for many years in Minnesota (before moving to Los Angeles), including doing work for the Minnesota Department of Transportation, Norwest Banks (now Wells Fargo), Pillsbury, 3M, General Mills, Lutheran Brotherhood, Ciba-Geigy, Anderson Windows, and others. His photography has been published in many magazines, ranging from National Geographic to The Farmer to, of course, Outdoor Photographer and PCPhoto.

credits

Acquisitions Editor

Michael Roney

Project Editor

Cricket Krengel

Technical Editor

Michael Guncheon

Copy Editor

Kim Heusel

Editorial Manager

Robyn Siesky

Vice President & Group Executive Publisher

Richard Swadley

Vice President & Publisher

Barry Pruett

Project Coordinator

Maridee Ennis

Graphics and Production Specialists

Denny Hager
Jennifer Heleine
Lynsey Osborn
Amanda Spagnuolo
Ron Terry

Quality Control Technicians

Charles Spencer

Proofreading and Indexing

Arielle Mennelle
Johanna VanHoose

This book is dedicated to the photographers who have struggled to master
new digital technologies, who have been determined to say,
"I can" and not, "I can't;" and to those photographers who love making images
and have found digital to offer an exciting realm of possibilities
to take their photography to new heights of
art and expression.

foreword

Digital imaging has revitalized photography as a whole. The number of SLR cameras being bought was declining into the early 1990's and fewer people were finding their creative selves in a darkroom. Along comes digital and all of a sudden photography is everywhere. My morning paper even had a discussion whether we should be shooting RAW or JPEG images with our digital cameras. I wonder how many general readers even knew what a RAW file was. But the interest is growing and the quality and ease of digital imaging is growing faster than I could have ever imagined. Ease is important to bring people to the medium, but quality will keep us interested and spur on our creative juices. RAW image capture is the foundation of quality digital images.

I keep hearing the comment "I'll fix it in Photoshop." The truth is that the better the image file is at the inception, the better the final presentation will be. RAW gives us the basis to get the most out of digital capture. Rob Sheppard's book will help those of us who want to get the most from our cameras without being caught up in a technical maze that will scare us off. He demystifies the RAW functions from first looking at a histogram on the back of the camera to making the adjustments in RAW conversion software when you get the image into the computer. Each step is a journey in optimizing your original vision, and he doesn't want you to lose any of the clarity that the process is capable of. Once you have read the chapters here you will not only know the how of capturing quality RAW images, but also the why so that you understand the process.

I have been involved with Outdoor Photographer and PCPhoto magazines from their first issues and saw a number of editors come and go. Rob Sheppard is the current editor of both and has brought to the magazines, and photography in general, a fresh and enthusiastic approach. These magazines are about teaching and the sharing of information. As you will see from this text, so is Rob.

George D. Lepp, The Lepp Institute of Digital Imaging

preface

There are a lot of books on Camera Raw or about Photoshop that include reference to Camera Raw. So I really had to ask myself why another? Sure, I could add another text to my resume, but why would any reader care? I really do like doing books that are helpful because I find digital photography to offer a lot for photographers, both in terms of very real benefits for better photography, and frankly, because it can be a lot of fun. I want to share that with other photographers.

Here it is, a book for photographers on Camera Raw. There are more technical books; I felt little need to duplicate them. There are more basic books; there was no point in making another book like them. I did feel that I could offer a unique perspective on how photographers can really benefit from RAW files and using Camera Raw. I have worked as a professional photographer, but more important, I have seen how photographers have adapted to and adopted digital technologies as I have worked on Outdoor Photographer and PCPhoto magazines. I know the pain that many went through — I got the letters that wanted our publisher to fire me for daring to suggest that digital might benefit photographers.

So I wanted to do a book that addressed photographers' needs and concerns, one that made photography as important as the technology. I have put together a series of ideas from the actual photography to the completion of working on an image in Photoshop that reflect what I have learned about how photographers can respond to and benefit from this technology. I truly want photographers to say, "I can!" and believe it. I do — I believe that every photographer who wants to master digital photography, to tame Photoshop, to benefit from RAW files can do it. As Henry Ford is quoted as saying, "If you think you can or you think you can't, you are probably right." I think you can!

One caution I do want to make. Photography is a creative endeavor. It cannot be controlled by formulas and recipes, whether written in this book or any other. The master of your images has to be you. Even if I say it is best to have a strong black in your photo, for example, and you don't like what that does to a particular image, don't do it! The idea of good or bad for your photos has to start with you. Anything written on these pages can only be a guideline because I cannot see your pictures. I will say that everything here is tested and does work, but I can never say whether something will work 100% of the time in your particular situation. Art and craft are just too subjective to allow that.

Most of the photos that are demonstrated in this book are available for download at www.robsheppard photos.com. These are full-size, RAW files, so you're going to need a broadband, high-speed connection to the Internet or else a lot of patience.

I hope you find these pages fun and informative. Don't be afraid to play with your photos to see how Camera Raw will work for you. It can work very well, indeed, but you'll get the most out of it and this book by trying lots of photos in Camera Raw.

A final note: if you buy a new digital camera, then try to use Camera Raw and it doesn't work, don't get frustrated. Because (as you'll see) Adobe has to back-engineer their software to work on new digital camera RAW files, you may have a version of Camera Raw that doesn't include your camera. You need to check Adobe's Web site for updates on Camera Raw that cover new cameras.

acknowledgments

There are a number of people who really helped me understand and adapt to new technologies early on so I could better explain them to photographers. Michael Guncheon taught me how technology can be used in service of visuals so that creativity and craft is not imprisoned by the tools. George Lepp was in there exploring digital photography at the same time as I was so we could share many ideas as we grew in knowledge. Bruce Dale gave me new perspectives on how digital could be used as an effective communications tool. The late Galen Rowell challenged me to prove the value of digital to photographers. Dan Steinhardt of Epson encouraged me to find a broader audience for showing how digital could help all photographers. Chuck Westfall and Rudy Winston of Canon have always freely answered any and every technical question I have had about digital technologies. Bill Fortney of Nikon has long been a great supporter of my efforts to help photographers better use digital photography. Steve Werner has constantly made me think how to best communicate about digital technologies to photographers. I also have to really thank all of the great folks who have been at my workshops and seminars who have taught me what photographers really need to know about digital photography and Photoshop.

I have to acknowledge my terrific parents who often wondered what the heck this photography business was all about when I was growing up but supported it anyway and now understand the beauty of it all. I have to especially thank my family, particularly my wife, Vicky, a terrific partner, who has had to put up with me writing on a laptop while between our daughter's soccer games, who tolerates me photographing all over the place saying I will just be a minute (but rarely am) then spending much time in my office working at the computer.

contents

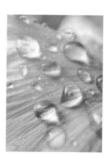

chapter 2 **Shoot Raw Right from the Start** 19

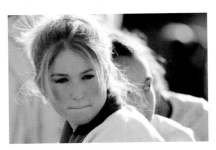

chapter 3 **The Histogram: The Key to Raw and Camera Raw** 35

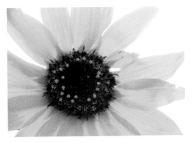

chapter **4 Color and Raw**   **55**

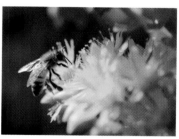

Part II Camera Raw Workflow   **71**

chapter **5 A Quick Look at Camera Raw Workflow**   **73**

chapter 6 **Workflow Applied**   95

chapter **7 Advanced Tonal Control   119**

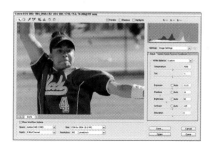

chapter **8 White Balance Decisions   133**

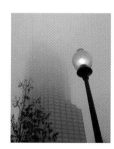

chapter **9 The Noise Problems No One Talks About 161**

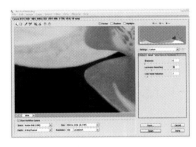

chapter **10 Tough Decisions 183**

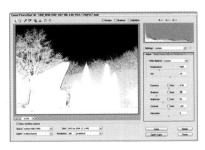

chapter **11 Compact Digital Camera Raw Processing** 211

chapter **12 Special Features of Camera Raw** 231

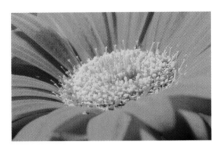

Part III Making Camera Raw Work Harder for You 263

chapter **13 Double Processing for Exposure 265**

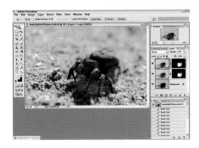

chapter **14 Post Camera Raw Processing   307**

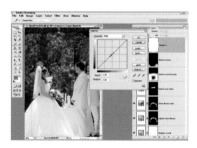

appendix **A Alternatives to Camera Raw** 327

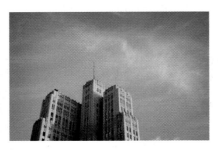

Pro Glossary 335

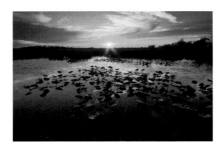

Index 339

CAPTURE WORKFLOW

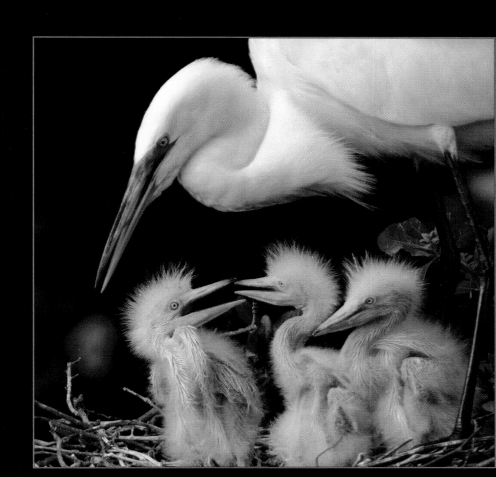

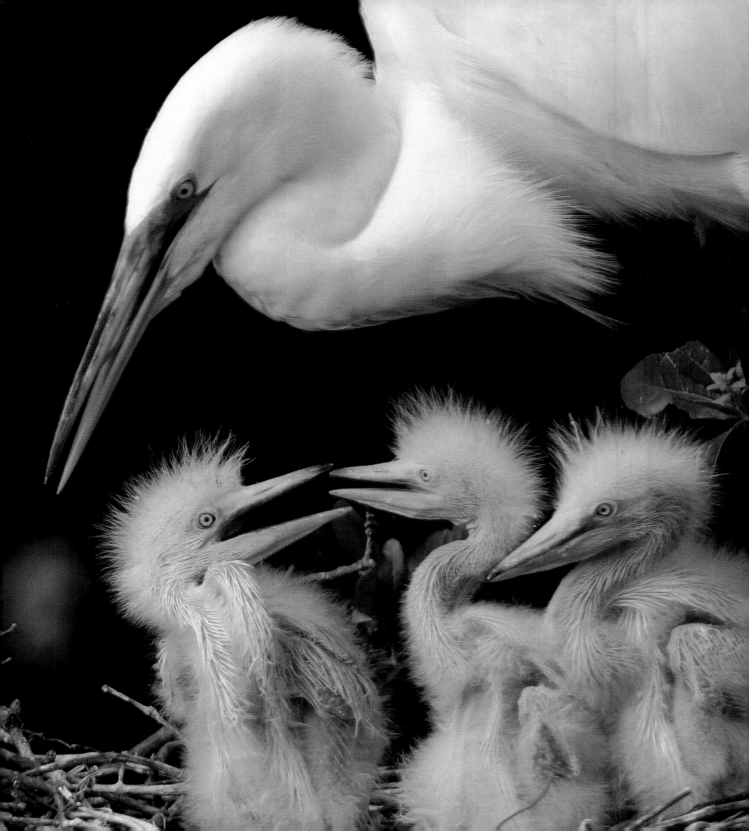

Chapter 1

WHAT ARE RAW FILES REALLY ABOUT?

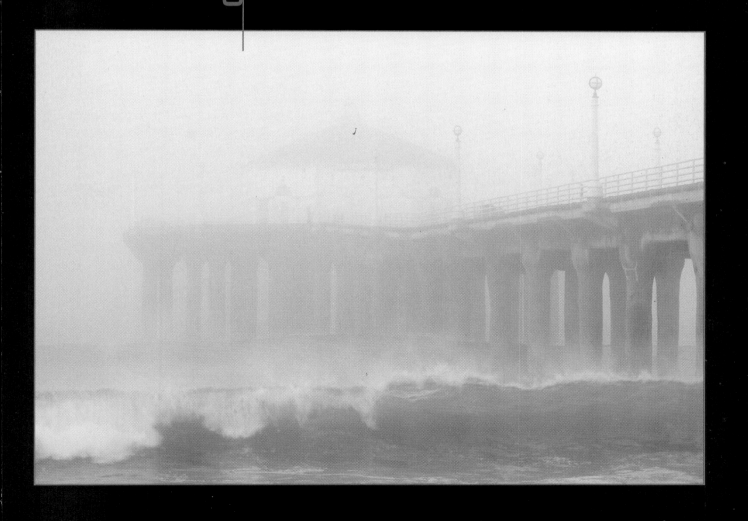

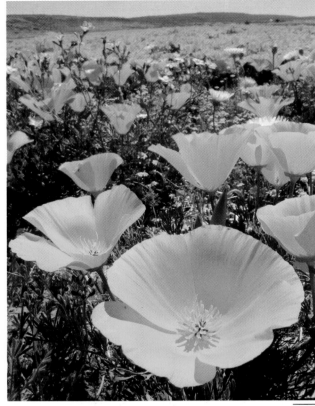

1-1

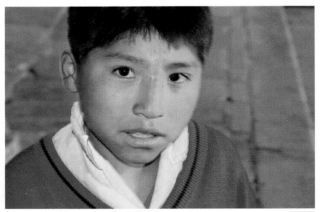

1-2

As a photographer, you need to understand something of what Raw is and is not in order to use Camera Raw file conversion software to its best. Raw is an important file format that offers a great deal of flexibility, but it is no magic bullet that can correct any problem with the original photography. The photo must be shot right from the start in order to get images like figure 1-1.

In addition, the debate of JPEG versus Raw often degenerates into one format being arbitrarily better than the other. Neither is automatically the best choice for a photographer. Raw offers much control, but also demands more in workflow. It is a terrific format for the thoughtful photographer and the careful worker who demands much from photography, but it has to be treated with a certain understanding of what it can and cannot do.

A RAW START

This is a tremendous time to be photographing. Cameras are better than ever and the whole digital transition has brought a new excitement to the craft. While film still has its uses, digital capture of images offers so many great advantages to the photographer that film is rapidly becoming a specialized way of shooting in everything from nature to people photography like figure 1-2.

One terrific innovation that came with digital photography is the Raw format, although technically, it is really the Raw formats. Every camera manufacturer has its own Raw format unique to its products. There are variations as the companies have made modifications, plus there can be unique formulations of the format for advanced compact cameras compared to digital SLRs. Confusing, true, but it only has to be if you want to know all the formats. Really, all you need to know is the one specific to your camera.

Adobe's DNG (digital negative) format has some potential to be a universal Raw format, though only time will tell about that.

HOW TO DEAL WITH RAW

This book also covers Raw as if it were one format. That's easy to do in a book specifically about Adobe's Camera Raw plug-in built into Photoshop CS and the program that comes with CS2 because Camera Raw treats all Raw formats equally well. It also deals with them seamlessly, without any need to think about format variations.

Raw is a unique format of image data that is unusable until opened and converted by a converter such as Camera Raw. Figure 1-3 shows a Raw file opened by Camera Raw (top) and the bottom image shows the file now converted. A Raw file holds a dense amount of information that you can mold and adjust in order to gain a high-quality image of your subject. You can also use other conversion programs, including those from the manufacturer, to achieve high-quality results, but other conversions require a more involved workflow because they do not have the integration with Photoshop that Camera Raw has.

A lot of confusing and misleading information on Raw has appeared in print and on the Internet — as well as much good and useful information. But misinformation, and even myths, about Raw can lead to unnecessary work in the computer in Camera Raw and could even yield results that might not truly enhance the image appropriate to your vision of the subject.

This book shows you how to use Camera Raw effectively and efficiently. You learn how Camera Raw works by seeing how it affects photographs and photography. I have a passion for helping photographers use new digital technologies to the photographer's benefit. I have no interest in working with computers unless they do something for the photographer, so every technical, computer-oriented aspect of Camera Raw stays grounded in terms the photographer understands.

THE JPEG VERSUS RAW DEBATE

Digital offers so many new things that the choices are confusing at times. And sometimes the choices are not perfectly clear, such as Raw and JPEG. In this book, you see why Raw is an important tool for photographers, and you get a lot of ideas on getting the most from it. My goal is to make Raw really work for the photographer by better use of Camera Raw.

Unfortunately, tech folks often push Raw without consideration as to how photographers like to work. Photographers sometimes use Raw even when it does not meet their needs but they feel guilty if they shoot JPEG. Well-meaning experts often promote one approach to digital, because that is how they do it, but unfortunately, they don't adequately explore alternatives as really used by photographers. Figure 1-4 shows a whole set of image files, both Raw and JPEG, and each file type has its advantages.

I've written a bit about JPEG and internal processing in cameras in a number of publications because there are photographers who are well suited to shooting that way. You need to understand a bit about using JPEG as well, because shooting 100 percent Raw is not effective nor

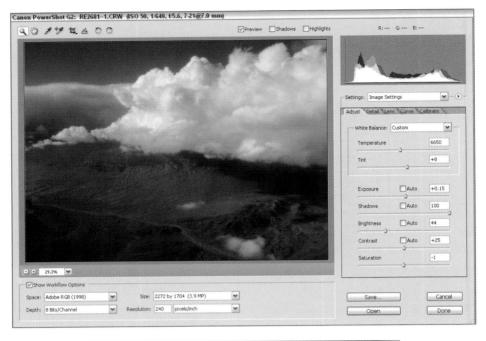

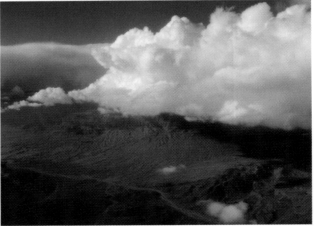

1-3

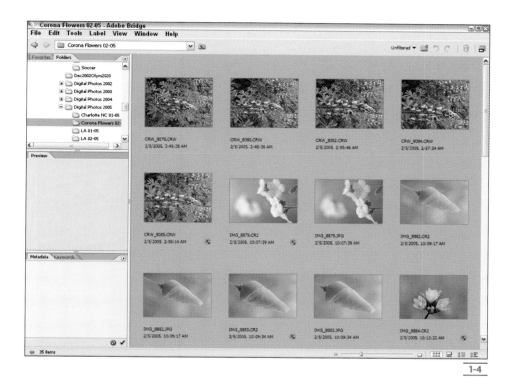

1-4

efficient for every photographer or in every situation. In spite of hype within the computer industry and from some Photoshop gurus, JPEG can be a high-quality format — it just is not as flexible and adaptable as Raw. In addition, for certain types of photography, JPEG has some advantages for any photographer.

WHY USE RAW?

Raw is an extremely valuable tool for the digital photographer, but not because of the math. Too many well-meaning computer types tell you it holds 16-bit compared to the 8-bit data of JPEG. Even if you don't know what that means, it sure sounds impressive. But photography is not about math unless you are a camera designer. Photography should be about the images. Yes, the higher bit depth in a Raw file can help, but that shouldn't be the

only reason for using a Raw file. There are some reasons that figure 1-5 does well coming from a Raw file, as you'll discover in this book, but if the photograph isn't adequate, no amount of Raw math will help it.

Raw is remarkable and important for its broad photographic capabilities. There are four key photographic reasons for photographers to use it:

> You gain some serious processing power for the image file.

> You need the increased flexibility that Raw offers.

> You have had problems due to the limitations that can come when shooting JPEG.

> You like working through an image to get the most from it.

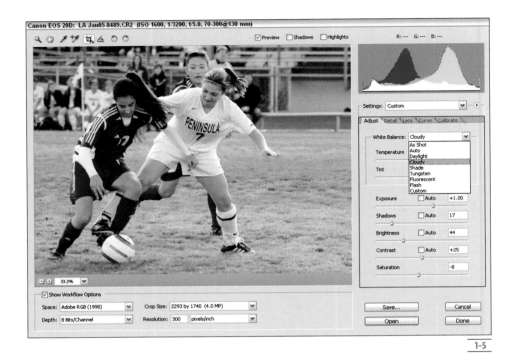

Canon EOS 20D: LA Jan05-8489.CR2 (ISO 1600, 1/3200, f/5.0, 70-300@130 mm)

1-5

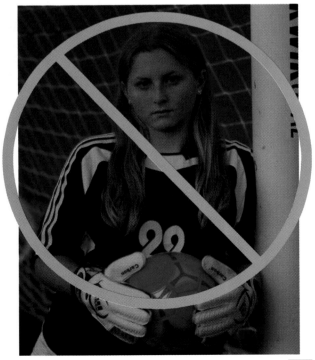

1-6

Once you do decide to work with Raw, it is very important to understand Raw requires a certain workflow to get the most out of it, a workflow you learn in this book.

UNDERSTANDING RAW

To use Raw to its best advantage, it helps to know a little about it. Raw cannot fix every lighting or exposure flaw in an image. Unfortunately, a mythology around Raw implies it can do this.

"Don't worry about exposure or color, you can fix it when you shoot and process in Raw!" That way of thinking is seductive, yet very dangerous. An image like that in figure 1-6 is a problem, no matter if shot in Raw or not.

Raw is:

> A type of image file with minimal change to the data coming from the sensor.

> Not unprocessed data as you may have read. The sensor creates analog information that must be processed into digital data.

> Image data that is converted from analog information with the A/D (analog/digital) converter and is a complex engineering challenge that luckily camera manufacturers have mastered for you.

> Affected by exposure as it is increased or decreased to the sensor's limits; the A/D converter will have problems dealing with those conditions.

RAW CAPABILITIES

A Raw file holds more tonal and color information than JPEG — 16-bit versus 8-bit — and offers a great deal of flexibility in how you can work the tones and color in an image. With Raw, you can frequently extract tones and details from the brightest and darkest areas of an image that have no detail in a JPEG file. This can be quite remarkable because it can at times allow you to show information in your photo that more closely resembles the real-world subject you want to preserve compared to what you find in a JPEG file or even from slide film. Figures 1-7 and 1-8 are two examples where the higher bit-depth of Raw helps. The light tonalities in the image can be difficult to manage if shot with JPEG.

Print film is a little different. Some people compared it to Raw, but there are significant differences between them. Both offer a great range of tones from black to white, but they handle the tones somewhat differently. That is neither

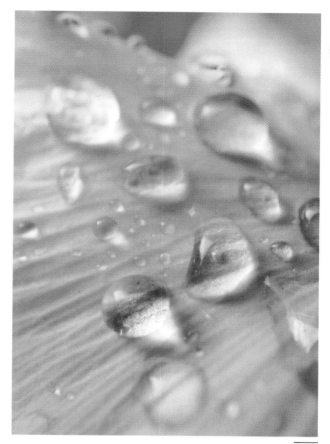

1-7

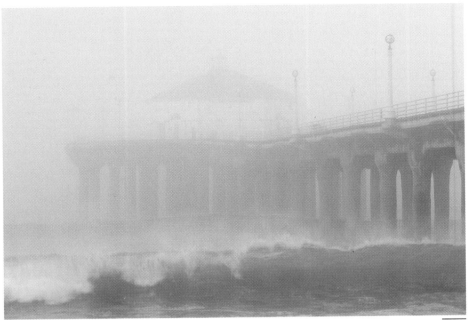

1-8

good nor bad; it is just different. Because this is a book about Camera Raw, you may wonder why this is mentioned at all. The reason: Some photographers, especially wedding photographers who have much to gain from Raw capabilities, traditionally shot print film and expected Raw (especially when it is compared directly to a film negative) to give them the same results. The two media require different approaches, so these photographers get frustrated and disparage Raw. It is not Raw's fault, but misplaced expectations. With proper use, shooting Raw can be easy and fun even for the traditional print-film shooter.

In addition, image tonal qualities can be maintained through greater adjustments done in Raw. You can creatively push and pull the tones of a photo to make it better do what you want when you use Raw. This format also allows you to enlarge digital images to a larger size with higher quality than if you enlarge them later in

Photoshop or using most other enlarging software. This allows the printing of very large prints from even small digital files that maintain superb quality.

DO NOT SHORTCHANGE RAW

The misconception that Raw is so adaptable that there is no need to worry about exposure or color shortchanges with Raw creates more work to do in the computer (which can be frustrating), and can result in less than the best tonalities and color. Consider these three things:

> Raw still comes from a sensor that has a finite range from black to white — if your exposure is outside of that range, nothing can bring it back, not even Raw.

> Because Raw comes from a digital translation of analog information given by the sensor (the A/D

converter mentioned previously), the old adage of garbage in, garbage out is definitely appropriate here.

> Raw does its best when it has good information coming from the sensor right from the start.

That's the key to any good picture, not just Raw: Shoot it right in the first place. If you have doubts, try another exposure. Following is a look at a few problems that come from poor photographic technique when shooting Raw.

These techniques are all covered in depth in the following chapters.

> **Underexposure:** This is the worst problem. If you underexpose a Raw file so that the tonal information is mostly in the dark areas, you do not have the best tonal or color information to work with (see figure 1-9). When you brighten those areas, you also bring out noise. Even the best of digital cameras shows annoying noise when an image is underexposed.

> **Overexposure:** Excess exposure causes tonal and color problems in later adjustments, again because of weaker colors and less tonal information. Added noise is not the problem here, but you get blocked-up, detail-less highlights that are a pain to deal with, as shown in figure 1-10.

> **White balance:** Shooting on auto white balance does not cause quality problems when shooting Raw, but it can create workflow issues later. If you set a specific white balance on your camera when using Raw, no pixels are harmed. But a tag of information about that setting goes with the file so that when it opens, it opens in the Raw converter with that white balance. You now have a specific point of reference to adjust from rather than the arbitrary and sometimes capricious white balance chosen by the camera as shown in figure 1-11.

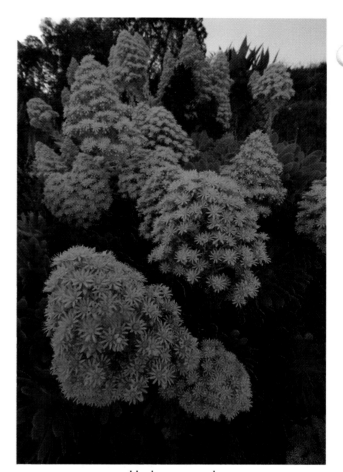

Underexposed

1-9

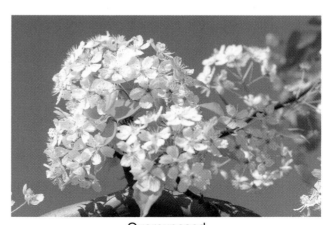

Overexposed

1-10

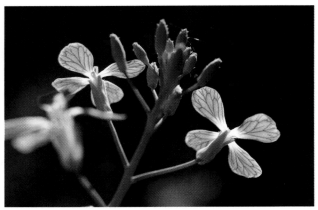

Wrong white balance

WHAT IS 16-BIT ALL ABOUT?

Image files work with data based on how many levels of gray tones exist between black and white for each of the three colors of digital: red, green, and blue (RGB). For a very long time, 8-bit data was the standard. It offers 256 distinct tones per color, for a total of over 16 million color values. This is a lot, obviously, and anyone who tells you that you can't get a quality image from 8-bit color is working by computer-ese and not photography. Photoshop is based on it, and digital camera files in JPEG use it. The use of 8-bit color does match how you see tonal and color information and can be perfectly capable of excellent results.

Problems with 8-bit occur if you have to stretch it a bit in processing as in figure 1-12. There is very little stretch room because as you stretch data, you lose steps of color and tonal information, resulting in problems with gradations of brightness and colors. If your exposure is off or

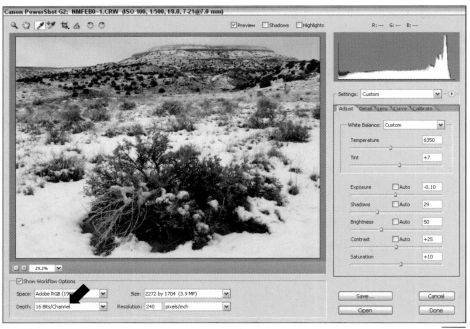

there are contrast issues in the image, you quickly run out of tonalities with which to adjust. In addition, the color of 16-bit expands the working range of colors and tones exponentially. You can do a lot of heavy-duty adjusting without the image suffering.

Technically, however, most digital cameras are only capable of capturing 12-bit color, which is still more than 8-bit. This 12-bit data is put into a 16-bit bucket, so to speak. At 12-bit, you get 4096 distinct tones per channel for a total of over 68 billion color values. That's 4,000 times 8-bit. That seems like a lot.

But remember, this is not expanding the capture range of the camera. For example, pure white and pure black still correspond to the limits of the sensor. What 16-bit (or the actual 12-bit of captured data) does is to give more steps in the working range, which increases the number of divisions between white and black, light and dark and provides a huge amount of flexibility and control over the tonality of the image. Frankly, you do not always need all those steps. Think of a staircase. The top and bottom stay put, but increasing the bit depth increases the number of steps

between the top and bottom. This can be critical if you try to push a heavy object up the stairs, but it makes no difference if you run up the stairs skipping steps anyway.

Those extra steps really do matter when you want to find more detail in certain parts of the range. You can stretch that portion without damage to the overall tonality of the image. In addition, those extra steps allow you to make major changes anywhere along the range of tones without causing problems to the tonalities and colors that are left (because there will be a lot of them left). Figure 1-13 is a converted but unprocessed Raw image to give you an idea of an image with lots of dark tones and a group of light tones, but much less in the midtone range. This is an ideal subject for Raw.

PRO TIP

Remember that your camera meter wants to create an image with middle gray tones. It makes a bright scene darker and a dark scene lighter. Metering something with middle gray tones in a scene can give you a good starting point for exposure. If you use auto exposure, also use the plus and minus exposure compensation control — plus for bright scenes, minus for dark scenes.

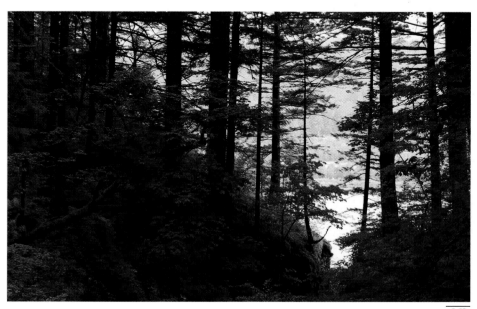

1-13

IS RAW THE PRO FORMAT?

Some photographers think that Raw is the format for professionals and JPEG is for amateurs. This can get you into trouble as it gives the wrong impression of what Raw does for you. Both formats are capable of the highest quality images.

Raw is a tremendous tool when you need it, but it is not for everyone, pro or amateur. If you arbitrarily use Raw at all times, and it doesn't always fit your needs, personality, or style, you may begin to find you have less enjoyment from working digitally. I don't shoot Raw all the time, and I have had many JPEG-shot photos published. Earlier in the digital changeover in photography, I shot mostly JPEG because the memory and processing overhead for Raw was a pain to deal with.

Raw no longer has that overhead problem. I like the rich capabilities of Raw, and now that large memory cards have come down in price, I use it extensively because it is such a valuable tool. Cameras that shoot Raw and JPEG at the same time are very useful but require larger memory cards as seen in figure 1-14. Raw is very important for digital photography, but it should never be used as an odd way of separating good photographers from bad. That comes from what's in the Raw or JPEG file, not from the file itself. Don't let any photo guru bully you into using either Raw or JPEG when they are not appropriate to your needs.

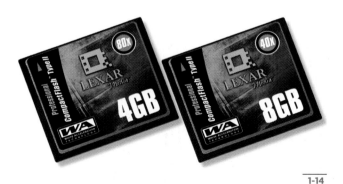

1-14

My goal in this book is to make Raw and Camera Raw work for you, to encourage you to have fun with photography through your use of this technology, and really enjoy digital photography. If you don't enjoy processing all of your photos in Raw, but feel guilty if you sometimes shoot JPEG, then that's sad to me. It means someone has made photography less fun for you. A push for Raw over anything else, regardless of the needs of the photographer, doesn't help anyone.

When should you shoot Raw or JPEG? Make that your own choice. Know that you can get top quality from both — figure 1-15 came from a JPEG file. Raw gives you a great deal of flexibility and control in processing your images to get the most from your subject, but it requires more work, more storage space, and slows down a camera. JPEG offers far less flexibility and control, but it is fast, requires less work, and needs less storage space.

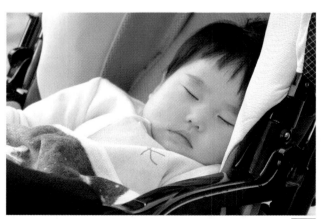

1-15

When JPEG Works

JPEG shot at the highest quality in modern digital cameras may look superior to Raw files when both are opened directly without much processing. The JPEG files often have a better tonal range (especially in the highlights) and deal with noise better. There is a good reason for this. All cameras today have advanced algorithms to convert the 12-bit data from the sensor to the 8-bit data that can be held in a JPEG file. Canon, for example, is well known for its quite remarkable DIGIC chip (in-camera processing circuitry), but all camera manufacturers include some amazing processing capabilities for the conversion of sensor data for JPEG files.

I know from talking to Canon that its DIGIC chip was designed to deal with highlights very, very well, and help minimize noise. The very powerful processing capabilities built into the camera (which essentially is processing the Raw file for you) can offer great results when shooting high-quality JPEG. It does require paying attention to how you work — exposure has to be done right, white balance chosen correctly, and so forth, as shown in this figure.

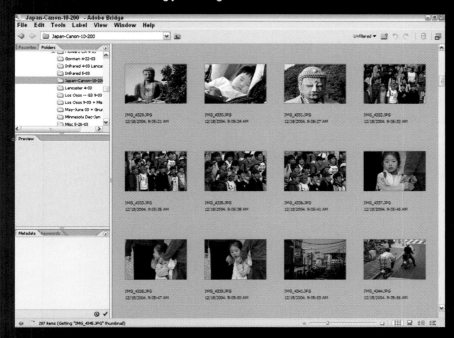

It is like having a little Raw expert doing conversions for you in the camera. That said, realize that this conversion is done automatically with no control by the photographer. Engineers working to maximize camera appeal and sales create algorithms that make good looking JPEG files, but if you want to have this control, then you must shoot Raw and make the conversions yourself. As you will see from this book, there are many benefits to doing exactly that, and you will be able to get files impossible to achieve from JPEG.

PROPRIETARY FORMATS

One of the big challenges for everyone shooting and processing Raw is that camera manufacturers have refused, so far, to create a common Raw format that everyone can use. Here are some of the extensions associated with varied Raw formats to give you an idea of how many there are (versions unique to certain camera types actually extend this list): Nikon (NEF), Canon (CRW, CR2), Kodak (DCR), Olympus (ORF), Minolta (MRW), Sony (SRF), Pentax (PEF), Fuji (RAF), and Leaf Valeo (MOS).

I have used multiple camera types from several manufacturers to take photos and find their Raw formats all equally good. Hard-core advocates of different brands, and especially their marketing folks, will tell you this isn't true and that there are significant differences worth really worrying about.

Not really. Yes, there are differences, but image quality is high among all of these competing variations of Raw. I challenge anyone to show me or anyone else a photograph that one could see differences that significantly affect the photographer's results. You cannot. Image differences among Raw images are far more affected by the sensors used by the cameras, A/D converters, lens quality, light, composition, and so forth. Different formats affect workflow, however, and some offer unique features that can be accessed only in a manufacturer's Raw conversion software.

Those features may or may not be worth it to you. They typically do little to affect actual image quality and more affect how you work on an image. On the other hand, the convenience of working with Camera Raw directly in Photoshop is huge. In addition, Camera Raw has been tweaked and refined to give you superb control over the photo.

DNG

Manufacturers do not really care about Adobe's challenges. However, having multiple and changing Raw formats presents a challenge to the consumer. First, you may have two cameras with two different Raw formats, even from the same manufacturer (especially if your cameras are very different in age). That can be a pain to deal with. Second, it is entirely possible that older Raw formats will be discontinued over time making them difficult to use in the future.

For these reasons, Adobe introduced the DNG or Digital Negative format. Adobe's engineers thought a lot about creating a consistent Raw format that can be used by all camera manufacturers and can be archived by photographers without fear that they cannot access it in the future as seen in the Save As dialog box in Camera Raw shown in figure 1-16. They even included flexibility in this format to allow camera manufacturers to add their own unique tweaks to it as well.

As of the writing of this book, camera manufacturers are not showing much interest in this format. In spite of

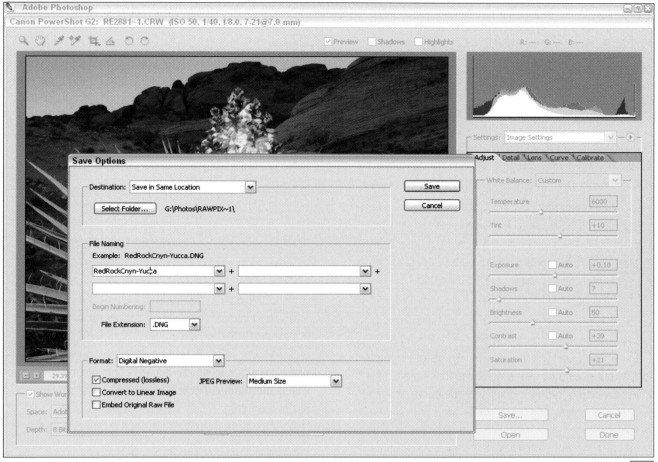

1-16

DNG's potential to reduce confusion and make it easier for the average photographer to work with Raw now and in the future, manufacturers show more interest in protecting their proprietary algorithms than in working together to help the photographer. Hopefully, this will change and there will be a consistent Raw format such as DNG that everyone can use.

For now, DNG is available for use in Photoshop CS2. Many photographers use it as an archiving format for Raw files because Adobe has said it is committed to preserving this format for use into the future for just that reason. You can save any Raw format file to a DNG file in Camera Raw in Photoshop CS2, or if you have Photoshop CS or 7, you can download a program from Adobe's Web site that can convert any Raw file to DNG.

When should I use Raw?

You can use Raw for any photography, but it should be used for how it can make a good photographer better, not as a substitute for craft. It is extremely valuable for the photographer who really likes to work his or her image, prodding tones and colors to get the most from the image file. Raw offers the greatest amount of tones and colors possible from your digital camera.

But it can also waste time and memory space if you shoot quickly and expect to make minimal changes to your images later. It can be a problem to use when you want to work fast, such as sports photography. Many cameras shoot faster and longer before having to stop to empty their buffers when shooting JPEG.

Raw is especially valuable when shooting scenes with a lot of important highlight or shadow detail. Its 16-bit capabilities allow much more adjustment of such tonalities than the 8-bit capacity of JPEG. This format is also very valuable when shooting under changing conditions where you cannot precisely control exposure or white balance. Its versatility and adaptability mean even problem images can often be brought under control.

Can any photographer use the DNG format?

Absolutely. It just is not being used by any of the major camera manufacturers, yet. What many photographers are doing is using this format as an archival Raw format. Some camera manufacturers have already changed their Raw formats in the relatively short history of digital cameras. Who knows if these variations of Raw will be supported in the future?

Because DNG is a broad-based format that any photographer can use at any time and can be made from any Raw format image, and because it is supported by Adobe, who does not make digital cameras, there is strong likelihood that this format will be around for a very long time. Adobe promises to always support it. This makes ideal to use for important images that you want to archive in a Raw format. You can convert any Raw file into the DNG format in free software available from Adobe (www.adobe.com) or in the Camera Raw converter.

What if I shoot in JPEG? Can it be changed to Raw?

In most cases, no. You have to set the camera to Raw (or Raw + JPEG) in order to have an image recorded in Raw. You cannot convert a JPEG file to a Raw file once the image is recorded, either.

However, Canon did something very unique with its advanced PowerShot cameras that would be well worth having on all digital cameras. In situations where JPEG works well and keeps the camera working faster, it is worth photographing simply in JPEG. But if you take a shot that begs to be recorded as Raw, for example, an image with a wide tonal range or lots of detail in bright areas, wouldn't it be great to instantly record in Raw? In these Canon cameras, you can do just that. As soon as the shot appears in the LCD for review, you simply press a button and you can record the image as a Raw file (on some cameras, you push the Function button; on others, the Flash button — check the manual).

Chapter 2

SHOOT RAW RIGHT FROM THE START

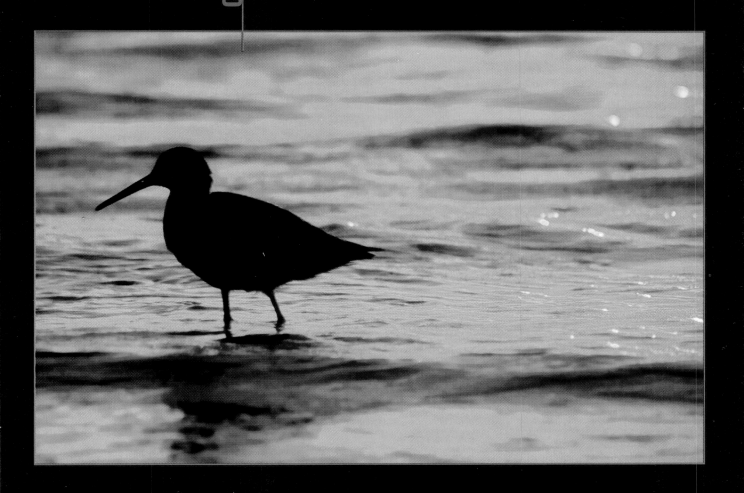

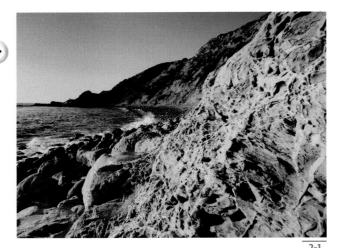

2-1

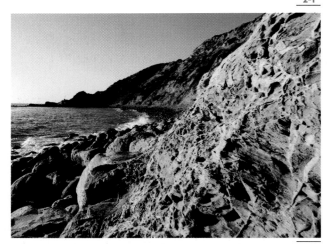

2-2

This is a book about Camera Raw, yet the first sections are not directly about the software at all. I really believe this is a key part of Camera Raw, however. To get the most out of Camera Raw, you must shoot Raw the best you can right from the start. Even though each camera manufacturer has its own Raw format, every Raw variation needs to be treated the same way, giving it the exposure, light, and color it needs to do its best. You may have heard that Raw is almost a magic technology that allows you to get great photos from any exposure. This is not true, and believing it can cause image quality problems.

It is interesting that as digital photography entered the photographic world, some photographers became frightened of it and said that craft would be lost. Craft, the control of the medium through skill, practice, and knowledge, has long been a core element of photography. The fear was that the computer would do everything by making decisions for the photographer and creating stunning photography without any work by the photographer. Even a rank beginner would now be able to match the practiced pro.

That last sentence actually appeared in a major news magazine about seven years ago. It is as much nonsense today as it was then. It represented, however, a fear about loss of craft because of automation.

In reality, there is technically less craft for photographers shooting slide film and using highly automated pro cameras than anything the computer can affect. There is still much craft involved in slide photography, but because little can be done to affect the image after the photo is shot, that is much less than what anyone who makes prints experiences. The need to know how to handle your medium is very important if you want to get consistently rich images like that in figure 2-1.

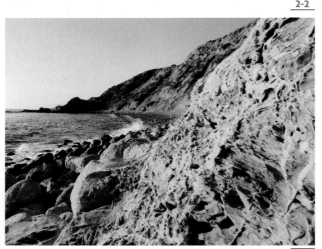

2-3

THE DIGITAL DARKROOM

Digital photography is far more like the traditional darkroom than anything else. It increases the number of points where the photographer can influence the image and offers new controls not possible before. It actually steps up the amount of craft that can go into an image. The use of Camera Raw is a craft if you want to use it in the most photographic way to get the most from your photos. It increases the opportunities for adjustment as you can see in figures 2-2 and 2-3, which are variations of figure 2-1.

Those increased opportunities concern people about the amount of work it takes. While it is true that shooting Raw requires more computer memory and time spent at the computer, like any craft it becomes easier to use with practice. And you get better at it, too. Once you start using Raw and Camera Raw in a consistent manner, you find it really can be done quickly and efficiently. And if you shoot Raw + JPEG, you can always go the JPEG route when you have to do a lot of images in a hurry.

An enjoyment and appreciation of craft is one of the joys of photography. Meet a challenging subject or scene head on in Raw, then master it in a great image, and you will feel satisfaction in that conquest, a conquest that comes from craft. Photography is part science and technology, part craft, and part art. The best images result when all of these work together.

PRO TIP

Viewing and editing Raw files can be a workflow challenge. The browser that comes with Photoshop or Photoshop Elements is very slow. It is okay for a visual cue as to what files to open and limited organizational work unless your computer is very fast and you have a lot of RAM. Browser programs like iView MediaPro (www.iviewmultimedia.com), IMatch (www.photools.com) and Extensis Portfolio (www.extensis.com) are much better suited to this task. They allow you to review, edit, tag, sort and manage your Raw as well as all other visual files, and do it quickly and efficiently.

UNDERSTANDING THE SENSOR

Because Raw files work with data that have had minimal processing coming from the processor, it can be helpful to understand a little about the sensor and how it works. This is not a technical discussion, but a quick overview of the key elements of a sensor as it affects the image in Raw. Figure 2-4 is an actual digital camera sensor used in the Canon EOS 1-Ds Mark II.

Here's how a sensor works:

> A sensor is a light-sensitive electronic device with multiple photosites (the pixels that make up the megapixels).

> Each photo site sees light coming from the lens and translates that light energy into electrical impulses (it does not actually create this electrical energy, but modifies currents passing through it).

> The sensor can deal with a certain range of light from dark to light so that too little light creates no reaction and too much light goes beyond its limits in handling brightness.

> The electrical charges are translated into digital data by the A/D converter as mentioned in Chapter 1.

> No detail can be captured if too much or too little light strikes the photosites — this is why exposure is so critical.

> The sensor also deals with color in a unique way. The color pattern in figure 2-5 is called a Bayer pattern, the most common way a sensor is set up to see color:

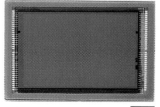

2-4

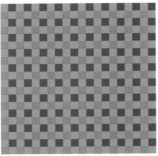

2-5

> The green sites measure both color and luminance (brightness), which is why they are more populous.

> All sites contribute to the resolution of the image. (A unique sensor from Foveon promised all colors for every sensor point, but it never caught on in the industry.)

If the camera processes the digital data for a JPEG file, the color of an image is built from the information provided by the unique combination of green-, red-, and blue-filtered photo sites. The file then has complete color data for each pixel. For a Raw file, this changes. Here, the data is saved with the color information separated by pixel and its original color. Then the colors are combined when the Raw file is opened and converted in the computer. This is why it is easy to make color corrections in Raw and why there is no quality change in doing it. The colors are actually reconstructed from the original data every time to make every color seen in an image like the willet against the sunset-lit water in figure 2-6.

> Each photo site only sees levels of brightness, not color.

> A pattern of colored filters (usually the Bayer pattern) is laid over the sensor, with green covering half of the photo sites, and red and blue split evenly among the rest.

> Each photo site then sees a color because it is seeing the brightness of light through a particular filter.

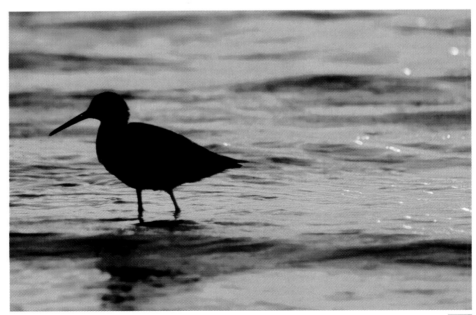

2-6

This does not, however, mean the Raw colors are always better — just more controlled. In most cases, that offers you a great deal of important flexibility. But the in-camera processing for JPEG sometimes makes certain colors look better, so pros often test both Raw and JPEG with varied colors to see when shooting Raw may be a limitation.

DEALING WITH LIMITATIONS

You can see from the way the sensor works that it has its limitations. The Raw file only holds what the sensor is able to register. The sensor is not a magic device that sees everything in the world so all that is needed is the Raw file, which would include all that detail, detail to be adjusted to as needed to match the world. If only that were true! The limitations of the camera sensor require that your photo technique matches the capabilities of that sensor in order to get the most from this technology. There is no sensor in the world that can handle the tonal range from the shadows to the backlit hair in figure 2-7, for example.

This also applies to color because color is constructed from the brightness of tones seen through color filters. It is important to realize that every photo site is affected by the limits of the sensor, regardless of the color filter in front of it. Proper exposure, then, also affects color.

This doesn't have to be hard. I am giving you ideas on how to use better technique with your digital camera, no matter what brand, so you can optimize your photography when shooting Raw and processing in Camera Raw. That said, I don't want you to tighten up and over worry your technique, either. No matter how much you try, there will be instances where your captured image is not optimum. But photography is a creative art, and you can always work with what you've got. If you like the shot, for whatever reason, but it isn't perfect or even shows tonal or color weaknesses, you can always just tell everyone you were being creative and meant to do it!

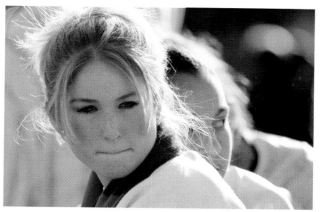

2-7

EXPOSURE — MORE THAN GETTING BRIGHTNESS CORRECT

Exposure is the key to getting the best from a Raw file. Because of the processing power of Camera Raw, you can often get a good-looking photograph from under- or overexposed images. However, that can cause problems with limitations with tonalities, weaker colors, increased noise, and less efficient workflow. I have consistently found that this is a misunderstood aspect of what a Raw file and Camera Raw can do.

It is important to understand what happens to an image file with exposure above or below the optimum for the sensor. The most obvious is that the sensor is now expected to perform its best with less than the best light on it. The middle range of tones in a sensor is very important to allow the sensor to best deal with a subject's tonal range and to capture the best colors. Under- or overexposed colors do not allow the sensor to capture the proper hues and saturations of a color. Underexposure like that seen in figure 2-8 is especially a problem.

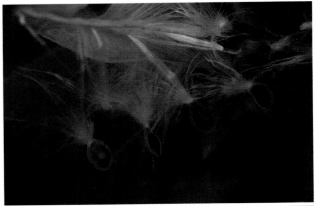
2-8

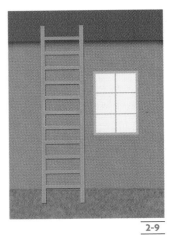
2-9

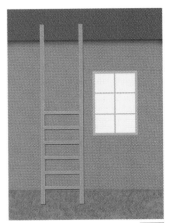
2-10

This is so important to understand that it is worth doing a mental exercise:

1. Think of a ladder.

2. Imagine that the ladder can only have rungs no closer than every six inches, like the illustration in figure 2-9. This obviously limits how many rungs will fit on the ladder.

3. Compare this vision of a ladder to a digital image — it, too, has finite steps between tones and colors. The six-inch restriction is like JPEG. As long as the ladder has rungs throughout, there is not a problem.

4. Now think of that ladder only with steps in the lower half (still six inches apart because the ladder can't have anything closer), as seen in figure 2-10.

5. Fix the ladder by moving the rungs. The problem is you can only use the rungs that are on the ladder (just like image capture, you only get a certain set of data), which is demonstrated in figure 2-11. Because you can allow more than six inches between rungs, you can get away with moving them farther apart, but to stretch them all the way to the top requires you to move them a couple of feet apart. This is a real problem with poor exposure with JPEG. There you have fewer original rungs (they might be a foot apart), so there is less to work with to stretch to the top.

6. With Raw, to continue the analogy, you have more rungs to work with. On the Raw ladder, you could think of them as showing up every three inches. Take the same reduction in height of rungs that was forced on the ladder of figure 2-10, and you can see in figure 2-12 that there are now more rungs available that can be used to fill in the gap at top. You don't need a rung every three inches, anyway, so you can move them easily and no one knows the difference. That is similar to what happens when processing a Raw file in Camera Raw.

7. Now suppose this Raw ladder was limited to having rungs at the bottom (see figure 2-13). This is like a strongly underexposed Raw file. Sure, they have the Raw spacing of three inches apart, but now there just aren't enough left to move to fill the ladder at the desired six inch rung interval. Stretching them now puts the rungs too far apart. A photo has less flexibility than the ladder example, too, because the tones of a photo change from top to bottom, unlike the rungs, which are identical. Exposure problems will force tones to be stretched separately in dark, light and middle tonalities and colors, and there simply won't be enough tones available for a quality image.

In a processed Raw file, this can mean you do not have the tones or colors you really want. The result means more work for you in Camera Raw. You move one control to where it looks good, but to correct problems, you need to make a counter-adjustment with another control. That may throw off color, so you need to make another counter-adjustment. Now, the first control looks off, so you have to go back and tweak it again. You may think you have it all right and make the conversion, then find the file still doesn't look right, so you have to start over again. It can become a major workflow problem.

FILTERS ARE STILL NECESSARY

A common, yet wrong, idea is that if you shoot digital, especially Raw, you no longer need filters. It is true that you really don't need filters to correct color, such as a special filter to shoot daylight film indoors and in order to get neutral color. You can get that with white balance either when shooting or when processing in Camera Raw.

But because the sensor has its limits, filters can help create better images from the start. The sensor can only capture what it sees, so if it can see a better image from the lens, it will capture that better image. Two important filters for digital photographers are the polarizing and graduated neutral density filters like that in figure 2-14.

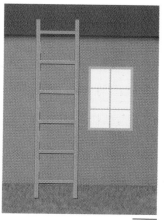

2-11

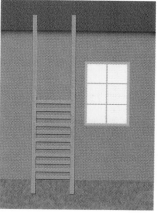

2-12

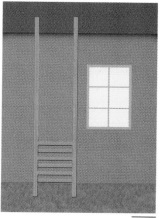

2-13

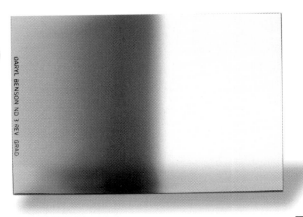

2-14

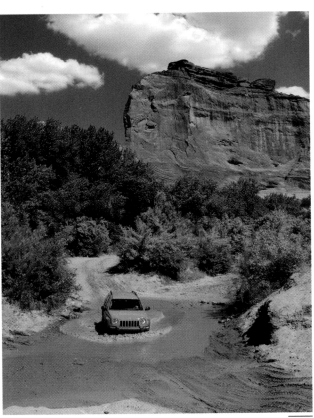 (side tab)

PRO TIP

When shooting with wide-angle lenses, a standard polarizer can be too thick and show up as dark corners to your photo. Look for special thin-mount polarizers for these lenses.

A polarizing filter changes how the scene is recorded and can make the digital workflow easier. This filter darkens skies when shooting at right angles to the sun (that is, when the sun is to the photographer's left or right). You rotate the filter for the desired effect. This can really make clouds pop. That can be somewhat mimicked in Photoshop, but why take the time if you do not have to because the image came into the program already adjusted in that way? A darker sky can also set certain subjects off better. Figure 2-15 is a good example of how a polarizing filter can darken the sky nicely.

This filter also removes reflections from glass, water, or other reflective surfaces. That is done at the time of shooting as this effect cannot be duplicated or mimicked in Photoshop. By removing diffuse sky reflections from shiny surfaces (such as leaves), color saturation is also increased (which can also be seen in figure 2-15), but in a very different way than can be controlled in the digital darkroom. Finally, a polarizer can reduce the effects of haze slightly, cutting its dulling effect.

The graduated neutral density filter (grad ND, grad, or split ND are other names) is a filter that is half clear and half gray in a specific neutral density amount. The line between the two is blended so it doesn't create a line in the image. The filter rotates to allow you to move the different parts over specific parts of the composition. Typically, you can

2-15

get one-, two-, and three-stop filters (sometimes labeled as 0.3x, 0.6x, and 0.9x). For digital photography, the two- and three-stop filters are most useful; the one-stop doesn't really do enough to make it worthwhile in the digital workflow. Figure 2-16 shows how a sunset is balanced with the lower part of the composition with a two-stop grad ND.

This filter allows you to bring tonalities of a scene into a range that is better captured by the camera sensor. It is commonly used by landscape and travel photographers to balance a bright sky with the ground. It can be used at any time to darken a bright area in a photograph to help the sensor better capture bright detail when the exposure for the darker areas may otherwise blow out the detail in that bright area. It is true that Raw and Camera Raw often allow you to pull out more detail in those areas, but that can also significantly increase your work time and adversely affect noise.

NOISE RAISES ITS UGLY HEAD

Modern digital cameras do quite well in controlling noise today, but problems with exposure and over processing of an image can bring noise back into the picture. Noise looks like the grain of film, like a fine pattern of sand across the image. Unlike film, however, it doesn't always appear in a consistent way over the whole image. It appears most strongly in the dark areas of a photo. Figure 2-18 is a detail of figure 2-17 so you can see what noise can do to an image.

Noise is strongly affected by the type and size of sensor in the camera, the ISO setting, and the exposure. You can't change your camera's sensor, but you can be aware of its capabilities. Smaller sensors are inherently more sensitive to noise. The smallest sensors in the otherwise very capable advanced compact digital cameras show noticeable noise very quickly when exposure is off or higher ISO settings are used. Certain larger cameras have a reputation for noise issues when used in definite ways at specific ISO settings. If you are aware of how your camera reacts to these conditions, you can shoot around them or just be willing to accept noise.

PRO TIP

Graduated neutral density filters come in screw-in, circular models and square or rectangular forms. The square and rectangular types fit special holders that allow you to shift the position of the filter, which allows you to better match its tonal change with your scene.

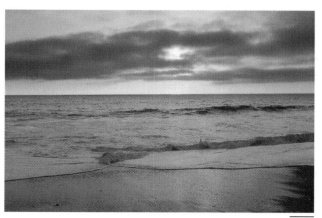

2-16

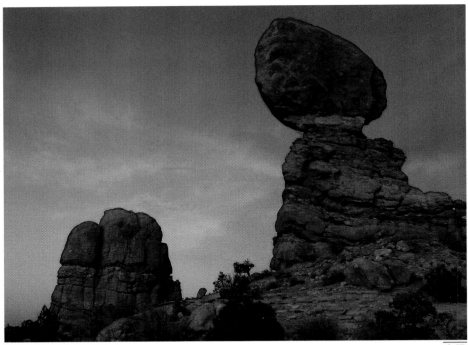

2-17

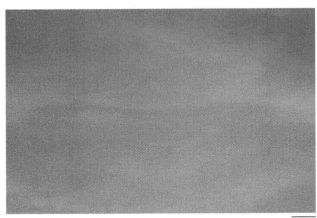

2-18

Underexposure can also add unwanted noise to any digital image. The reasons for this are related to how darker tones change with increases in light. A relatively small increase in the quantity of light at the sensor can raise the level of dark tones, yet will have little effect on bright tones. This continues in the computer — as dark areas are brightened, it takes much less intensity to make them lighter as compared to making light tones lighter. Because a big change in light to go from black to dark gray is not required, the intensity of light seen by the sensor by the time the lightest tones are reached is increased exponentially. Greater amounts of light can obscure noise. When you make a bright area brighter, you are dealing with solid tonal information. This changes at the low levels of tonality. As you make those areas brighter, you deal with much weaker tonal information and noise is quickly amplified along with the brightness values.

Here's a way you can check your camera to see its noise characteristics:

1. Take photographs of several subjects with medium tones, and severely underexpose them. This should be done by setting your exposure at least three f-stops below what your meter suggests. Try scenes with very different subjects that are typical of what you normally shoot. Include dark areas in the image as seen in figure 2-19.

2. Take one photograph that is exposed properly for your control, shown in figure 2-20.

3. Shoot Raw, auto white balance, and at a normal ISO setting of 100-200.

4. Take another set of exposures using the highest ISO setting of the camera.

5. Process your photos very simply in Raw. Don't worry about perfect pictures. Just adjust exposure and brightness settings until the images are somewhat normal in brightness (ignore the fact that there may be other issues of contrast and color).

6. Use Unsharp Mask to sharpen all photos to Amount 150, Radius 1, and Threshold 0 (this will show the noise).

7. Now compare all of the photos against the properly exposed control. You'll see the underexposed image looks harsher; its tonalities are not as smooth nor its colors as good as the properly exposed image, as can be seen even here when you compare figure 2-21 with the control, figure 2-20.

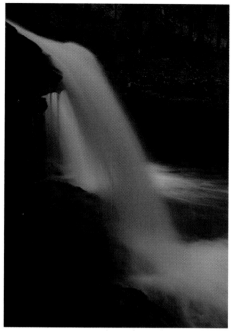

2-19

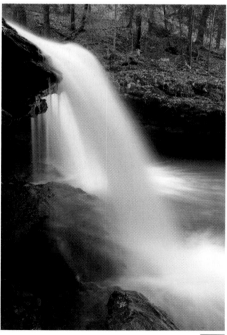

2-20

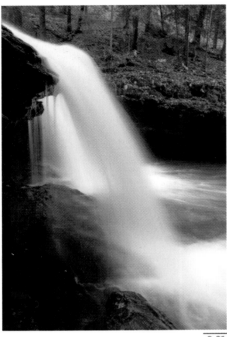

2-21

8. Enlarge the photos because they do not show all the differences when seen small. Look for the noise (which will be very obvious in many or even all parts of the photo). You can see a dramatic difference in the enlarged areas from the correctly exposed image (figure 2-22) and the underexposed shot (figure 2-23). Also compare the colors and tonalities to the control photo (figure 2-24 compared to figure 2-25). Admittedly these illustrations are extreme, but many photographers have never been advised of this effect at any exposures. These examples clearly demonstrate why proper exposure is so important.

It is true that you can limit the noise in the image to a degree in Camera Raw and in the noise reduction filter of Photoshop CS2. But this is not a simple fix, and there are trade-offs. The first is a workflow issue. You do not always see the noise until later in the process and you

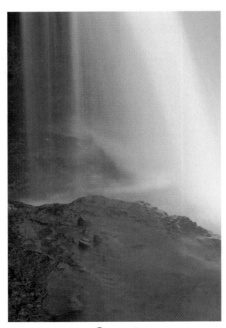

Correct

2-22

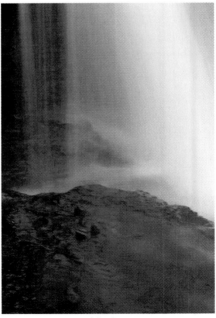

Under

2-23

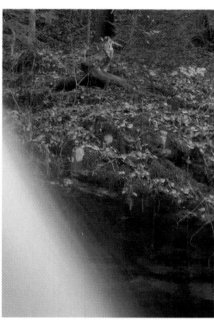

Correct

2-24

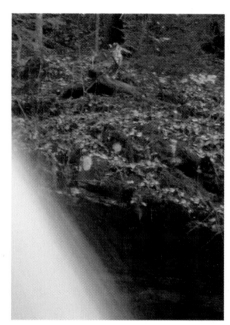

Under

2-25

have to reprocess the image. At the minimum, you have to spend more time tweaking the photo in Camera Raw.

The second is that removing noise can affect details in a photo. Noise, in a sense, is a very fine detail in an image. If you remove it, other fine details will be affected as well. So you have limits as to how far you can go without causing problems to the photo. Over processing a photo to control noise can make it look very unnatural with odd-looking tonal and color transitions. You are much better off minimizing noise to begin with by shooting at the right exposure and minimizing your use of higher ISO settings.

VARIATIONS AMONG CAMERAS

As you might have guessed from the noise discussion, cameras vary in the way their sensors work to capture an image, and this affects what can be done in Camera Raw in processing their images. The size of a sensor's photosites, for example, has a big effect on image quality, although to really see differences, you have to compare two sensors at the same level of technological development. New innovations in sensor manufacturing allow manufacturers to pack more photo sites into a given sensor size (which results in smaller photo sites, too), yet gain increased performance from them.

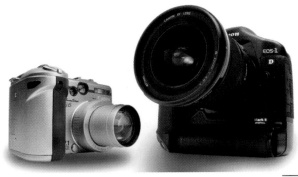

2-26

Still, you see a significant difference in image capabilities when comparing a digital SLR to an advanced compact digital camera (as seen in figure 2-26). The latter is capable of superb image quality and offers some unique photographic advantages; however, its small sensor size with higher megapixels limits its sensitivity and increases noise as described above. At low ISO settings, these cameras are capable of superb results and they have the facility to capture Raw files. This makes them very versatile, but also limited in range. A digital SLR's larger sensor with its corresponding larger photosites allows it to react to larger amounts of light, resulting in more sensitivity and greater response to light and color.

In addition, different sensor designs affect how a sensor sees light and color. Many photographers are surprised to discover that when they set two different camera models from the same manufacturer to the same white balance, for example, that the colors do not match (regardless of whether the white balance is set in the camera or in Camera Raw). This does not always happen — it depends totally on specific camera models but is frequently noticeable when comparing a newer camera to an older model.

In addition, the response to various colors can change from one camera's sensor to another's sensor (different camera models — they will be consistent in a given model) so that you cannot precisely match images shot with two camera models. This can be a challenge when you deal with skin tones as seen in figure 2-27. If you need images to match, you need to shoot with the same camera models at this point in digital camera development. Even the great flexibility of Raw and the power of Camera Raw do not allow you to otherwise easily match colors and tones. It can be a real workflow nightmare if you have not checked how your cameras match in color and tone.

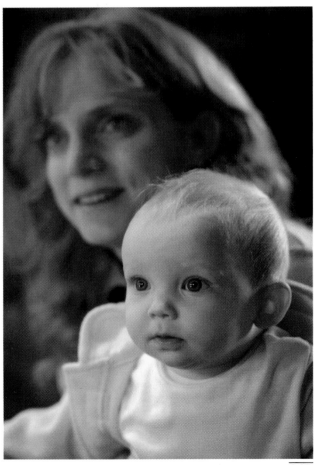

2-27

Q&A

How can I know how the sensor of my camera deals with noise?

This is not an easy question to answer because there are no noise standards in the industry and camera manufacturers do not like to deal with it except to say their cameras have low noise. There is no way to directly compare cameras short of shooting the same scene at the same exposure with them to get a subjective feel for the noise. No one has established a noise meter that allows you to objectively compare different cameras. Even to interpret some of the hard-core digital camera Web sites, you have to know who is doing the review and have access to a camera that has been reviewed by that person in order to have a point of reference.

There are some guidelines to keep in mind, however. One is sensor size — you usually find that if you compare cameras with the same megapixels that the one with the smaller physically sized sensor produces more noise. This is why an 8-megapixel compact digital camera produces more noise than an 8-megapixel digital SLR. In general, camera manufacturers are aware of the noise issue and are working very hard to create new cameras with less noise. The latest cameras will typically have better noise characteristics to their images than older models.

How can exposure affect color in Raw even if the exposure is within the range of my camera's sensor?

A sensor captures color differently depending on the intensity of the light hitting the sensor (which is affected by exposure). Consider this: If a color is greatly underexposed, it looks nearly black. There is very little chroma or color information in it. You can make it as light as you want, but it still looks more gray than colored. Increasing exposure increases the color information available for use, but when exposure is low, there is less chroma within the tonality. No matter how hard you try, you cannot get the full color that was originally there in the actual subject. The same thing happens when you expose colors near the bright end of the tonal range — colors wash out so that even if you darken the tone, you can never fully show the original color of the scene. This is why proper exposure is important for colors, too, so that you can get the richest and most accurate colors from your scene.

Will my sensor be damaged from too much light?

In the past, inappropriate exposure to light, especially the sun, could damage a camera. For example, if the lens of a rangefinder camera was left uncovered and pointed at the sun, a hole could be burned in the shutter, which would cause little overexposed spots to show up in every shot taken after that.

When sensors are manufactured, they are completely in the light. They aren't constantly photosensitive like film or a solar cell that creates electricity from the light. They become photosensitive when charged — when the proper current goes through the unit. When an excess of light hits the sensor, the pixels become overloaded and have to dump their charge. In a small, defined area of pixels, this causes something called blooming. The bright light forced overloaded pixels to interfere with surrounding pixels.

While this cannot put a hole in the sensor or cause spots to appear (which is what used to happen with video sensing devices), too much light on the sensor can affect its sensitivity over time. This is not so likely with a digital SLR because the exposure of the sensor is limited to the actual point of exposure, unlike compact digital cameras. Because the latter's sensors are live — always on when the camera is on — it is possible to give them too much light. This could happen if you shoot on manual for dimly lit situations then go into bright light without changing the exposure.

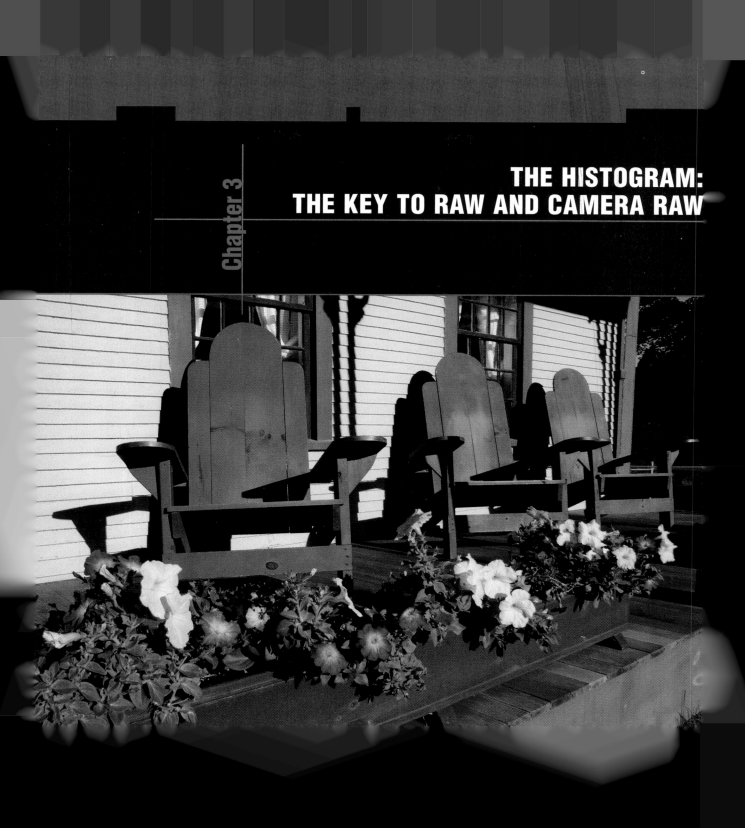

Chapter 3

THE HISTOGRAM:
THE KEY TO RAW AND CAMERA RAW

As you learned in Chapter 2, how you capture a digital image has a critical effect on the tones and colors. An important part of a digital camera that helps you evaluate your images to be sure you get the right exposure and more is the histogram. Very few places tell you much about it beyond the basics or give you the tools needed to interpret the histograms attached to your photos. In this chapter, you learn how to interpret a histogram to get the best images possible from your photos.

I want you to be able to use this important tool — not be intimidated by it — to gain the best possible image files for use in Camera Raw. This gives you both the best images and an efficient workflow. Realize, however,

that you will not always get perfect images or perfect histograms. The real world isn't like that. But if you understand how to use the histogram, you will consistently get quality image files that process nicely in Camera Raw.

This chapter includes a series of specific photographs with their histograms. The unprocessed images give an idea of how photos with certain histograms look coming straight from the camera. Look at them by evaluating the colors and tones and comparing that to the histograms. The actual subjects are not important.

WHAT IS THE HISTOGRAM?

The histogram sometimes looks a bit intimidating to photographers at first. The black-and-white chart of figure 3-2 is what you would see on a camera as it comes directly from the photograph, figure 3-1. It seems like it is a technical graph — and actually it is! But it is also a very visual way of seeing exposure in a very direct way.

A histogram is a graph of the number of pixels at certain brightness values, with dark values on the left and bright values on the right. You can read it without knowing any math, becoming an engineer, or even if graphing was not a highlight of your high school years (which it was not for most of us). You simply compare one side to another. If most of the hills and mountains are at the left, the photograph is very dark. If they are in the middle, the image will be average gray in tone. If they are at the right, the photo is light.

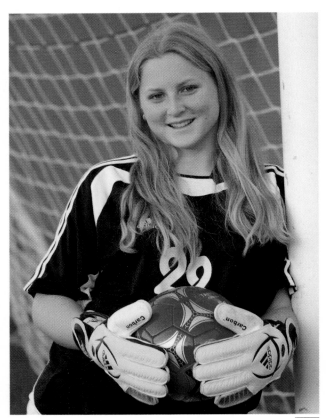

3-1

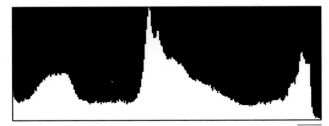

3-2

You can get into a detailed analysis of the math used to build a histogram, such as that seen in figure 3-3, but it cannot tell you much about the photo if you don't actually see it, and such an abstract analysis would be unlikely to help you understand exposure any better. It is enough to realize that the visual representation of exposure values in the histogram is available to you when shooting and when using Camera Raw to help you interpret the exposure of an image and then use that information to make a better exposure (or to correct it in Camera Raw).

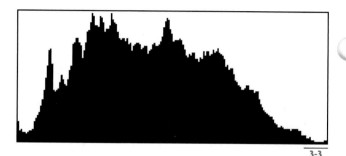
3-3

I'm going to help you analyze some photographs and their histograms to see what can be done to the various types of images. It is enough to get a visual feel of what histograms look like rather than getting too technically involved in all the details. The histogram can help ensure your exposures are good, and that your tonalities and colors are captured adequately.

BLINKING HIGHLIGHTS

Many modern cameras offer blinking highlights (blinkies) when you review a photo on the LCD. This is an indication of overexposure, which can be very helpful in letting you know where the problems in an image are located. It is not a perfect match to where the limits of the sensor's highlight capabilities are being reached, but it does offer a good approximation. This tool is simulated in figures 3-4 and 3-5 and also in figures 3-6 and 3-7.

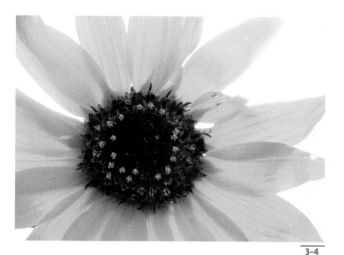
3-4

Blinking highlights are excellent to use with a histogram, but can be misleading if you rely on this feature alone. It tells you where there are highlight limitations, but it does not tell you anything about the balance of tones in an image. Some scenes need an exposure that blows out some highlights to pure white (which would activate the blinking highlights) in order to properly capture other tones and colors. If you simply go by the highlight warning and give the image less exposure, you may underexpose the rest of the scene, and not make the choice to let those highlight details go.

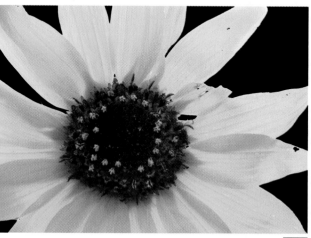
3-5

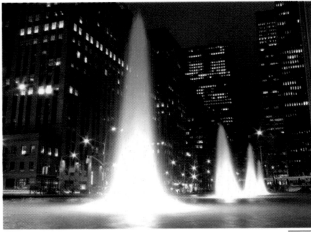

3-6

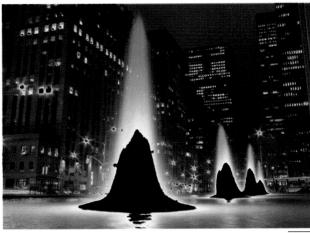

3-7

PRO TIP

Many digital cameras rotate vertical photos by default in the LCD. This reduces the size of your image, which can make it harder to see blinkies and other compositional details. I recommend turning the Autorotate function off so images display full size, though on their side. It is easy enough to rotate the camera or your head!

Or you may figure those highlights are unimportant for detail and ignore the warning. If the tonal range of the image is limited, you may have wasted those tones needlessly, but you are unable to know that from the blinking highlights. Use them as another indication of exposure, a warning for you to consider what is happening in the bright areas of the photo, but use them with the histogram.

READING THE HISTOGRAM WITHOUT BEING AN ENGINEER

As you work with digital photography, you eventually learn to read a histogram almost intuitively. At first, you may not remember which side is for the dark parts of the photo and which side is for the bright. Don't worry about that. The great thing about digital photography is that you can instantly see what a histogram does and at no cost. There are some advanced compact digital cameras with a live LCD (and sometimes an electronic viewfinder) that also have a live histogram. You can change exposure to make the scene lighter or darker and instantly see the effect on the histogram as seen in figures 3-8 and 3-9.

Because digital SLRs do not have live LCDs, there is an exercise that can help you understand how a histogram represents exposure. Here are the steps:

1. Put the camera on a tripod so there is no variation in tonalities due to composition changes.

2. Take three photographs of the same scene: one exposed correctly according to the meter, one overexposed by one full stop, one underexposed by a stop (less than a full stop shows differences, but it will not be as dramatic for learning purposes).

3. Set your playback display to show the histogram (unfortunately, all cameras do this differently, so no specific guidance can be given as to how to do this — you'll have to consult your manual).

4. Compare the three shots as demonstrated by figures 3-10, 3-11 and 3-12. You see that overall the hills of the histogram shift to the right with more exposure (as the scene gets lighter) and to the left with less exposure (shapes of the hills change, too).

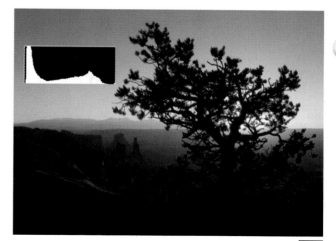

3-10

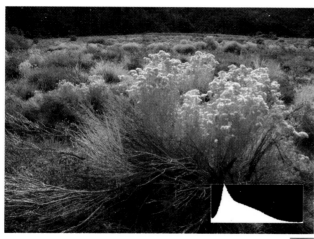

3-8

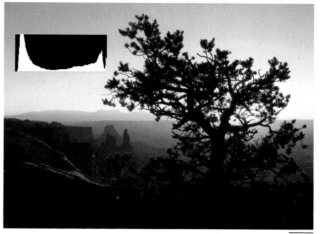

3-11

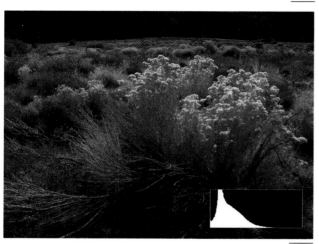

3-9

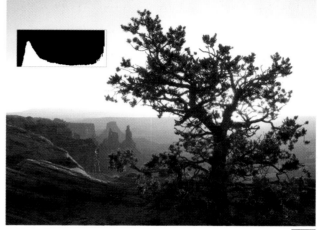

3-12

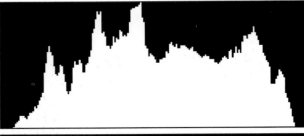

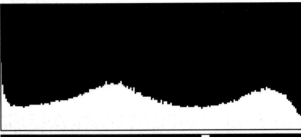

3-13

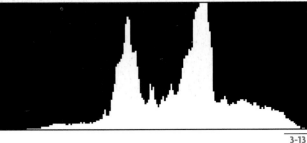

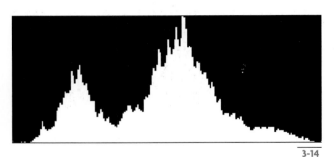

3-14

That's all there is to reading a histogram — data on the left is dark, data on the right is light. It is the interpretation of the histogram that is important to getting your exposure (and ultimately color and noise) right.

INTERPRETING THE HISTOGRAM

Remember these things about exposure with digital photography:

> Underexposure causes problems with noise and weaker colors.

> Overexposure causes problems with tonalities, detail, and color.

> Good exposure makes the most of your sensor's capabilities.

If you keep these ideas in mind, you quickly learn to interpret any histogram such as the range of graphs seen in figure 3-13. An underexposed image puts most of the histogram on the left side of the graph. An overexposed image puts the histogram hills to the right side of the graph.

If the histogram starts from the bottom of the graph at the left (no cliff), moves into a hill or a series of hills of brightness values, then drops down to the bottom of the graph before it hits the right (no cliff — small bits of graph may appear because of stray highlights, but that is not a cliff), then your sensor has captured a full range of tonalities as seen in figure 3-14, and Camera Raw allows you to bring out a great deal of detail in the image.

If parts of a scene are so overexposed or underexposed that no detail can be recorded by the sensor (tonalities are beyond its capabilities at that exposure), then the values are clipped. This means that detail is clipped from the image at that point and that the histogram is clipped off at either end (or both). The hills that make up the histogram's information are chopped off at the end when clipping occurs, such as seen in figure 3-15. The right side of this histogram looks like the hill has changed to a cliff.

If this cliff is at the right side, then highlights are clipped, meaning they lose detail. If the cliff is at the left, then shadows are clipped, also showing a loss of detail. By loss of detail, I mean total loss of detail at this point. No amount of work in Camera Raw can get that detail back as the sensor can capture no detail in areas with brightness values beyond the ends of the histogram.

HISTOGRAM PATTERNS

Several other patterns can occur with the histogram. Actually, the central part of the histogram can vary considerably, from one big hill to many smaller hills to tall spires, and so on. All that means is that there are varied brightness levels in your scene as displayed in one unique histogram in figure 3-16. Or if you have mostly middle tones with a few bright spots, you might find the histogram will have a moderate level through the center with some spikes at the right, for example. After observing a lot of histograms, you will actually be able to interpret how those hills and spikes relate to the image, but this is not critical for our use of Raw and Camera Raw.

What is important is how the brightness values play out on the graph compared to the dark and light sides. Clipping at the ends is a critical thing to look for, obviously, but you should also be careful of having all of your data at the left and a big gap to the right as seen in figure 3-17. If detail is important in those areas, then you need to alter your exposure to bring the histogram into the main part of the graph.

In general, you want to avoid a histogram with most of its data on the left side or with everything crunched to the right, even if nothing is clipped as seen in figure 3-18. If you can have the main part of the histogram running through the middle of the graph, you are using the optimum part of the sensor. You want to avoid having a big

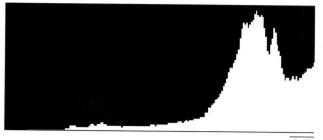

3-15

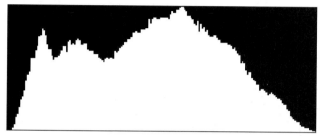

3-16

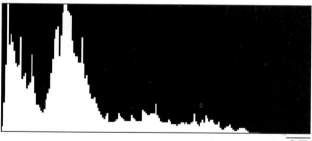

3-17

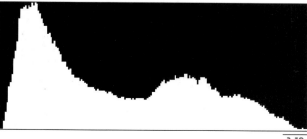

3-18

gap at the right or left going to the ends without data. That is a waste of the sensor's capabilities, can cause you more work in Camera Raw, and may weaken your scene's colors. This is especially true if there is a big gap on the right, which means too much of your data is in the dark areas.

But you may have a scene that is mostly light or dark. In that case, it is okay to have the histogram favoring the appropriate side. However, meters underexpose light scenes, putting data too much to the left, without exposure correction. And meters overexpose dark scenes, putting that data too much to the right, without correction, too. A slight bit of overexposure for dark scenes (as long as important highlights aren't lost) can give you benefits of lower noise (or even none at all), better tones to adjust and stronger dark colors because you can always darken the image later in Camera Raw or Photoshop. Underexposure for light scenes is more of a problem as correcting it can create noise and you might find it a lot of work to get the purity of light color that the scene needs.

You might also run into subjects with an overall good histogram but a big spike at the left or right as figure 3-19 shows. Usually, that isn't a big problem. There are scenes where a bright light or a very dark shadow appears, but need no details in them. In film, you often find certain subjects and scenes have tonalities beyond the range of the film and you just accept that. Sometimes you have to accept the same with Raw (although later in this book you learn some ways to deal with such issues and get a greater tonal range than you are used to seeing from film or digital photography).

Finally, you often see a small hill histogram that doesn't reach to either end of the graph as seen in figure 3-20. This simply shows that the scene doesn't have enough contrast to fully use the sensor. This is not a problem, and Camera Raw handles it beautifully. The only thing to be careful of is watching where the bulk of the data sits on the graph. If it is all in the dark side, this can cause you problems with noise and color and give you less than optimum tonal information. You are well suited to give the scene a little more exposure to move the histogram data to the right — remember, you can always darken it later. If all the data is at the right, it is good to give less exposure so that the histogram data moves more toward the middle to better use the sensor's capabilities for tonal and color capture.

CHECKING METER BIASES

A good exposure is critical to getting the most from your subject's tonalities and color as you have seen. In an ideal photographic world, all meters, in-camera or not, would give the same exposure for a given scene and the digital cameras' sensors would respond the same way to that exposure. Unfortunately, such a world does not exist, so you need to know a little about your camera or handheld meter's biases. I have found, for example, that some digital cameras consistently underexpose low-light scenes, and that must be accounted for when you shoot the photo.

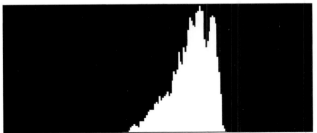

3-19

3-20

You can check your camera or other meter in this way:

1. Set your camera to automatic exposure, no exposure compensation, and auto white balance. Using a hand-held meter, you will obviously be shooting on manual exposure.

2. Photograph a series of scenes in different lights, such as those in figures 3-21 through 3-24. Photograph something in daylight, in the shade, indoors in bright light, indoors in dark light, and at night.

3. Now go through them all on your camera's LCD screen with the histogram turned on. See where the values end up on the histogram. If you see a bias toward the right or left side in certain situations, keep that in mind when you need to photograph and then compensate for it. Or at least keep it in mind as you check your exposure.

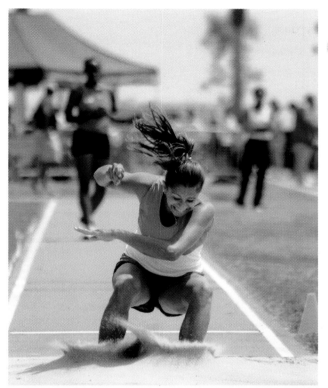

3-21

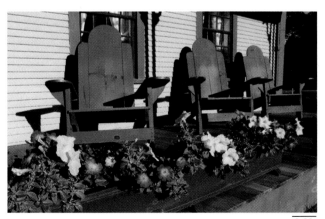

3-22

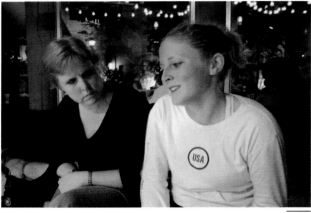

3-23

LOOKING AT HISTOGRAMS: EXAMPLES OF GOOD EXPOSURES

In this section, you take a look at actual photographs with their histograms to get an idea of how to examine and evaluate them. It is important to understand that you are seeing images that have had no adjustment; they come straight from the camera except for some sharpening. They do not all look as good as other photos in this book because most images will need some adjustments, especially for the black and white points in a scene. These examples start with good histograms with data from right to left and no clipping and move to more challenging situations so you can get a feel for what these scenes and their exposures mean.

GOOD EXPOSURES

A good exposure, obviously, is one that works for your subject. However, when you are shooting with digital capture, a good exposure is also one that respects the limits of the sensor. This section shows you a series of photographs with histograms to give you a better idea of the range of good exposures and what they mean to an image.

Perfect exposure with ideal histogram

Figure 3-25, wild lupines blooming along a Southern California highway, represents a perfect exposure with an ideal histogram, although most histograms (even good ones) do not look quite like this. Most of the tones and colors are captured by the optimum part of the sensor's range (the middle) and appear as a hill nearly centered on the histogram. That's key to this image because so many of the tones and colors of the actual scene have middle gray tonalities.

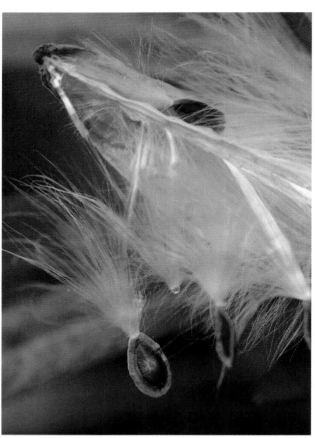

3-24

There is slight, unimportant clipping of blacks at the left and no significant clipping of whites at the right. This is critical for this photo as some very important bright tones are in the flowers (there actually is some minor clipping to the bright top left of the front flower cluster, but this will not affect much).

The whole graph is slightly to the left side, which is normal for an image with a lot of darker gray tones. If more exposure is used, the graph shifts to the right, but that also shifts the brightest tones to the right. That would likely cause highlight problems that cannot be easily fixed.

The picture may seem a little low in contrast (although the book printing process can affect this — it looks gray on the monitor), which is good for coming into Camera Raw with this look to the histogram. This range of full tonality in the sweet spot (the range of best sensitivity) of the sensor means you have a lot of flexibility with adjustments to change both tonality and color.

Nice range of tones from left to right

Figure 3-26, clouds viewed from an airplane, shows a nice range of tones from left to right with no clipping. I love photographing clouds. They come in such fantastic shapes and forms — they can make flying an exciting time to be photographing (it is true they can represent turbulence, too, but I still love to fly among them). They can be a challenge for the photographer because they can have a very large range of tones, especially in the light grays to white. Be careful not to clip important highlights when you photograph such subjects — pure white, burned-out areas of a cloud are not very attractive and cannot be fixed in Camera Raw.

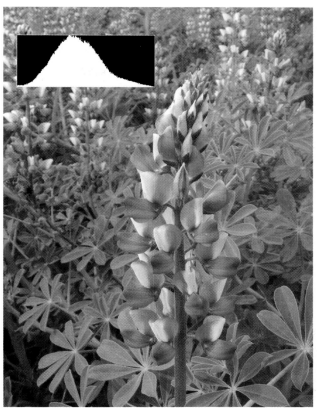

3-25

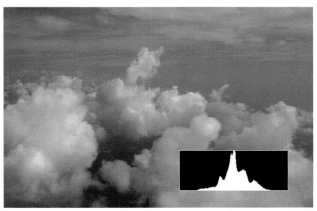

3-26

Notice that the histogram fits completely between the left and right sides. It actually drops to the bottom line well before either end. This means there is no pure black (total underexposure) or pure white (total overexposure) in the image file. Most of the tones are, however, toward the right side, which is good because it means you are working with light grays exposed as light grays.

The reason the exposure does not have pure black or white is because of haze in the air (and from the airplane window). Sometimes the air has a bit of moisture or dust in it that can create some haze. The result is only dark and light grays at the extremes in the photo. This is easily corrected in Camera Raw, as long as you are careful that the exposure gives you a histogram with most of its range through the middle.

Histogram has visual relationship to scene

Overall, figure 3-27, a photo of pond lilies and the pond environment is a good exposure. The left part of the graph slopes up from the bottom after the far-left side, but close to it, meaning no blacks are clipped and the exposure is not wasted with a big gap on one side of the histogram. The right part slopes down to the bottom before the far-right side, also close to it, meaning that no tones on this side, the light side, are clipped and there is no wasted gap of information. The tonality of the scene essentially

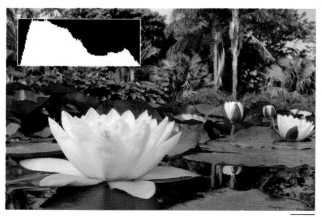

3-27

matches the capabilities of the sensor. You can readily adjust an image like this for more contrast and drama, but if you need the delicate details of highlights or shadows to work with, they are there.

This picture is interesting because you can really see how the tonalities in the scene relate to the histogram. The large hump on the left side is basically all the dark tones of water, leaves, and shadows. There is a depression of fewer tones, then another hump to the right. This represents the lilies and the sky. This is also very important to note. Those subtle bright tonalities of the petals of the flowers can really make a difference in this sort of subject. Imagine if the very light grays were not in the white of the flower in the foreground. That would make it lose texture and form.

It is true that you can deliberately underexpose this image in order to ensure all tonalities in the white flowers register on the sensor. However, this shoves the big block of dark tones to the left. Some are then clipped, which might not be important because this photo is really more about the whites. However, the dark greens would drift into tones with less color so the overall image would have less color tonalities and would not adjust into as rich an image that is possible from this exposure.

Light tones kept in range

Figure 3-28, a California poppy in the early morning, is almost an inverse of the previous shot of the pond lilies. California poppies do not open until fully exposed to the full sun for some time. On this day, light clouds were keeping the full sun away, which also left the dew on the closed flower. This is the reason for the photograph and influenced the exposure.

The image has two humps to the histogram like the pond lilies, but in this case, the left side is smaller than the right (representing how many pixels hold certain tones). The image is not as clearly defined as to the dark and light areas as the previous example, as the tonalities are more dispersed in the photo. Most of the darkness comes from the shadows on the flower itself, while the bright hump is from the large amount of light colors in the photo.

There is a slight bit of clipping at the right. This is mainly from the highlights on the dewdrops. You can give the image less exposure, but this causes a problem with the dark colors starting to move too close to the left side. A little bit of washed-out highlights on the top parts of the dewdrops actually gives them some sparkle and certainly does not hurt them. By keeping the exposure bright enough, all the important colors (the two humps in this case) are well within the range of the sensor. It is easy to bring up the blacks on the left side in Camera Raw or Photoshop without killing the dark colors or the bright tonalities of the image.

Black-and-white challenge

A really tough situation challenges us in figure 3-29 — black and white, not as accents, but as the major part of the uniforms of the two soccer players. Luckily, the clouds in the sky knock down the contrast of the light somewhat and keep the tonalities within the range of the sensor. This is a very difficult angle to shoot from on a bright, clear day because the shadows on the black uniform cover a large area, and the highlights on the white uniform are also big enough to create a problem if overexposed to no detail.

You see most of the exposure is to the left side of the histogram. In this case, that is quite important because of the low part of the graph that goes to the right side. Notice that while it is not as high as the peaks in the middle and at the left, it is also not at the bottom. This is no gap of data, but a range of very important whites to the uniform. If exposure headed to the right (which uncompensated automatic exposure may encourage), there would quickly start to be clipping on the white uniform. While it is true the action is what catches the eye, a glaring, detail-less white uniform is very distracting.

The peak in the center is mostly the dark parts of the white uniform, the skin tones, and the light grass. The peak at the left is mostly the dark uniform and the dark

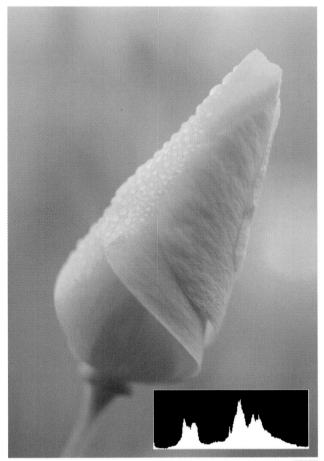

3-28

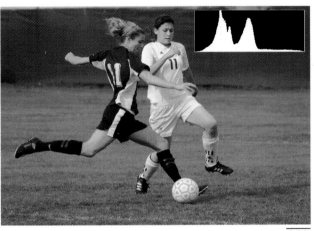

3-29

47

windscreen behind the players. Because the graph is not clipped at the left, the blacks are fully revealed. The unadjusted image seen here is too gray, for sure. There should be a solid black somewhere, but that can be easily adjusted in Camera Raw.

Restricted tonal range still needs good exposure

Foggy days can make for quite interesting photographs, as seen in figure 3-30. The tonalities of a scene can shift dramatically from the usual and allow you to capture quite striking images. The heavier the fog, the narrower the tonal range will be of the scene. Fogs, though, usually do not look their best if exposed to look too heavy. They need a bit of lightness to them, but you do not want to overexpose them, either. You find that most cameras set to autoexposure tend to underexpose a fog and give it an unneeded heaviness. If too dark, overall tonalities can be difficult to separate into the light tonalities expected in a photo of foggy conditions.

Probably the best thing to do is to get an exposure with the tonalities in the middle, but weighted toward the right side, as seen in this photo. The dark tones of the pier appear in the left hump of tonalities (which is nearly in the middle of the histogram) while the light grays of everything else appear in a hump to the right. This can easily be stretched in the 16-bit space of Raw when adjustments are made in Camera Raw.

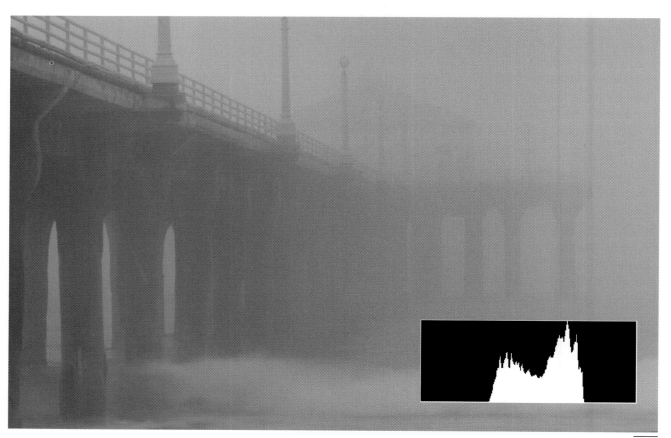

3-30

Some people have the mistaken idea that a restricted tonality like this is just as easy to photograph with JPEG. While you might be able to get an acceptable image in that format with a bit of work, you are likely to find some tonal breaks or banding in the gentle fog tones because of the problems with stretching 8-bit tonality. This image needs to have some stretching of tones when adjusted in order to look right — how much is very subjective, because you will not have a pure white or black in such a photo.

BAD EXPOSURES

Any exposure that doesn't work with what the photographer expects from a scene is a bad exposure. In the digital realm, a bad exposure is one that causes problems in the processing of the image. The mythology around Raw files is that they cannot have a bad exposure. This is definitely not true, as you will see.

Poor exposure causes color problems

Figure 3-31 is another soccer example that allows some direct comparisons to the previous soccer shot, figure 3-29. This one is poorly exposed. Because this is a Raw file, Camera Raw allows you to fix the image so it looks much better than this, but it still will not match a better exposure. The light was changing this day due to a storm that had moved through, and I did not compensate for the change when this action happened. As a sports image, the action is more important than subtle color details, so the final image from this file may be okay, but it will take a bit of work.

Images like this can be a pain to deal with. Because the tones and colors are compressed to the left, dark side of the histogram, there is less chroma or color information in them. This means a lot of adjustments, then readjustments are required to balance brightness and color just to

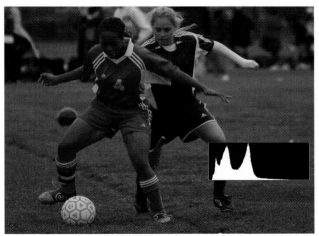

3-31

make the image look normal, let alone good. You can see there is a significant gap of data to the right, meaning that the best part of the sensor has not been used. It also means exposure can be increased easily without clipping the white tones. Actually, in this photo, the white on the girl's sleeve doesn't need a lot of detail, so if it clips, it is not a problem.

In addition, noise hides in tones compressed into the dark tonalities, ready to reveal itself as the tones are expanded. Because action shots are often taken with higher ISO settings (this one was), more noise is there anyway, so any adjustment to make these dark tones and colors just look normal also makes noise more visible.

Bad light causes exposure problems

Figure 3-32 probably should not have been taken. As a photographer, you always have the choice of not shooting a photo if conditions are bad for the subject. Truthfully, I deliberately shot this photo to push the camera a bit and

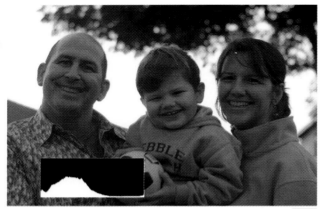

3-32

see how it handles a very extreme tonal range. I thought the out-of-focus tree was enough to knock down the brightness of the sky, but it was just too bright all over.

What happened is that the bright light behind the subjects overpowers the dark areas. The exposure is low because of the influence of the bright light — you immediately notice the histogram has a big hump on the left side of the graph. This means all of the important skin tones of the people are recorded as dark grays, not the best place for light skin. More exposure can bring those tones up, but that causes another problem. Flare begins to cause problems around the man — more exposure makes this worse. In addition, there are very bright skin tones (especially at the edges of the man's head) that wash out with more exposure.

This composition is a no-win situation for the photographer. You cannot expose it properly to capture the skin tones without other problems and there is no way even Camera Raw can make this a shot with great color and tonality. This is an example of a shot in which you just need to move to find a different angle. Otherwise, you can

spend a lot of time in Camera Raw just making it look okay rather than enhancing an already good shot you might have gotten by choosing another angle.

Poor exposure causes background problems

Figure 3-33 is another shot that probably should not have been taken (or at least erased right away). The flowers are properly exposed with good middle tones and color that can be adjusted quite nicely.

But check out that background! You can see the histogram is weighted toward the right side. It is severely clipped, too, while pixel brightness levels continue to rise as they hit the right edge. The background will never have good color or tonality. It just is not in the image file. No matter what you do or how much work you do in Camera Raw, this image will always look bad because the background will have big, ugly, and distracting areas of no-color, washed-out white.

If you must keep this shot, however, you must process the image twice in Camera Raw for the flowers first and then to get whatever you can from the background. You combine the two images in Photoshop to get the best tonalities from each. The final image still looks washed out, so you add a layer and paint in colors to the background. That is the only way you can do anything with this photo. You do not have to check every exposure with the histogram, but it helps to look regularly to be sure your photo technique is consistent.

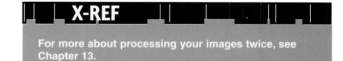

X-REF

For more about processing your images twice, see Chapter 13.

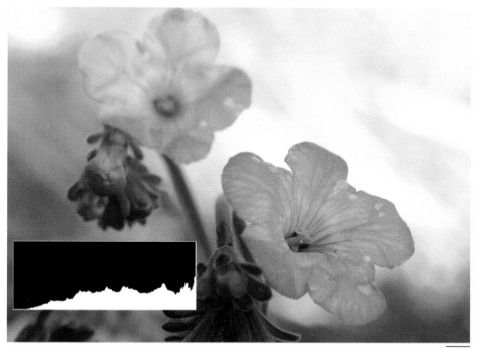

3-33

Exposure for shadows washes out highlights

Figure 3-34 is a very old structure that is part of the seventeenth-century Nijo Castle in Kyoto, Japan. The building has some fascinating detail that needs enough exposure to really show it off. You see immediately, however, that this exposure causes major problems. It shows a great example of this type of scene, but the exposure itself is actually part of a bracketed series. I knew the scene had too much range for the sensor, so I shot for the cloud and buildings separately with the idea of merging these shots together later. The use of a graduated neutral density filter would have improved the results, but because I had none as well as no tripod, this idea did not work.

But you can see what happens to the histogram and the image with such an exposure. If you look at the left side, you can see that the important dark tones are recorded perfectly. There is no clipping and there is a significant hump of data on that side. The right side of the histogram is where the big problems appear. A very bright hump of

bright tonalities climbs at the right, only to be abruptly cut off. Basically, the beautiful bright tones that make a cloud so attractive are totally gone. This cloud is a mere shell of itself.

There is nothing that can be done in Photoshop to fix such an image. Important bright highlights like the cloud must be exposed correctly, even if they are not such a big area in the photograph.

PRO TIP

As mentioned, a graduated neutral density filter would have helped immensely and is an important tool for anyone who regularly photographs outdoors. A graduated neutral density filter is clear on one half and a dark neutral gray on the other. The two areas blend at the middle in a nice gradation of tone. The clear area goes over the dark part of the scene — like the buildings in this image — and the dark area goes over the bright part, the cloud (this doesn't always perfectly match the scene, but it helps). This brings such tonalities into a range that the sensor can capture.

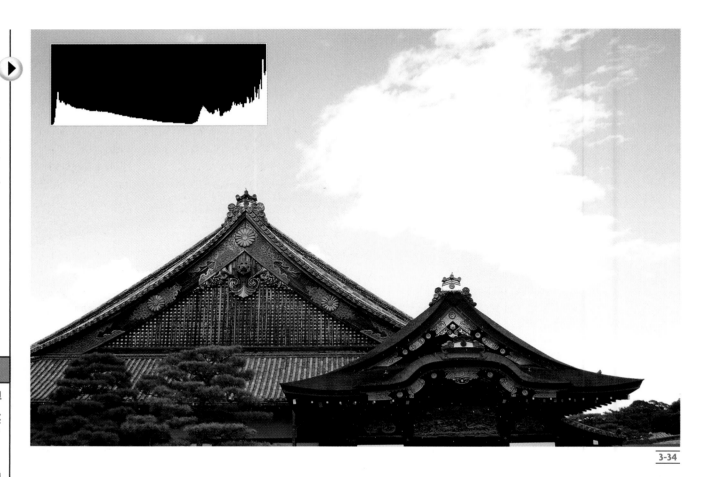

3-34

Q&A

I've seen some camera histograms that have additional vertical lines in them as part of the graph. How important are they?

Those lines simply give a clear visual indication as to how the captured tones are spread throughout the tonal range from black to white. Usually, they represent thirds of that range so you can more easily see where the bulk of the histogram or its humps sit (these lines vary in number and placement, but they are all designed to help you read the histogram better and more quickly). If the histogram hump is all in the left third of the graph, you know you may have problems depending on the subject. The same thing applies for the right third. If important midtone tonalities are represented in the middle section of the graph, then you know your exposure is probably good.

Some histograms have colors for the graph. How can I use them?

The colored lines represent the color channels of your digital image file — Red, Green, and Blue (RGB) — and tell you how exposure affects them. But reading them depends partly on the type of photography you do. For photojournalists, nature photographers, wedding photographers, and others who are basically dealing with natural light conditions occasionally enhanced with flash, the separate colors are of little value. If you can turn them off, you find the histogram easier to read and understand for these types of photography.

However, when there are critical issues with color, which can be an important concern for some types of advertising photography, the color histogram can provide additional information worth considering. It is harder to read than the standard histogram because the different colors interact. On a broad view, you can think of it as showing where the colors are in terms of tonalities in the photograph and if you are getting such bright colors that there is clipping in a channel.

Because the color channels of the histogram are not heavily used by most photographers in-camera, I am not going to go into much more analysis of them. I know very few photographers who pay much attention to them while shooting. If you want to experiment and see what happens with exposure, try photographing subjects with one solid red, green, or blue color, such as a blue ball. Change exposure and see how the colored histogram changes with these broad colors.

Can I measure how the sensor of a particular camera deals with tonal range?

To a degree, yes, although to get a really precise measurement, you need some sophisticated measuring tools. Here's one simple way to do this that works, but it isn't particularly for the really technical minded:

1. Set up a subject with a few different, but flat tones. A good way to do this is to put a middle gray, white, and flat black together (you can buy special exposure cards with this combination).

2. Set your camera to JPEG, not Raw, for this test. JPEG processes the file simply and the camera tries to get the most tonal range possible. Because it has trouble with the very bright and very dark when shooting directly to JPEG, the camera will give you an image that is more easily examined to see tonal range extremes. It gives you information that provides a good feel for the tonal range possible from your camera.

3. Shoot the combination cards after metering (in manual exposure) on the middle gray card. Then gradually add half a stop of exposure for about five f-stops (this puts you out of range for the sensor). Repeat this by decreasing exposure by half a stop at a time, also for about five f-stops.

4. Examine your images on your computer screen (do not use the camera monitor). Find the exposure in the dark sequence when the middle gray turns to black and matches the tone of the black area.

5. Find the exposure in the light sequence when the middle gray turns to white and matches the tone of the black area.

6. Check the metadata for each of these exposures and compare them. See how many f-stops of exposure difference there is between these shots and you have a rough idea of the sensor range.

Chapter 4

COLOR AND RAW

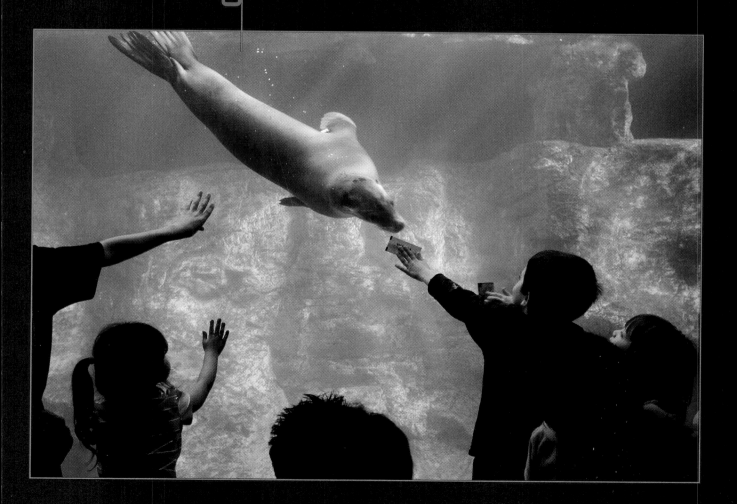

Color is a critical issue for photographers today because color photography is the most common use of the medium. From snapshots to advertisements, color is the main way we see photographs as seen in figure 4-1. Black-and-white photography is still important, but now it is seen as something special and unique — not the everyday photography it used to be when Life magazine was at its peak.

Raw has not often been discussed in terms of color quality. Mostly, color has been connected to Raw when talking white balance and the ability to change color in Camera Raw. This, I believe, is unfortunate. Colors in a photo are strongly affected by exposure, as discussed in Chapter 3. In addition, exposure and white balance choices you make while shooting will affect your workflow, and sometimes in a rather negative way. You may be able to get the colors you want, but at a cost of time and even frustration while working on the images.

This doesn't have to be a big burden for the photographer. Understanding how you can deal with color in Raw and then keeping a few simple things in mind can be all you need. There is no question that shooting digital, and especially Raw, requires learning some new tools, and it elevates the level of craft in photography. But like any craft, work with it a while and it becomes second nature. Cameras used to be very simple, but over the years many great features were added which did complicate their operation. Still, photographers learned the controls and gained new possibilities from them. The same is doable with digital.

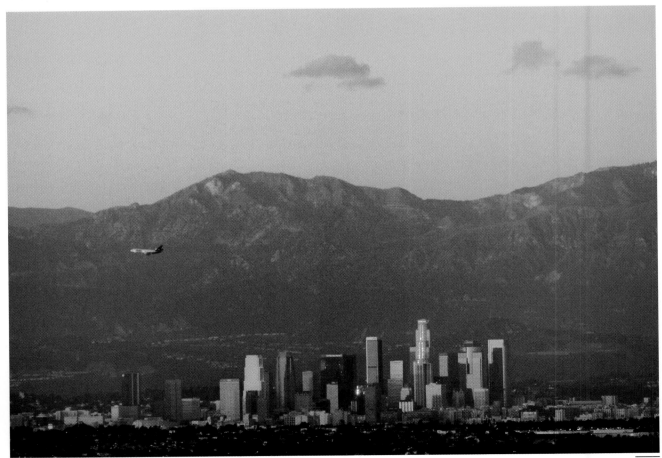

4-1

GOOD RAW IS GOOD COLOR

In Chapter 3, you learned why good exposure is important to getting the best results from Raw. I touched on color, although the example there of good and bad exposure was not selected to show off color. The photos in figures 4-2 and 4-3 are. The changes between these shots are strong — figure 4-2 is purposefully overexposed while figure 4-3 is deliberately underexposed. This allows you to see such changes easily so you can recognize what can happen. You can compare your own camera's results by doing a similar exercise:

1. Set your camera to a specific ISO and white-balance setting (do not use auto white balance). Shoot in Raw.

2. Shoot two exposures of a subject with a wide range of color tonalities and good gradations between them. Shoot one exposure correct for the subject (following the histogram guidelines of Chapter 3) and one that is 1 to 1.5 f-stops underexposed.

3. Process the good exposure in Camera Raw just enough to make it look good. Process the other exposure to match, as best you can, the good exposure.

4. Compare the two images.

The only difference between the way these two images were shot is exposure. Adjusting the good exposure in Camera Raw takes very little time. Adjusting poor exposure can easily triple the time involved. Even then, you may discover the color does not match (it is not as obvious on the printed page of a book compared to a print you make from an inkjet printer). There is a color shift with certain colors, but there shouldn't be. This is strictly because of the underexposure and the processing necessary to compensate.

You also notice in figures 4-4 and 4-5, the magnified versions of figures 4-2 and 4-3, that the underexposed image's color is harsher and has poorer tonal gradations. This also is not as obvious on a printed page in a book as on an image produced by your own printer. Some of the

problems with color also occur due to a distinct increase in noise that, even when it does not show up directly at a given image size, still affects the tonal gradations of the image. Good exposure always means you have the best chance of getting the best color.

PRO TIP

Remember to regularly check your histogram. You do not need to do it after every shot — that is a waste of time. But check it as the light changes or after a long set of shots to be sure your exposures are giving you what you will need.

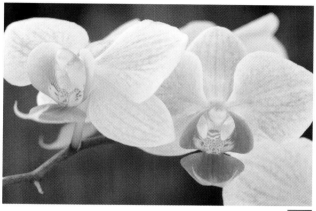

4-2

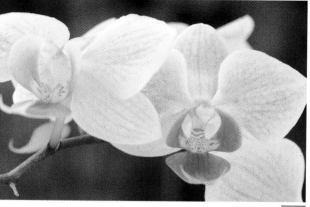

4-3

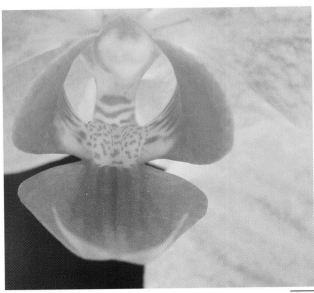

4-4

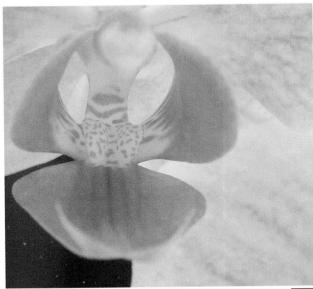

4-5

ADOBE RGB VERSUS sRGB

An important choice has to be made about color space when shooting digital. It so happens that this choice can be changed at the time of processing a Raw file, but for workflow reasons, it is usually best to make this choice in the camera. (When shooting Raw, this choice is registered in the metadata — information about the file — that is recorded when the camera saves a Raw file. This is then read by the Raw converter and serves as a starting point for you to work with.)

Adobe RGB and sRGB are color spaces that you can use to control and adjust color. A color space is a defined range of colors with which a digital file can work. The Adobe RGB space is larger than sRGB. This means it has a wider range of colors with which to work. Figure 4-6 illustrates this point with two buckets of pigments — Adobe RGB is a bigger bucket. Because sRGB was developed to make good use of the capabilities of the computer monitor, a myth has evolved that sRGB is only for images that will be displayed on the monitor, especially Web photos. Belief in this myth can lead photographers down a path that may be inappropriate for them.

There are far more color challenges that come from shooting the image at the wrong exposure than you can

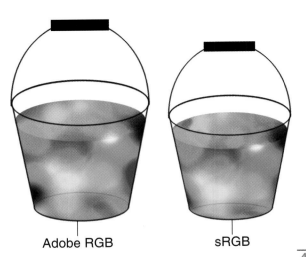

Adobe RGB   sRGB

4-6

ever get from comparing how much Adobe RGB has versus sRGB. While sRGB offers a somewhat smaller color space than Adobe RGB, this is no different than choosing a film. Digital photographers who once shot film touted one film over another because they liked the color, not because one film gave more color to work with than another. For example, Fujichrome Velvia has a far more limited color space than Fujichrome Astia, yet most professional nature photographers preferred Velvia for its color. I find it odd that now some of them claim you should use Adobe RGB for its space when sRGB may be better for many photographers because of its color. I guarantee that you cannot look at a photograph and tell whether it comes from one working space or the other — it is actually difficult to show you the differences in a photo printed in a book like this, and the two spaces are not adjustable in ways to easily make them match. Figures 4-7 and 4-8 show the same image with different color spaces. If they weren't near each other, you would be hard pressed to say one is "better" than the other except for personal color preferences. They will adjust differently in Photoshop, with Adobe RGB offering more flexibility, but not every photographer needs it.

COLOR SPACE FOR THE PEOPLE

Both Adobe RGB and sRGB are excellent color spaces that provide professional and solid color results from your image. The choice comes down to what you need in color, personal preferences, and workflow. Don't ever let any digital guru make you feel incompetent for using sRGB. If it gives you the results you want, then it is the color space to use.

You can test what each space looks like for you (assuming you have a calibrated monitor, which is always important):

1. Open any Raw file with significant color in it into Camera Raw, a photo like that in figure 4-9.

2. Look for the field called Space below the image. This is the color space field.

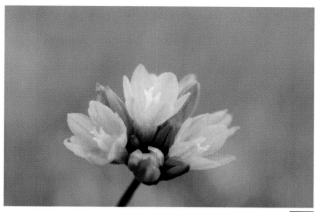

4-7

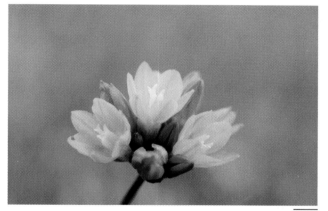

4-8

PRO TIP

When I try to balance the sRGB versus Adobe RGB claims, I receive odd comments from some professional digital processors that I favor sRGB and that this can lead the faithful astray. I do not favor sRGB over Adobe RGB. I actually use them both. What I defy is the blind recommendation of using Adobe RGB by everyone regardless of individual needs. Use whichever space works best for your particular situation.

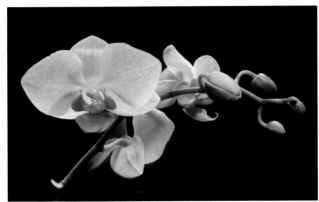
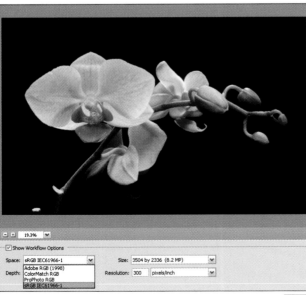

4-9

4-10

3. Click on the words or the down arrow at the right to open the menu for this box as seen in figure 4-10. Adobe RGB and sRGB appear (there are other letters after sRGB — it comes in different flavors, but that has little meaning here), along with some other choices. Some color workers like the options available in those other choices, but for photographers, Adobe RGB and sRGB are plenty.

4. Alternate clicking Adobe RGB and sRGB. The colors and contrast of the image change.

ADOBE RGB AND sRGB DIFFERENCES

So how do you make the choice between these color spaces as seen in figures 4-11, which shows Adobe RGB, and 4-12, which shows sRGB? Here are some things to consider when comparing them.

> sRGB looks snappier with brighter colors and stronger contrast. While you can match that in Adobe RGB, many photographers prefer these colors and tones (sort of like the preference for Velvia) and find sRGB gets them to an image they like faster than working with Adobe RGB.

> Adobe RGB has more adjustment capabilities. You can push and pull colors into precise hues and tones with more accuracy in this color space. This can be critical for the commercial photographer shooting products for a manufacturer.

> sRGB matches many output devices better, especially digital printers at labs that print from digital files.

> Adobe RGB includes colors that do not exist in sRGB, so if you have special color needs for a photograph, Adobe RGB is the only choice.

> For average photographers, sRGB gets them to a print that they like faster than Adobe RGB. That does not mean a better print is not possible with Adobe RGB.

> Adobe RGB is ideal for the careful worker who enjoys spending time in the digital darkroom.

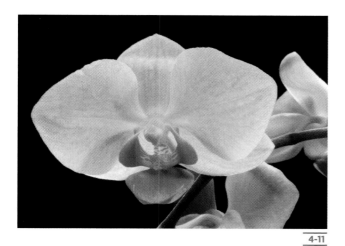

4-11

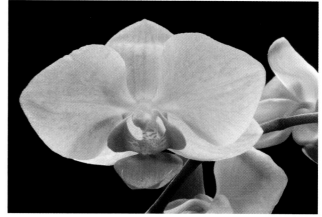

4-12

WHITE BALANCE: A RAW WORKFLOW ISSUE

White balance is one of the greatest features of digital photography. In the days when film dominated photography, it was a real pain to balance the colors of the scene to the capabilities of the film. It took a lot of filters, special meters, and much trial and error. Many photographers just said, "Forget it!" and strictly shot under controlled light (usually electronic flash, which was balanced for daylight films).

White balance changes all that. Now, you can get great-looking color from most natural light situations without filters or controlled light, plus you can control the rendition of that scene's colors for creative effect as seen in figures 4-13, 4-14 and 4-15. This can be done in the camera or in Photoshop. Shooting Raw makes this very easy to do and with no quality loss. You can even change a setting made in the camera to a different setting in Camera Raw.

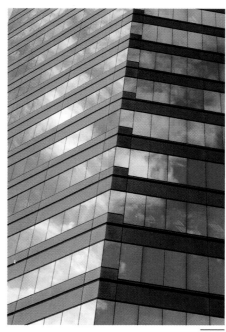

4-13

PRO TIP

White balance removes the need for many color correction filters. However, you can control color in interesting ways by shooting your camera on a white-balance preset, such as daylight, and then using a particular color filter, such as a fluorescent correction filter, for its unique characteristics.

61

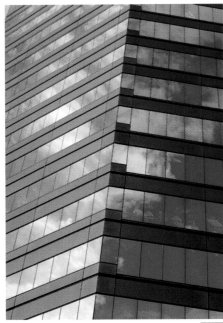

4-14

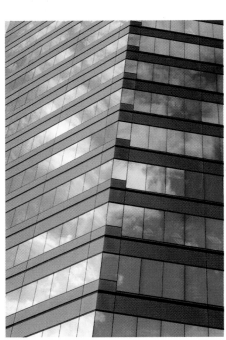

4-15

White balance actually comes from the video industry. This has always been a standard part of professional video production. Cameras are pointed at a white card in the scene and the camera makes the white card a neutral white. White balance in a digital camera tries to do the same thing. When the camera sets white balance and you are shooting Raw, it keeps that information in the metadata recorded along with the actual image. Then when you open that photo in Camera Raw, the software recognizes that setting and adjusts the image appropriately.

WHITE BALANCE IN THE CAMERA

But why white balance in the camera? You can, after all, change it at any time later. There is no quality difference and leaving the camera on auto white balance just means one less thing to think about when photographing. That is 100 percent true and there is absolutely nothing wrong with working that way. However, I like to choose my white balance while shooting for several important reasons, all related to workflow and image consistency. Consider these ideas:

> By choosing a white balance while on the scene with your subject, you can compare what you are seeing in the LCD with the actual scene such as that shown in figure 4-16. You now can be confident that your white balance can be used as a solid reference for dealing with adjustments to the scene.

> Auto white balance can be a compromise and give you a weaker interpretation of the scene, which is then what you first see when opening Camera Raw.

> Locking down a white balance on critical color situations, such as product photography (figure 4-17), can mean a much more efficient workflow in finishing the images in the computer.

> Auto white balance can often change white-balance readings as you select a new focal length or reposition your camera in a scene (so that it sees a different background, for example). If the resulting photos have to match, you have more work to do in the digital darkroom to make them the same.

> Choosing a specific white balance while shooting brings a stronger discipline to the craft, encouraging you to get the shot the best you can, even in difficult white balance situations as seen in figure 4-18. It leads to a more hands-on experience.

> Auto white balance can be a compromise of color that looks right when the image is opened in Camera Raw so that the photographer does not go any further to find a better mix of color.

> Apparent exposure can be affected by the white-balance setting. Technically, white balance is only a set of instructions in the image file's metadata, so it can't actually change an exposure. But it will affect the appearance of brightness in an image so if you set it yourself at the time of photography, you can be sure you make the proper exposure corrections.

WHITE BALANCE CHECKUP

It is a very helpful exercise to shoot the same subject with all of the white-balance settings your camera offers. It gives you a more intuitive feel for white balance. Try this:

1. Set your camera up to a constant f-stop — aperture-priority exposure works well for this. Changing f-stops changes focus, which affects color tonalities. You want to keep them constant.

2. Find a scene in light that will not change for the five minutes it might take to do this exercise. Also, look to include light and neutral tones, as these are very sensitive to white-balance changes.

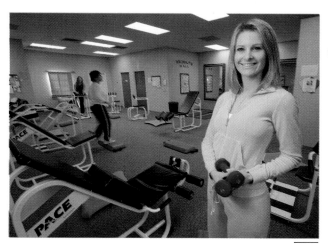

4-16

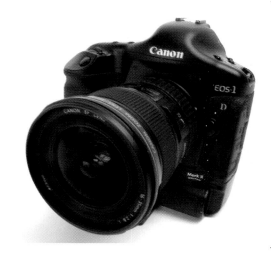

4-17

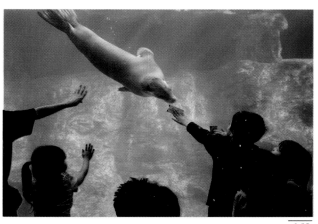

4-18

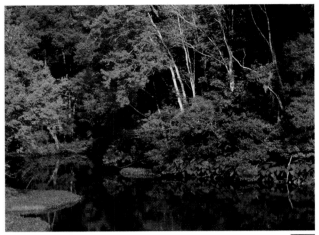

4-19

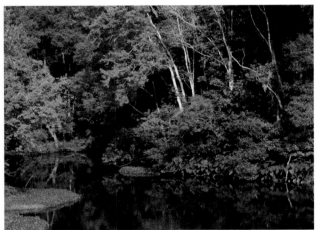

4-20

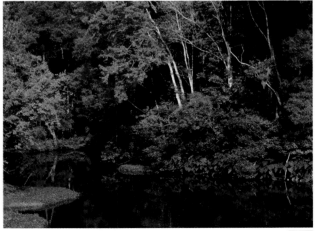

4-21

3. Shoot a series of images changing your white-balance settings for each as seen in figures 4-19 through 4-22. Follow the order that your camera control takes you from auto through all the presets, or take careful notes with shot numbers. This is important because the metadata of most cameras does not specify which preset was used, so you need to be able to compare your shooting with the actual images to find that out.

4. Open all images directly without changing them in Camera Raw. Compare the colors.

AUTO WHITE BALANCE

Auto white balance was once a poor choice in the early stages of digital camera development. It was inconsistent and undependable. That's no longer true. Manufacturers have worked very hard to make auto white balance work well. It really is to their advantage to make cameras do well on automatic for the great mass of amateur photographers because that translates to camera sales.

And auto white balance is not just for amateurs. Pros use it in mixed and changing lighting such as that seen in figure 4-23 because, frankly, that is the only way to get good white balance. If you are a photojournalist following the president of the United States from meeting hall to hallway to outdoors and must constantly change white balance, you miss shots. For the photojournalist, good white balance is a real help because it means acceptable color is always possible in an area where the action and context of the image is far more important than precise color. Plus, news photos are usually used singly so they do not need to match others.

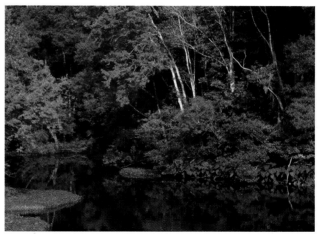

4-22

But auto white balance can have problems. When the colors are critical, important colors can have the wrong hues or an inadequate balance with the rest of the scene. In addition, auto white balance frequently gives weak color renditions of natural scenes compared to the way photographers expect such scenes to look based on experience with film. It does not know that you want a sunset rich with warm colors — it may try to neutralize some of them, for example. Finally, if you shoot three photos of the same scene, each with a different focal length or background, which color of your subject is correct?

PRESET WHITE BALANCE

Digital cameras come with a set of preset white-balance settings. These allow you to lock white balance to a specific adjustment. Most cameras include presets for daylight, shade, cloudy, tungsten, electronic flash, and fluorescent. The continuous quartz light used for the subject in figure 4-24 was balanced with a tungsten preset. Each one produces a consistent and reasonable interpretation of the light under those conditions. You can change lenses or move around, but as long as the light doesn't change, the colors of your subject stay firm.

Some cameras include additional presets and controls to tweak the presets. This can be very useful for very precise work as you can adjust a preset to better match the specific conditions you find in a particular shooting situation. The important thing to remember about a preset is that it

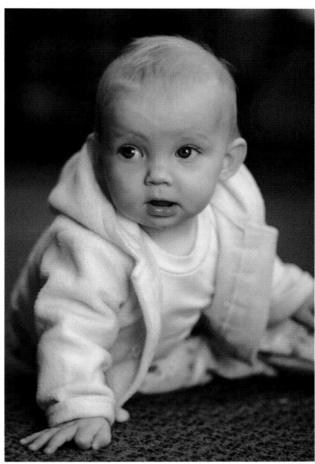

4-23

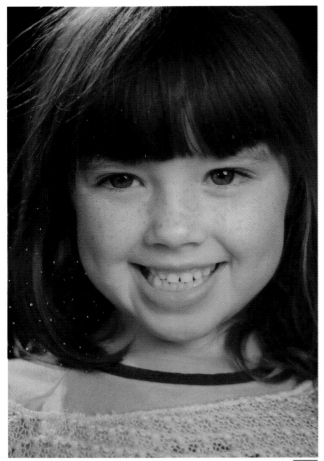

4-24

PRO TIP

Try custom white balancing on a pale color, such as a paint sample from the hardware store, for controllable color effects. When the camera white balances on a pale blue color, for example, it removes that color, making the whole scene warm up dramatically.

locks your camera to a specific lighting condition such as using a daylight preset for a sunset (figure 4-25), and in Raw, that preset is interpreted by Camera Raw when the file is opened in it.

You can also use white-balance presets to change the response of the camera to the scene. For example, you can

use a setting like cloudy when shooting in daylight in order to warm the scene, or at sunset to make it look richer in warm colors. Or, in daylight, the daylight preset keeps things pretty neutral, while shade, cloudy, and electronic flash warm it up, and tungsten cools it down. Fluorescents have varied responses. If you aren't sure about this, try the setting, shoot a photo and check the LCD. While the image in the LCD is not perfect in its renditions of color, it gives a good idea of what is happening.

CUSTOM WHITE BALANCE

This is a secret weapon of a select group of pros and photo enthusiasts. While custom white balance has been on every digital camera I have seen (I have not examined all of the inexpensive point-and-shoots, however), few photographers use it or even know about it. I have even asked some pros about their experience with custom white balance and received a blank look in return.

Custom white balance allows you to precisely balance your camera's response to specific lighting conditions on your subject. This often gives you the most neutral colors possible for the scene. You use a white or gray card, have the camera measure the card's colors, and then make the card neutral. You can put that card in exactly the light on your subject, in exactly the position of your subject (or nearby if the subject doesn't allow this) so you can create a white balance customized for it.

Unfortunately, cameras, even models from the same manufacturer, do not have consistent ways of measuring a custom white balance, so I can't give a step-by-step outline for this process. But to give you an idea of the process and show you certain things to look for, here is the process used by the Canon EOS 20D:

1. Shoot a photograph of something white or gray in the light that hits your subject as seen in figure 4-26. This does not have to be in focus in spite of some camera manual's recommendations, but it does have to fill most of the image area. And it does have to be exposed reasonably well, but all tones should be in the mid range.

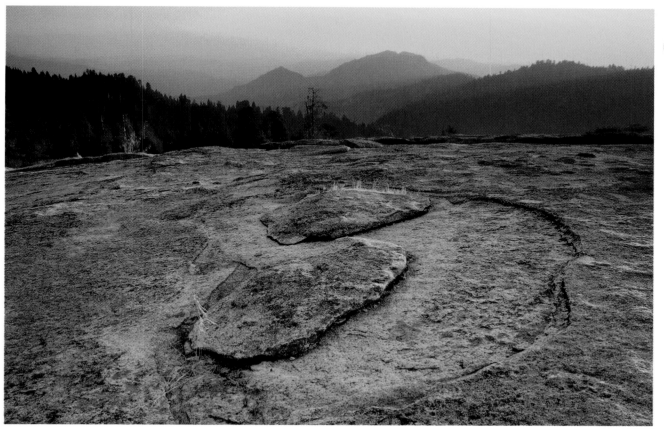

4-25

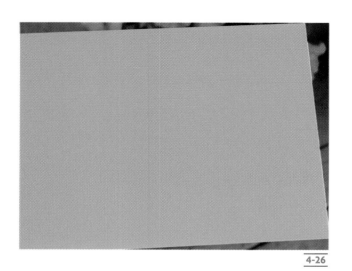

4-26

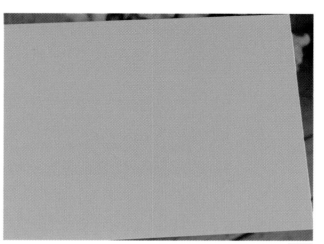

4-27

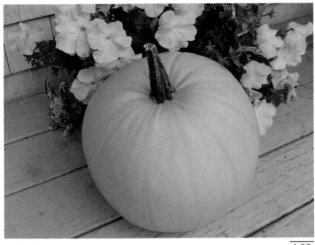
4-28

2. Push the menu button and go to the shooting menu.

3. In the shooting menu, find the Custom WB entry and select it.

4. Now the image you just shot should be open with some instructions.

5. Follow the instructions by pushing the set button — the color in the card will be removed as seen in figure 4-27. Now, set the white balance mode to the custom icon (it is a small black dot over a V-shaped depression in a small horizontal rectangle).

6. The camera saves this as a preset for this particular light as shown in figure 4-28, even if you change to other settings, until you do a new custom white balance.

Color Temperature of Light

The color of light is referenced by a scale that starts at 0 and essentially goes to infinity. It is based on the heating of a theoretical sphere and is warmer (red or orange) at low temperatures and changes to cooler colors (blues) at high temperatures. This is the Kelvin scale, and though it uses "temperatures," numbers are not referenced with the degree sign.

Two things are critical for the photographer: the warm/cold color range and the relationship of different colors on the scale. Color temperature is based on a palette of warm and cold colors, which is essentially an amber to blue scale. Other colors, such as the magenta to green range, are affected, but are not directly related to it. In addition, if you compare two points on this scale, the one with the lower temperature is always warmer than the higher temperature.

This is directly applicable to color balance in a digital camera. If you balance to a specific color of light, that light will be neutral in color, but then other lights will be warmer (lower in temperature) or cooler (higher in temperature), which is one thing that separates real-world light from studio light (which is consistent in color temperature). Typical color temperatures include: tungsten lights (2400K to 3800K), quartz lights (3200K), midday daylight (5000K to 5800K), cloudy day (6000K to 10,000K), and open shade (8000K to 20,000K).

Q&A

How much can I trust the camera's LCD for judging color?

A simple answer is to use it as a guide, not an exact rendition of the image, but it also depends on the camera and LCD. I have seen cameras with horrible LCD output that give you little idea of what the color of the photo will look like. They can only be used as a way of checking things like focus and composition. But I have also seen cameras that had a great correlation between their LCD screens and image color.

You can test this very simply:

1. Shoot some casual photos within walking distance of your computer.

2. Check the LCD for all of them, and then download them immediately onto the computer.

3. Review the shots on the computer. Do they match what you remember?

4. Put the memory card back into the camera and play back the images on the LCD. Now compare them to the computer screen. I give you both steps 3 and 4 because they give you different reference points. You will not have a computer to compare images to when shooting most of the time, so it helps to consider both the direct comparison and the memory check.

5. See where the biases are with your camera's LCD and keep that in mind when evaluating images on it in the future.

Really, isn't Adobe RGB a better color space than sRGB?

That all depends on what the criteria for better is. If more is important, as in more color range to adjust, then Adobe RGB is better. On the other hand, if faster and easier is important, than sRGB may be the better color space.

A lot of things in the digital color world are very subjective. Having an absolute better only works when the criteria for that better are defined and known. For example, which is better — four-wheel drive or front-wheel drive? The answer depends on driving conditions and needs of the car owner. If you only drive the streets of Los Angeles, four-wheel drive has some distinct disadvantages, including poor gas mileage. But if you need to go off-road, four-wheel drive is the way to go.

The same thing applies to color space. When I am shooting quickly with JPEG, I often use sRGB for its speed benefits. Because a Raw file can go either way, I can leave the camera set to sRGB, knowing that I can choose Adobe RGB with that file later in the processing with no loss in image quality. I do typically process Raw files to Adobe RGB, but depending on the situation, there is a strong benefit to just setting the camera set to sRGB when I shoot Raw + JPEG (which I frequently do).

CAMERA RAW WORKFLOW

Part II

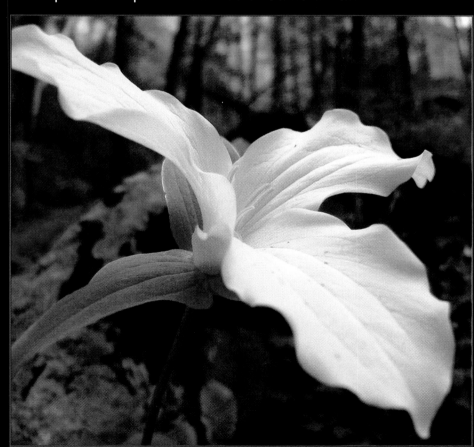

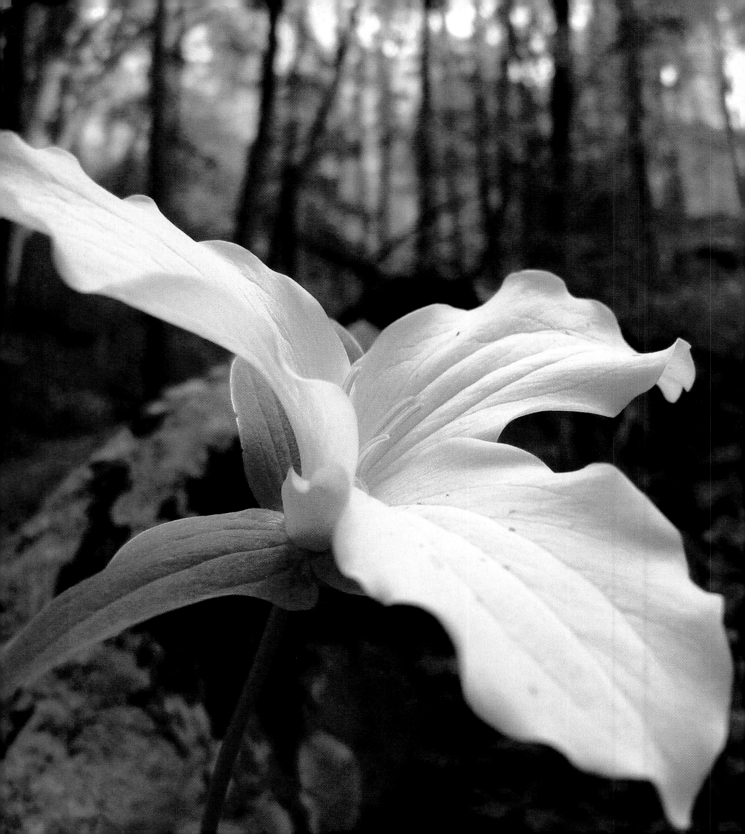

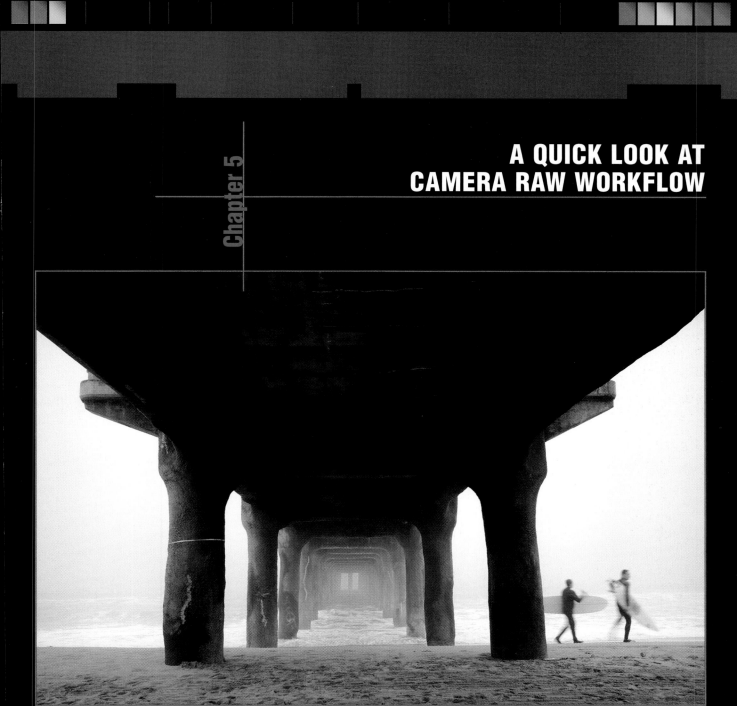

Chapter 5

A QUICK LOOK AT
CAMERA RAW WORKFLOW

Camera Raw is both simple and complex. It is simple in that it uses an uncomplicated, easy-to-follow interface with all the controls directly related to photographic concerns. If only Photoshop had such a straightforward interface! But unlike Photoshop, Camera Raw was designed strictly for the photographer dealing with a purely photographic need — processing an image directly from the camera.

This chapter gives you a quick overview of Camera Raw and some of the key parts of its workflow. You can use this chapter as a reference to the interface and how it can be interpreted. While you see many screen images from Camera Raw, you may find it helpful to open Camera Raw with any image and follow along with this overview.

It is important to note that your version of Camera Raw matches what you see here if you work with Photoshop CS2. If you work with Camera Raw in Photoshop CS or earlier versions of Camera Raw when it was an add-in plug-in, you will discover there are additional features in Camera Raw such as new tools and adjustment tabs as expressed in Adobe Creative Suite 2 shown in figure 5-1. Use what you have and don't worry about the additional features until you can upgrade to Photoshop CS2. All of the major adjustment controls are in all versions of Camera Raw.

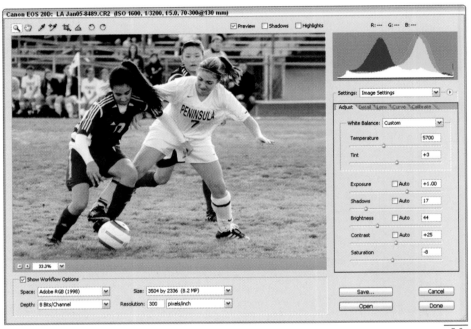

5-1

FINDING YOUR RAW PHOTOS

Before you can open a Raw photo, you obviously must know where to find it. Filing and editing your photos is not part of this book, but it is an important part of your workflow. The computer really is just a virtual filing cabinet. If you had trouble finding slides or negatives before, you probably have the same problems on the computer, although there are some techniques that can make it easier to organize your images.

Browsers that recognize Raw files are an important way to deal with image files on the computer. These photographic programs show all files in a folder as small thumbnails on the screen. It is like looking at a lightbox, and just like on a lightbox, the photos can be quickly sorted, edited, and selected. Browsers let you rename whole groups of images, tag them with special edit criteria, print out contact or proof sheets, add IPTC data (personal information added to the metadata of a file), and much more.

Photoshop came with a browser in earlier versions; Photoshop CS2 uses a unique browser called the Bridge, shown in figure 5-2. It is actually a separate program that bridges multiple Adobe programs in the Creative Suite, such as InDesign or Illustrator if you have them. This is a very versatile browser with a lot of power for organizing your images. It does have one downside, however — it is slow compared to other browsers on the market. It is great for finding a specific image to open in Photoshop, but it is frustrating to use for editing unless you have some power to your computer.

Independent browser programs can be a great option for actually editing photos. These include iView Media Pro (shown in figure 5-3), Extensis Portfolio, and others. These programs are much, much faster in accessing images for editing and sorting. They allow you to quickly tag and sort images into specific groups. Plus, they have many powerful and automated organizing tools as well.

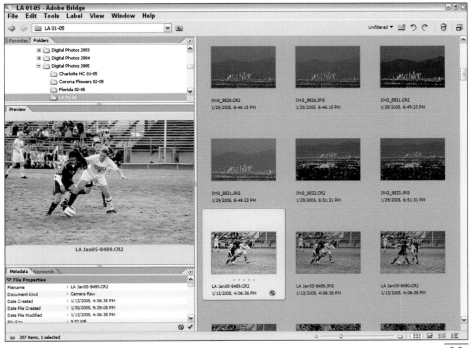

5-2

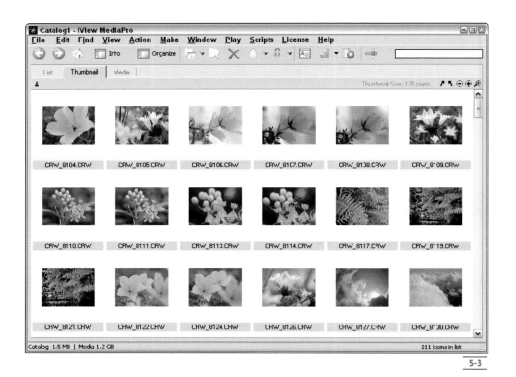

5-3

PRO TIP

Color-coding images in a browser is a very fast way of editing a shoot. In almost all browser programs (including Adobe Bridge), you go through either multiple thumbnails or full-size images on the screen as a slide show. You then quickly tag each image as it comes up, for example — red for selects, blue for trash, black (default) for keeping for other reasons. Then you can sort for each group and refile them (or create a new browser catalog for them).

OPENING CAMERA RAW

Photoshop automatically opens Camera Raw when it detects that the file you want to open is a Raw file. This can be through the standard file open dialog box in Photoshop as seen in figure 5-4. Simply click the desired file, a thumbnail appears that allows you to confirm this is indeed the photo you want, and then click Open.

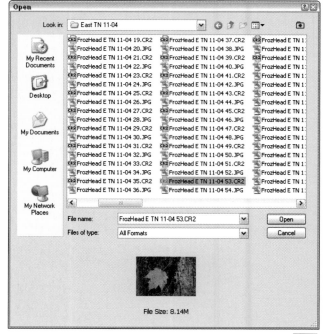

5-4

This requires you to know the photo name and location. Unless you have an idea of which file or even folder you need, this can be a frustrating hunt. Printing a proof or contact sheet of images either from Photoshop or an image browser program can be a quick and easy way of finding a specific image. I find that it is important to name file folders for specific shoots or subject matter, then group them under larger folders, such as a month or a big project. For example, I have a section on my hard drive called Digital Photos — this is where I put all my images that I download straight from the camera's memory card (I download from a memory card reader). Then I have folders for each year broken down into folders for

projects and months. A browser helps you find the images quickly.

You can open multiple Raw images with Camera Raw. If you double click individual shots one at a time you will open multiple Camera Raw windows. This is not the most efficient way to work (it uses more RAM, for example). A better way is to select multiple files in the Bridge (Ctrl/⌘ click them one at a time), as shown in figure 5-5, then choose File ⇨ Open in Camera Raw. This opens the group in a new interface that shows Camera Raw with the first image (in chronological order) open in Camera Raw and the others ready in a filmstrip to the left (see figure 5-6).

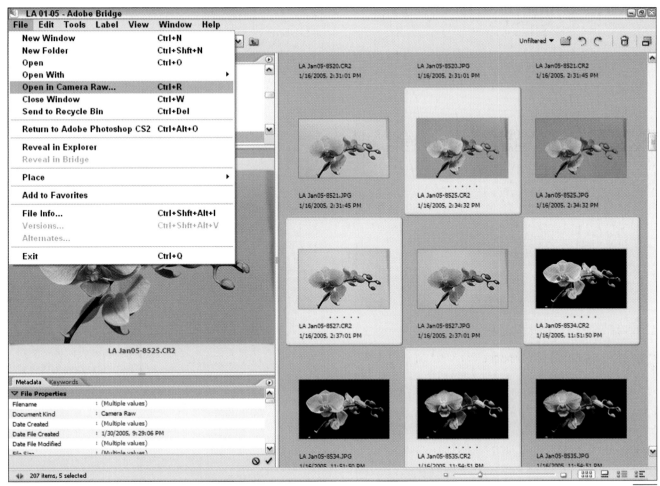

5-5

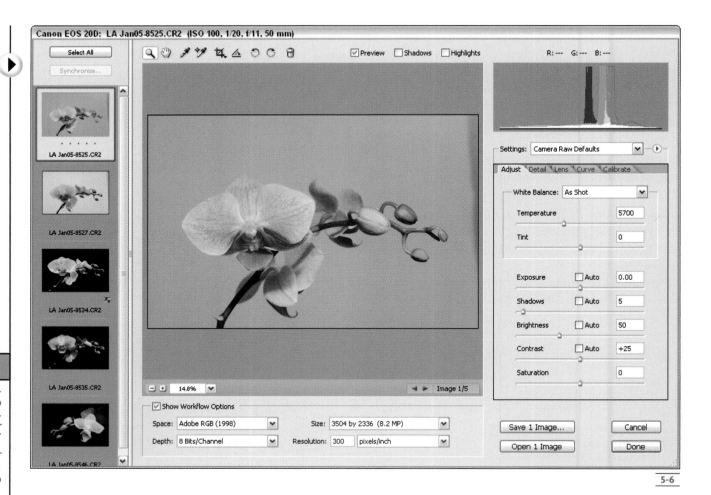

Canon EOS 20D: LA Jan05-8525.CR2 (ISO 100, 1/20, f/11, 50 mm)

5-6

PRO TIP

When downloading images, it helps to set up specific places to store them before you start downloading. This makes it easier to find your photos when working with Camera Raw. Create a special place on your hard drive for downloading images that you always go to in order to make the process more structured. I find that it is important to name file folders for specific shoots or subject matter, then group them under larger folders, such as a month or a big project. For example, I have a section on my hard drive called Digital Photos — this is where I put all my images that I download straight from the camera's memory card (I download from a memory card reader). Then I have folders for each year broken down into folders for projects and months. A browser helps you find the images quickly.

THE IMPORTANCE OF RESET AND UNDO

With Camera Raw open, there are two important and absolutely essential tools that you need to know about: Undo and Reset. These are decidedly not very exciting, but that makes them no less important.

Of course, most people who use the computer regularly know they can execute Undo by pressing Ctrl/⌘+Z or access by choosing Edit ⇨ Undo. That backs you up one step and undoes whatever you did last. It works the same within Camera Raw. This is really important because it means you don't have to worry about trying anything in the program. Not sure how something might work? Try it — you can always use Undo to remove that adjustment as demonstrated by figures 5-7 and 5-8.

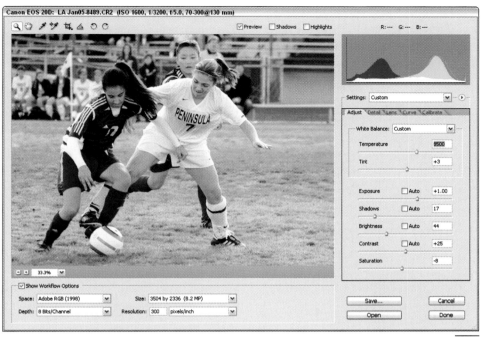

5-7

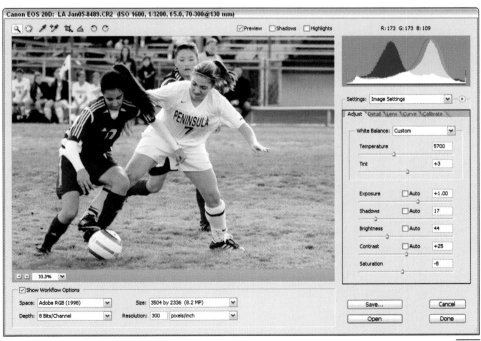

5-8

Reset is a complementary tool, a core part of Photoshop, yet it is surprising how many photographers do not know it is there. It is a feature that lets you reset any open dialog box back to its original state when it opened with your photo. You can totally mess up your photo in Camera Raw and always have an out — Reset. This button isn't visible while you are working on your photo. But as soon as you press and hold Alt/Option, the Cancel button changes to Reset, as shown in figure 5-9. It can be a lifesaver.

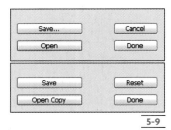

5-9

CAMERA RAW IN SIX-PART HARMONY

It helps to mentally divide the Camera Raw interface into six sections as seen in figure 5-10. This way it isn't just an amorphous bunch of stuff, and you can more quickly find and understand this software. Each section deals with similar aspects of the image controls, and each is quite different from the others. Take them from the top, left to right (earlier versions of Camera Raw look slightly different):

1. Camera Raw toolbar — these are the cursor tools that operate with a click or drag of the mouse. They are, from the left, the Magnifier (or Zoom tool), the Hand tool for moving around in the image, the White Balance tool (an eyedropper), the Color Sampler tool (another eyedropper), the Crop tool, the Straighten tool, and two image-rotating tools (counterclockwise and clockwise).

2. Image preview — six separate pieces here, although most photographers find the first three most useful: Preview, Shadow clipping, Highlight clipping, and channel information for Red, Green, and Blue.

3. Image — the image itself has a nice big view to show you what Camera Raw is doing.

4. Image adjustments — this is a big block of very important adjustment tools, starting at the top with the histogram. Below that is a settings menu, then a flyout menu appears to the right of it. The block below holds a wealth of adjustment capability, from exposure change to color correction and enhancement to noise reduction and much more.

5. Workflow options — at the lower left is a group of small menus with a series of choices (this can be hidden if you always use certain choices by deselecting the Show Workflow Options check box). You choose color space, color bit depth, final image size, and pixel resolution when the image leaves Camera Raw.

6. Execution commands — last are basic, but key, controls to allow you to finish working on an image in Camera Raw.

PRO TIP

Right-clicking the image gives you a menu for whatever tool is active. Both Windows and Macintosh systems support a two-button mouse. Get rid of the stylish Apple mouse with the Mac (a one-button mouse) and purchase a USB two-button mouse for much more versatility.

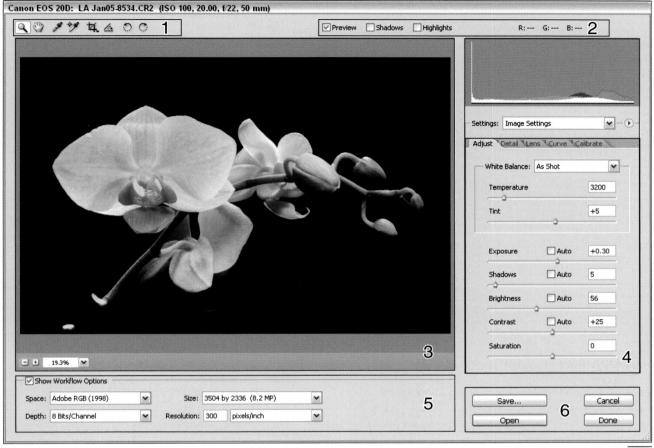

Canon EOS 20D: LA Jan05-8534.CR2 (ISO 100, 20.00, f/22, 50 mm)

☑ Preview ☐ Shadows ☐ Highlights   R: ---   G: ---   B: --- **2**

1

Settings: Image Settings

Adjust Detail Lens Curve Calibrate

White Balance: As Shot

Temperature   3200
Tint   +5

Exposure   ☐ Auto   +0.30
Shadows   ☐ Auto   5
Brightness   ☐ Auto   56
Contrast   ☐ Auto   +25
Saturation   0

4

3

19.3%

☑ Show Workflow Options

Space: Adobe RGB (1998)   Size: 3504 by 2336 (8.2 MP)
Depth: 8 Bits/Channel   Resolution: 300   pixels/inch

5

Save...   Cancel
Open   Done

6

5-10

CAMERA RAW TOOLBAR

Start to look at the Camera Raw interface by opening a photo in it. The controls in the Camera Raw toolbar are similar to the standard Photoshop toolbar, as shown in figure 5-11. You are just going to see what they do before doing a lot of work on an image. However, remember that you can't hurt anything in Photoshop if you recall that you can always Undo and Reset. This is very freeing because if you aren't sure about a particular control, try it! So try the toolbar controls.

1. Click the Zoom tool or Magnifier (figure 5-12). This acts just like the Photoshop Magnifier/Zoom tool.

5-11

5-12

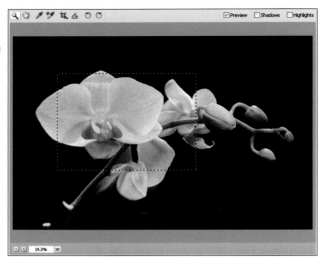

5-13

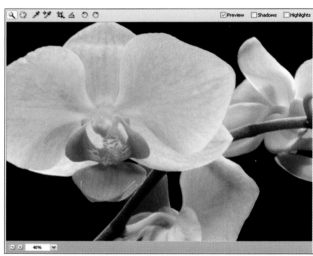

5-14

5-15

5-16

Click the photo and it enlarges. Press and hold Alt/Option, click, and the photo gets smaller. Use the Magnifier like a cursor to outline a box on the photo (see figure 5-13); that area enlarges (figure 5-14).

2. After magnifying the image, click the Hand tool (see figure 5-15). Use it to move the magnified photo around inside the viewing area (it has no effect on the image). You can also instantly access the Hand tool by pressing the space bar.

3. The White Balance tool (see figure 5-16) is designed to make neutral tones such as white or gray neutral (it does not work as well on black). Click anything that should be a neutral tone and Camera Raw makes it so.

4. Use the Color Sampler tool (see figure 5-17) to click a color in the image that is particularly critical for you. As soon as you click, you find the preview image resizes to allow a new thing to appear in the interface, a box for RGB numbers. You can click up to four colors and each one appears as a set of RGB numbers. This can help you know how colors are changing as you make adjustments to the photo. Remove individual points by pressing and holding Alt or Option and clicking on a point. Remove them all by clicking the Clear Samplers button.

5. The Crop tool (see figure 5-18) is an interesting choice for Adobe. Try it, using it just like the Crop tool in Photoshop; but it doesn't exactly work like the Photoshop Crop tool. A cropped image appears in the preview (and in Adobe Bridge). However, this crop is not permanent! The preview shows the cropped area, but the rest of the photo is still there. When the image is opened, it is cropped, but the original Raw file is not. You clear the crop using the Escape key or by pressing and holding the cursor on the Crop tool and a shortcut menu appears with Clear Crop visible.

6. The Straighten tool (see figure 5-19) lets you do just that. Find a line in the photo that should (or could) be either horizontal or vertical. Click on one part of that line,

then move the cursor down the line and click again. A crop box appears at an angle that makes the lines horizontal or vertical. This is applied when the file is opened.

7. The two Rotate tools (see figure 5-20) simply rotate the photo 90 degrees at a time, either counterclockwise or clockwise.

5-17

5-18

5-19

5-20

PREVIEW OPTIONS

Camera Raw lets you see your image in several ways to help you make decisions on how to adjust it. Previews are important when you use Camera Raw, although not every photographer will use all of them. Still, it is worth playing around with all of them to understand how they might be used.

> **Image.** A preview shows you the image itself as seen in figure 5-21.

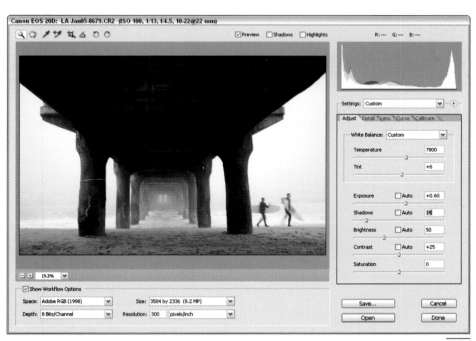

5-21

> **Sizing.** You can enlarge the image in the preview to better see details. Use the Zoom tool, the size settings drop down menu (at the bottom left of the preview), or the plus and minus buttons next to the size settings, as shown in figure 5-22. Press Ctrl/⌘+0 to instantly go to the full image.

> **RGB data.** Specific RGB data lets you see relationships of the Red, Green, and Blue channels, as seen in figure 5-23.

> **Histogram.** This histogram shows exposure information in the separate channels as also seen in figure 5-24.

> **Clipping warnings.** Photoshop CS2 added a couple of useful new tools: the Shadow and Highlight clipping warnings. These show you where detail in shadows and highlights is lost, as seen in figure 5-24, but I do not use them much. I favor the techniques described in the next chapters because the colors in this feature can be distracting. I suggest you try these warnings on an image to see where your detail is clipping and see if it helps your workflow.

PRO TIP

Right-clicking the image when the Zoom tool is active gives you a sizing menu immediately. This is a quick and easy way to resize the preview — and another reason why Mac users should get a two-button mouse.

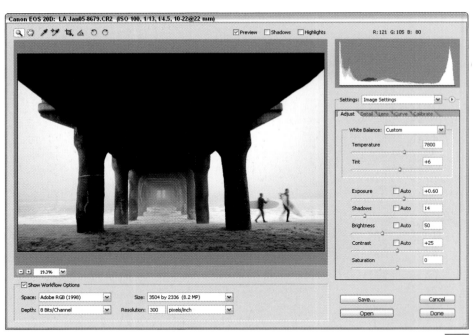

5-22

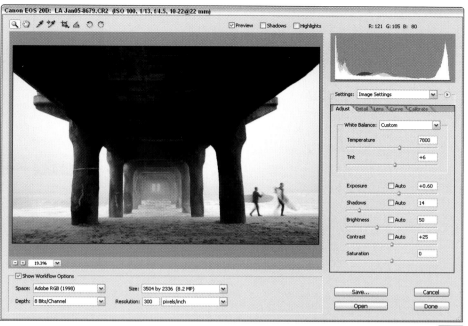

5-23

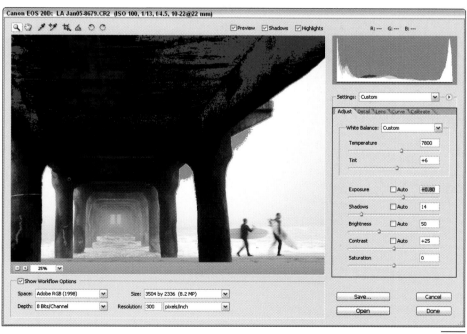

5-24

THE IDEAL WORKFLOW

Starting in Chapter 6, you learn how to go through an image with Camera Raw from start to finish and experience workflow firsthand. However, because workflow overview is a popular subject, I present the ideal workflow in outline form now. This is meant to offer you an overview of the process and not get into detail as to where all the controls are or how to use them. I want you to think about a process and way of working in this section. It is also worth considering that every photo and photographer is different, which often means modifying this ideal workflow to meet individual needs. After opening the image in Camera Raw, you can follow these steps:

1. **Base settings:** Check your base settings at the bottom left as shown in figure 5-25. Be sure you select the color space and bit depth you prefer, the size you expect the photo to be, and a resolution appropriate to your end use.

2. **Problems:** Check to see if there are any major problems with the photo (if you are shooting to get the most from your file in the first place, this will rarely be your problem). Correct a very dark or light photo; fix any white balance imbalance.

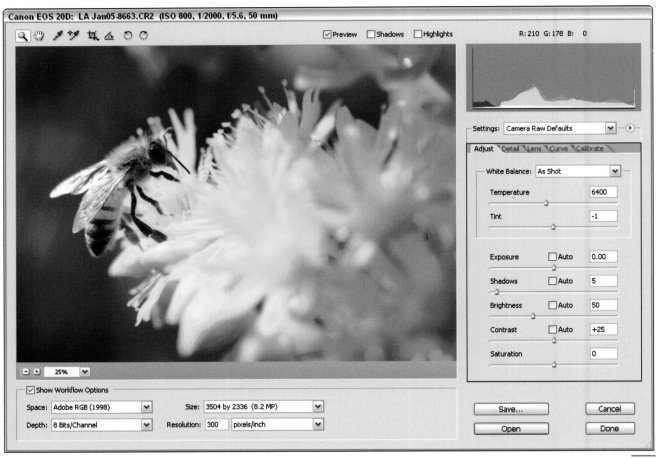

5-25

3. **White:** Check white and light areas and where they appear in your photo. Use the Exposure slider for whites. In figure 5-26, the highlights are corrected to bring detail back into the brightest areas (especially noticeable in the wings of the bee).

4. **Black:** Check black and dark areas and where they appear in your photo. This is a critical issue and something that I come back to again and again. One problem that I consistently see in images from workshop participants and even from pros contributing to Outdoor Photographer and PCPhoto magazines is weak blacks. This results in poor color and contrast. Use the Shadow slider to adjust blacks. In figure 5-27, the photo looks dark, which is okay, because the highlights and blacks have been set correctly. The overall darkness is corrected next through a midtone adjustment.

5. **Midtones:** Adjust midtones by setting the overall brightness of the image with the Brightness slider, or use the Curves tab to use curves for overall adjustment, as done in figure 5-28.

6. **White balance:** It is difficult to fully evaluate white balance until the overall exposure is set. Tweak white balance as needed as shown in figure 5-29.

7. **Saturation:** Use Saturation to boost color if needed, but use it cautiously.

8. **Noise:** If noise is an issue, go to the Detail tab. Remove sharpening if present, then add Luminance Smoothing or adjust Color Noise Reduction, as shown in figure 5-30.

9. **Other:** Use Lens adjustments if needed.

10. **Finish:** Save or open the image.

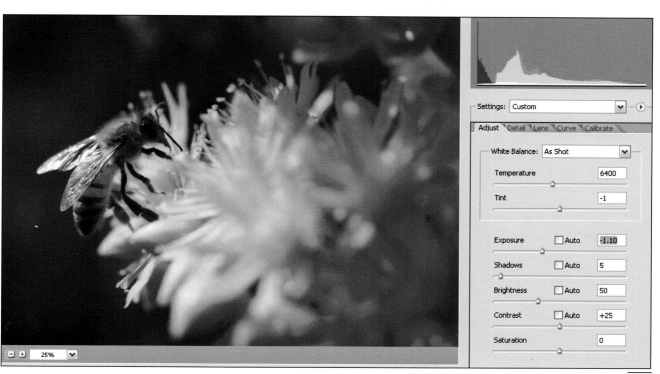

5-26

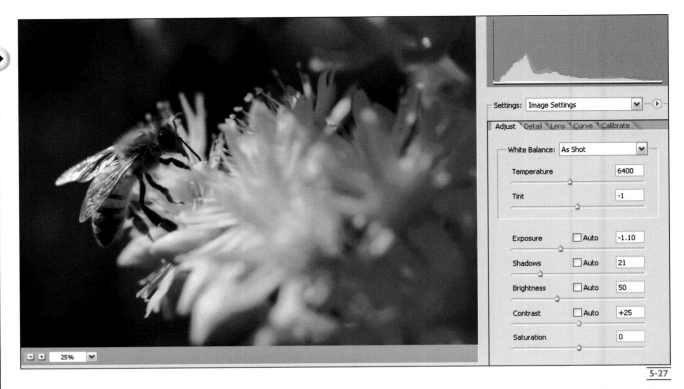

5-27

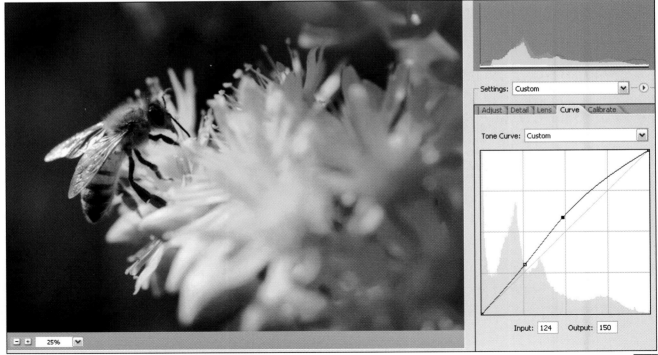

5-28

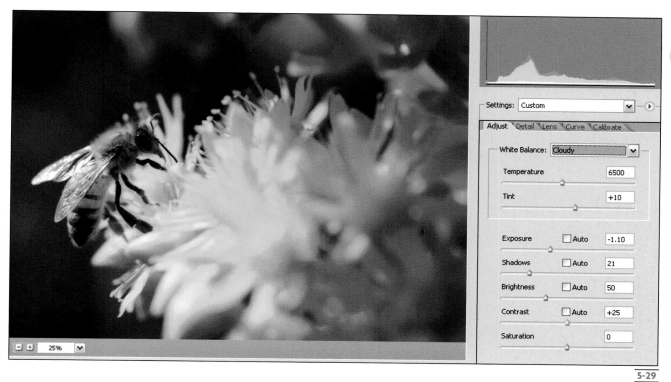

5-29

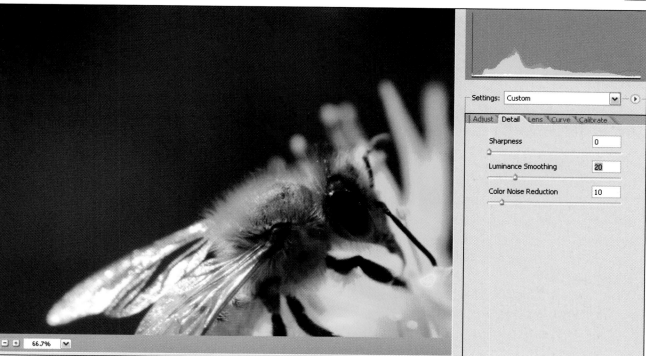

5-30

BASE SETTINGS

As you go through the rest of the book, you will notice that the base settings of color space and bit depth, the size you expect the photo to be, and a resolution appropriate to your end use will not be discussed repeatedly. These are settings that you change infrequently depending on your way of working (see figure 5-31, which is from the lower left portion of the Camera Raw interface).

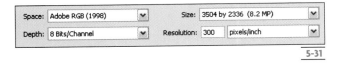

5-31

> **Space.** Typically, you use one color space for most of your images. You can choose either Adobe RGB or sRGB, whichever setting gives you the most consistent results for your workflow. A quick review: Adobe RGB is the larger space and allows more adjustment of color; however, sRGB often looks better to photographers and may allow you to more quickly get to a photo you like. In spite of the rather arbitrary pronouncements of some Photoshop experts, you do not have to use one or the other. The choice of sRGB is okay for any work, and you can achieve great images with either color space.

> **Depth.** 8-bit usually works just fine and is easier to deal with than 16-bit. You are adjusting the image in Camera Raw in a 16-bit color space, and if you do the big adjustments there, you really do not need 16-bit for most purposes back in Photoshop. 16-bit just requires too much memory overhead with too little benefit in Photoshop for the majority of photos. If you do have an image with delicate tones in the highlights that are really critical to the photo or some dark tonalities that you want to continue to develop in Photoshop, then 16-bit can be helpful.

> **Size.** This is one area that you may change more than the others. Typically, you size your image to either the native size of the file (your original megapixels from the camera) or the most common large usage of your photos — if you need larger prints than the native size gives you, for example. The actual pixel dimensions of the photo are given along with the megapixels. A plus sign shows the photo is bigger than the native size, a minus sign shows it is smaller. No sign after the numbers represents the native size. Sizing a photo to a bigger image size than you need will cost you in terms of RAM and storage needs.

> **Resolution.** Most photographers have one need for output resolution and leave this set to one number, typically either 240 pixels per inch (for inkjet printing) or 300 (for publication purposes). This is not a setting that affects image quality and can easily be changed later in Photoshop without affecting the photo. It only affects how the computer reads the pixels and spreads them out along a given dimension.

HOW TO APPROACH CAMERA RAW

All of these pages of computer screen shots, all of the numbers, the histograms, the sliders, and so forth, make processing a Raw photo seem very technical and computer-ish. But they can be a smokescreen and distract you from the important and real purpose for using Camera Raw: better photos for you.

Not better photos by my standards, not better photos by any Photoshop guru's standards, but better photos that meet your specific needs, whether that is a great print for the wall or a submission to a photo buyer at a magazine. Only you can know what that ultimate goal is. All work in Camera Raw, then later in Photoshop, must be to support that goal. Figures 5-32 and 5-33 represent better photos for me, following this philosophy.

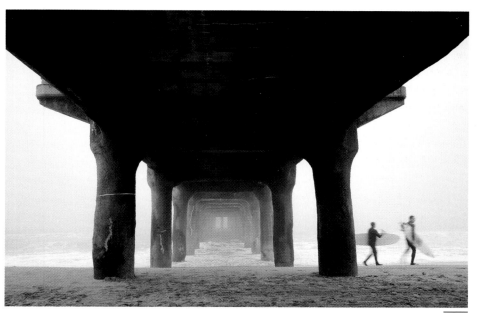

5-32

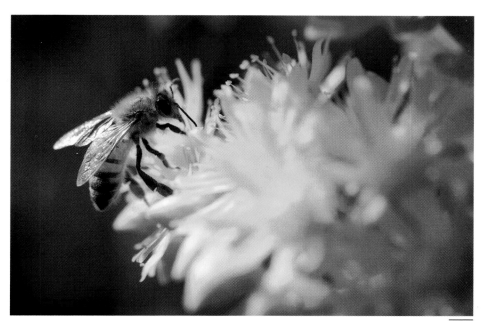

5-33

I emphasize that the ultimate decision of what is a good photo really is yours even though there are some well-meaning Photoshop folks who give their way as the only way, implying that if you don't do it their way, you won't have a good photo. That's great if their way works for you, but sometimes it does not, and I have seen photographers get frustrated and unhappy with the digital medium, thinking it is all their fault, when in reality, it is because they are trying to do something not really suited to their way of working.

This is definitely a craft that takes practice. This book gives you many ideas on how to do that practice and how to get the most from your Raw photos. But it is up to you as to how you interpret that information on your particular photos. Follow the workflow described in this book to get you going, but do not be afraid to take off on your own path to better meet your photo needs.

MONITOR CALIBRATION

I have to spend a short time talking about monitor calibration. For those of you who have calibration hardware and software, and use it, you can skip this section. For everyone else — and I know there are a lot of you who have not calibrated — this is for you.

Monitor calibration used to be a painful, difficult process that required expensive tools. That is no longer true. Monitor calibration packages of software and sensor are available at reasonable cost from ColorVision, X-Rite, and Greytag. Less important than which one is best (they all work quite well) is that you use at least one of them. You must let your monitor warm up before calibration (even before serious adjustments) at least 15 minutes for an LCD and 30 minutes for a CRT. Figure 5-34 shows monitor calibration in progress.

Without a calibrated monitor, you will not get the best results from Camera Raw. Any concepts of color space or bit depth are meaningless because un-calibrated monitors throw colors off more than either. A calibrated monitor gives you a consistent and predictable workspace for your image processing. It does not guarantee perfect prints because that is a different medium, or for the pro, images that look the same on an art director's monitor because the photos have to leave your system (it is no longer closed and controllable).

What monitor calibration does is make sure that the colors and tones you adjust are being adjusted from a standard, measured place so that your results are consistent and predictable, too. It lets your computer know how to interpret the data it reads from an image file for display on your monitor. It is important to calibrate your monitor regularly. How often depends on the monitor type and how much it is on. CRT monitors need calibration much more often than LCD's. If a monitor is on continuously, a CRT may need calibration as often as every two to three weeks. If an LCD is on continuously, you might not need to calibrate it more than once a month or so.

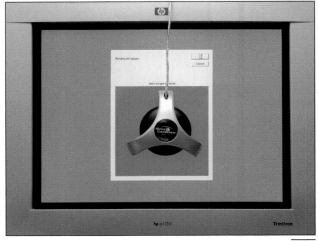

5-34

PRO TIP

Just as important as a calibrated monitor is a neutral workspace. Your eye compensates for bright lights and colorful hues around your computer — avoid them. Go for a neutral workspace around your monitor.

Q&A

What is the best way to bring images into the computer from the camera?

Many photographers download photos directly from the camera. A high-speed connection to the camera, such as USB 2.0 or FireWire, is a good way of doing this, but I recommend using a memory card reader. A memory card reader is a simple device that plugs directly into the computer then allows you to insert your memory card for direct download. Use a USB 2.0 or FireWire reader (be sure your computer supports these standards before buying one, however).

There are several reasons why I believe a memory card reader is a better solution than downloading directly from the camera:

> **Speed.** Card readers are always as fast as downloading from a camera and are usually faster.

> **Convenience.** The card reader is always plugged in. You never search for a cable or a space to put your camera.

> **Power.** Card readers need no external power. With a camera on batteries, a memory card can be corrupted if the camera loses power during transfer of images. Using an extra power cord for the camera works, but it is a nuisance.

> **Drag-and-drop convenience.** Cameras are often recognized differently by the computer than a card reader. A card reader simply shows up as another drive. You can drag-and-drop photos from the card to your hard drive.

What if I change the order of the ideal workflow? Even though you say I can modify this to meet my needs, won't changing the order also affect the image?

Changing the order of the workflow affects how you adjust the individual elements of your image in Camera Raw. If you adjust color first, for example, this affects how you see tonalities, which may mean you make some changes to tonalities that you might not have done if you had done them first. But adjusting an image in Camera Raw is not a science. You are the ultimate arbiter of what is right or wrong about your image. If you find a different order of work is effective for you, then that is probably the right way for you to work. As you go through the next chapters, you see how to interpret an image as you adjust it. This is probably more important than any specific way of making the adjustments.

What if I change my mind about a photo after I have processed it in Camera Raw? If I then make additional changes, will the image quality suffer?

A great thing about Camera Raw is that no adjustment is permanent. This is not true for other formats. If you process the image and save that as a TIFF or PSD file, any further changes may affect the quality of the image because at this point, you are now working with the actual pixels in the photo rather than the Raw file that has to be converted to actually work on pixels.

You can always go back to Camera Raw and open that image again. You can go back to how the original file looked or make changes to the image as much as you want for everything from correction to creative options. There is then no change to the quality of the image as everything done in Camera Raw is recorded by Photoshop as instructions. It is only when the photo is converted and saved to a specific file format that these instructions are translated into actual pixels.

Chapter 6

WORKFLOW APPLIED

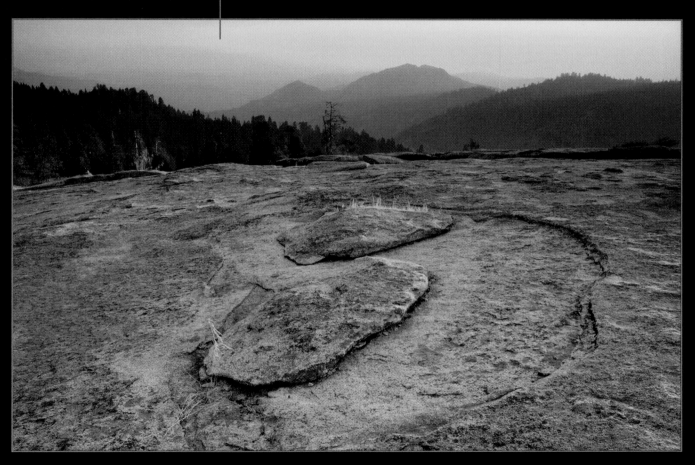

In this chapter, you look at a simple, uncomplicated image for processing in Camera Raw. The landscape from Sequoia National Park (shown in figure 6-1) has a good range of tones throughout, and the exposure is correct for the scene. Because it was shot in Raw, it can be adjusted quite strongly, if needed, without causing problems with tonalities or colors.

This chapter does more than take you step by step through processing an image in Camera Raw. You learn the basics of working with an image in terms of key Camera Raw controls, but you also consider the thought process involved as to why you choose certain controls. There has always been a good news-bad news mentality about processing digital images. The good news is that you have a lot of control that you can adjust in nearly infinite ways. The bad news is that you have a lot of control that you can adjust in nearly infinite ways. Control lets us make our photos better, but many choices it provides can freeze our thought process.

So I want to give you some ideas on how to approach all that control, how to think about your adjustments. You see how a good image — figure 6-1 — is processed to reveal the true potential of the photo, which is seen in figure 6-2. It is not easy to give specific numbers or slider positions, though I know some photographers want it to be simple like that. Unfortunately, every subject demands different approaches to its processing. With some practice and a thought-process to deal with the choices, you develop a workflow that allows you to process most Raw images quickly and efficiently.

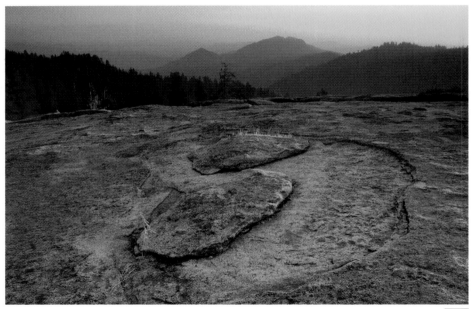

6-1

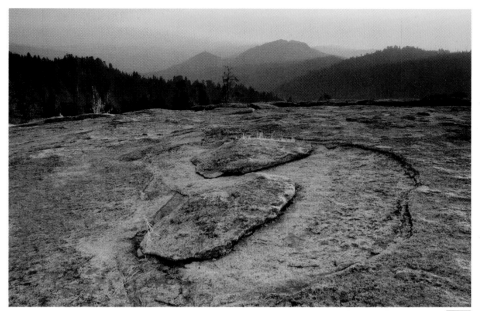

6-2

WHAT IS YOUR PHOTO ABOUT?

The landscape image I use here is a good one for this chapter on Camera Raw basic workflow. I am not going to jump in and start changing this photo for you, though. How do you think about adjusting a photo? I believe it is important to know what your photograph is about and why you shot it, as this influences your choices. Arbitrarily adjusting an image based on some sort of objective criteria sooner or later gets the photographer into trouble, or at the least, gives less than pleasing results. Know the purpose of the photo, and make adjustments that support that purpose.

This example used throughout the chapter is an image of the very famous Beetle Rock in Sequoia National Park at sunset. The area was made famous by a classic nature book, One Day on Beetle Rock, by Sally Carrighar; however, if you are of the baby boomer generation, you may remember it from the Disney movie of the same name. It is a big granite dome with little vegetation on it, so if you go out onto the rock, you can see quite well over a large part of the horizon.

NOTE

When Camera Raw is first opened, a warning sign that looks like a road sign with an exclamation point may appear. This just means your computer is still working and processing the file for your use.

I found the exfoliation patterns (the places the rock had broken up in the foreground) interesting (see figure 6-3) and wanted to balance that with the sunset. This is why I shot with a two-stop graduated neutral-density filter. Without that filter, the sky would be too bright. Sure, I could have done some Photoshop gymnastics to bring the sky into balance, but why bother when you can shoot it right in the first place and save the trouble? So obviously, I want to retain that detail in the final shot. In addition, the sunset color is important, so that's something else to be careful of in adjustment.

There is no need to overanalyze every photograph you shoot before opening Camera Raw. That is counterproductive. However, you do need to respect your photograph. Using Camera Raw should be about getting the most from your photo, not getting the most from Camera Raw. I believe in the photograph and the photographer.

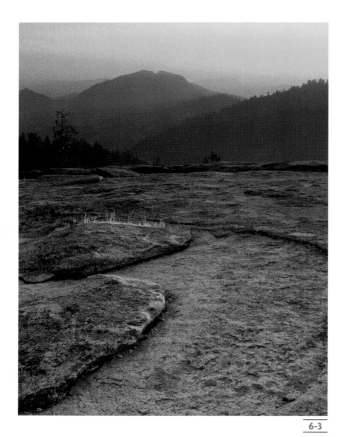

6-3

AUTO SETTINGS

When Camera Raw is first opened in Photoshop CS2, all Auto settings are selected by default as seen in figures 6-4 and 6-5. I highly recommend you deselect all of them, as seen in figure 6-6, and then click on the arrow-triangle to the far right of Settings to access a menu that gives the choice Save New Camera Raw Defaults. Choose that and all other files of that type will open the same way.

The auto settings work — but with varied amounts of success on different photos. They can be misleading if Camera Raw opens with them. You can always reselect any individual Auto setting choice to see if it helps (and sometimes it will). But it seems odd to use Auto settings for Camera Raw, because this program, Camera Raw, is the epitome of control. Auto settings relinquish your control and allow arbitrary mathematical formulas to decide what your photo should look like.

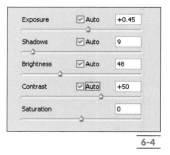

6-4

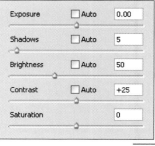

6-5

I love what the Adobe engineers have done in creating Camera Raw and Photoshop. These are stunning, powerful programs. They have tried to be helpful in creating auto settings that apply what they believe are effective ways of adjusting images. As much as I love the engineers' brilliant computer work (and it is brilliant — I can't begin to understand what happens under the hood of Photoshop), I don't think they are capable of looking into the future and knowing what you or I had in mind for a specific photo. Auto settings simply look at the tones of a photo and adjust them according to what Adobe engineers think a photo should look like based on arbitrary analysis of your photo compared to their mathematical ideal.

WORKFLOW OPTIONS

Once you open the photo, start at the bottom left of the Camera Raw interface and begin your adjustments from there. Make sure the Show Workflow Options check box is selected, as shown in figure 6-7.

This section of the Camera Raw interface is pretty straightforward. It is definitely not the creative part. It defines how Camera Raw will interpret standard parts of an image, such as the color space and image size. You will usually set this once based on your most common workflow needs and leave it alone for most photos (after using the Save New Camera Raw Defaults choice described earlier in this chapter). The only part that is commonly changed on even a somewhat regular basis is the Size choice to match specific image size needs.

1. Check the Space field. By clicking in this box or on the down arrow you get a drop-down menu of a number of available color spaces, as shown in figure 6-8. You can use any of them, but I recommend Adobe RGB or sRGB (you are always safe with Adobe RGB). Adobe RGB provides the wider color gamut, which is important when working with all the subtle colors seen in the photo that you are working with. In this photo, Adobe RGB seemed to be the best choice for these colors. The preview can give you an idea of the difference. You can

click back and forth between these two color spaces. I saw a potential problem in the sky with sRGB, so Adobe RGB is the best choice for this example.

PRO TIP

In Windows, double-click the Space box to highlight it and use the up- and down-arrow keys to quickly move among the color-space choices while watching the photo.

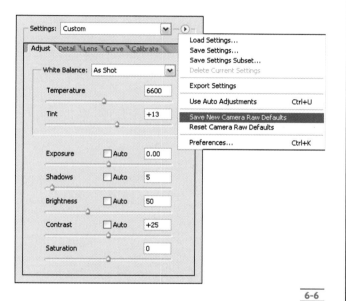

6-6

6-7

6-8

2. Click in the Depth field to choose a bit depth. You have a choice of 8 Bits/Channel or 16 Bits/Channel as seen in figure 6-9. This is an output choice and has no affect on what you are doing in Camera Raw. For most photographs, 8-bit is plenty (16-bit greatly increases the file size). For this photo, there is an argument that could be made that further adjustments in Photoshop might be helped with 16-bit because of the subtle tonal gradations throughout the image.

3. Select an output size by clicking in the Size field, as seen in figure 6-10. You can start with the native file size that your camera produces by selecting numbers without a plus or minus sign (plus means the file is

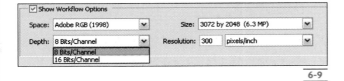

6-9

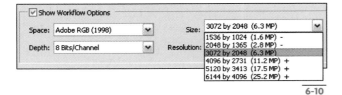

6-10

increased from the original; minus means it is decreased). If you know you need a large file from your photo, this is the best place to upsize your image. While you can resize the photo inside Photoshop to get good results, resizing in Camera Raw builds the size better because it is using more basic data from the camera and because the sizing algorithms that are used with this data are superb. It makes a much larger file, and if you decide to use 16-bit, it could be a problem if your computer lacks adequate processing power and RAM.

4. Click in the Resolution field to choose an output resolution. This has no effect on image quality; it is here purely for workflow reasons. For this photo, 300 pixels per inch is selected, as shown in figure 6-11 to process the photo for publication purposes. Having your image with an appropriate resolution for its final use means less work later checking image size. Output resolution only changes how close or far apart the computer puts pixels and does not affect their quality. You can always change this later without any harm to the photo.

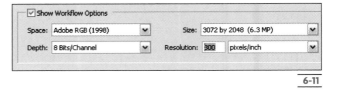

6-11

TONAL ADJUSTMENTS

The brightness (or darkness) of a photo and its contrast have a great impact on how it is perceived by a viewer. Composition is affected, but mood is probably the most strongly changed element of a photograph when it is made brighter or darker, or the contrast is adjusted. Color also has a big effect, but generally, it is better to start with tonal adjustments unless there are color problems. Camera Raw offers three key tonal adjustment controls, plus a weaker fourth. The first, Exposure, is not particularly intuitively named for what it is used for, but the others are. Here is a quick summary of them as seen in figure 6-12.

> **Exposure.** This seems like it might be for overall adjustment, but it is actually used for highlights and bright areas of a photo. The whole image gets brighter or darker, but use this slider to change highlights. If you press and hold Alt/Option while adjusting this, you can see where the bright areas clip detail — pure white is no detail. The colors represent channels that are full in the sense that they are at their maximum. Camera Raw in Photoshop CS2 introduced highlight warnings (select the Highlights option check box at the top right) — this can be helpful, but it can also be confusing compared to using Alt/Option.

> **Shadows.** This slider affects the shadows and black levels of the photo. The whole image darkens, but the key to this adjustment is the dark parts of the photo. If you press and hold Alt/Option while making this adjustment, you can see where the dark areas clip detail — pure black is no detail. The colors represent channels that are at their minimum. Camera Raw in Photoshop CS2 introduces shadow warnings (select the Shadows option at the top right). While this can also be helpful, it can be less clear compared to using Alt/Option.

> **Brightness.** Once highlights and shadows are adjusted, you can tweak the overall brightness of the image with this slider (it is affecting midtones). As

you change it, you may find highlights (Exposure) and shadows affected such that they have to be slightly refined in their own adjustments.

> **Contrast.** This slider affects the overall contrast of the image, but it is a bit too heavy handed for my taste. You can gain better control of the contrast by separately adjusting the highlights and shadows. Most of the time you can leave it at its default setting.

Exposure, Shadows, and Brightness can be compared to Levels adjustments in Photoshop. The black slider at the left of Levels is like Shadows, the white slider to the right is like Exposure, and the middle slider is like Brightness. The Curves adjustment of Camera Raw (Photoshop CS2 only) is an excellent way to adjust the overall brightness of the image (affecting midtones), but the Beetle Rock photo does not need it, so this group of tonal adjustments is enough for now.

Here's how to continue work on this image:

1. Press and hold Alt/Option, and click and drag the Exposure slider. The whole image usually gets black except for a few small areas as shown in figure 6-13 (on some photos, your exposure might make it all black to start). This screen shows the threshold of tones as they change to pure white. As you move the slider, the bright or colored areas represent highlights. The white is pure white, no detail. You can alternately click on and off or press Alt/Option on and off to see how these areas relate to the whole image.

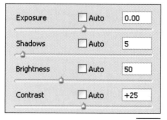

6-12

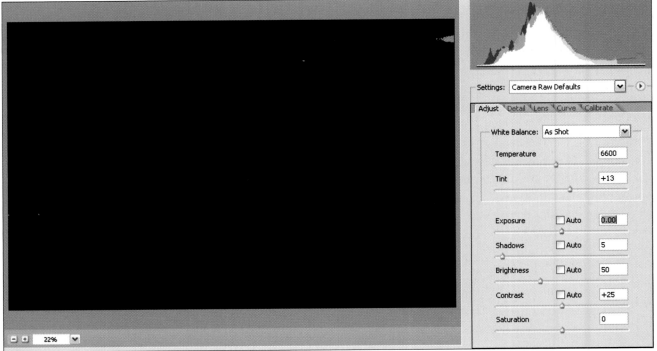

6-13

2. While continuing to press and hold Alt/Option, click and drag the Exposure slider right to increase bright areas, or left to decrease. This is a subjective decision, but generally you want at least something very bright in most photos. In this photo, the sky should remain bright without clipping (losing detail and color). You can always try moving the slider too far and see how the image is affected, as seen in figure 6-14. In this photo, the highlights brighten a little in the rocks as the sky gets brighter (see figure 6-15), but if you go too far, the sky loses some of its color because it gets too bright.

3. Press and hold Alt/Option click and drag the slider for Shadows. Just the opposite of Exposure, the whole image turns white except for a few small areas, as shown in figure 6-16. This screen shows the threshold of tones as they change to pure black. The black or colored areas represent the darkest shadows — the black is pure black, no detail. Again, try alternately clicking on and off or pressing Alt/Option to see how these areas relate to the whole image. Depending on your image's original exposure, this may also appear as pure white at first until you move the slider.

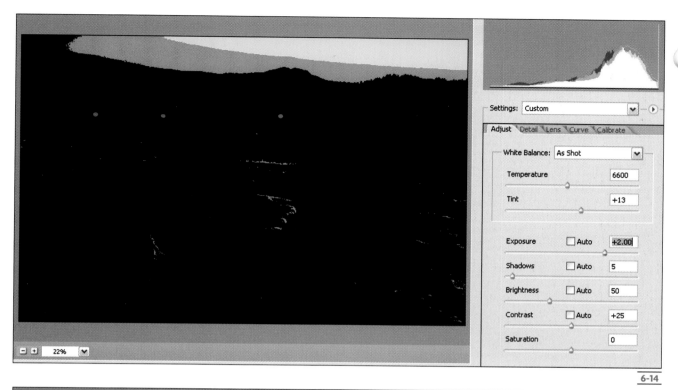

6-14

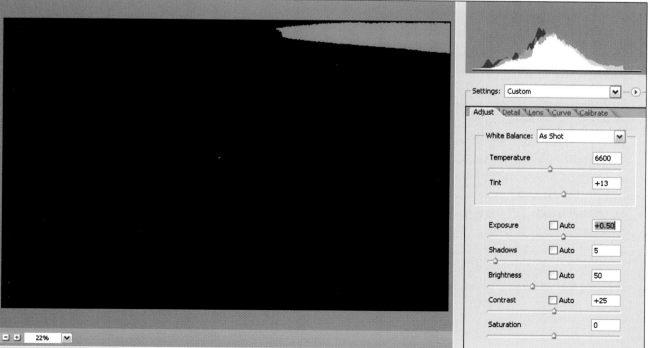

6-15

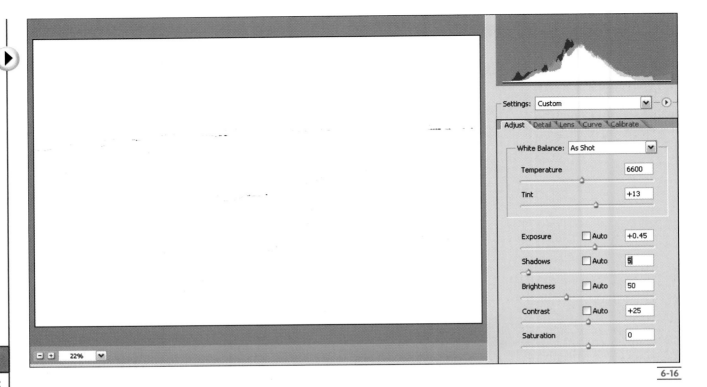

6-16

4. While pressing Alt/Option, click and drag the Shadows slider to the right to increase dark areas, or to the left to decrease. This is also a very subjective decision, but generally you want at least something black or near black in most photos. In this photo, the blacks show up in ways that are quite clearly defined. I like picking up the blacks where they outline some key features in this particular composition. You can always try moving the slider too far and see how the image is affected, although the whole thing gets rather dark. In this photo, if you go too far, the dark areas block up as shown in figure 6-17, and the image looks too harsh. This image looks best when the black areas barely outline key features as seen in figure 6-18. You will note that the trees show up as a color. This means

that the color channel is clipping, but without it being black, it also means there is some tonality in it. If I wanted the trees a pure, clipped black, I would move the Shadows slider farther to the right.

As noted before, photographers often do not get the proper blacks in an image. Without a strong black, colors and contrast will often look weak. Deep blacks in the shadow can be very attractive in the right image. This is not true for highlights. If highlights get washed out, they become pure white. That will generally be a distraction to the image as people tend to be attracted by bright spots in an image. Plus, large areas of white can be very unattractive in a photo while large areas of black can just be dramatic.

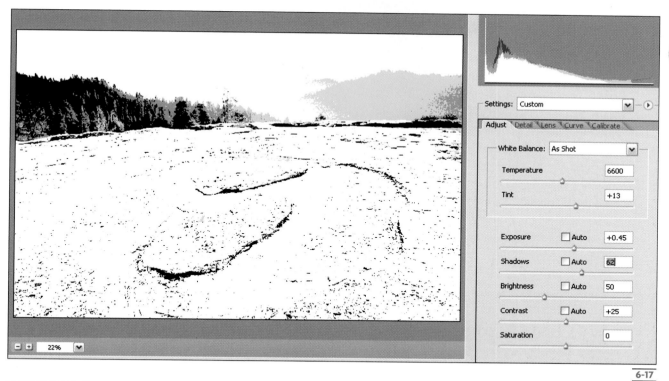

6-17

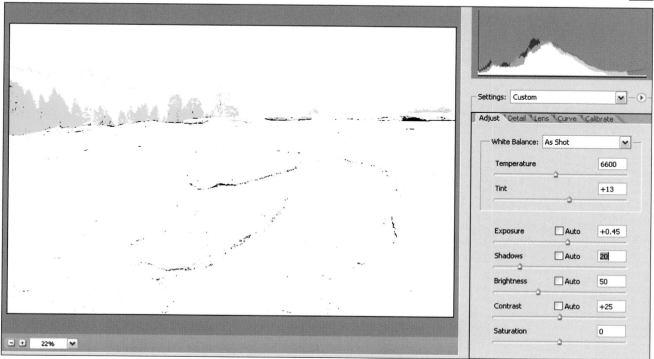

6-18

5. Making the highlight and shadow adjustments makes the photo too dark. To correct that, click and drag the Brightness slider to the right, as shown in figure 6-19. This adjustment is even more subjective than the others and is totally a matter of taste. This also demands a calibrated monitor for best results. A brighter image allows you to see more details, but it can also lose some of the drama of a darker photo. Do not press and hold any keys for this adjustment; however, it can be useful to try the auto setting here. In this particular photo, the auto setting makes the image too dark, so the Brightness level is moved up to give the image the airy, colorful feel that I remember from the scene.

6. Leave Contrast at its default setting. In general, you are setting the contrast of the image by your use of Exposure and Shadows. I find that if you need more contrast, you are generally better off using a stronger Shadows setting and/or working with the Tone Curve, which will be explained later.

7. As a final check, select the Shadows and Highlights options (select them one at a time) to see where the darkest and lightest areas end up in the photo, as shown in figures 6-20 and 6-21. Selecting these options enables you to see colored areas — red for highlights, blue for shadows.

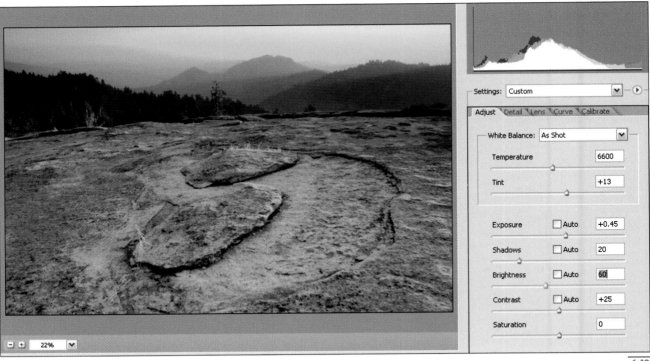

6-19

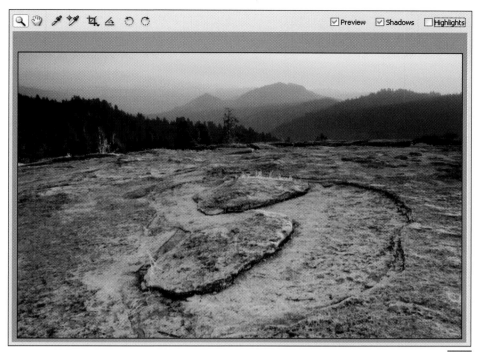

6-20

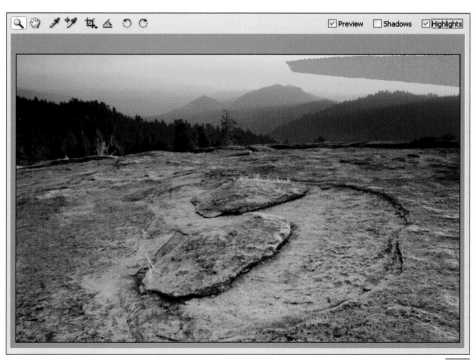

6-21

Colorful Warnings in Camera Raw

Showing the whole image as black with light highlights or white with black shadows is using Photoshop's ability to show you the threshold of when detail changes to pure white or black. Bright areas without any detail appear as pure white in the black field and dark areas without any detail appear as pure black in the white field. This is far easier to use than the highlight and shadow warnings that are included now in Camera Raw. If you check the Highlights and Shadows checkboxes above the Preview image, you will turn on these warnings. Colored areas will now appear (red for highlights, blue for shadows) when highlights or shadows in your photo exceed the thresholds for white or black, respectively. These colored areas actually show you the same detail-less areas that the Alt/Option threshold technique shows you, but with less clarity because you have to disentangle these colors from the rest of the photo. You can quickly go back and forth from the threshold view to the real image to compare what is happening when using the technique described above, but the colored parts of the warning settings make this a little harder to interpret. You can certainly try the warnings, and if they help you, use them.

PRO TIP

It can help to look at the histogram for additional information. Unfortunately, Adobe has not provided the ability to change it from a full-color, channel-based histogram to an overall, luminance-based histogram. The colors make reading the tonalities in the histogram more difficult. However, if you look closely at the colors, you can get an idea of what is happening to them at the extremes (shadows at the left and highlights at the right). In this photo, you can see the overall tones are well within the histogram range. There is slight clipping of the Red channel at the right, which is okay because it represents the strong warm color of the sunset. There is also slight clipping of the Blue channel at the left, which is fine for shadows.

8. It also helps to select and deselect the Preview option to see how the image has changed from how it came into the program (the effect is shown in figures 6-22 and 6-23). If you find you have lost something in comparing the preview with the old version, you can readjust the image.

9. You can always reset the whole thing by going to the Settings box above the sliders. Click in it and find a setting called Image Settings, which you can choose to reset Camera Raw to the original image settings. You can also press and hold Alt/Option at any time — when Cancel changes to Reset appears at the lower right, click it.

10. Small adjustments can make a big difference. Sometimes I wish this interface had two sliders for each control — one for adjustment here now and another for finer tuning. But it doesn't, so realize that small changes can be enough. If you really have trouble doing a small enough adjustment, you can type new numbers in the box above the adjustment or you can highlight the number and use the up and down arrow keys to change it

X-REF

For more on understanding the histogram, see Chapter 3.

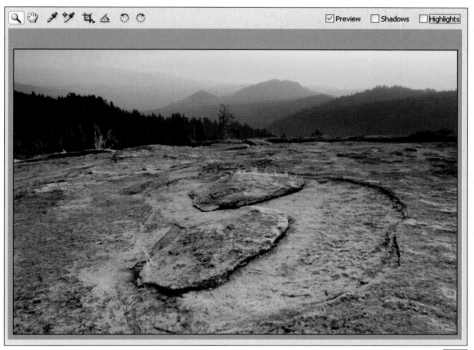

6-22

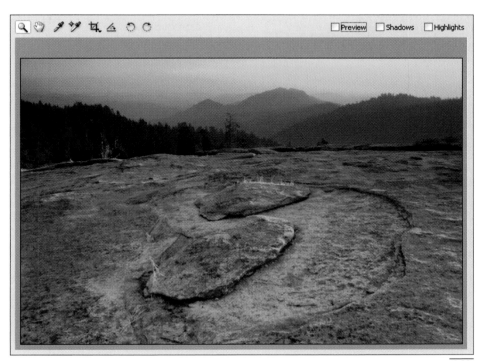

6-23

Color Adjustments

Color of an image is a tricky thing. Some images like the scene in figure 6-24 have a natural colorcast that can be expected from a landscape at sunset. On the other hand, other photos demand a neutral tonality with no colorcast at all. Camera Raw lets you do both.

In Chapter 5, you learned about the main color tools for Camera Raw: White Balance (how shot, temperature, tint), and Saturation. The Beetle Rock photo looks good right now, but there is more that can be done to get the most out of its color. For your own images, it is always worth looking at these key color tools and what they do for your photos. You may be surprised at how even a small adjustment for any of them can help. Here's how to deal with color using the Beetle Rock photo:

1. White Balance set to As Shot looks pretty good. This was actually shot at the Cloudy white-balance setting, although if you set Camera Raw to Cloudy, a different look appears. The settings in figure 6-25 do not directly correspond to camera settings, but they give you a quick way of changing white balance. Looking at this image, Cloudy also looks right (as expected), Shade is too strong, and Daylight makes the sunset too weak. Daylight may actually be closer to what the eye sees, but this is not how people see photographs

PRO TIP

Sunset (and sunrise) photos look richer and more natural when settings such as Shade or Cloudy are used when photographing the scene.

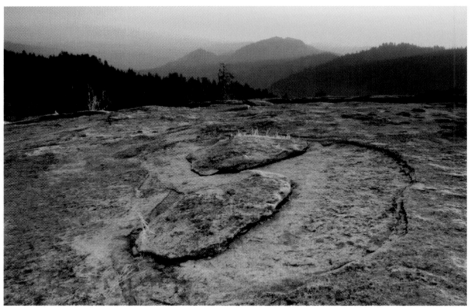

6-24

of sunsets. Everyone is used to the way films like Fujichrome Velvia and Kodak Kodachrome warm up sunrises and sunsets and expect those conditions to look like they did with film.

2. It often helps to try a little tweak of the Temperature slider. Adding a slight bit of warmth enriches the colors, but too much makes them look unnatural. A photographer friend of mine loves to shoot many outdoor subjects with strong warming filters, so he is willing to go farther than I am with this adjustment. Be careful, however, that you do not go too far and make the photo look artificial. Strong Temperature adjustments usually need some Tint tweaking. This photo needs no additional Tint adjustment other than what it came into Camera Raw with, as shown in figure 6-26.

3. Check Saturation, although this is a very personal decision that you come to over time working with Camera Raw. Be careful about overdoing this control — a little goes a long way. For this shot, a big jump of about 10 points helps the contrast between rocks and sunset colors, and it doesn't hurt the overall color balance (see figure 6-27). Look at Saturation changes in that way — what does it help, what does it hurt?

NOTE

Changing the color temperature is actually a relative thing. What you are doing is changing the color temperature setting relative to the original color temperature of the scene as captured, but the effective result is a warming or cooling of the photo. Cooling comes when the color temperature is higher than the comparative temperature, warmer when it is lower. Slight changes make a big difference, so you can type smaller number changes in the box above the slider scale.

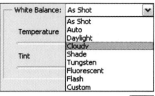

6-25

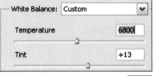

6-26

PRO TIP

Saturation is another highly subjective control, and you must be very careful with it. A little addition of saturation (the intensity of color) goes a long way. Many photographers make the common mistake of increasing saturation too much so that the image either looks garish or does not reproduce properly outside of Photoshop. That said, many subjects, especially nature, sky, architecture, and travel, look good with a slight addition of saturation of perhaps 5 to 10 points. On images of people, be very careful as this control can make skin tones look unnatural at best and blotchy at worst.

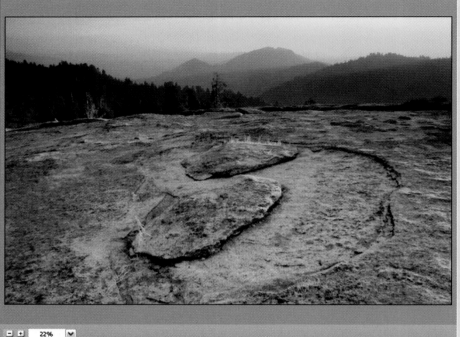
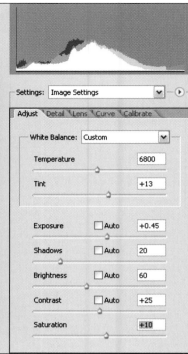

6-27

DETAIL ADJUSTMENTS

Noise issues are the next elements to check in the photo. You find this in the Detail tab next to the Adjust tab in the adjustments area. There are three new adjustments here: Sharpness, Luminance Smoothing, and Color Noise Reduction, which are all seen in figure 6-28 which also shows an enlarged area of the main image so noise can be better seen.

> **Sharpness.** Set this to 0 for now. It is best not to sharpen the photo at this point in the process.

> **Luminance Smoothing.** This affects the general noise that comes from a sensor and may be seen in skies and other smooth tones.

> **Color Noise Reduction.** This affects color noise effects that often appear in dark parts of an image, especially when that image is underexposed.

Noise reduction settings are not for getting rid of problem noise but to reduce normal levels of noise so that the image goes into Photoshop as good as possible. If you use these controls to try to remove high levels of noise, you can cause problems with details in the photo. You are better off, in those situations, in using noise programs specially designed to deal with noise problems (including Photoshop CS2's noise reduction, although it is not as effective as some independent software such as Noise Ninja, Kodak ASF GEM, or nikMultimedia Dfine).

Back to Beetle Rock (and figure 6-29). It is very important to enlarge your image in order to see the noise. You will not see noise if the image shows 100% in the preview. Good areas to see noise are in smooth toned segments of the image, such as sky. Noise can be hard to see in highly patterned areas.

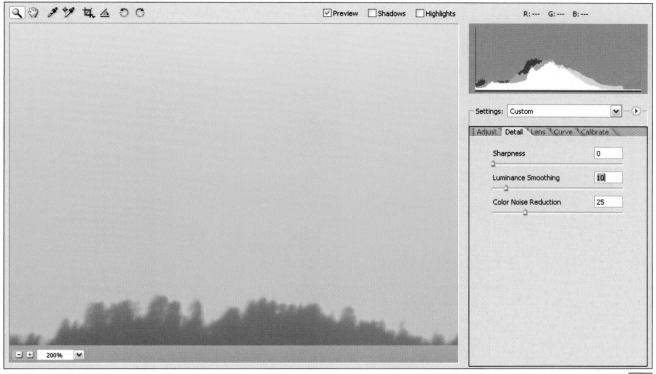

6-28

1. **Check for noise.** The Magnifying tool is used to greatly enlarge the sky to see what noise might be there. Because this image has very little, a setting of about 10 for Luminance Smoothing works fine. You can try moving the slider in big jumps back and forth to see any changes that might be possible. I move the image around, looking for luminance noise, by pressing and holding the space bar, which transforms the cursor into the Hand tool. This allows you to click and move the photo inside its preview window.

2. **Continue searching for noise.** I again use the Magnifying tool, this time to greatly enlarge a dark tree area as seen in figure 6-29. Now I look for chromatic or color noise. This image is very clean, so no Color Noise Reduction needs to be added. Actually, I reduce it to a minimal amount because Color Noise Reduction reduces color in the little details — in a photo like this, all of the color that comes from the sunset light is important.

PRO TIP

When you greatly magnify an image in Camera Raw, it can be hard to move around to another location in the photo. Use Ctrl/Cmd 0 to get the full size of the photo. That way you can quickly find a new place to magnify in a totally different area, then use the Magnifying tool to go to a new area. This saves a lot of searching at magnified levels.

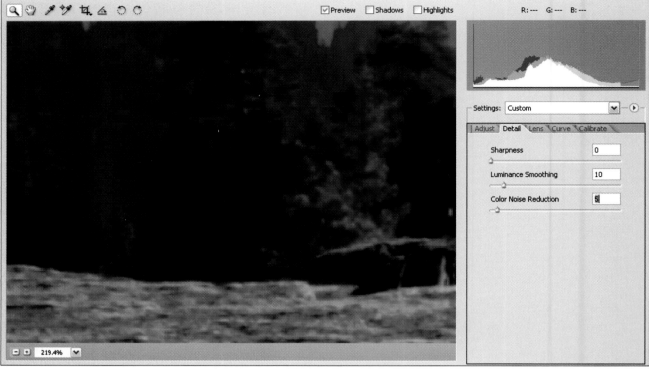

6-29

CHECK YOUR RESULTS

Before committing to all of your adjustments, it is a good idea to do a final check against the original image as it came into Camera Raw. If you are still in the Detail tab, you can click the Preview on and off to see the effects of these adjustments, but Preview only shows what is happening with a specific tab.

To see the overall effect again, go back to the Adjust tab, fit the whole image into the preview area (double-click the Magnifier icon or press Ctrl/Cmd+0), then select or deselect the Preview option to turn Preview on and off (using the P key also does this). If you have any questions about small areas of the photo that are not easily seen at full photo size, magnify those areas and again turn the preview on and off.

SAVE YOUR WORK

The default for Photoshop CS2 is to automatically update your adjusted Raw file's thumbnail in the Bridge. This is not a permanent change — actually, nothing at all in the file itself is changed, only the instructions about processing this file have been changed so that this file reopens in Camera Raw with these settings.

To keep this photo with its adjustments, you have several choices at the bottom right of the Camera Raw interface: Save, Open, Cancel, and Done. Open simply applies the settings on your photo as it converts it to the Photoshop working space. This is the most common use of Camera Raw. Cancel cancels everything and returns you to Photoshop. Done merely updates the metadata of the file and returns you to Photoshop without actually opening or saving the image. All of your settings are retained, but this is a specialized and not very common way of using Camera Raw.

However, when you click Save, the Save Options dialog box appears, as shown in figure 6-30. It offers a few different options.

The Save Options dialog box offers options to let you choose a destination for your file, give it an new name, and save an adjusted image as one of four file types: DNG, JPEG, TIFF, and Photoshop (PSD) (see figure 6-30).

> **DNG.** This is Adobe's all-purpose Raw file, Digital Negative, and keeps the Raw data of your original intact. This format is still developing; it is a good format for archiving Raw files. For most purposes, you can use the default settings (lossless compression and medium JPEG preview).

> **JPEG.** This type of image file can be opened on any platform. JPEG also lets you compress the image when you quickly need a smaller file to send to someone over the Internet (or if you have to use a device with limited storage space).

> **TIFF.** This type of file can also be opened on any platform. TIFF is an uncompressed (or losslessly compressed) larger file.

> **Photoshop**. This file is saved with a PSD extension and is the ideal working file for an image that you want to work on more in Photoshop (you can just open the image to do this — click Save to keep a file to work on later).

SETTING UP CAMERA RAW FOR YOUR CAMERA

Camera Raw recognizes image files from your digital camera. You can set Camera Raw up for some common ways you prefer to work on them. Once you set a new file to some standard adjustments, you can tell Camera Raw to save them by using the Save New Camera Raw Defaults. This choice is in the drop-down menu to the right of Settings as seen in figure 6-31. However, do this at the beginning of processing an image so that only

those repeatable settings have been saved, or you will include settings for adjusting a specific photo, adjustments you do not want to use for all images.

To set up Camera Raw for your camera, you need to do some very specific things to the interface, and then save those changes. You turn off all of the automation, check basic resolution, and so forth as follows:

1. Deselect all auto settings.

2. Put in the most common color space that you want to use (if you are not sure, use Adobe RGB for now).

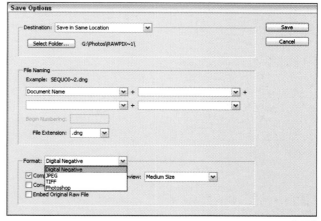

6-30

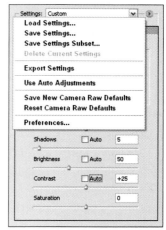

6-31

3. Choose a size that is appropriate for most of your photography. You may find it best to use the native size of the photo (the original megapixels — the choice that does not have a plus (+) or minus (−) after it) or the first larger size.

4. Choose a depth. Most work will look fine at 8 Bits/Channel.

5. Choose a resolution. If you are making prints from an inkjet printer, 240 is a good number. If you shoot for publication, use 300. Also, use pixels per inch.

6. Choose a white balance. Use the setting As Shot.

7. Do not sharpen images in Camera Raw. Leave the sharpening until last in the image adjustment process in Photoshop. Set Sharpening on the Detail tab to zero.

8. Go to the drop-down menu next to the right of Settings (click the circle/arrow button) and choose Save New Camera Raw Defaults. These settings will now occur any time you open a Raw file from the same camera.

There are several other options in this menu.

> **Load Settings, Save Settings, Save Settings Subset.** You can choose these when you work on an image from a shoot that has consistent conditions, such as a studio shoot. You can save the settings used to adjust one photo, and then use those same settings on other photos without changing the Camera Raw defaults. You simply make the adjustments needed, save the settings, open a new photo, and then load the settings. You can even make variations of such settings by choosing Save Settings Subset.

> **Export Settings.** This allows you to save the settings for use on another computer. Use Auto Adjustments turns on all auto settings, which I do not find very useful. Reset Camera Raw Defaults takes you back to the original Camera Raw settings, which is useful if you think the default settings have changed and you need to return to the original starting place.

> **Preferences.** This opens a Camera Raw Preferences dialog box (see figure 6-32) that lets you control a couple of small features. One is how image settings — the adjustments you make to your file — are saved. Remember that when settings are saved with a Raw file, nothing is actually changed on that file — this is only processing information or instructions that are applied when the file is opened. They can always be changed. Sidecar XMP files are small system files that Photoshop keeps with your photo and let Camera Raw and the Bridge know how you have adjusted this file, so an adjusted image appears as a thumbnail in the Bridge and when the photo is opened in Camera Raw. The Camera Raw database will remember changes to the file, but this is not used to update the Bridge thumbnails.

Apply sharpening to is a choice you have in how sharpening is used. You can simply deselect sharpening altogether in Camera Raw by clicking and dragging the slider in the Detail tab to 0 (my preference) or you can choose Apply sharpening to: Preview images only to see how final sharpening appears when you sharpen at the end of the process. You can generally leave Camera Raw Cache set to the default, unless your main hard drive is short on space. This is the thinking room that Photoshop uses for working on Camera Raw images. If you have multiple hard drives, you can set it to your fastest, most open drive.

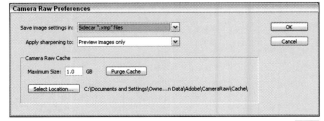

6-32

Q&A

What if I sharpen photos in Camera Raw?

Sharpening affects everything in a photo, including noise and out-of-focus areas that should not be sharpened. By sharpening at this point, you are also sharpening those things that you do not want to be sharpened. Having noise sharpened, for example, can cause problems as you do further work on an image because other adjustments find and enhance that noise.

In addition, sharpening is best applied to a specific size. A good workflow is to complete all of your adjustments to an image, then save that image as your master. Then you size that master to your finished image size and sharpen for that specific size. You then save that file as a TIFF file — I like to label it with the size, which I then know also means it has been sharpened. You do not need a new image size for every little size you want from a file, but it is a good idea to have differently sized and sharpened files for radically different sizes, such as 4 × 6, 8 × 12 and 16 × 24.

What if I use auto settings? They seem to give good results...

There is no question that the Adobe folks want users to succeed with Photoshop. They aren't going to create anything that automatically results in bad photos, so auto settings do work. The problem is that they are one-size-fits-all sorts of settings. They work by analyzing a photo then arbitrarily making adjustments based on what is usually correct. But whose standards determine what is usually correct? That's the problem.

If the image looks okay, aren't these standards also okay? They can give you an image that does indeed look okay, but then so does the high-quality JPEG setting from your camera. It seems to me a waste of time and the power of Raw if the auto settings are used because you can get similar results with JPEG and the camera's internal processing. Raw offers so much more, that to relegate it to auto seems like such a waste.

In addition, the auto settings can be misleading. They can make the photo look acceptable and cause the photographer to miss important adjustments. That's why I turn them off so that they do not appear when I first open the photo. Getting a really good image, rather than one that is mediocre, comes from really interacting with the actual photo and not following auto paths.

Chapter 7

ADVANCED TONAL CONTROL

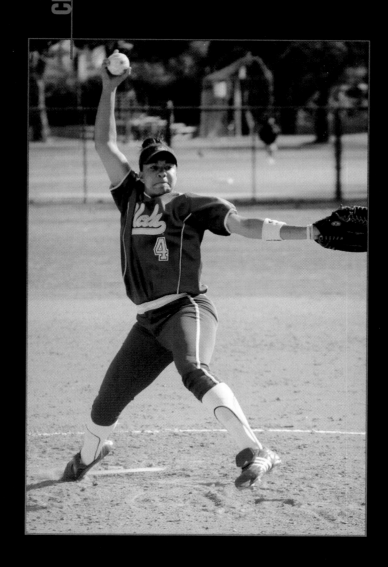

In Chapter 6, you saw a complete adjustment of an image. This chapter features a more challenging photo to continue the quest to master Camera Raw. You see some of the same things done for the Beetle Rock landscape, but this photo requires different decisions, including looking at the new Curves tab of Camera Raw in Photoshop CS2.

The photo shown in before (figure 7-1) and after (figure 7-2) versions is important for a number of reasons that affect how it should be processed. This is one of the pitchers from the very strong UCLA women's softball team. The team has consistently reached the NCAA championships and has won the championship more times than not in recent years, yet this fact is hard to find in the sports pages, let alone a photograph of a winning pitcher. Women's sports don't get the attention of men's sports, yet women athletes are at least as dedicated to their sport as men, and compared to the top three men's sports — football, basketball, and baseball — women athletes tend to be better students, as well. How you feel about a subject should always guide your interpretation of the image file.

This photo is a challenge because of the light and the range of dark and light tones. You cannot reposition players for better light during a game, so you shoot with what is available. In addition, there is an intensity to action during games that cannot be matched during practice or warm-ups. Using this photo also allows continued use of a very practical workflow for Camera Raw.

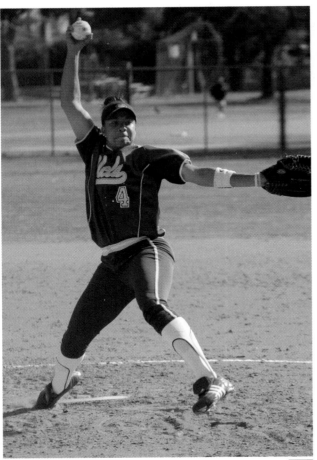

7-1

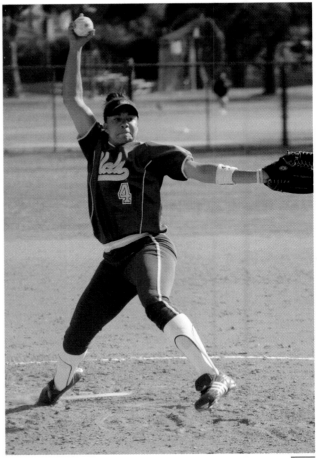

7-2

EVALUATE THE IMAGE

For every photograph opened in Camera Raw, the first step should always be to look at the image and evaluate it as a photograph. Although they may follow all the rules and guidelines they have learned for using Camera Raw, photographers sometimes start to adjust the image too quickly, before they really appreciate what the photograph is all about.

This process does not have to take a lot of time, although like any craft, working with Camera Raw requires more time in evaluating images at first if you have never done this before. You want to quickly look over an image to see what its strengths and weaknesses are. But even before that, you need to think about what the photograph is about. What is the subject? What are you trying to say about the subject? (This does not have to be anything deep, but it is important to know what should be communicated.) Why is this photograph important to you? Look at the photographic details to gather additional information. What are the highlights? Where are the shadows? Are there contrast issues? What is happening to the color?

In the introduction to this chapter, I point out a few things about this photograph. It is important to me because it shows off a premier female athlete in action. You need to see the action and the person. The tonality and color of the image should enhance both and not take away from either. This especially supports the idea that auto settings should be avoided. A photograph of action should have a different appearance than a simple portrait, even if the light for both is the same.

Looking at the photo in figure 7-3, you can quickly see from the arrows the highlights, especially on the white socks. While you don't need to see perfect texture in those areas, if they are totally blown out, they can be distracting. In addition, the color of the uniform in the shaded areas is important and a viewer of the final photo will definitely want to be able to see this dark-skinned woman's face.

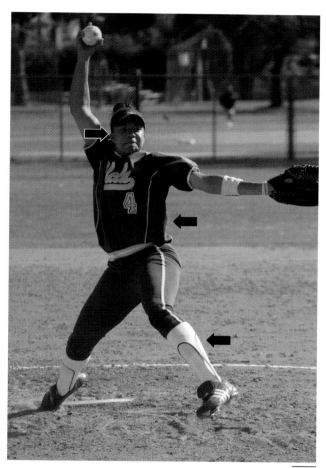

7-3

FIRST ADJUSTMENTS

This photo comes into Camera Raw on its side. While you can work on it that way, it may be distracting. If you do, you can rotate the image to a vertical position so that it looks normal. The two rotate buttons are on the Toolbar at the top of the interface — they are pretty self-explanatory, rotate left or rotate right. One problem, obviously, is that the photo now shrinks to fit vertically in an essentially horizontal preview box (compare figures 7-4 and 7-5). Maybe Adobe will someday have an interface that senses horizontal versus vertical photos and adjust its space accordingly.

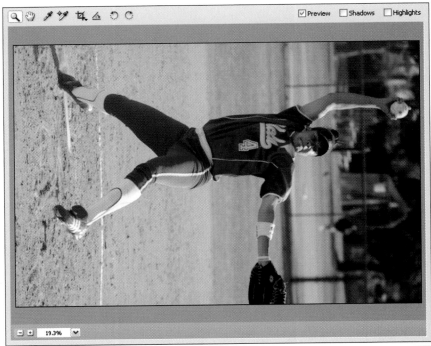

7-4

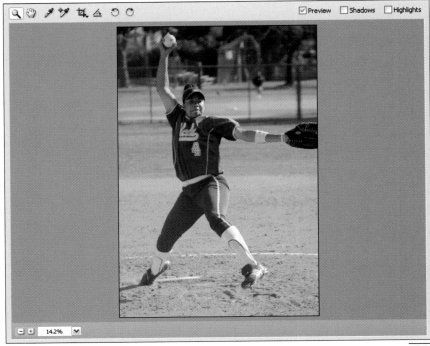

7-5

So here are the basic adjustments for this photo:

1. Rotate the image to vertical.

2. This photo looks good from the start, so no big corrections to tones or colors are needed.

3. Adjust Exposure. Press and hold Alt/Option, then click and drag the Exposure slider and watch for highlight action. This photo's highlights are already at the edge as shown in figure 7-6, so they should not be increased. Backing Exposure off a little to tone down the highlights is probably the best action.

4. Adjust the Shadows. Again, press Alt/Option to check black areas in the photo. This photo is a bit weak in the blacks, so it helps to increase the shadow setting as demonstrated in figure 7-7. Do not go too far or the colors will be lost in the shadows.

5. Adjust the midtones. This photo needs a more versatile tool for dealing with midtones than the Brightness slider. It is time to move to the Curve tab. Final color will be adjusted after working on midtones.

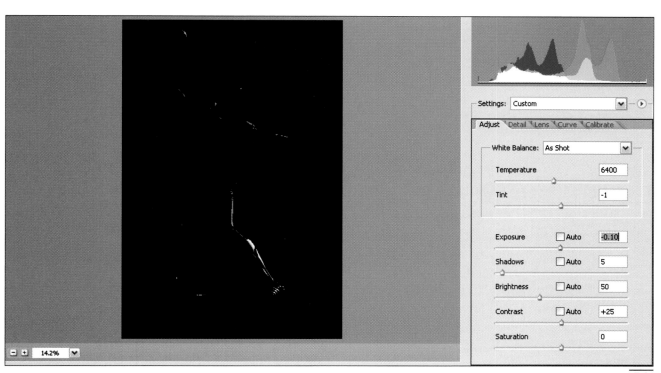

7-6

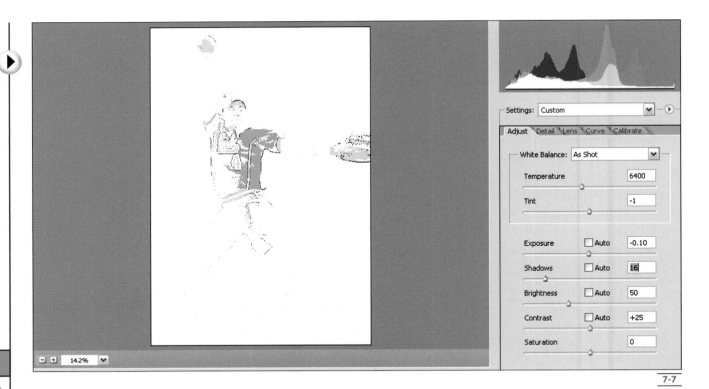

Settings: Custom

Adjust | Detail | Lens | Curve | Calibrate

White Balance: As Shot

| Temperature | 6400 |
| Tint | -1 |

Exposure	☐ Auto	-0.10
Shadows	☐ Auto	16
Brightness	☐ Auto	50
Contrast	☐ Auto	+25
Saturation		0

14.2%

7-7

TONE CURVE ADJUSTMENTS

Curves has always been an important part of Photoshop's adjustment capabilities (although Adobe's naming convention is a little confusing — the tonal curve control in Photoshop has always been called Curves, but it is in a tab labeled Curve and is called Tone Curve). This is a graph of tones from black (bottom) to white (top) that you can change by clicking on the line from the bottom left to top right and dragging it up or down. It is true that a lot of work can be done on a photograph without ever using the Curve tab or Curves at all. In fact, Photoshop Elements does not include Curves, yet you can do excellent work with that program.

The advantage of the traditional Curves adjustment is more flexibility in tonal adjustments and a more blended way of adjusting. With Curves, you can make one tonality lighter and another darker, for example, and smoothly blend all the tones in between. That is simply the way Curves works. You get into the Curves function of Camera Raw by clicking the Curve tab, shown in figure 7-8, in the adjustment area.

If you have used Curves in Photoshop, you will quickly understand how to use the Tone Curve. While you can affect black and white with this curve, it mainly affects the gray tones from darkest to lightest tones (and the colors that match those tones). The adjustment interface does, however, have a few special choices not available in Curves. Here's how to use it:

1. Once the Tone Curve tab is opened, try the choices in the actual Tone Curve box first, shown in figure 7-9. Photoshop does not include this with Curves. I think it is a great idea because it is automation that you can control! There are four choices: Linear, Medium Contrast, Strong Contrast, and Custom. In Windows,

you can quickly check the effect of each on your photo by double-clicking the box, then using your up- and down-arrow keys to go through the choices. Linear is very straightforward; Medium and Strong Contrast offer simple S-curves to give some contrast to the image; Custom automatically appears when you make any changes to the first three curves.

In this photo, Linear is a little too flat, Strong is too strong, and even Medium isn't quite right. But by going through these choices, you get a good idea of what might be needed. An adjustment of Medium Contrast works here, although in this case it is easier to start with the Linear curve.

2. Adjust the curve for midtones. After choosing Linear for this photo, click the middle of the curve to set a control point and drag it upward as shown in figure 7-10. This brings up the midtones quite nicely. The colors and the pitcher's face gain better tonalities. However, some of the contrast of the image is lost — contrast that is appropriate to an intense sports moment.

3. Adjust the curve for darker tones. The darker tones are at the lower part of the curve. By clicking and dragging that part of the curve down, the tones deepen. This photo needs two points set for the dark area of the curve, which is a great advantage of a tonal curve. The first one can bring is set near the first quarter tones (the Curve is divided into four sections by guidelines) and then brought down to the original linear line (which shows up as another guideline running diagonally through the graph).

4. Make further dark tone adjustment. The darkest tones need some darkening to build overall contrast, so I click again on the line for the curve, this time closer to the bottom left (which would be pure black). I drag this below the original linear curve as seen in figure 7-11.

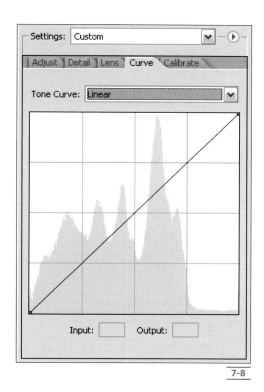

7-8

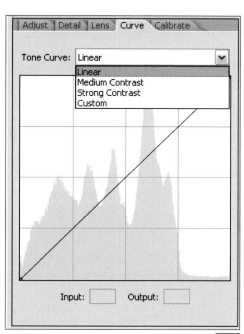

7-9

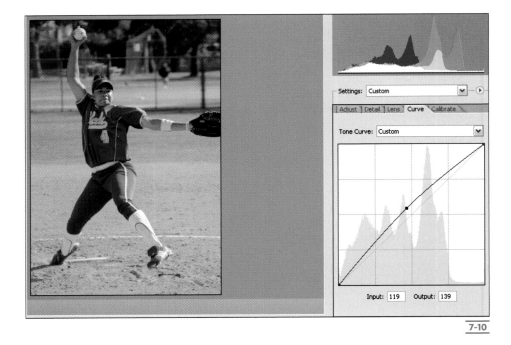

7-10

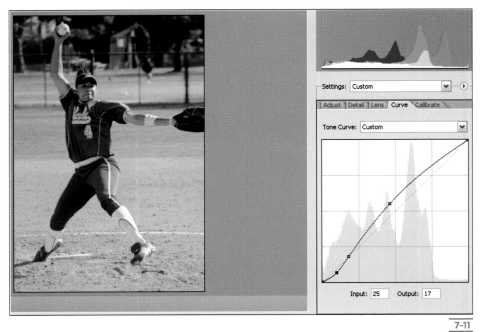

7-11

5. Check the highlights. In pulling down the lower part of the curve, some of the upper part shifts, making bright areas a little brighter. You can try pulling the top part of the curve back toward the centerline, but only slightly. You do not need to make big changes in order to see a change in the image. If you do not like the added point on the curve, click on it, then drag it quickly off the entire graph to remove it. I like the brighter high-lights so I left the top part of the curve alone.

6. Compare the adjustments with how the photo appeared without the new tonal curve. Select and deselect the Preview option to see if you like what has happened with the Curve tab adjustments. If it doesn't look quite right, try readjusting the points. You can always delete control points by clicking and dragging them out of the box.

Here are the keys to using the Curve tab as represented by the finished curve in figure 7-12 for the softball player:

> Things get brighter as control points are dragged up and darker as they are moved down.

> Multiple points can be selected to change different tones in an image.

> Darker tones are at the bottom of the line; lighter tones are at the top.

> Small adjustments go a long way.

> Contrast increases when the bottom of the curve moves down and to the right while the top moves up and to the left (the curve gets steeper). It decreases when the bottom moves up and to the left while the top moves down and to the right (the curve gets flatter).

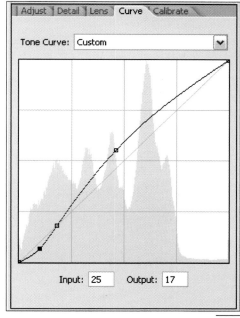

7-12

127

Back to Color

With the tonalities of the photo looking good, adjustments can go back to the Adjust tab. Overall, the color looks good, but it can be tweaked a little. One thing that happens in photos like this is that a blue sky can cause blue to appear in shadows (you typically do not see that color in such a scene — our eyes adjust to it). This is a problem with African-American skin tones — they pick up an unattractive bluish tint very quickly.

This photo could use a slight White Balance adjustment. It looks reasonable using the As Shot setting seen in figure 7-13, but it can be improved. You may find this to be true with many photos, meaning the As Shot version looks okay. I almost always will check other settings to see how the Temperature is affected and if any changes will help the photo. This does not negate what I said earlier about choosing a white balance when photographing — the advantages for consistency and for getting you quicker to good colors still apply.

1. In Windows, double-click the White Balance box to highlight the settings. Use your arrow keys to go quickly through the presets. This is not so much to choose a new preset for this photo but to see what changes seem to improve the image. When using a Mac, you have to go through each choice down the menu by clicking open the drop down menu every time.

2. Warm up the photo. In this case, the shaded areas of the subject pick up blue from the sky. The settings used on the camera help a lot (compare to the Daylight preset if you are not sure), but by moving the Temperature setting up slightly, the whole image warms and the skin tones improve as seen in figure 7-14. You do not have to move the slider very far — if you do go too far, the whole image will gain an unpleasant warm colorcast.

3. Check the tint. In this case, the way it came in from the camera seems just right.

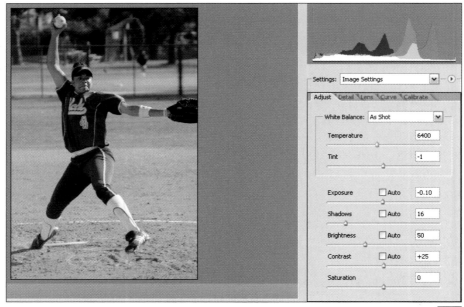

7-13

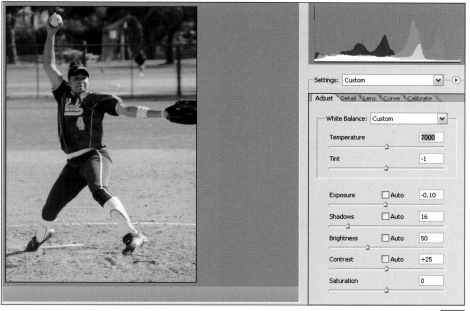

7-14

PRO TIP

Color is greatly affected by the tonalities around it, especially the white and black tones in a photograph. Setting these before final adjustment of color can help you get better, stronger colors.

EVALUATE THEN OPEN OR SAVE

I always like to make a final evaluation of the image before committing to opening it in Photoshop or saving it. There are three things you can do to check your shot before moving on:

> **Preview the image.** Select and deselect the Preview option to see the changes.

> **Check highlights and shadows.** Are they appropriate to the image? Do you need more or less detail in them? Enlarge your image to better see these areas if needed. Figure 7-15 shows an enlarged area to examine highlights, while figure 7-16 features shadows.

> **Determine if the image works.** Are all the adjustments to the image appropriate to the subject? Look at the photo in the preview (figure 7-17): do your changes make a better photo that communicates more effectively? Are the creative effects you may have wanted doing the job you expected?

Now open the image in Photoshop if you plan on doing additional work or save it for later use.

PRO TIP

If you close Camera Raw while working on an image by clicking Done, the settings are saved to the Camera Raw file (that is the sidecar XMP file in preferences). The original pixels of the file are not affected, but the Preview will not give you the original image. You must choose Settings ⇨ Camera Raw Defaults to see it. You get back to your present settings by choosing Settings ⇨ Image Settings.

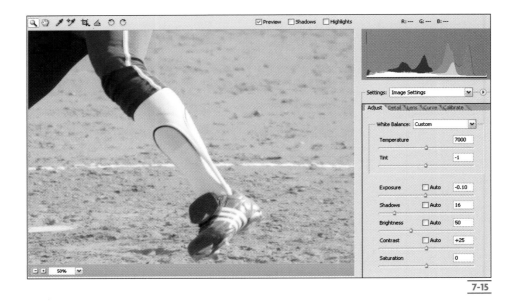

7-15

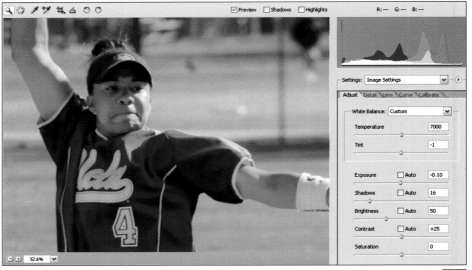

7-16

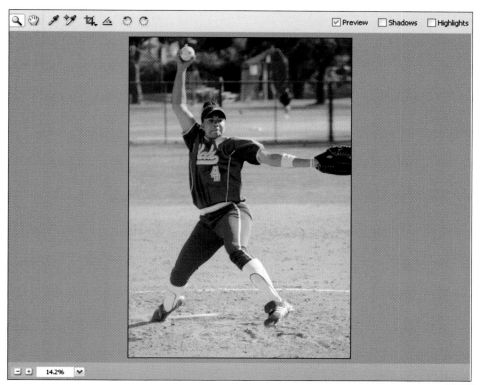

7-17

Q&A

■ **How does adjusting the tonal curve affect color in an image?**

This is a very important question. Colors are changed in two major ways by adjusting the tonal curve:

> Colors get darker and lighter. Perhaps this is obvious, but as colors change in tonality, they also frequently shift slightly in hue. That may be of little consequence in many images, but for critical color work, that can be an issue. You may have to do final corrections in Photoshop.

> As tones darken or lighten, the perception of adjacent colors changes. This is a key visual tool of artists who often deliberately change tones around essential colors so that those colors have a different impact in the image.

When should Brightness be used and when should the Tonal Curve be used to adjust midtones?

There is no absolute rule for this. Obviously, if you have an older version of Camera Raw, there is no choice — the Curve tab is not a choice. But with CS2, you do have that choice.

In general, do not be afraid to do moderate midtone adjustments with the Brightness slider, although technically, you get better tonalities by using a curve. If you have an image that has a lot of gentle, blending colors and tones (for example, a portrait with skin tones), you often find that a curve is best from the start. If you have to do stronger midtone adjustments, the curve is usually the best way to go.

A lot of this depends on the subject. Portraits, as mentioned, do well with curves, while many landscapes and architectural subjects are easily (and effectively) adjusted with the Brightness control.

What if I never use the Tonal Curve? Brightness seems easier.

It is indeed easier. You just have to deal with one slider that affects midtones. It is a little like the middle tone slider of Levels in Photoshop. The Tonal Curve, on the other hand, has infinite variety to its use because you can put multiple control points on the curve and use them to bend it every which way.

If you find that you get the results you want from the Brightness slider, don't worry about the Tonal Curve. After all, Camera Raw before Photoshop CS2 had no such adjustment and photographers did just fine with it, creating superb images. However, there are two basic advantages to the Tonal Curve:

> **Control over tonalities is definitely increased.** You can click on the bottom of the curve where the dark areas reside, increase their level, click on the top of the curve, home of highlights, decrease their level, and then click to add another point in a different place in the bottom of the curve in order to further adjust the dark areas. This offers much flexibility.

> **Gradations between dark and light tones are improved with the tonal curve.** This is because of the way it gradually makes the change between the dark and light tones, which can be especially helpful in images with a lot of fine gradations in tone.

Chapter 8

WHITE BALANCE DECISIONS

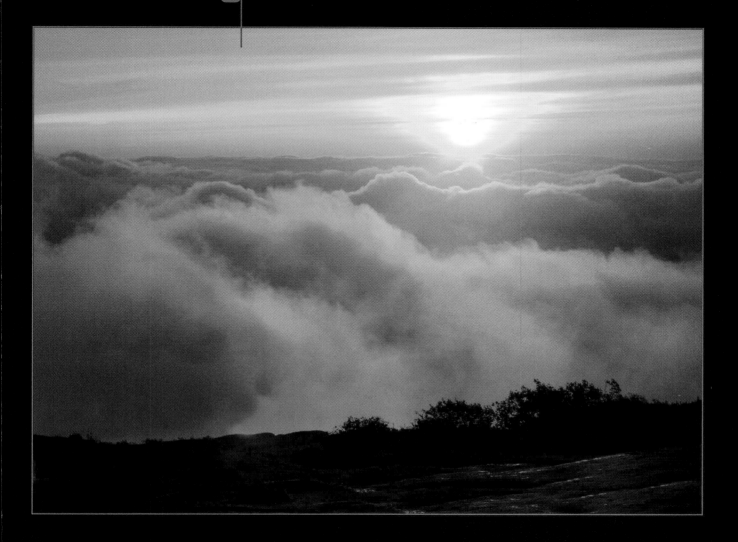

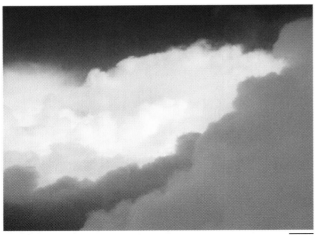

8-1

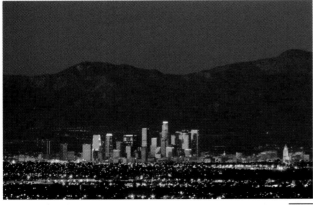

8-2

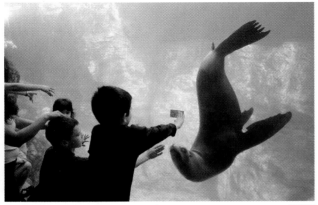

8-3

Color is a critical issue for color photography, obviously. Yet, because it is so obvious, it is often taken for granted. Less than satisfactory color in digital images frequently appears because color balance (white balance) is treated too casually.

You have the ability to control color very critically in Camera Raw through the use of the white balance settings. White balance relates to a specific technique that originated in video production, but here it is essentially the same as color balance — creating a balance of colors that is appropriate for the subject and the purpose of the photograph. As mentioned before, a calibrated monitor is critical for best results in evaluating color.

Three examples in this chapter show the range of possibilities of color adjustment using the white balance controls. The finished versions of the three photos — clouds, a dusk/night scene, and a very colored image of kids playing with a seal — are seen in figures 8-1, 8-2, and 8-3 —. The tonal adjustment process is included, but it is abbreviated from the previous chapters.

A NEUTRAL SUBJECT IS RARELY NEUTRAL

If you fly a lot, takeoffs and landings can offer some wonderful photo opportunities. As weather conditions change, clouds break and the picture possibilities are terrific (though such conditions can result in some bumps when flying through them). Even if you don't expect much, it can still be helpful to keep a camera out early in the morning when the light can be especially good on clouds.

The photo in figure 8-4 was taken when the weather pattern was in flux. This is a time I always have a camera ready. As soon the plane broke through the lowest clouds, wonderful scenic vistas of cloudscapes appeared. You shoot fast in these conditions because of the speed at which the plane moves through the clouds.

Looking at clouds superficially, they seem to be mostly neutral white and gray, except at dawn or dusk. This scene fits neither condition. But clouds are not neutral, but their neutral tones show off slight color variations due to decisions you make in choosing a white-balance for your camera. These changes become critical to the overall appearance of the photo, too.

Unfortunately, there is no easy way to discuss what is the best color for the clouds because you respond quite differently to the same shot as slight changes occur in the color balance. You may prefer a different balance than another photographer. You have the right to interpret your image the best you can, and white balance is a key area of interpretation.

CLOUD TONALITIES INTERPRETED

Go through the cloud shot from the beginning and continue to examine how to evaluate an image as it is processed in Camera Raw.

1. In this photo, the subtle tonalities among all the clouds are a very important part of the photo. This is a good candidate for 16-bit output, as shown in figure 8-5, which allows further adjustment of subtle highlight tones, especially, without problems.

2. Adjust the highlights. Overall, the photo looks fine, with excellent tonalities and no color problems, so the next step is to go right to Exposure and check the highlights as shown in figure 8-6. It's really critical in a photo like this to retain good, rich detail in the brightest areas. If the very bright center of the clouds was blown out to nothing, it would be an annoying distraction.

3. Check black levels. This photo has no real blacks, nor should it, as seen in figure 8-7. Clicking and dragging the Shadows slider until blacks appear gives the photo a harsh and unappealing appearance. However, bringing some black into the image can build more contrast between the middle, bright clouds and the outer, dark clouds and sky. You can achieve the right amount of dark tones by moving the Shadows slider to the right. Press and hold Alt/Option until dark tones just start to show. Then back up until they just barely appear in this threshold screen.

> **PRO TIP**
>
> People see neutral tones as neutral in real life. The human eye/brain connection interprets the world in a very specific way, regardless of the color of the light (under normal light conditions), so that neutral grays have no colorcast. The camera does not see this way and always responds to the color of the light, adding a colorcast to it if the white balance does not match that light. Look for parts of your photo that absolutely need to be neutral in tone and work to keep them neutral as the photo is adjusted.

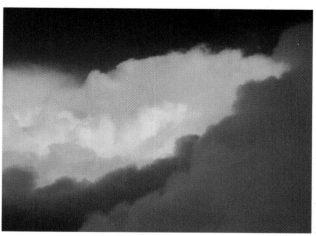

8-4

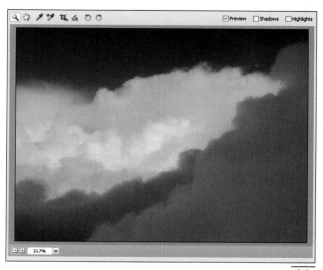

8-5

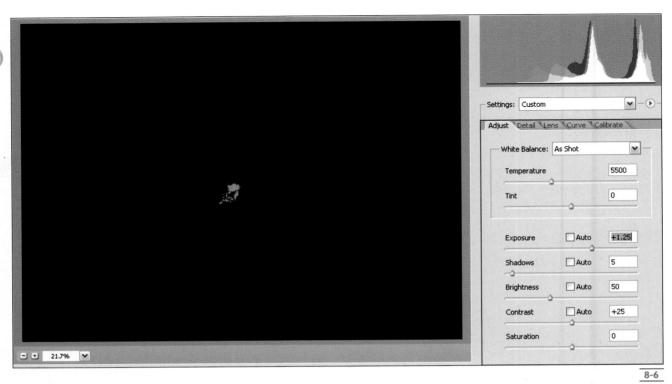

8-6

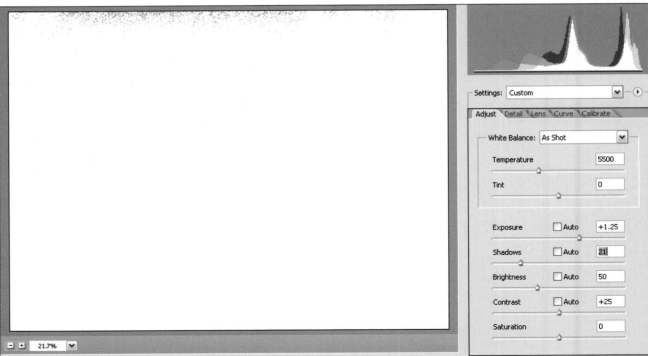

8-7

4. For midtones, not much is really needed. Kicking the Brightness down just a little makes the image look a little richer, as demonstrated in figure 8-8. The Tonal Curve can always be checked for midtones. Here it was left on Medium Contrast after quickly comparing the other settings.

5. Review the details. There is a bit of noise in the sky as seen in figure 8-9. This is not unusual with small digital cameras like the one used to make this image, a Canon PowerShot G6. While such cameras are very convenient and perfect for this sort of shot because you don't have to deal with a big camera, their sensors are inherently more noisy than those in a digital SLR. Luminance Smoothing is increased all the way

up to 60 as demonstrated in figure 8-10 — this is high and can cause problems with fine details, but there is none in this photo. This is also unusual, even for small cameras, and occurs because of the way the small sensor deals with the subtle gradations of the high-altitude sky (and parts of the dark clouds). Chrominance Noise Reduction is not a factor (it is more a problem in underexposed images).

PRO TIP

If noise reduction by Luminance Smoothing or Chrominance Noise Reduction is not enough in Camera Raw without extreme settings (or at any setting), don't try to do it all in Camera Raw. Use another noise-reduction procedure or plug-in later in Photoshop.

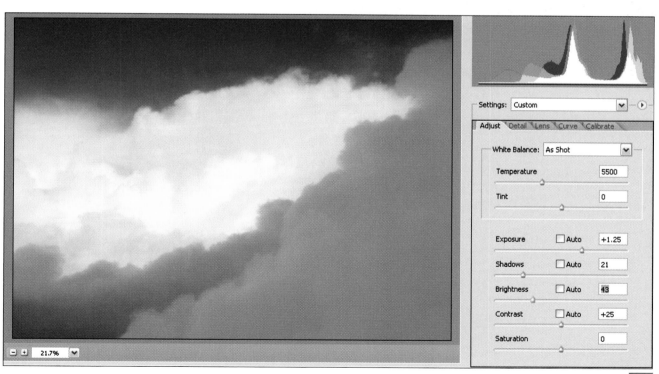

8-8

137

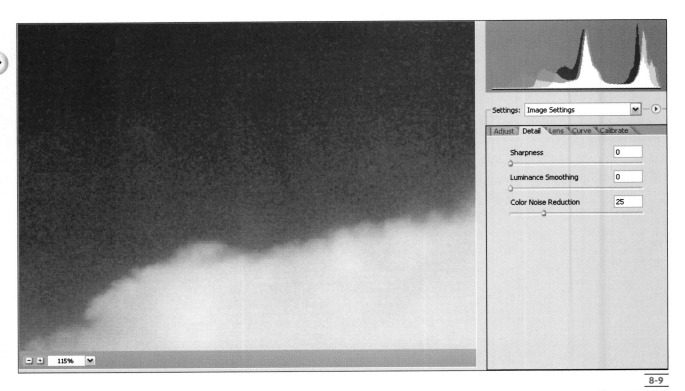

8-9

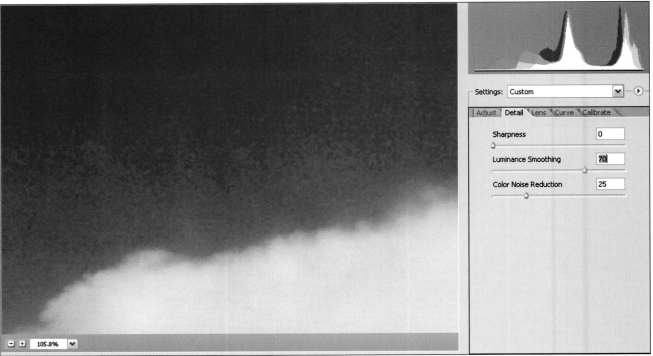

8-10

CLOUD COLOR

Overall, the photo looks a little blue at this point, but then, the image is in the sky, surrounded by blue, so that can be a valid interpretation of the image. I don't like the blue, however.

1. This is an ideal job for the White Balance tool because there are so many different shades of white and gray to work with. This tool has minimal effect on tonalities, and it is mainly used to remove color from neutral tones. You can click in various places in the clouds and see many different, though slight, variations in color. Both the Temperature and Tint settings change as you click.

   Click the center, bright clouds to remove the warmth in them and make them neutral. That makes the photo even bluer. You can click the dark clouds to the right to maintain the color temperature of the original image, but it boosts Tint in the magenta direction, warming things up slightly.

   Clicking in the lower-left clouds greatly increases the color temperature, but perhaps to an excessive level, as shown in figure 8-11.

2. Click around the photo and watch the Temperature and Tint numbers change. You can see that the overall effect of warming has a nice look, but something in between the warmth from the right cloud click and the warmer conditions from the left cloud click works best from my perspective. The right cloud was clicked, and then the Temperature setting was increased slightly, as seen in figure 8-12. You don't need a big change for an image like this that is dependent on the gentle coloring of its neutral tones, as seen in figure 8-13.

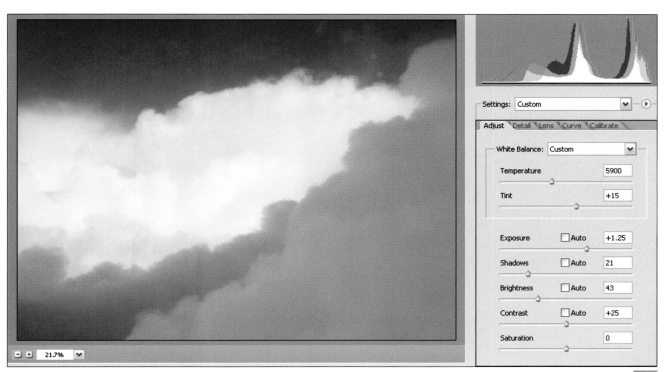

8-11

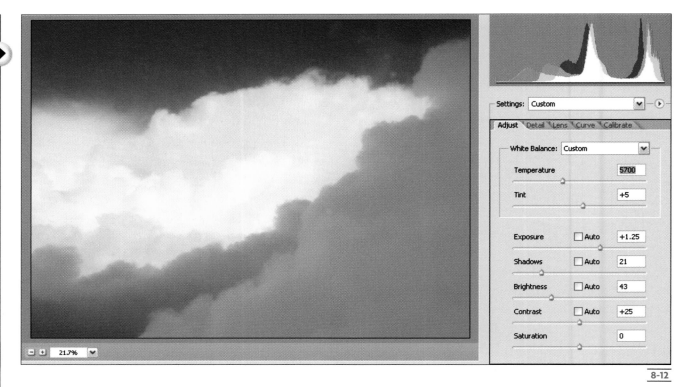

8-12

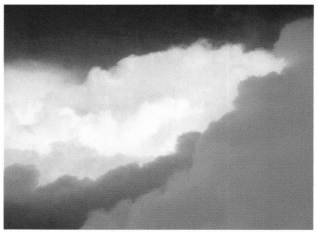

8-13

PRO TIP

The Spot Healing Brush tool in Photoshop CS2 actually gets better with multiple clicks. If the first try doesn't work, try again and again. It reevaluates the sampling points each time so that the image repair gets better.

If you look closely at parts of the photo in Camera Raw and the adjusted shots, you notice a slight change. Imperfections on the window of the plane that affected the quality of the image were removed with the Spot Healing Brush tool once the photo was completed and moved into Photoshop. This is a great new addition to Photoshop CS2 because it fixes little problems like these with a single click on the offending pixels. It smartly looks at what is around the problem and fills it in.

DUSK LIGHT

When photographers shoot film, they are stuck with one basic interpretation of a night scene's colors depending on the color balance of the film. Tungsten film has a different look than daylight film, for example. Some adjustment can be made with print film, but this is not always completely satisfactory.

Film and digital cameras see night a little differently than the eye does. The eye/brain connection compensates for color differences among lights and sees things more neutrally than film or digital capture. This is not so bad because it gives wonderful color to a scene by intensifying color differences among light sources. The problem: Which light source color is right? Different color or white-balance settings change how the colors of lights appear (and their effects on surroundings) in the photograph.

The photo I'm using for this next example is affected by the warm, late light from the sunset sky (the sun has already set) as well as the street and building lights. One thing to keep in mind is that the color of the actual light source will not appear as anything except white if the exposure allows that light to wash out. That is normal, however, and trying to retain such color in most lights will likely damage other tonal relationships in the photo.

DUSK INTERPRETED

Figure 8-14, an image of Los Angeles about 20 minutes after sunset, captures colors of the western sky reflecting off the buildings, plus the mountains are enhanced by the light created by the afterglow of dusk. Street- and other city lights add contrast and color to the image.

The photo has a serious adjustment problem. Haze in the sky weakens its contrast and tonal qualities. This haze-induced problem needs to be fixed as obviously haze can't be removed from the air at the time of exposure. Otherwise the photo will never quite look right and colors will never reach their potential. In most cases, those tonalities must be adjusted first before critical work is done on the white balance.

> **Exposure.** It's just about perfect in figure 8-15. Any increase removes colors from the lights. Any decrease only makes the photo dark.

> **Shadows.** This is the critical adjustment, not just for contrast and tones, but also for color, as you quickly see. Increase this setting until blacks begin to appear in the shadows at the bottom of the photo as shown in figure 8-16 and figure 8-17. Immediately, a more dynamic dusk shot appears.

> **Curve.** Brightness could be used to adjust midtones, however, in this case, a livelier downtown and mountain tonality and color is achieved with the Tone Curve as demonstrated in figure 8-18. The dark midtones need to be brightened slightly, which is done by setting the curve to Linear and then clicking about a third of the way up the curve from the bottom and dragging that point up. This makes the darkest tones a little too bright, so a second point is added slightly above the bottom of the tone curve and this point is pulled down. This movement of the curve down also makes the upper part of the curve rise, pivoting on the first point. This brightens up things like the buildings, which could be a problem in some photos and would need to be corrected. In this example it looks good, so there is no reason to change the upper part of the curve.

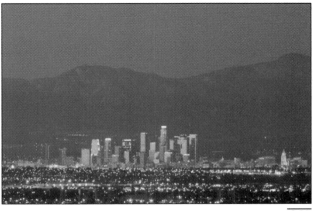

8-14

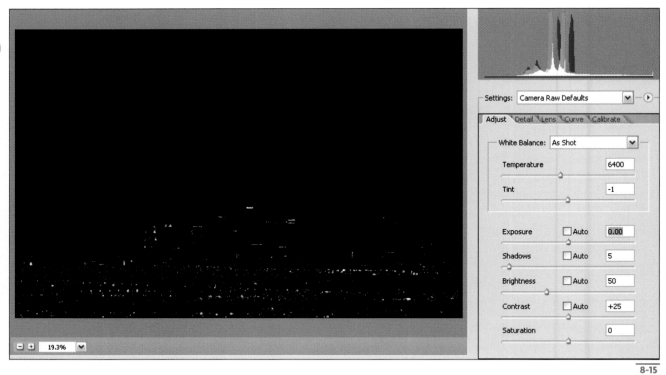

8-15

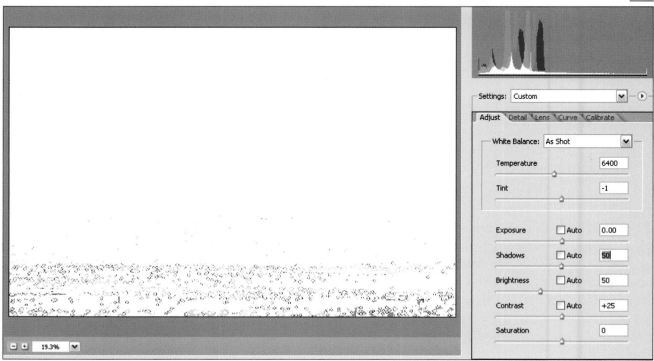

8-16

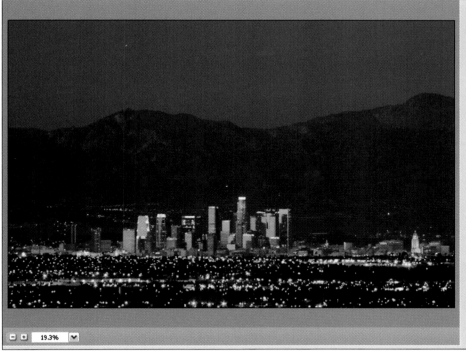
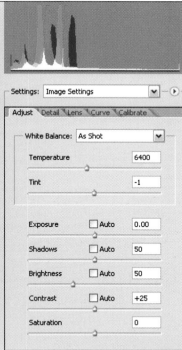

8-17

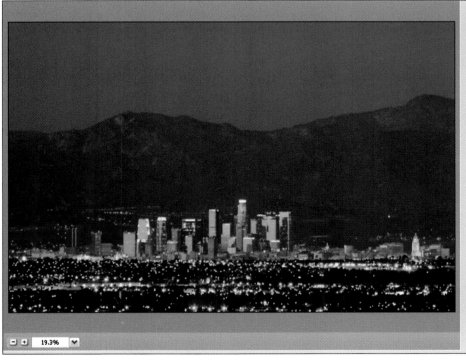
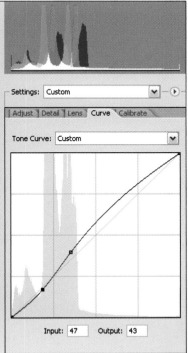

8-18

Haze, whether it comes from fog, morning air, or smog, affects both the color and contrast in a photo. If the air is very hazy, don't try to over adjust the white and black points through Exposure and Shadow. This can lead to an unnatural contrast for the conditions so that the photo looks harsh and unrealistic. Look for a balance that reflects the mood of the scene. Color is another story. Sometimes, you want to get rid of smog color completely, but on the other hand, a sunrise fog results in beautiful color that should be retained.

> **Detail.** There is a faint bit of noise in the sky. In a picture like this, I would avoid doing any big Luminance Smoothing (there is little color noise), because as Luminance Smoothing increases, details in the buildings may be affected. A little added smoothing can help, however, as seen in figure 8-19.

DUSK COLOR REVEALED

Now that you've adjusted the tonalities, adjust the White Balance. This can have a great effect on a dusk photo. Figures 8-20 (Daylight), 8-21 (Shade), and 8-22 (Tungsten) show three radically different interpretations of color due to changes in white balance.

> **White Balance.** The As Shot setting looks good as seen in figure 8-23. This is why setting your camera to shoot a specific white balance can really help your workflow. If you can bring a photo into Camera Raw looking good As Shot, that means less time needed to make new choices or to figure out what the photo really should look like.

However, this type of shot really shows off how much control you have over the image in Camera Raw. By double-clicking the White Balance settings in

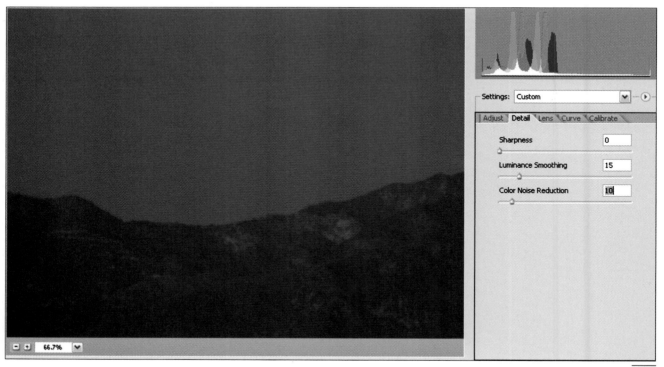

8-19

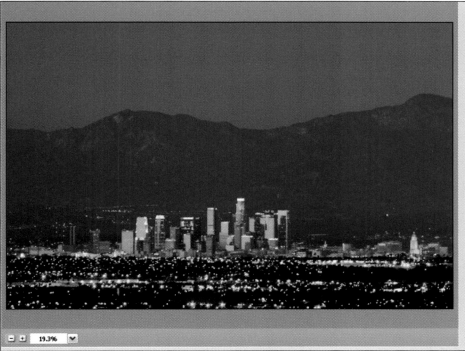
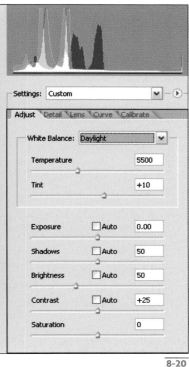

8-20

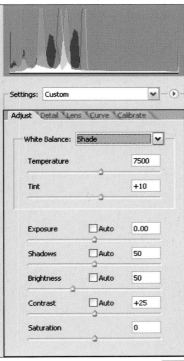

8-21

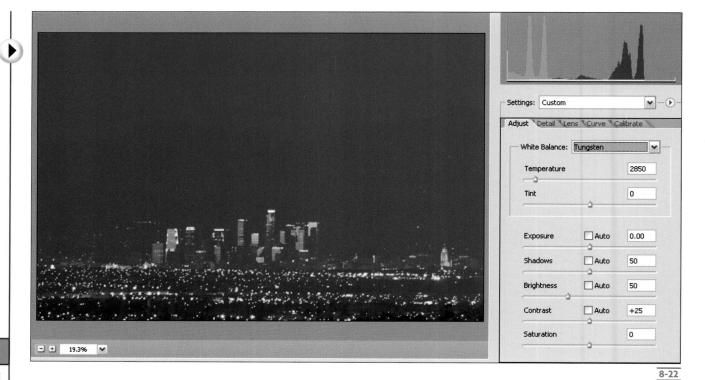

8-22

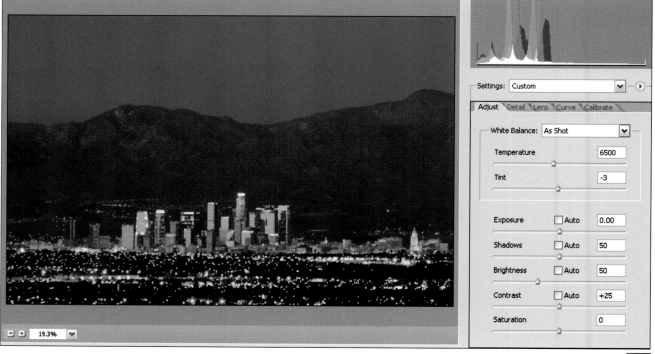

8-23

Windows, you can then use your up- and down-arrow keys to move from one setting to another. If you work on a Mac, you must select each setting manually by opening the menu and clicking on each. Daylight is an interesting interpretation that makes the scene look more like a night shot. Cloudy warms it up, a little warmer than As Shot (which actually was Cloudy, but Camera Raw's interpretation is slightly different), including adding a lot more magenta tint. Shade really warms it up, but so much so that it starts to look like pollution more than an attractive time after sunset. Tungsten and Fluorescent give a total night look, but they don't seem natural because of the reflected sky on the buildings. Flash is much like Daylight.

> **Temperature and Tint.** Using the Cloudy setting gives a Color Temperature setting of 6500. This is higher than the As Shot setting and offers a nice afterglow sort of color, except that it is too magenta. Here's where the tint comes in (minus is green, plus is magenta). By pulling it back from the +10 of the Camera Raw Cloudy setting, the tonalities and colors of the scene start to look more believable (the White Balance setting will automatically change to Custom). Going into the minus Tint settings (which adds green to counterbalance the magenta) gives the photo much better colors.

The White Balance tool is not of much use in a photo like this, seen in its final version in figure 8-24. Where are any good neutral tones that you can click? They are difficult to find. This photo does not need neutral tones to look natural. That would not reflect the lighting conditions.

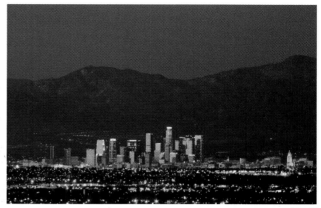

8-24

SEAL GREENERY

In the image (see figure 8-25) of kids playing with a seal at the Aquarium of the Pacific (or maybe it is the seal playing with the kids), the colors are difficult. These colors are not very attractive, although from a purely documentary viewpoint, this photo has accurate colors only in terms of what the camera saw in the light, but not what the eye sees. The clear plastic walls and water in the seal pool are green. But no one sees this the same way the camera does — the eye-to-brain connection makes adjustments to give more natural-looking colors.

Frankly, the photo's colors, real or not, just don't look right. They need to be adjusted. This is one case where the off-color is so strong that it needs to be adjusted before making any tonal adjustments. This is important because the color is distracting. Adjusting blacks, whites, and midtones before the color is fixed can lead to poor judgments in making those changes.

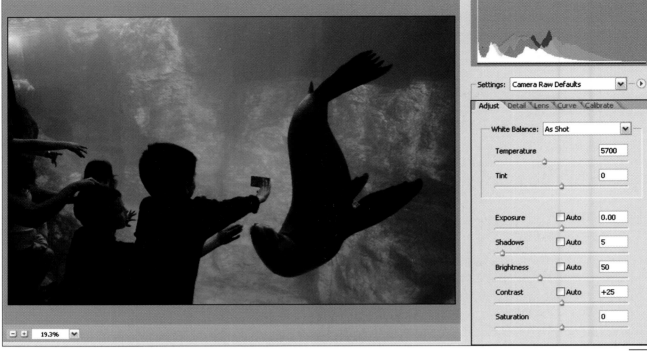

8-25

1. Adjust the color with the White Balance tool. This is the type of photo where this tool really shines. There are always going to be some nice neutral tones to work with. By clicking around on the rock behind and above the seal and the kids, the photo quickly gains better color, as shown in figures 8-26, 8-27, and 8-28. The area behind the seal makes the image too yellow. The rocks to the left of the seal, just above the boy, seem to work best, giving the image a pleasing, more natural coloring.

This example really demonstrates the power of Camera Raw and the White Balance tool. Most photos will not have this kind of color problem, but it is nice to know that the software can correct it.

2. Adjust the Tint. Temperature increased a bit from the use of the White Balance Tool, but the most dramatic change was in the Tint. The magenta component of the color soared to take out the green. It seems to be a bit too much, however, so it is worth backing it down somewhat as shown in figure 8-29.

PRO TIP

When shooting real-life scenes, it really helps to pre-set your camera and have it ready for action before you start photographing. Fumbling with the camera or just randomly shooting continuously in hopes of getting something usually won't get you the best shots. Know your camera. Be prepared so that you can just watch and wait for the action to develop.

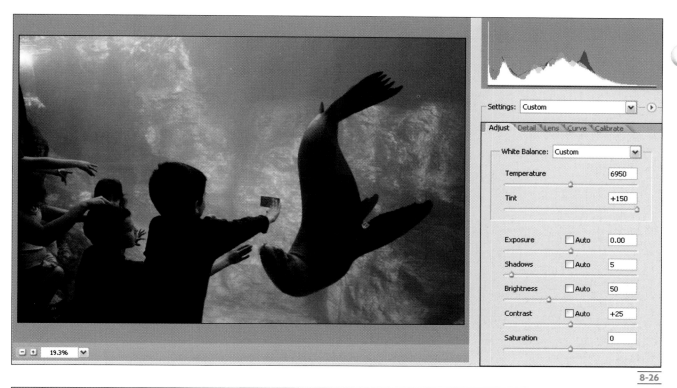

8-26

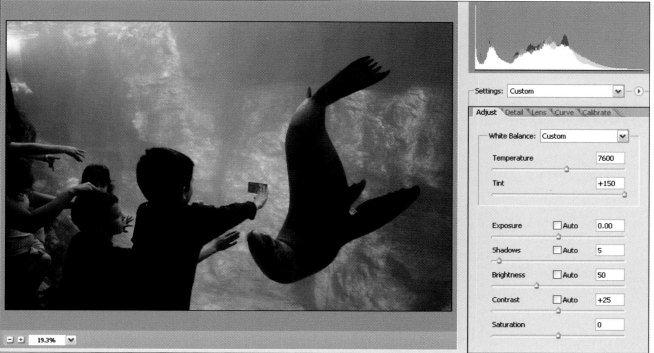

8-27

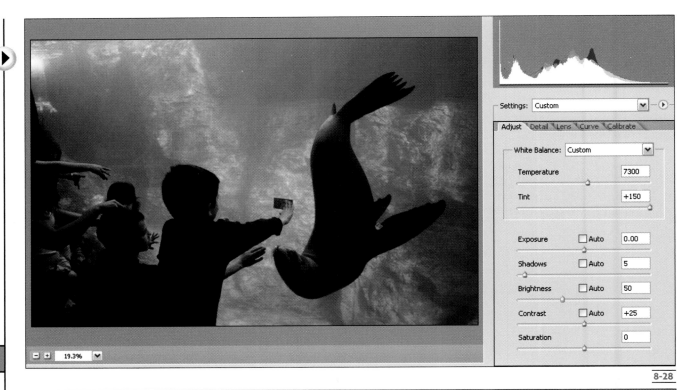

8-28

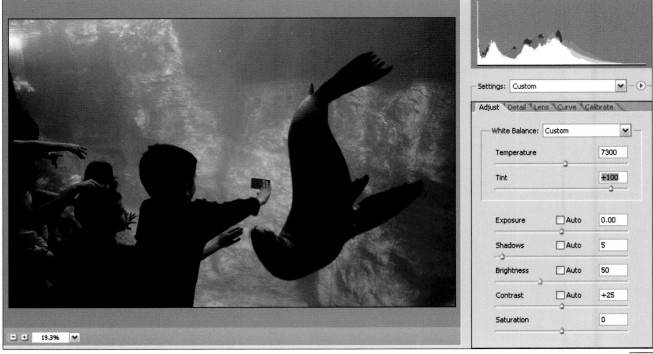

8-29

Now that the color has been corrected, the tonal adjustments can be made.

> **Exposure.** You don't always have to start with exposure, but because this is the order the interface has, it doesn't hurt anything to start there, as demonstrated by figure 8-30. Brightening up the whites gives the photo a little more snap. It also makes the bright light at the upper left annoyingly bright, but this can be easily cropped without affecting the overall composition.

> **Shadows.** The strong blacks in the children's clothing are all that is needed (see figure 8-31).

> **Midtones.** The midtones need to be adjusted slightly. You can adjust the Brightness slider. However, this photo has many varied midtones with many different gradations among them. This makes it ideal for the Curve tab as shown in figure 8-32. The Medium and

Strong Contrast settings are okay, but Linear makes the seal look better. By raising up the middle of the curve, then using a second adjustment point in the upper area to bringing that part of the curve back to the center line, the midtones of the seal and water are improved.

> **Detail.** The water disguises the noise in this photo, so you have to look at the dark areas with tone, the seal's body in this case (see figure 8-33). There is a little of both color (or chromatic) and luminance noise here because an ISO setting of 800 was used. Luminance Smoothing and Color Noise Reduction need to be increased somewhat. Note: First edit, In the Detail tab, etc., is redundant for what has already been discussed. This is not the first time this has been discussed.

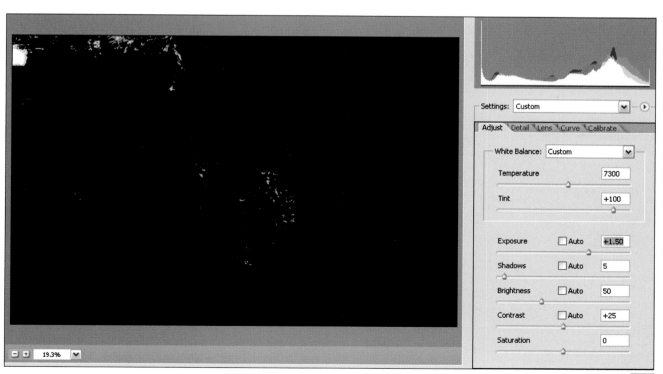

8-30

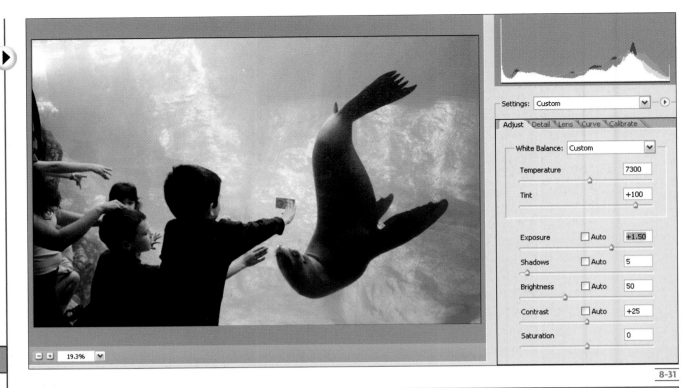

8-31

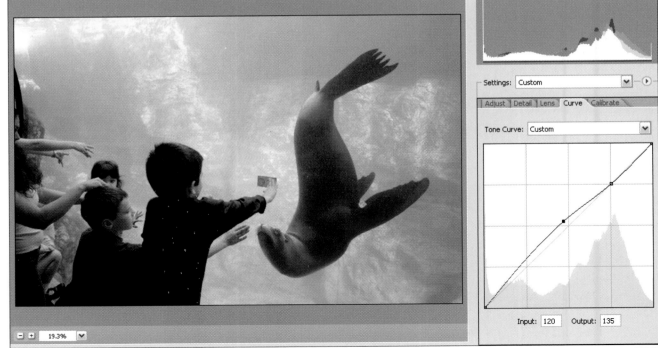

8-32

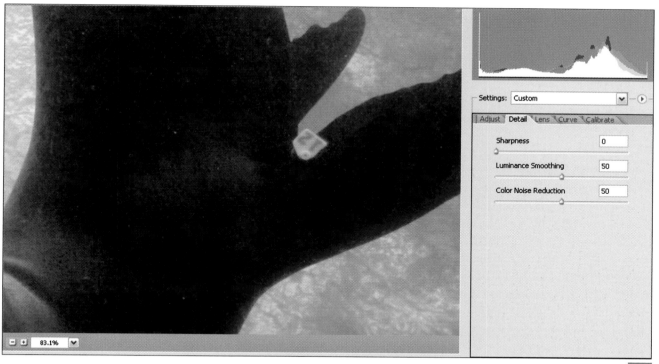

8-33

PRO TIP

If you are ever unsure about the noise in a given photograph, always check the dark areas. Pure black might not show the noise, but dark grays will, especially if they are smooth-toned areas of the subject.

Grab shots of interesting street action can be have good color, too, as seen in this example. Often, the colors you have to deal with for a street shot do not record in ways that help the photo. However, it still helps to set the white balance on the best you can, then Camera Raw lets you get the colors right in the processing of the image, as shown in figure 8-34. There is much potential for this kind of photography, but many news photographers simply accept what the sensor captures. That is often not appropriate or even accurate to the scene. The procedure shown for this example is a good one for this type of situation.

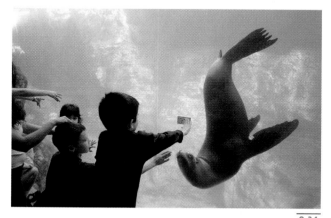

8-34

EVALUATING COLOR

What is the right color for your subject and scene? Ultimately, this is up to you and what you think is best for the photograph. However, there are some tips you can use to help you better decide just what is right or wrong about the color in an image.

KEY COLORS

In many photos, there are key colors that are critical to the subject or to the composition. These are colors that you and everyone else recognizes, therefore if they are off in some way, everyone will believe the whole photograph is wrong even if the rest of it is perfect. In figure 8-35, it is the color of the skin tone of the woman that makes the photograph read right, even though technically, the fluorescent lights in the background give an "off" color to it.

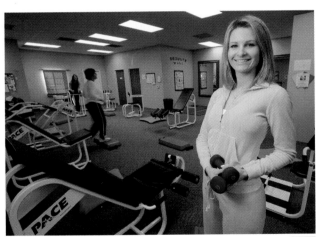

8-35

You need to pay attention to such colors, whether they are the hue of the sky or the color of skin. Even if these colors are technically recorded correctly yet do not look right, the rest of the photo will not look right, either. It is sometimes surprising how much influence a key color has over the image. If you hold your hand over that color, the rest of the photo often changes.

CRITICAL COLORS

For any pro shooting product photography, it is critical that certain colors of the product are adjusted properly. They may or may not be key colors, however; that depends on their dominance in the image. This is where the right exposure, light color, and white balance settings from the start help immensely. If any of these are off, the adjustment takes longer and often results in an unsatisfactory image overall. This is also where a calibrated monitor is absolutely critical — you don't want to be changing a color that is already biased by the monitor display.

You'll usually find it best to enlarge the image in the preview so that mainly the critical color (or colors) is displayed, as seen in figure 8-36. It can also be very helpful to have either samples of the product or color available when working on your image in Camera Raw if they are small, but don't view them casually. Put them on a neutral background (gray or white, with no strong colors) that can be lit with a color-corrected, daylight-balanced light such as those from Osram.

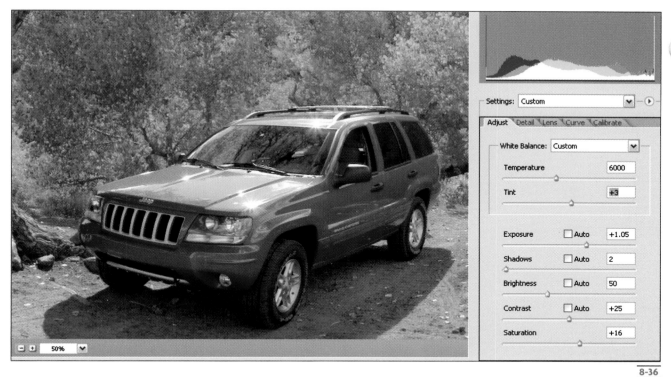

8-36

MEMORY COLORS

There are certain colors that are always remembered in a certain way. Green grass, blue skies, skin colors, red apples, and more, each has an expected color based on what everyone remembers about it, such as the sky in figure 8-37, even if that memory isn't real-world accurate (this is a little like Key colors, but they don't always affect the entire photo like a Key color does). Even if color in a photograph is dead-on accurate, the photo will not look quite right if a memory color is off even if that just means the subject has an unusual color. People will not believe it. If a color doesn't seem to read right to you, look closer and see if it is one of those memory colors that comes with its own expectations. If it is, try to adjust for it. Sometimes you can't get that color right in Camera Raw, and you have to wait until the image is in Photoshop.

COLORCASTS

Colorcasts can be good or bad for a photo. A colorcast is simply an overall color that gives a color to neutral tones and influences all colors in the photo. It can be left in the photo, removed, or modified depending on what you need from the image.

At sunrise or sunset, a photo looks normal with a warm colorcast such as that seen in figure 8-38. That's what photographs of these times look like. You certainly don't want to remove that colorcast. But indoors, your eyes adapt to many lighting conditions, making colors look perfectly fine in ways that the camera won't. Colorcasts like the warmth of an incandescent light bulb might be welcome if not too strong, while a green cast from fluorescent bulbs is never wanted (unless you are going for some creative effect — visually, the human mind does not like green casts in a photo lit by fluorescent lights).

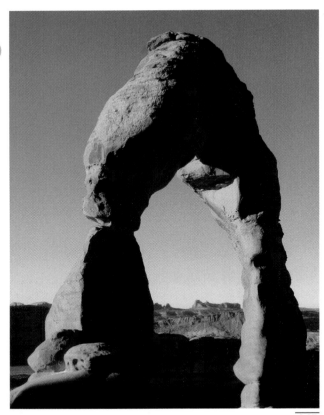

8-37

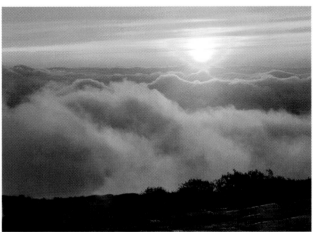

8-38

PRO TIP

Sometimes a problem colorcast is not obvious while processing the image in Camera Raw, yet it appears later when printing the photo, for example. If you suspect a colorcast at all, it is helpful to correct it in Camera Raw. To find it, you can do two things: first, use the White Balance tool and click in the photo to see if colors improve (you'll see how the colorcast changes); second, increase the Saturation slider dramatically and see if an overall, undesired color shows up (move the slider back afterward).

Sometimes colorcasts seemingly just appear due to a variety of reasons, as seen in figure 8-39 and corrected in figure 8-40 (the latter is more accurate, but the first may be more interesting depending on your preferences). When they contaminate neutral tones inappropriately, then it is time to remove them. In a spring woods, for example, white flowers often have a greenish tint. Also, in low-light situations, for example, you may find a magenta flavoring to colors that doesn't help them and needs to be removed.

WEAK COLOR

There are a number of factors that can cause color to appear weak:

> **Black adjustment.** If blacks are dark gray instead of black, colors suffer.

> **Low saturation.** Digital cameras record color differently than some films so the Raw file may need a color boost.

> **Color interactions.** A very bright color in the image can strongly influence other colors and make them look weaker, as seen in figure 8-41. There is nothing you can do about this in Camera Raw. You have to make corrections later in Photoshop.

> **Color corruption.** A colorcast can corrupt the key colors, even if it is not an obvious colorcast.

COLOR INTERACTIONS

Colors do not act alone. They interact with each other. If you have the same red in two photos, one on a green background and one on a blue background, that red appears like two different colors. This is also affected by tonalities — put the same color on black, then on white, and the change is dramatic, even though the color has not changed at all. Obviously, you can't change those interactions in Camera Raw, but it is important to be aware of this effect so that you can adjust the image accordingly, especially when dealing with critical or memory colors.

For example, you might enlarge the image so much in the preview that you are missing certain colors in it. Then you adjust the image to make the enlarged area look right, but when you go back to the whole photo, the colors now look off. This is why you always need to check color adjustments critically with the whole image, even if they all look right in the enlarged view. This is also why it is critical that the workspace around your computer has only neutral colors.

CREATIVE COLORS

Of course, you can do anything you want to the image and create colors far beyond what you might normally use. This can be a good thing to try in order to create more interest in an important image that just isn't coming to life otherwise. You might, for example, use an indoor light setting, like Tungsten or Fluorescent, for an outdoor scene (like the one in figure 8-42) or a Cloudy setting for an indoor scene, just for the color effect that you get. Because you are doing all your adjustments in Camera Raw and will never replace the original Raw file, there is no quality loss doing this. There are no limits to the possibilities here, but I recommend you be careful and use this technique sparingly. On many images, it just looks like a mistake.

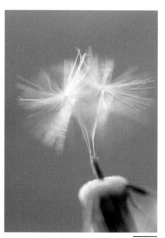
8-39

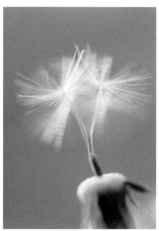
8-40

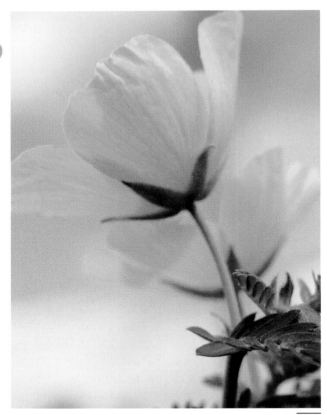

8-41

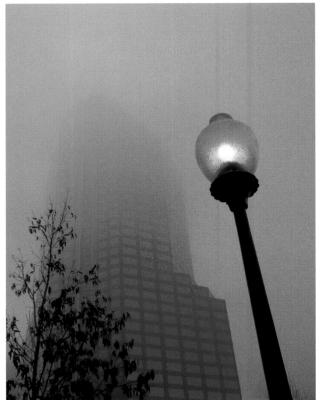

8-42

Q&A

It seems too complicated to shoot white balance presets in the camera. What if I just shoot auto white balance? I can see I can correct a lot of color in Camera Raw.

You can do exactly that without affecting the quality of the image. It may mean, however, that you have more work to do in Camera Raw because of the additional changes you often need to make. This is especially true when working with images that have strong colorcasts in them, such as the seal playing and dusk city shots in this chapter. By setting a specific white balance preset with a shot like the seal playing, you can change your angle, move around, zoom in or out, and your colors are consistent, making that series of photos easier to adjust. With the dusk shot, using a consistent preset white balance lets you actually see the changes in the light as the sun goes down and the city lights come on. Otherwise, the camera is likely to keep changing the colors so that when you do make adjustments in Camera Raw, you may miss some of the color changes that were there because the camera itself overcompensated.

What if I use black-and-white settings with my digital camera? Do I need to worry about color adjustments in Camera Raw?

Cameras that offer a black-and-white setting record just that, a black-and-white photo, but only in the JPEG file. The Raw file holds all the original color information from the sensor. The camera records information in that file that you shot this in black-and-white, but Camera Raw does not recognize those settings for most cameras (I actually don't know of any that it does recognize for black-and-white, but this is a constantly changing thing, so by the time you read this, it might). If you want the black-and-white translation made by the camera (and some offer color filter settings that change black-and-white tonalities), you must either shoot Raw and JPEG at the same time (so you have both files) or use the camera manufacturer's Raw converter to recognize the choices. You can use the Saturation slider in Camera Raw to remove the color from the file, but that won't necessarily give you the same results you saw in the camera LCD.

Shooting Raw plus JPEG is a great advantage when you use unique settings on a digital camera, such as black-and-white. This gives you the best of both because you get the black-and-white image you expected (from the JPEG), plus a complete Raw file that can be adjusted for either color or black-and-white.

What if I use Camera Raw for black-and-white? I know you can just remove the color with the Saturation slider.

I really can't recommend this for every photo. You can certainly try it and see if you are satisfied with the results. Image quality is fine, but a good black-and-white photo demands careful consideration of how colors are changed into different tones. There is a huge difference in a black-and-white photo in how reds and greens are interpreted, for example. This was what made Ansel Adams work so great — his ability to use filters, film processing, and printing to create expressive black-and-white tonalities. The change of a color image to black-and-white through the Saturation slider is a rather heavy-handed and arbitrary way of doing this.

A much better way of creating a black-and-white image is to make the best possible full-color image in Camera Raw and output that image to Photoshop as a 16-bit file. There, you can use Channel Mixer set to monochrome for a great deal of control in changing colors into black-and-white tonalities. Channel Mixer starts with the emphasis on the Red channel. Play around with the mix as you watch how tonalities change.

Another option is to again process the full-color image to 16-bit, but then use nik ColorEfex, a Photoshop plug-in, to make the black-and-white change. nik ColorEfex does a lot more than black-and-white, but it has three different ways of making a black-and-white conversion, and each one is very intuitive and easy to use (Channel Mixer is not very intuitive).

What if I just adjust the white balance first in a photograph? Why should I always do black, white, and midtones first?

You certainly can do white balance first. And in many cases, you'll get similar results. In addition, you should always do white balance first if the image comes into Camera Raw with the color way off.

I recommend doing the black, white, and midtones first because they can strongly affect color. Setting the black point in an image is especially critical and can have a big effect on how colors appear. Two things happen then: first, as the black point is set, all dark tones get a little darker, which makes many colors look a little richer; second, black sets off colors, and any bright color will look different in saturation when next to black.

Chapter 9

THE NOISE PROBLEMS
NO ONE TALKS ABOUT

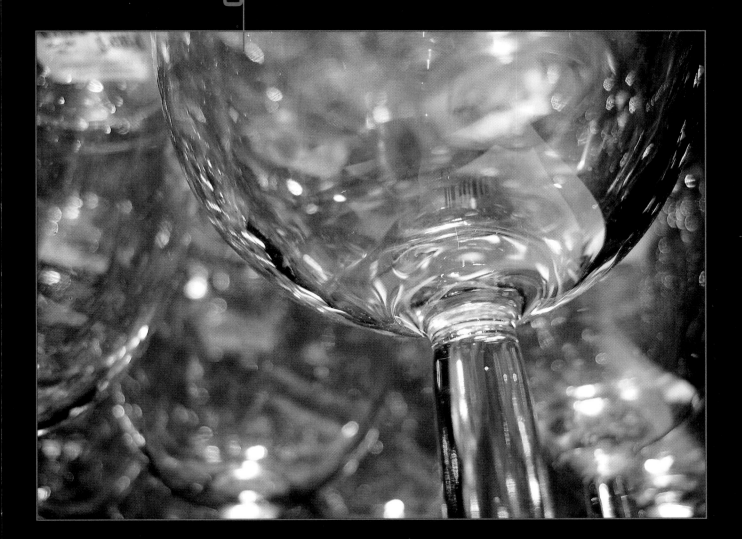

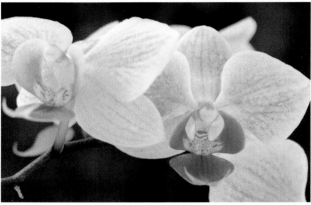

9-1

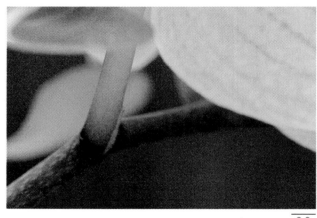

9-2

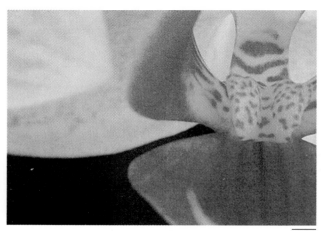

9-3

Noise is not a new issue with photographers. As discussed in Chapter 2, it just had a different name in the past: grain. Grain and noise may come from different things, but visually, they are essentially the same — an artifact of the medium (an artifact is something that comes into a photograph that doesn't exist in the world but is introduced into the image from the technology used to make the photo). Noise and grain make an irregular, sand-like pattern over the photo that can range from difficult to see to annoyingly obvious.

The most recent digital cameras have great noise-reduction circuits and even sensors with much lower noise characteristics, so noise is much reduced from a few years ago. It still exists, however, and continues to be a critical issue for the photographer. It is curious that it is not often discussed in Photoshop books (although perhaps it will be now with Photoshop CS2's new noise-reduction filter). Noise can be a big problem with any digital camera if exposure is not ideal, ISO settings are high, or you have to do major adjustments to a photo in the computer. Figure 9-1 shows what noise can do to a photograph, but it won't show up as strongly at the size used here, so details in figures 9-2 and 9-3 better illustrate what noise problems can look like.

How the image is processed in Camera Raw affects the noise in the final image. You have seen some basic approaches to working the image in Camera Raw in previous chapters, and noise is discussed, but only in a very basic manner. In this chapter, you see a very different approach compared to what has been discussed so far, or for that matter, in most books about Photoshop. You will start to understand what can and can't be done with noise, and why some of the most common approaches to noise reduction might not be best for your photograph.

WHEN NOISE BECOMES A PROBLEM

Noise becomes a problem when it distracts from the subject (see figure 9-4) and its detail (see figure 9-5). Sometimes noise can be an interesting creative effect (you can even add it in Photoshop, if desired) that you can use to make a photo look older, or at least, give it an interesting texture, as seen in figure 9-6. But this is not something most photographers want in the majority of their photographs. However, it is important to note that in certain, very dramatic photos, especially news or sports photography, you might not notice noise at all because the subject is so strong that it overpowers any attention the viewer might put on the noise.

In photos of subjects like people, flowers, landscapes, architecture, and more, noise can be a distraction to your subject and take away from the appreciation of the photograph by a viewer. Noise can especially be a problem when big prints are made, where noise that you never saw on the computer monitor can appear. I find this is consistently an issue for anyone making prints. It is very easy to overlook certain patterns of noise on the monitor, especially if strong colors or graphic elements overpower it. That noise, unfortunately, appears all too well in the print.

The source of noise starts in the shooting due to several factors influenced by the electronics and digital elements of the camera. Processing an image in Camera Raw and Photoshop can reduce the appearance of noise, but making a noisy photo into a smooth-toned image is not easy. A smooth-toned image needs to be shot that way from the start. You can also increase noise in Camera Raw, if you are not careful in your processing, as you learn in this chapter.

PRO TIP

Noise is often more obvious in a print than on the computer screen. Once you have a photo you think you are going to like but have not finished all the processing in Photoshop, try making a print to check out noise problems as well as to get an overall view of the image as a print.

X-REF

For more about the sources of noise, see Chapter 2.

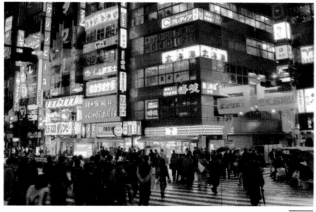

9-4

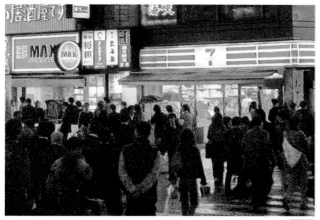

9-5

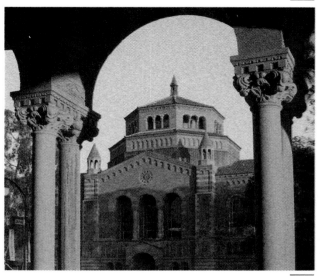

9-6

WATCHING FOR NOISE

The first step in controlling noise is to be aware that it exists and to look for it. For most images, that doesn't begin until well into the processing workflow when you go to the luminance and color noise controls in the Detail tab of Camera Raw. However, there are some things to watch for that can alert you to noise problems, as seen in figures 9-7, 9-8, and 9-9 (figure 9-7 is the full image; the others are details from it):

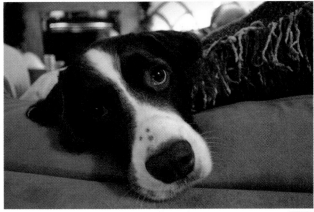

9-7

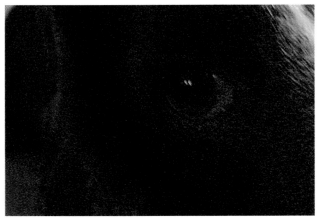

9-8

> **Dark areas.** Noise quickly appears in dark areas that are strongly adjusted to bring out detail in them as seen in figure 9-8. Be careful about overprocessing dark areas. You may want to keep them dark (to minimize noise) or work on them in Photoshop (keep the file 16-bit for that) because you gain some more control then.

> **Underexposed photos.** Comments made about dark areas can also apply to underexposed areas: noise can be a problem. You may need to create an image with more contrast so that the dark areas stay black (hiding noise).

> **Saturation.** The Saturation control in Camera Raw and Photoshop can increase the appearance of noise when used too strongly. Figure 9-9 is a simple detail of figure 9-7; however, 9-10 has had the saturation boosted too much. This control doesn't know the difference between broad colors that need changes and small details that don't (which is exactly what noise is). High saturation settings can especially intensify chromatic noise (color noise) and they may affect luminance noise as well.

The solution to all of this is obvious: Shoot the photo the best you can in the first place, but that doesn't help much when the photo is in front of you in Camera Raw. At that point, you must deal with whatever noise you find. While you can't change the underlying noise, you can be alert when conditions (such as underexposure) might make noise more prevalent. Then you need to watch the image as you process it, being aware of changes in how strongly the noise begins to appear. When you suspect noise problems, enlarge the preview at times — you can press Ctrl/⌘+0 to instantly return to the full image — so you can check for noise.

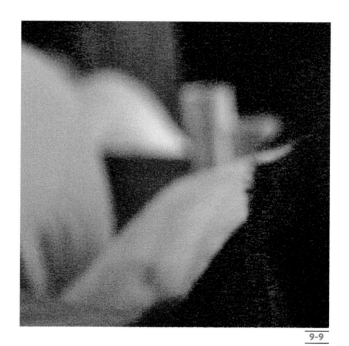

9-9

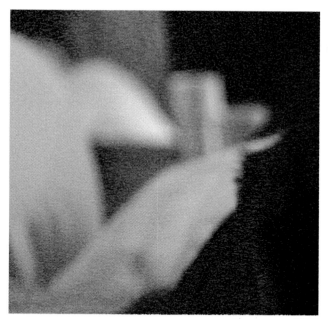

9-10

REDUCING NOISE IN CAMERA RAW

With a little experience, you begin to recognize when noise is more likely to appear in a photo. Because adjustments in Raw don't actually change anything in the original file (or anywhere, for that matter, until you tell the program to create a file in Photoshop or you save the file), you can always back up the adjustments until noise problems are reduced. As you become more aware of noise issues, you can use the following key techniques in dealing with noise in Camera Raw:

> **Standard photos.** On many photos shot with newer digital SLRs, you do not notice much noise as seen in figure 9-11. Check continuous tone areas such as sky or out-of-focus areas for any noise, as shown in figure 9-12, which is a detail of 9-11. A very slight pattern under high magnification is not really

a problem (film always had that pattern from grain), but if it seems a little high, you can always try the Luminance Smoothing adjustment in the Detail tab of Camera Raw (usually minor background noise in a standard, well-exposed digital photo is of the luminance type).

> **Moderate noise.** Higher ISO settings or slight underexposure may cause moderate noise in the image, as seen in figure 9-13 and its detail, 9-14. This can be reduced slightly by using the Luminance Smoothing and/or the Color Noise Reduction sliders. You have to look at an enlarged portion of the image to see what effects these have.

> **High noise.** Unfortunately, when high noise appears in an image from the start (such as from a high ISO setting, as seen in figure 9-15 and its detail, 9-16,

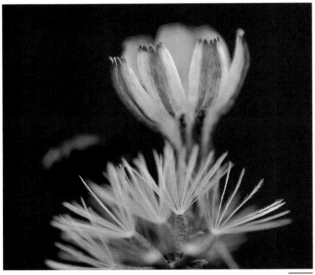

9-11

9-12

or a very underexposed photograph), compromises are involved in order to reduce it. The Luminance Smoothing and Color Noise Reduction sliders have some effect, but as their strength is increased, fine details in the photograph are also lost. Your best choice at this point is to adjust the image as well as you can and apply moderate noise reduction, but above all, do everything you can to not increase noise (not increasing noise is different than reducing it). After processing and opening the image in Photoshop or saving it, you can then use noise-reduction software on it such as that built into Photoshop CS2 or an independent program such as Digital GEM, Noise Ninja, or Dfine.

> **Dark areas.** As you lighten areas that are too dark and noise starts looking bad, reduce that adjustment. Sometimes you must make a choice between putting up with some annoying noise if you must see the detail, or keeping the area dark to reduce the noise and lose the detail altogether. You can actually make the area blacker (which will make the photo look more contrasty), which removes or reduces the appearance of noise.

> **Saturation.** If you increase saturation, you may notice broad areas of color, such as sky, start to look grainy (sky is a common place for noise to show up with saturation changes). When this happens, back off the saturation adjustment.

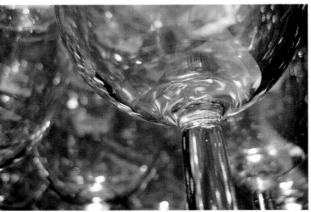

9-13

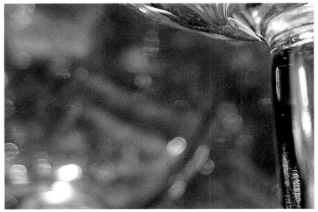

9-14

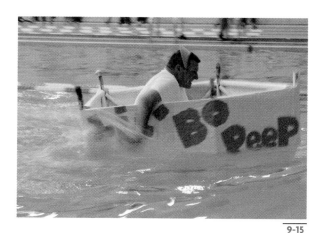

9-15

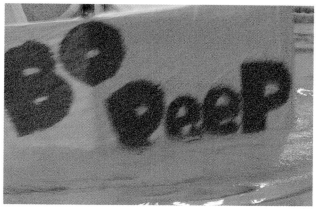

9-16

PROCESSING AN IMAGE WHILE CONTROLLING NOISE

The following photo processing example works through a photo of orchids with some noise issues. This photo also appears in Chapter 2, which covers shooting the image right from the start. The image has some serious exposure problems. Even though it was shot with a digital SLR with a reputation for very low noise, the image is underexposed resulting in very high noise. This is not a normal photo in the sense that it is more underexposed than photographers normally see, but it is a superb example for demonstrating how processing an image affects the appearance of noise and how you can make new choices to adjust a photo to reduce what noise does exist.

PRO TIP

One great thing about digital photography (among many) is that it never hurts to try a shot — so go for it, even if you think the shot might not be perfect. Sometimes you just have to experiment to see what a particular exposure does for a subject. So what if you are wrong about a hunch? You can't waste film and you'll often learn from the problem images. It doesn't cost anything to bracket your exposure, either. After all, I did get a good example to use for noise issues in Camera Raw!

This orchid should have been exposed so that the white areas registered white in the photo. This is one problem that comes from the often-heard recommendation to be sure you don't overexpose a digital image. Over attention to that idea results in underexposed photos with noise problems that can be avoided.

START WITH THE BASICS

You always start processing an image with the same basic workflow. You don't absolutely have to follow the order of steps used throughout this book, but I can tell you this workflow works and it won't let you down. If you find your that images require some tweaking of this order, that's fine, but once you discover what works for you, be consistent and always use that workflow. This makes it much easier to process your images.

1. Press Alt/Option and click and drag the Exposure slider to quickly set highlight levels using the threshold screen that appears from pressing Alt/Option while adjusting. This photo comes in with the whites very dark. They need to be brought up until white just begins to show in the blackness of the threshold screen as seen in figure 9-17. This immediately improves the photo as demonstrated by figure 9-18.

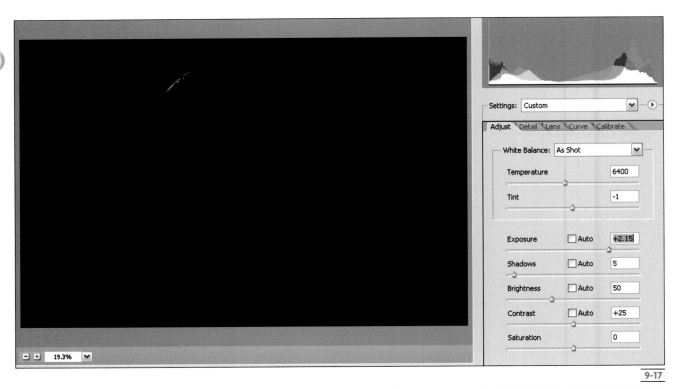

9-17

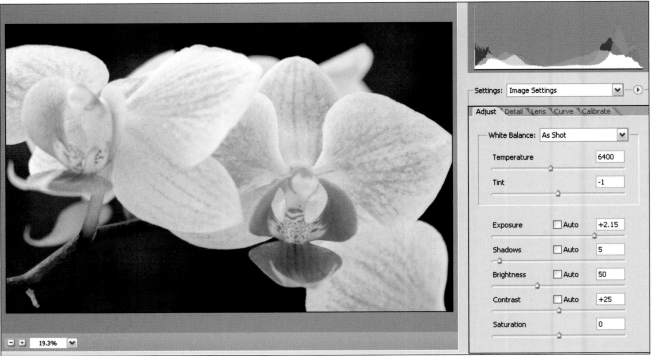

9-18

2. Press Alt/Option again and click and drag the Shadows slider to adjust the darkest parts of the photo, as shown in figure 9-19. The obvious choice is to drag the slider to the right just a little, but as you see later in this chapter, that may not be the best choice. For now, a slight increase in black level is all that is done to the photo (see figure 9-20).

3. If the Brightness slider is used on this image, the flower color appears a little dull probably because it is somewhat of a blunt-instrument as a tool. I often find the Brightness to be much less effective than the Tone Curve, but sometimes you just have to try it and see what happens. In this case, the Tone Curve in the Curve tab helps this problem. Because the lower portion of the curve represents the dark areas, it can be moved up slightly where the darker colors reside. This is basically in the second quarter of tones from the bottom (the Tone Curve is divided into a 4 × 4 grid). The upper portion is the light part of the photo, so it can be moved back toward the middle so that the light colors are kept. Both of these adjustments can be seen in figure 9-21.

4. The color is a little weak because of the underexposure, so increase the saturation setting. Click and drag the Saturation slider slightly to the right, as shown in figure 9-22.

5. The photo looks fine with the White Balance setting of As Shot (also seen in figure 9-22). It has a slight warmth that works well with the colors.

The photo now looks about as good as it is going to get for this set of controls. But look closer and you'll quickly see the noise problems.

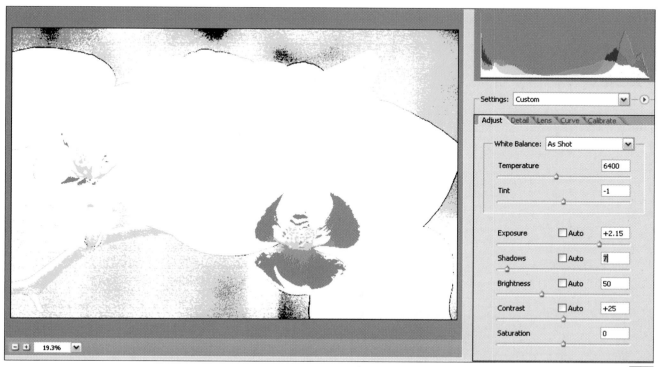

9-19

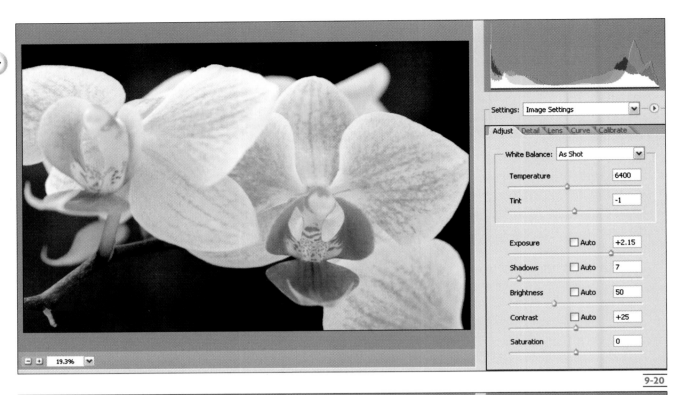

9-20

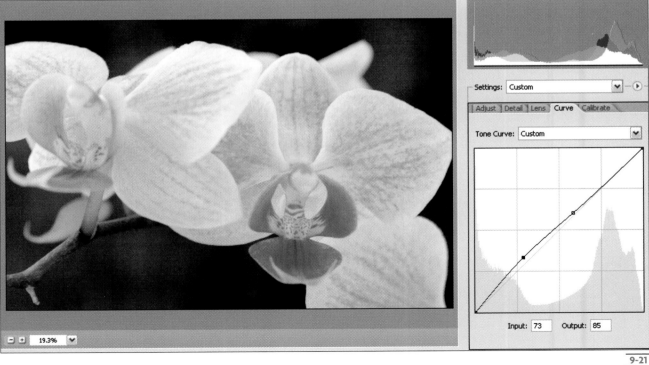

9-21

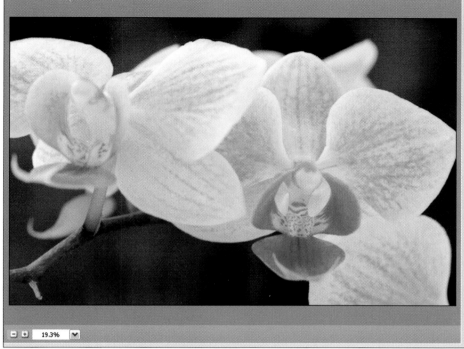
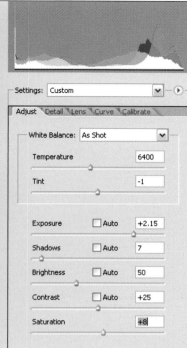

Settings: Custom

Adjust | Detail | Lens | Curve | Calibrate

White Balance: As Shot

Temperature   6400

Tint   -1

Exposure   ☐ Auto   +2.15

Shadows   ☐ Auto   7

Brightness   ☐ Auto   50

Contrast   ☐ Auto   +25

Saturation   +8

19.3%

9-22

TRYING TO CONTROL THE NOISE

With even moderate enlargement of the preview, the noise becomes very obvious. You can actually get away with more noise than normal in the flowers themselves because the noise looks a little like a color pattern in the petals. However, the noise in the rest of the photo is very noticeable. There is a lot of chromatic and luminance noise in the dark background of the photo, as seen in figure 9-23. There is actually some of both in the darkest parts of the main flower, but the chromatic noise is disguised by the color of the flower, as shown by figure 9-24. Noise typically appears worst in the dark areas, as seen here in the background; that is one place to look for it initially. In addition, you might look for it in smooth areas of a photo, which in this photo also happens to be the background.

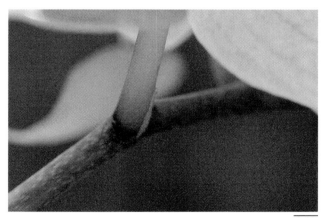

9-23

PRO TIP

Remember that if you are faced with two choices, always deal with a stronger problem first.

The first thing to try here is the Detail tab to see what the noise reduction sliders can do. The color or chromatic noise is so strong in the background that it is worth starting with that problem:

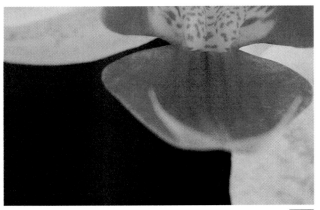

9-24

1. A good amount of color noise can be seen in the dark background behind the darkest part of the right flower, as shown in figure 9-25. A lot of color noise can be reduced here, but whenever you do such noise reduction, check the rest of the photo. High settings of Color Noise Reduction affect small color details in the photo. In this photo, for example, as this setting is increased, the color noise is definitely reduced in the dark background, but some weird things start to happen to the color in the flower as well. This definitely reduces the liveliness of the color there — not a good thing. So in this case, I would not drag the slider to a setting higher than 10, as done in figure 9-26. This is a very subjective move — the amount varies depending on the photo and the amount of noise. It helps to check several areas of the photo as you make a final choice.

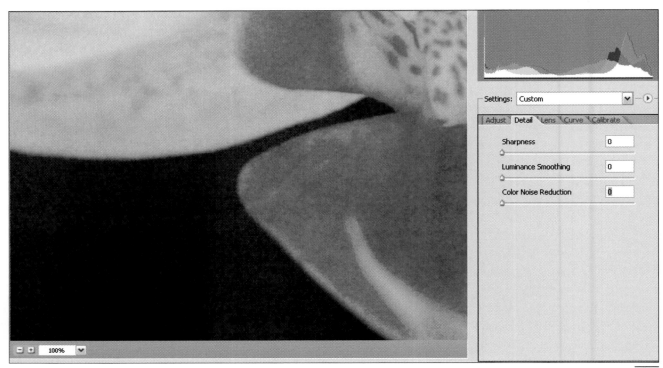

9-25

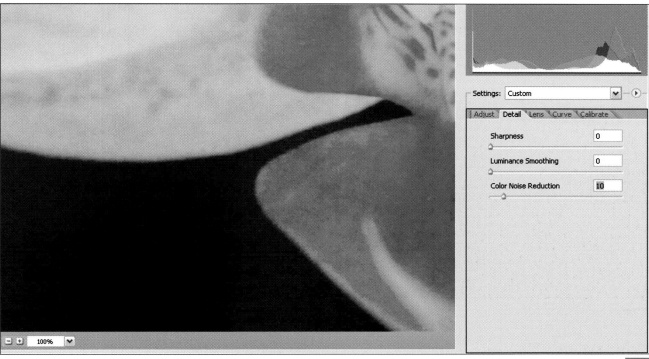

9-26

2. Luminance noise often appears in the darker, smooth tones of the photo. It is quite obvious in the background and midtone areas of the flowers. Because adjusting Luminance Smoothing also affects subject details, it helps to find something with detail as you do this. The stem on the left has some detail in it as well as luminance noise. Increasing the slider setting to about 30 does a good job of reducing the noise somewhat without making the stem look unnatural, as seen in figure 9-27. If you move the slider far to the right, as done in figure 9-28, it seems to dull the whole photo and it appears to lose focus, yet there is still noise. Little details in the photo disappear if you make such a move.

Again, this is highly subjective and totally dependent on the photo and what you need from it. Your level of acceptable noise may not match what I find acceptable, but if it meets your needs, that is okay. In addition, a photo with

more fine detail that is dependent on a strong feeling of sharpness may not be able to handle a lot of Luminance Smoothing. On the other hand, a photo of clouds may be able to handle a great deal of smoothing because clouds don't have a lot of fine detail.

PRO TIP

When looking at the affect of adjustments on noise, it always helps to enlarge the image as mentioned. But this doesn't help you see what the effect actually is, or how it is affecting small details. Select the Preview option above the preview image. Select and deselect the check box to turn the preview on and off, which then turns the effects you are adjusting on and off as well. This is a big help in seeing what is happening to the photo's noise and details. If you use the Hand tool (which appears by pressing and holding the space bar) and move the photo around, you also turn the effects on and off as you move the photo.

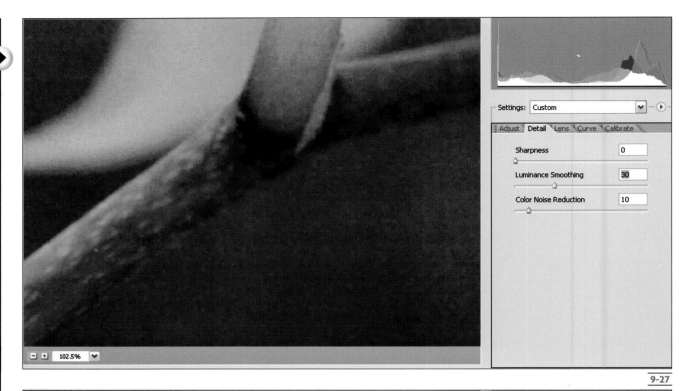

9-27

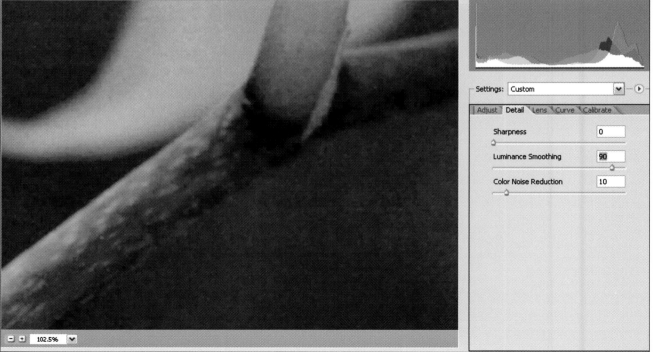

9-28

LOOKING DEEPER AT NOISE

The workflow just described — make normal adjustments, then check noise — works for most photos. However, it is worth taking a little deeper look at this image to see what else is affecting the noise and how that knowledge may lead to different choices in adjustment.

By turning off the noise reduction in the Detail tab for this photo, the noise returns with a vengeance. However, if you go to the stem or the sharp center of the main flower, the photo actually looks sharper and a little more detailed, as demonstrated by figures 9-29 (no noise reduction) and 9-30 (noise reduction). This is an optical illusion. A trick that experts who work with out-of-focus old photos use is to add some sharp noise to the photo to make it look sharper.

Another example comes from film. Tri-X is an old film technology that photographers have loved for a long time. Even when Kodak created newer films and threatened to remove Tri-X from the market, photographers still stuck to Tri-X. They love its tonality even though it is a grainy film. Everyone prints it with the grain as sharp as possible, which gives the film a unique appeal and make it often appear sharper than it is.

This is why noise reduction is always a compromise. You can often smooth out noise quite strongly, but it comes at a cost of making the photo look less sharp and changing small tonalities and details.

But things other than noise reduction can help you deal with noise — adjustments that can be done either right from the start or later on when noise problems become more obvious. Sometimes these can be well worth trying because they have less effect on sharpness and details. This photo shows these effects when noise reduction in the Detail tab is turned off and it is adjusted differently in the Adjust tab.

1. Increase the Shadows slider setting a little to make the dark areas go quickly darker. This hides a lot of the color noise and some of the luminance noise seen in figure 9-31. It definitely affects the darkest areas of the photo, increasing the overall contrast. This can be valuable in too ways: noise is reduced without affecting sharpness and the image gets more dramatic, as seen in figure 9-32. In this case, its quite effective, although further adjustment is needed.

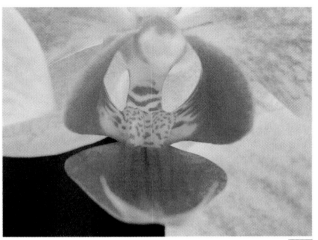

9-29

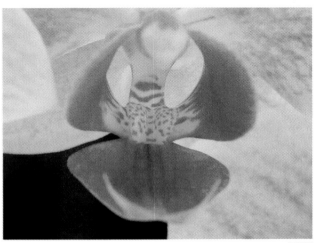

9-30

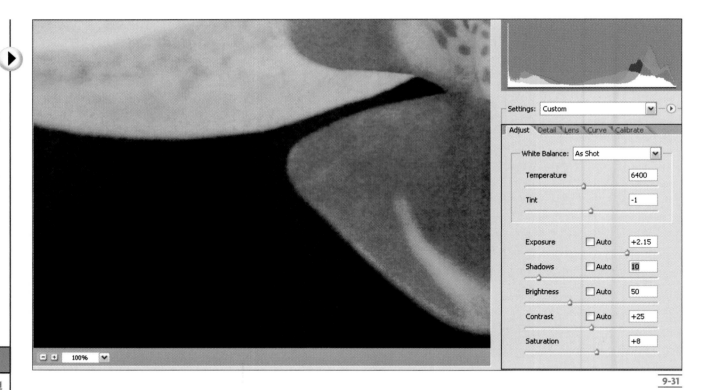

9-31

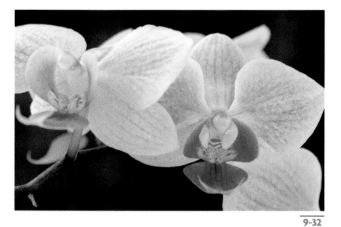

9-32

2. The Brightness slider does not do much for the mid-tones in this sort of image. It just doesn't give enough control. The dark colors of the flowers need to be lightened, but not at the expense of the darkest areas that were just deepened when the Shadows

slider was adjusted. This is definitely a place for the Tonal Curve.

3. Here is where some of the fancy capabilities of Curves (as known in Photoshop) come into play. The Tonal Curve in the Curve tab can be limited in its adjustment to ranges of tones. Here, the darkest areas can be kept dark (to keep noise down) while the dark colors can be enhanced. Click on various sections of the curve to place additional control points. You can use them to pull up or down specific parts of the curve while not affecting other parts. In this image, the parts of the curve in the second quarter from the bottom (the second quarter tones or the darker midtones) strongly affect the dark colors of the main flower.

By clicking on a point in the bottom of the curve to anchor it then clicking again in the lower part of the middle of the curve and dragging that part of the curve up (readjusting the original points, too), the dark colors get lighter without brightening the darkest parts of the photo with the noise, as seen in figure 9-33. Even with the Luminance Smoothing and Color Noise Reduction sliders set to 0, this image shows significantly less noise than appeared in a more normal adjustment. This photo also needs a little tweaking to the upper part of the curve to brighten the light parts in a natural way.

Rather than trying to bring out all the dark detail, which just means more noise, working the image this way gives it more interesting tonal and color relationships, while at the same time, less noise. There is still noise in the moderate toned areas of the background, but this can be affected by the Detail tab controls.

4. The Saturation slider has a strong affect on chromatic noise. This photo needs a little extra saturation, so undoubtedly this has an effect. You can actually see how the Saturation adjustment affects color noise if you magnify an area of the photo that has some noise, then click and drag the Saturation slider way to the right, as demonstrated in figure 9-34. That chromatic noise practically jumps out at you. Luminance noise is also increased because as color noise intensifies, the tonal differences that affect luminance noise also increase. In this photo, the extra color saturation is important because the flower colors are a little weak due to the exposure, so a compromise is needed. The Saturation slider is increased, but color noise is watched carefully.

5. When the Detail tab is selected, much less adjustment is needed. Both the Luminance Smoothing and Color Noise Reduction sliders can be kept low (they are both set lower, as seen in figure 9-35). This has a significant effect on both the appearance of sharpness and the liveliness of the color in the flower petals.

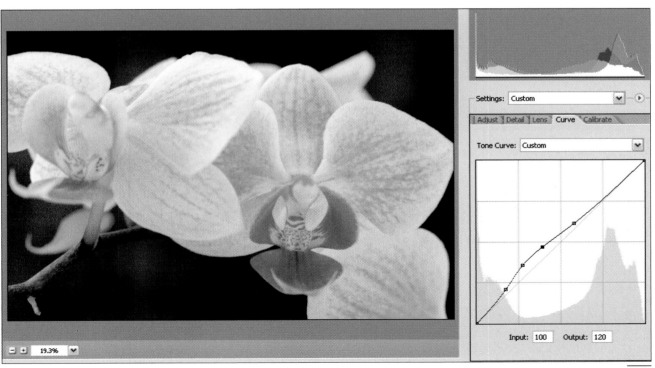

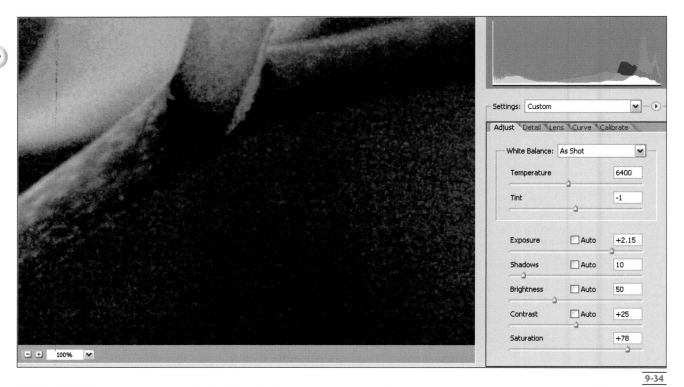

9-34

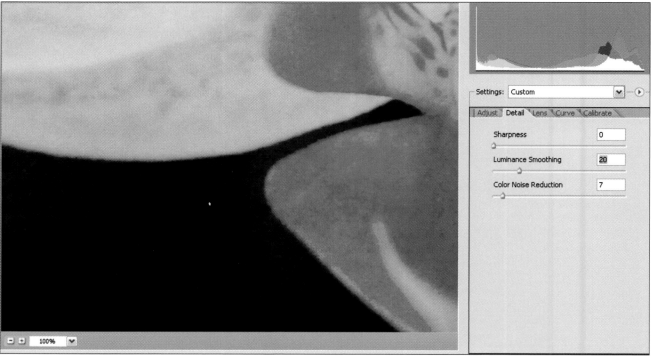

9-35

READJUSTING THE IMAGE

Once you make your best noise adjustment using all the techniques described in the previous sections, it is very important to look at the whole image again and see if it needs any final adjustments. There is a tendency (and a real danger to good processing) to check the noise details in a magnified preview, see that they look okay, and then tell Camera Raw that you are done. You open the photo in Photoshop or save it, when you might be better off making some final tweaks to the photo in Camera Raw.

1. Set the Preview to show the whole photo (pressing Ctrl/⌘+0 is the easiest way to do this).

2. Step back visually and try to see the photo as a whole. It is really too easy to only focus on the details you have just worked on. Force yourself to see the overall photo. The scene illustrated here needs a boost in Brightness, which is shown in figure 9-36. Don't mess with the Tone Curve at this point because of the very particular changes made earlier. You also have to keep an eye on noise to see if this new change does something you don't like.

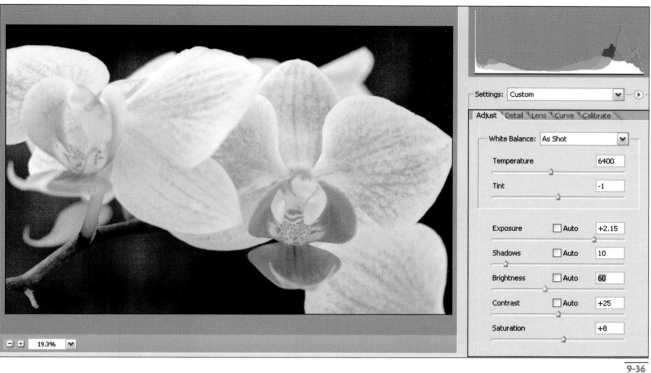

9-36

3. This photo doesn't need any Saturation boost, but you may notice that a final tweak of this slider is needed on other images.

There is now quite a difference between the before adjustment photo and the one seen in figure 9-37. This is by no means a perfect photo. A better exposure would have made a better image. It has taken a lot of work to get here, but the image is much improved from its start.

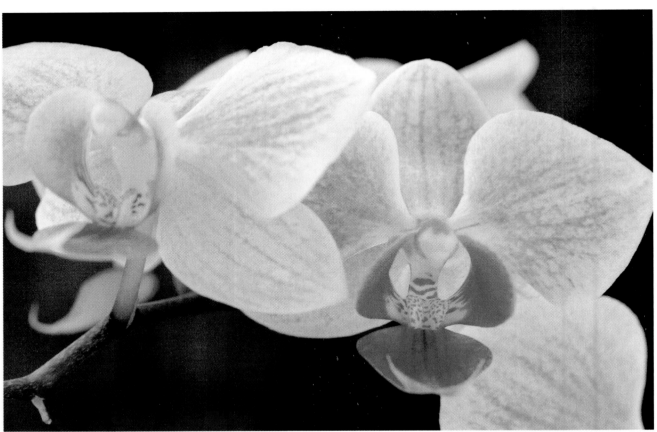

9-37

Q & A

What if I find the compromises are too much? Can I just leave the noise as is?

On some photos, you may need to do exactly that. The orchid photo in this chapter does not have a lot of fine detail. If your photo has that kind of detail, you may want to be very careful how much noise reduction you do. Also, as mentioned, sometimes a bit of noise in the photo makes it look sharper. Don't overdue it, however, because a high degree of sharp noise is very distracting to the viewer unless you have a very special effect in mind.

When working with soft forms such as clouds or subjects that may have problems with noise, such as a traditional portrait, you can often increase the noise reduction settings quite a lot without harming the photo. They may even make the skin tones look smoother.

Noise is a very subjective thing. Fine-art photographer Robert Farber is famous for his images with deliberately enhanced grain and noise. On the other hand, you never see a bit of noise in the large-format landscapes of Jack Dykinga. Find where you and your subjects work best with noise.

What if I just used the Sharpness slider to compensate for having to use the Luminance Smoothing slider?

That line of thinking makes sense. After all, increasing the Luminance Smoothing slider setting often makes the photo look a little softer, a little less in focus. Adding in the Sharpness control balances this a little.

The problem is that as the Luminance Smoothing adjustment is increased, fine details start to blur and disappear. At that point, using the Sharpness control won't help. In addition, it can actually mislead you into thinking that there is more detail in the photo than there really is because the preview looks sharper.

You are still much better off doing sharpening in Photoshop after you do your initial image processing in Camera Raw. You have much better control over that sharpening in the Unsharp Mask control, plus you can try the Smart Sharpening tool of CS2.

After applying a lot of noise reduction techniques to a photo, I notice it doesn't seem to have the same crispness and brilliance of other photos. Is that true?

This is a real danger of the noise reduction controls in the Detail tab. The crispness and brilliance of a photograph comes from tiny highlights that a lens resolves and the sensor captures. Unfortunately, those tiny highlights appear the same to Camera Raw as noise, so as you increase Luminance Smoothing (mostly) and Color Noise Reduction (to a lesser degree), these tiny highlights are dulled and blend into the photo. The result is that the whole photo loses a little of its crispness and brilliance. In some cases, the noise may just be too distracting and annoying, so you have no choice. You lose something as the noise is reduced. But in other photos, you may prefer leaving some noise so that other factors in the image, such as image brilliance and sharpness, are less affected.

Chapter 10

TOUGH DECISIONS

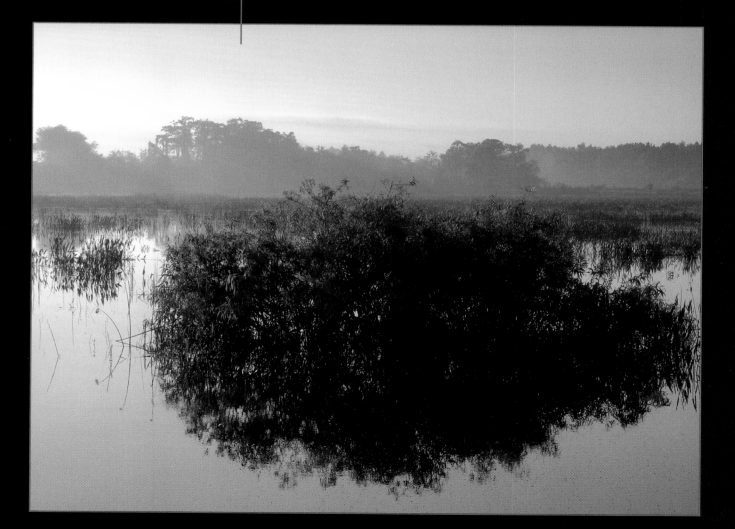

Wouldn't it be great if every photo had a perfect range of tonalities and colors that you could quickly and easily adjust in Camera Raw? Unfortunately, the real world doesn't offer that possibility. Some scenes are dark; others are light. Lighting is uneven; subjects and backgrounds don't match, and so on.

Scenes that do not have a perfect range of tonalities and colors may force you to make some tough decisions on processing in Camera Raw. There are a lot of classes and books about Photoshop that discuss very important general image processing and working with problem images, but tough decisions are rarely discussed. Yet, every serious photographer faces them sooner or later.

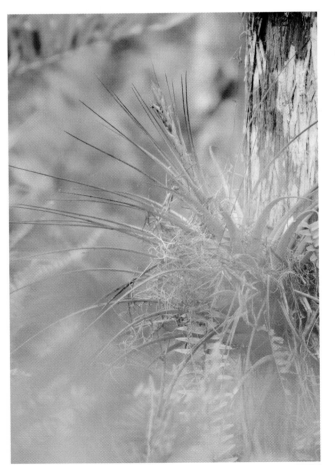

10-1

This chapter gives you more insight on working with Camera Raw while offering some advice on making tough decisions about challenging images. Learning to use Camera Raw to its potential is not about learning all the sliders and adjustment controls. You already know them all by this point in this book. To truly master Camera Raw (and this applies to Photoshop, too), you need to learn to read photos and be able to make the right decisions on how to adjust them. There are three images shown in this chapter — a photo with soft and subtle colors, a high-contrast image dawn shot and a night shot with totally artificial lighting. Remember that there is no absolute right decision, because any adjustment to an image is always based on your particular style, preferences, and use of the photo.

SOFT COLORS

Photography has the potential to show all sorts of interpretations in the world. The photo in figure 10-1 is a soft look at the colors in a cypress swamp (this is the final, adjusted photo). This is a highly photographic way of seeing. Such an image does not exist for human vision. Yet, it is an interesting and impactful way of shooting certain subjects, from flowers to people.

The image was taken in Loxahatchee National Wildlife Refuge in Florida in the northern part of the Everglades ecosystem. A cypress swamp is an interesting place, and the refuge includes a very nice boardwalk through it. It can get a bit mosquito-ridden at times, but in February and March when the bromeliads (or airplants) bloom, it is a very pleasant hike.

I deliberately shot the photo in figure 10-1 for the effect. The swamp is so filled with plants that I wanted to give a visual impression of that growth. The photographic technique for this soft effect is fairly simple:

> Shoot with limited depth of field using a wide f-stop and a telephoto lens. This particular photo was captured at 250mm of a 70-300mm zoom lens, shot wide open at f/5.6.

> Shoot deliberately through foreground elements. In this case, I moved the camera until I could shoot through leaves, but the main plant in the background (Northern needleleaf, a tillandsia starting to bloom) is clearly seen and sharp, as emphasized in the cropped detail of figure 10-2. You must use manual focus and be careful of your focus point.

HARSH CONTRASTS

If this photo starts looking too harsh, the soft feel of the colors is quickly lost. If it were simply processed by the numbers, so to speak, based on what was discussed in earlier parts of this book, that is exactly what would happen. Here's how that would work:

1. This is a vertical shot, but it comes into Camera Raw as a horizontal (see figure 10-3). It must be rotated to vertical by clicking the Clockwise Rotate icon at the top of the preview image (as done for figure 10.4 and on). Many cameras allow you to rotate the photos in the camera, but because this limits the size of the image in the LCD I don't like to do it.

2. Standard procedure is to press Alt/Option while clicking and dragging the Exposure slider to set the highlight level, as seen in figure 10-4.

3. Continuing the normal way of working an image, press Alt/Option while clicking and dragging the Shadows slider to set blacks, as seen in figure 10-5.

PRO TIP

Your camera records exposure information for each shot in the metadata (information about the file) kept in the image file. With many lenses, the camera also records focal length. This can be a great way to check how you made a particular shot. Camera Raw does not offer a way to access this metadata; however, the Adobe Bridge does (the old Photoshop CS browser does, too).

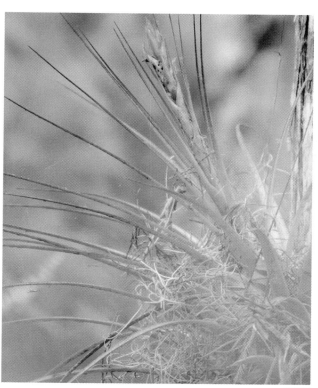

10-2

Tough Decisions

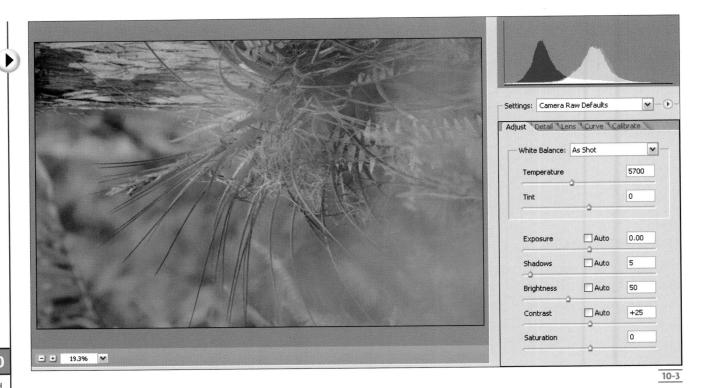

10-3

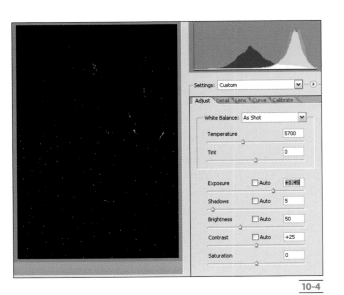

10-4

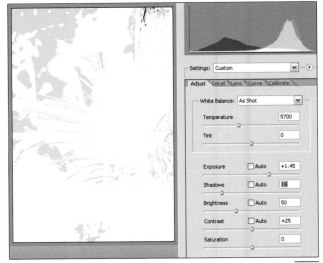

10-5

How a soft image like this is exposed in the camera can be a very important issue. Often, soft colors are attractive because they are light in tone. Dark colors never really look soft and don't make this effect work its best. An overall light-toned subject (including the soft, out-of-focus colors) is often underexposed if the camera meter is used without interpretation. That can mean less quality to the soft colors when adjusted in Camera Raw.

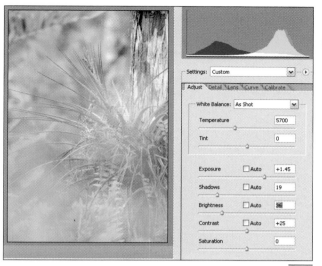

10-6

4. Once the brightest and darkest parts of the photo are determined, check the midtones. In this image, they could go darker (see figure 10-6).

Basic choices have been made and the result in figure 10-7 is certainly a snappier image than the original. It is okay, but it really doesn't support the original intent. Such adjustments certainly are acceptable in many applications, but they really aren't what is needed in this case. The original shot as it first came into Camera Raw was also okay, but rather flat, as seen in figure 10-8. The image needs something in between this juiced-up version from standard adjustments and the original capture from the camera.

ADJUSTING WITH SOFT IN MIND

This photo really looks its best when it shows off the softness that the shooting technique captures. To do this, take a more studied approach to the standard adjustments:

1. If you press Alt/Option to adjust Exposure to its normal place where the highlight threshold appears, the image is too harsh. You can also see in this image that the histogram is restricted. There is very little

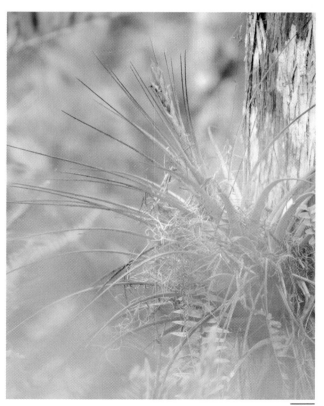

10-7

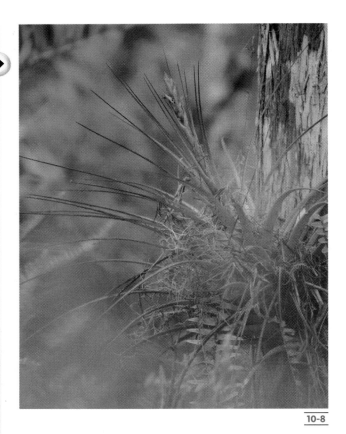

10-8

data on the right side. You may also remember how far the Exposure had to be moved to the right (brightening the photo) until the threshold was reached. So you know that a movement of the slider to the right is going to help, but just something far less than the threshold. One way of doing this is to press and hold Alt/Option and click and drag the slider until the threshold is reached, then back it off a bit. Release Alt/Option and move the slider until the highlight brightness of the image seems good, as shown in figure 10-9.

2. Adjusting Shadows is tricky. Generally, you want some sort of dark areas in a photo (even if they are very small) for contrast and color. This does not work for this photo. Increasing the Shadows setting slightly does make the photo a little richer, but too much and it quickly becomes harsh. The Alt/Option and threshold technique helps you visualize where the darker areas are, but on a shot like this, however, you need to adjust the Shadows slider purely by the way the image looks in the preview (see figure 10-10).

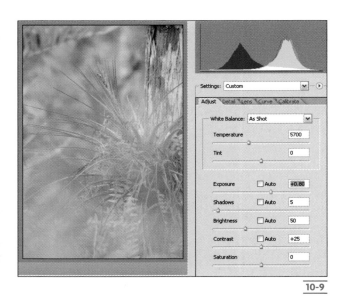

10-9

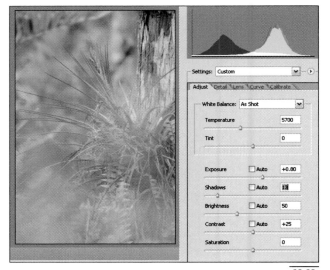

10-10

3. Because subtle tonalities are a real key to the softness of this photo, the Tonal Curve is really the best way to deal with midtones. The Medium Contrast setting doesn't actually look too bad, but it could be improved. It does, however, point to a direction of adjustment, namely darker dark tones and brighter light tones (this is not the same as blacks and highlights, but refers to dark and light gray tones that are very important to the photo). By placing two points on the Linear Curve setting (which changes it to Custom), one at the bottom quarter intersection to anchor the dark tones and one in the upper third quarter to lighten the mid- and brighter tones, the image can quickly be brightened and the contrast boosted slightly without hurting the soft colors (see figure 10-11).

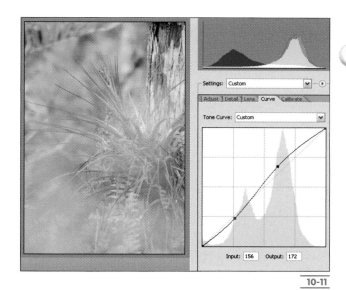

10-11

4. Because the dark areas have been really tricky in this photo, it is a good idea to re-examine Shadows after changing midtones (see figure 10-12). It appears that it can be increased slightly to give the darker tones a little more emphasis.

COLOR ENHANCEMENT

Overall, this photo has pretty good color after adjusting tonalities. But it seems to have a little too much yellow (you can even see this in the histogram that is very strongly yellow to the middle and right side). Here's how you might fix that:

1. Trying different White Balance settings, such as seen in figures 10-13 (Cloudy) and 10-14 (Auto), makes the color worse, so it goes back to As Shot, which is shown in figure 10-15.

2. The photo seems a little too warm, so clicking and dragging the Temperature slider to the left reduces some of the warmth of the photo, as shown in figure 10-16. Too much and it starts looking a little cold in the grays. A change of about 600 degrees seems to help.

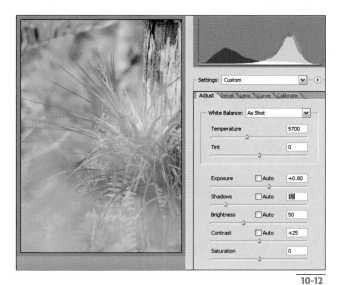

10-12

PRO TIP

It is important to remember that with the Saturation slider, a little can go a long way in most photos. Oversaturated colors often lose tonality and can look garish. Oversaturation can be a sure sign that an image has been Photoshopped (or perhaps, over-Photoshopped).

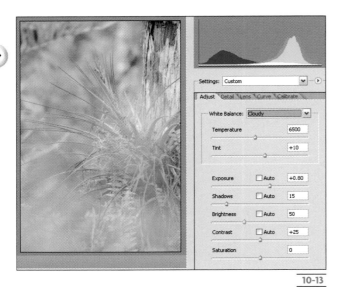

10-13

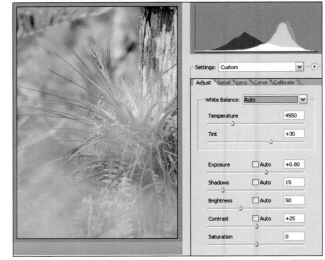

10-14

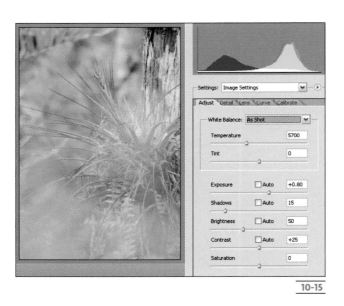

10-15

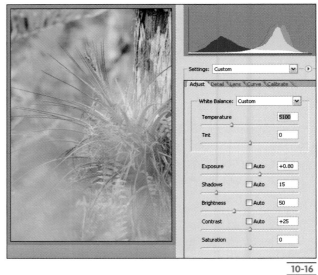

10-16

3. Click and drag the Tint slider to the left to increase the green and to the right for magenta. Adding a little green makes the foliage look better, but gives the whole photo too much of a colorcast. I prefer to drag the slider slightly to the right to make the back and flower a little richer, as seen in figure 10-17.

4. This photo has so much color in it that increasing the Saturation setting can quickly result in some ugly overkill.

THE DETAIL TAB

This photo has so much soft, out-of-focus areas that noise can be a real problem. However, enlarging the photo preview shows that there is very little noise in the image. No Luminance Smoothing is needed or should even be used, as seen in figure 10-18.

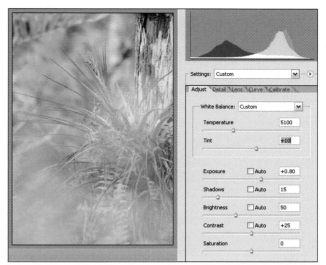

10-17

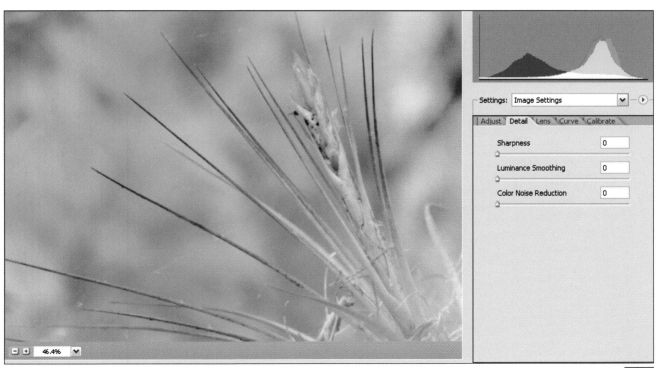

10-18

This is also true for Color Noise Reduction. On first glance at the photo, you might think that this control does very little on such an image. Overall, that is true. However, when the fine parts of the bromeliad are enlarged, the fine red color on the thin leaf tips is damaged when you drag Color Noise Reduction slider to the right. None should be applied to this photo. It is important to check multiple points in your photograph as you adjust the Color Noise Reduction slider. You don't want to gain noise reduction in one area at the cost of losing important color details in another.

The final image has excellent color yet the soft effect is still obvious, as seen in figure 10-19.

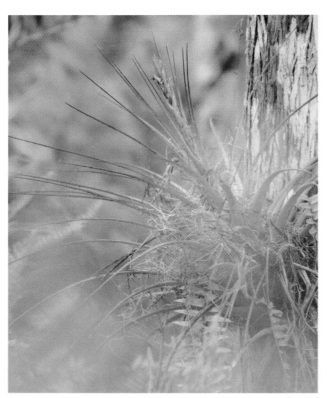

10-19

BACKLIT CONTRAST

Any image with high contrast such as that from backlight conditions will always challenge you when working in Camera Raw. Camera Raw offers many choices, but the contrast of the image limits what you can and can't use, especially if you want a realistic photo. One problem is that Camera Raw can only adjust the whole photo. Sometimes high-contrast images need special work in Photoshop where you can control the adjustment of small areas of the photo separately from each other. If your image needs a lot of adjustment, it can help to bring it into Photoshop from Camera Raw as a 16-bit file.

That said, Camera Raw offers quite a bit of capability with a contrasty image, such as figure 10-20 taken in a swamp in the Everglades wetlands southeast of Lake Okeechobee, shot toward the rising sun. This figure shows unadjusted form. It is bright because the sun has just risen and should retain that feeling of brightness. Yet the shrub in the foreground is rather dark, and the overall contrast seems a bit harsh for the humid atmosphere of a swamp in the early morning. This cannot be changed at the point of exposure. More exposure would totally blow the sky out; less exposure would give the shrub even less color.

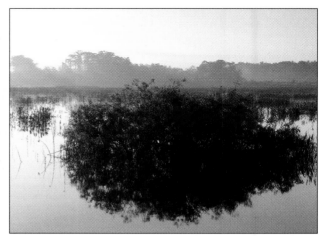

10-20

CORE DECISIONS

As I stress throughout this book, it always helps to follow a consistent workflow when working an image. This automates the process and gets you to think less about Camera Raw and more about the photograph. The photograph and your interpretation of it should always color your decisions on how to adjust it, not arbitrary rules about processing a photo that are sometimes given. Here's one way of interpreting this high-contrast photo:

1. The Exposure slider is typically teamed with Alt/Option. In this case, however, the photo comes into Camera Raw with a lot of brightness at the upper left. This is a good exposure because there is adequate detail in the dark areas, but the highlights need to be toned down.

As the slider is dragged way to the left, some clouds in the bright area appear in the top left of the image, but this actually occurs beyond the threshold point shown with the Alt/Option key. That's okay to a degree. However, the feeling of brightness is lost and that bright area appears a bit flat and gray if the Exposure slider is dragged too far to the left, even though some clouds in the bright area show up more, as seen in figure 10-21.

This is an important point. I don't believe in making a photo serve some arbitrary standards that aren't necessarily appropriate to the needs of the photo itself (it is interesting that the automatic choice for Exposure makes it even grayer than figure 10-21). This photo needs brightness where the sun is rising. That's a

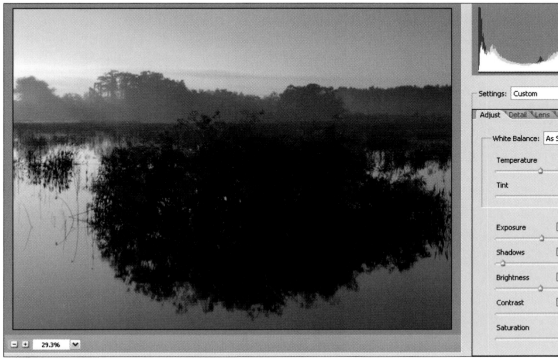
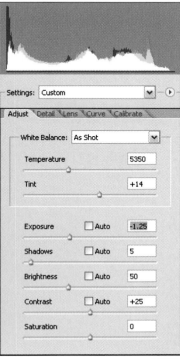

10-21

normal way you see such an area. If the brightness is arbitrarily toned down just so you can see the clouds, you have to ask, so what? Does that really help the photo? In this case, I don't think so, so I like what is happening in figure 10-22. Note how much airier the background atmosphere looks.

2. Moisture in the air makes the shadows a little weak. Using Alt/Option and the Shadows slider, they can be strengthened by bringing them up just a bit to encourage some blacks in the shadows, as seen in figure 10-23.

3. The Brightness slider is way too blunt a tool for the subtle tones and extreme contrast of this photo. This is where the Tone Curve in the Curve tab really helps (see figure 10-24). Working with four points on the curve (use the Custom setting) allows some significant changes: one point is placed at about the bottom quarter tone intersection and moved up to lighten the darker midtones; a second point is placed below that and dragged down to keep the darkest tones dark; a third point is placed about a third from the top and

pulled down to bring the brightest areas down slightly in tone (which also helps their color); finally, a fourth point is placed near the top of the curve to bring down the very bright areas back to the midadjustment line (which allows the bright clouds to be kept). By using the curve to selectively affect different tonalities, the photo now starts showing some of the atmosphere that one expects from a swamp at dawn.

PRO TIP

The numbers available in Camera Raw can help in photos like this. For many situations, I feel they take you away from the real photograph and make the process too mathematic and arbitrary. However, this photo does point out a situation where the numbers can help, such as very bright or dark areas. Check the numbers for RGB at the top right of the interface when your cursor is over a part of the image (in figure 10-21, it was over the brightest part of the sunrise at the top left). White happens when all three numbers approach 255; black when all three numbers approach 0. In figure 10-21, the brightest part of the photo is not pure white (the numbers are in the low 240s).

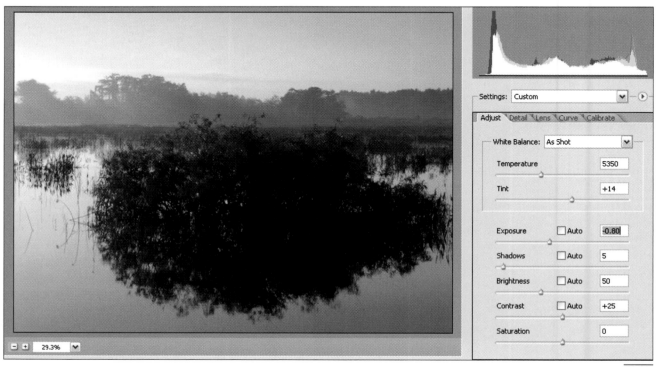

10-22

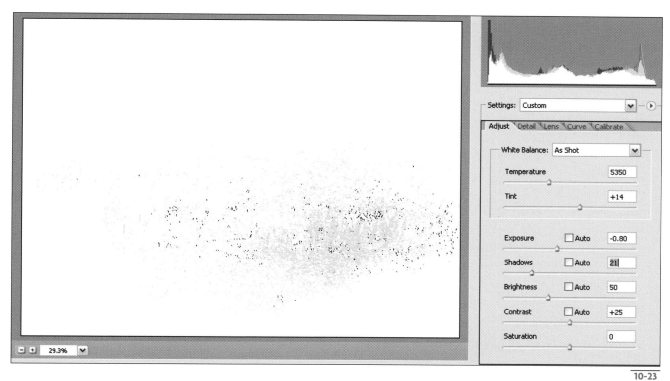

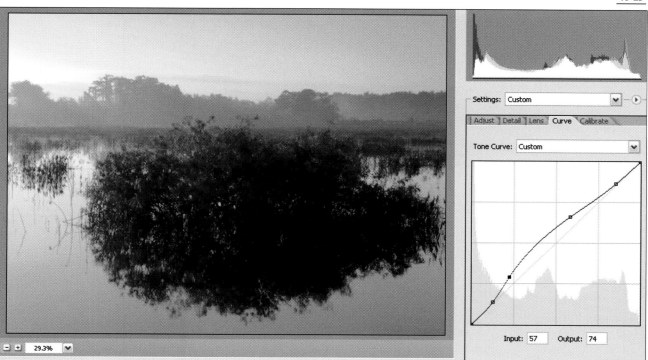

COLOR ENHANCEMENT

At this point, the image looks good, but the color is a little weak. Sunrise and sunset are definitely enhanced by a warm interpretation of the scene. This has become the way such conditions are seen in photographs (because traditionally, a color film balanced to be neutral in the middle of the day was used, making the sunrise or sunset far warmer than seen by the human eye). A real documentation of a sunrise or sunset often seems false to most viewers. To give this photo a more traditional sunrise feel, it needs some more warmth and even more color overall.

1. This is a perfect photo to click down the choices of the White Balance setting menu from top to bottom to see what the different choices offer the image. The indoor settings are way too blue and daylight seems a bit wimpy. Cloudy and Shade add quite a bit of warmth to the scene. Shade, as seen in figure 10-25, is too strong for my taste, so I stick with Cloudy, which is demonstrated in figure 10-26. This immediately evokes a strong feeling of sunrise in the Everglades.

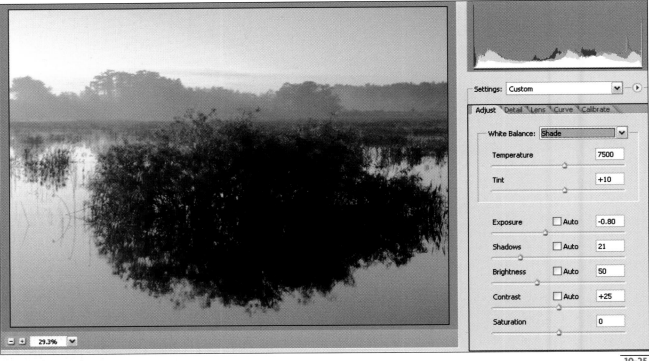

10-25

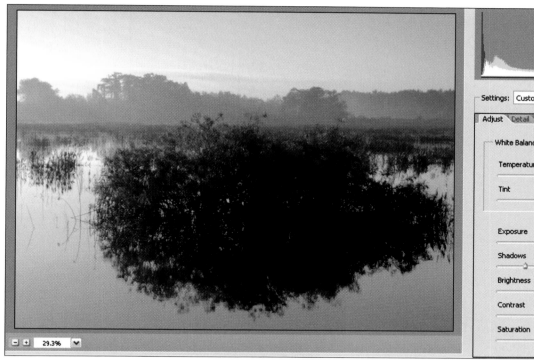
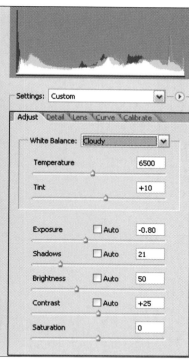

10-26

2. If you click and drag the Tint slider to the left, it makes the whole photo greener, but if you drag the slider just a little, as seen in figure 10-27, it makes the sunrise look a little more yellow, which is a very natural look for a sunrise.

3. For a richer look, Saturation is increased slightly (see figure 10-28). Be careful how you use Saturation. Too much and the photo looks garish in a hurry. Kicking it up a little, however, gives the colors a stronger early-light look.

Once the image is in Photoshop, I am tempted to add some color to the top-left corner to bring it down in tone a bit and increase the blue content of the water in the lower right (a very natural look). Both of these are selective, small area adjustments that cannot be done in Camera Raw.

Overall, however, the photo now has a nice feel to it, as seen in figure 10-29. There is color in the leaves in the foreground bush, plus there are some nice tonalities in the humid air around the trees in the background. There is an excellent fall-off of darkness from foreground to background, which gives the scene excellent atmosphere.

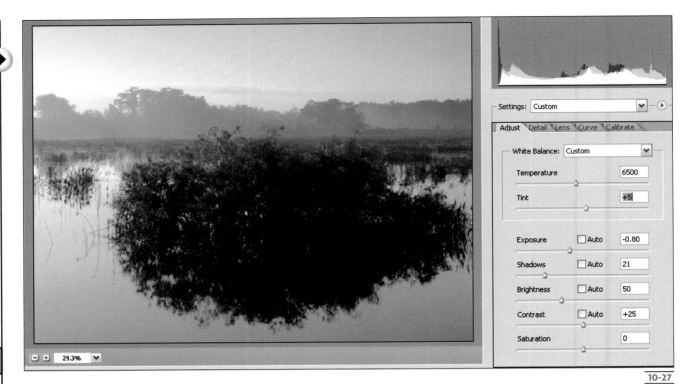

10-27

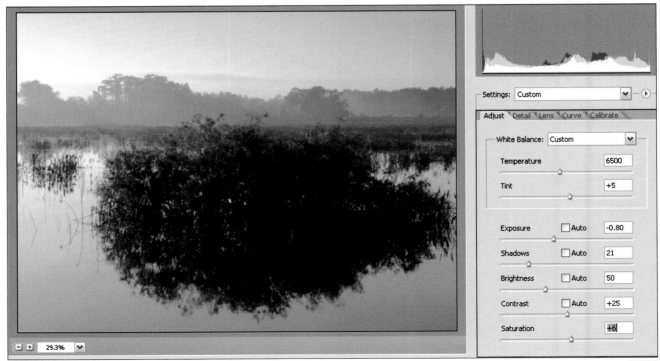

10-28

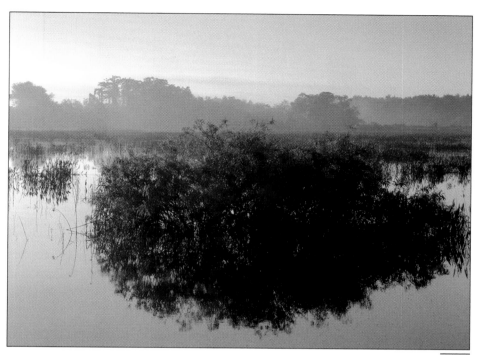

10-29

NOT THE NORMAL LIGHT

When the light on your subject is not the normal daylight or indoors lighting, you are faced with some interesting choices as to how to deal with the subject. Do you try to make it look like its real colors (if you remember what they are)? Do you try to make it look natural (which can be something entirely different than the real colors)? Or do you go for an unexpected interpretation that is far from an accurate rendition of the scene?

Figure 10-30 is the unadjusted shot of a plaza in San Jose (actually right across the street from the Adobe headquarters), an image that would be fairly flat and ordinary during the day. At night, it comes alive, yet what colors are real or natural? Or should it have a completely different rendition than the camera captures? I lean toward a

natural look for this scene. Camera Raw interprets how the camera recorded the image as a bit warm, so that should be adjusted. But tonalities are all over the place in this image, which allows for some very distinct choices when adjusting them.

PRO TIP

Digital cameras are great for shooting night scenes. Night shots used to be difficult with film because of reciprocity failure (a change in light sensitivity of the film as long exposures are used) and because exposure was so hard to judge. With a digital camera, you can freely take pictures, check the exposure immediately, and then adjust as needed. In addition, you can play with white balance settings to gain a color interpretation that seems reasonable and still change that later in Camera Raw if needed.

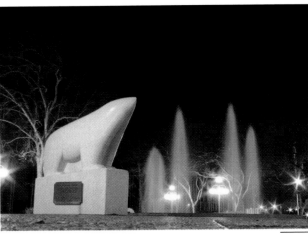

10-30

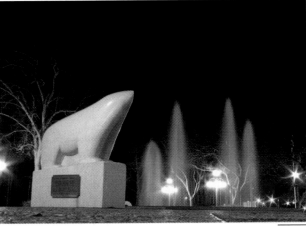

10-31

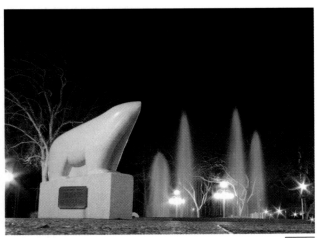

10-32

COLOR OR TONALITIES FIRST?

In this photo, a different workflow attack may be warranted because of the color, but before you start to work on a photo like this it is important to understand how viewers perceive such an image. Generally, people like to see some warmth in the light from night photos. Whether that is realistic or not isn't the issue. People are used to seeing photographs taken at night with film that has imperfect color balance. For a variety of reasons having to do with film types and color temperature of lights, traditional color films recorded nighttime scenes with an amber or red-yellow bias, even though the human eye sees the same scene in a more neutral manner. So people expect a color night photograph to look somewhat warm and consider it unrealistic if it is not, even though it can be corrected to a neutral condition in Camera Raw or Photoshop itself.

In figures 10-30, 10-31, and 10-32, you can see three different interpretations of the color in this scene:

> **Figure 10-30.** While the color in this night photo is okay as interpreted by Camera Raw from the camera settings, it seems a little too warm. The bear statue is especially a bit yellow.

> **Figure 10-31.** You can see that while this more neutral image is probably closer to what the eye sees, it does not look as realistic as the others. Most people would consider it a bit cold compared to the two other images. Still, it is a valid interpretation of the scene, and there may be situations where it is required.

> **Figure 10-32.** This is the interpretation I like. It keeps some warmth, yet has a more naturalistic feel to the night.

There is no absolute right way to deal with the color in this image. Any photo similar to this with mixed, artificial light requires you to experiment a bit and see what you like. Because color is so variable in such an image, it is a good idea to deal with color first in the workflow. Color is affected by further adjustments, so I like to deal with odd or off-color first so that I am not bothered or distracted by the color as the image continues to be processed. Here's how the color was determined to get to figure 10-32:

1. A quick way of fixing colorcasts like this one is to use the White Balance settings. Because this is night with tungsten lighting, that is certainly a logical choice. Tungsten does indeed take out the warm color, as seen in figure 10-33, making the whites and grays of the scene fairly neutral, although it is too neutral with too much blue for my taste.

Note that the neutral tones are different in color (compare the statue with the water fountain, for example). That is because tungsten and other artificial lights do not have a consistent color temperature (unless you supply lights designed for photography). Wattage and variations in manufacture will change that. This is one reason why you can never get a perfectly neutral scene in a photo like this that has different light sources (if you wanted to do that, you'd have to go into Photoshop and adjust the areas individually).

2. The little gray eyedropper, the White Balance tool, works quite well in any photo with easily found neutral tones, as seen in figure 10-34. In this night scene, the bear statue and the fountain both have neutral tones, and clicking on different places with the White Balance tool actually gives quite a range of results. That's normal because different parts of the statue see different lights, for example. Sometimes by just clicking around, you can get a perfect color. When you try this on your photo, some of the adjustments look good compared to others, so note where the Temperature and Tint sliders end up with the adjustments you like.

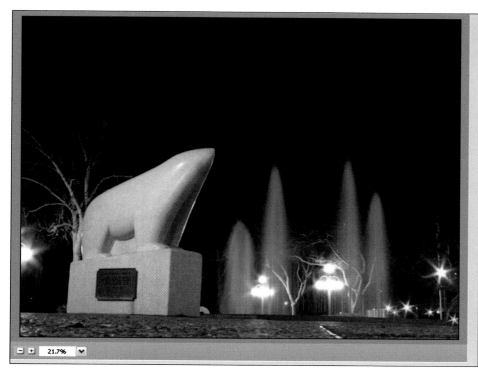
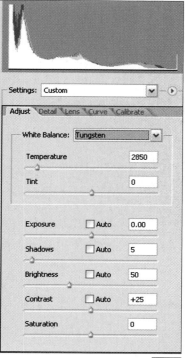

10-33

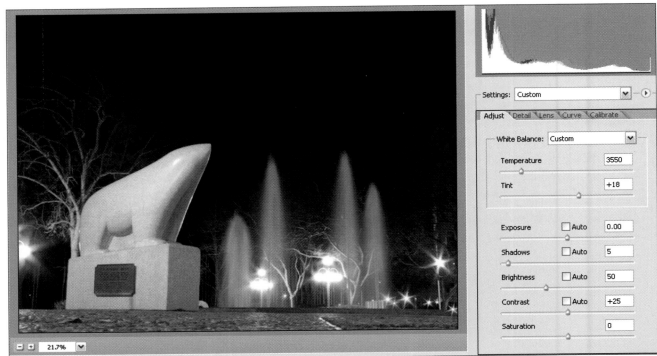

Settings: Custom

Adjust | Detail | Lens | Curve | Calibrate

White Balance: Custom

Temperature		3550
Tint		+18
Exposure	☐ Auto	0.00
Shadows	☐ Auto	5
Brightness	☐ Auto	50
Contrast	☐ Auto	+25
Saturation		0

☐ ☐ 21.7% ▾

10-34

3. Because neither the White Balance settings nor the White Balance tool provided exactly what I want, I decided to adjust the Temperature and Tint sliders manually. The notes I made about the Temperature and Tint slider numbers in Step 2 give me a starting point. I knew I didn't want the high number used for the original Camera Raw interpretation of this photo of 5500 for Temperature. I didn't like the numbers below 3000 for Temperature that came from the White Balance tool, but I did like some of those around 3500 with Tint adjusted toward magenta. So I tried around 4400 for Temperature and Tint at 8 (see figure 10-35). This gave it a nice night feeling without looking too yellow or amber.

NIGHT TONE INTERPRETATION

The night sky is important to this composition as it defines the time and accents the lights. Seeing a hint of trees in the sky also seems helpful, though how much

needs to be scene is debatable. When looking to interpret a photo, you often have to make compromises. To get a very dark sky may mean the loss of some of the highest parts of the trees, yet that darkness may be more important to the scene than an arbitrary capture of the twigs just because Camera Raw can bring them out.

Another thing to consider here are the bright lights. The lights are overexposed, but that's pretty much normal for night shots. You can tone them down a bit in Camera Raw or they can be exposed for their detail, but you have to ask why? I'm not sure what that would accomplish other than underexposing important parts of the image. Pure white, bright highlights in lights is an accepted way to see night lights in a photo.

Some people wonder about the star patterns on the lights as seen in the detail (see figure 10-36). This is not from a filter. This is a diffraction pattern along the diaphragm blades of the iris of the lens. As you stop a lens down to

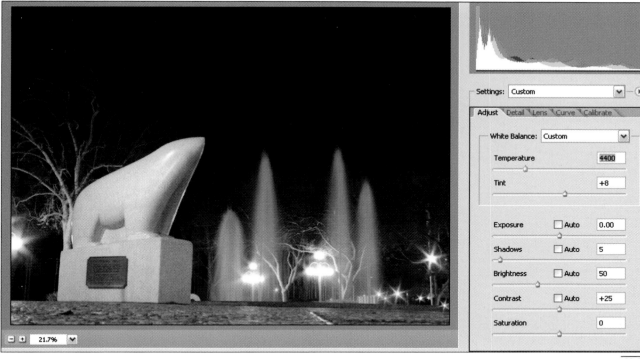

10-35

its smaller apertures, the opening for light gets smaller and bright highlights diffract as they pass that opening. A pattern is created that is related to the actual shape of the diaphragm. This particular shot was made with an advanced compact camera that has a very small lens to begin with, which makes even moderate apertures act this way.

ADJUSTING FOR THE NIGHT

This photo could be made brighter or darker, and frankly, who would know that either condition wasn't an accurate rendition of the scene? Probably both would be! Still, a night photo should be tuned to keep its feeling of night, and here's how this one is adjusted:

1. To get the feeling for the night sky for this composition, the workflow changes again and starts with the Shadows slider. I really feel the night sky needs to be black, and this is easily done by pressing and holding Alt/Option while clicking and dragging the slider to the right, as shown in figure 10-37. The pure black part of

the sky does not go all the way down to the trees and fountain. That is important. Having a dark tone there with a slight color to it gives some atmosphere to the night.

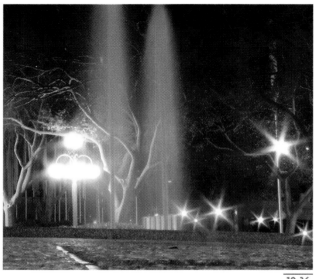

10-36

203

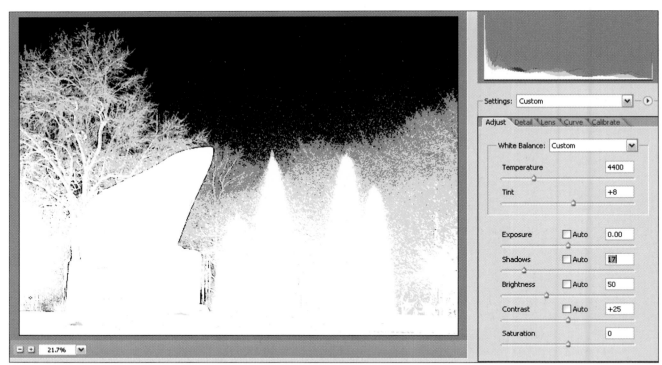

10-37

2. There isn't much that you can (or should) do to the bright lights. However, there is a bright highlight on the statue that can be toned down a bit with the Exposure slider, as shown in figure 10-38. Bringing that down darkens a few other things but doesn't really have a big effect on the rest of the photo.

3. The midtones important to this photo are the grays of the statue and water, plus the darker tones of the tree branches. The Brightness slider is a little too heavy handed for this adjustment. Going to the Tone Curve, it is important to set some points that won't change much. You do not want to brighten the lightest tones much, so click a point high on the curve at the three-quarter-tone intersection to limit higher changes. In addition, the darkest areas should stay the same so, click near the bottom, about halfway to the first-quarter-tone intersection to help in that area.

Next, pull the curve up from the center (see figure 10-39). Two points work well: one in the center and one down near the first-quarter tone. This allows the midtones to be pulled up with a little extra emphasis in the darker tones (which helps parts of the trees).

CROP FOR EVALUATION

At this point, the photo looks good, but it seems a bit spacey, that is, it could be cropped. This is a fairly large image file (from a 7.1-megapixel camera), so a bit of cropping won't hurt it much. I am a firm believer in always trying to fill your camera's image area with important elements in your composition. This does two things: it ensures you have maximum quality to work with from your camera file (you paid for that sensor, so why not use it!), and it forces you to really look at all parts of your composition while you are with the subject. It is very frustrating to be working on a photo in the computer and tell yourself, "If only I..."

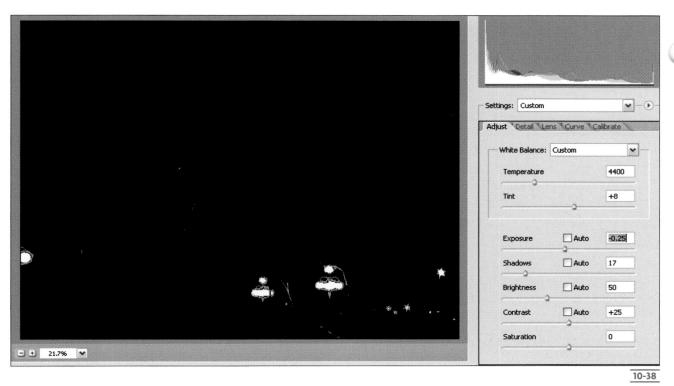

10-38

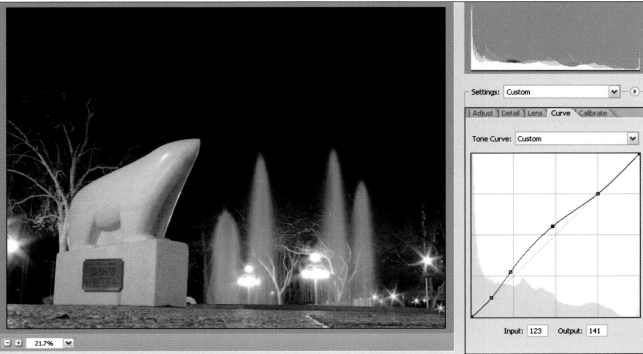

10-39

This image has too much space at the top for me, and the light that sits on the left side of the photo is a little distracting because of its placement. Because Camera Raw allows cropping now, why not? Actually, some Photoshop pros feel it is better to crop later, in Photoshop. As far as quality goes, there is no difference between either approach. In addition, any crop in Camera Raw is not permanent. If I need to crop, I often crop an image early in the process (at least a rough crop), such as in Camera Raw, so that I can remove annoying elements (they are actually just subdued in the Camera Raw interface) that might be distracting as I adjust the image.

This image is cropped with the Crop tool. Simply use it like a cursor — click and drag the cropped area to a rough size, as seen in figure 10-40. Then tweak this adjustment by moving the sides in and out. You can also rotate the whole cropped area if the photo is crooked.

Once you make the crop, you still see the rest of the photo, though it is grayed out. It would be nice if you could now give a simple command (such as Ctrl/⌘+0) to see the cropped area filling the preview window, but Adobe has not provided that yet (actually, Ctrl/⌘+0 still gives you the whole image, even that which is being cropped, which is a bit silly as this makes the active photo smaller). I find it helpful to use the Zoom tool and use it to outline the active, cropped area of the photo, which now makes it close to full preview size.

PRO TIP

You may notice that the Crop tool has a little triangle at its lower-right side. This means it has a flyout menu if you click on the tool and hold the mouse button down. You now have a choice of cropping ratios. This is very helpful if you need a specific size. The Crop tool gives you the specific ratio you pick, allowing you to very carefully place the crop over the elements in the image. The numbers, however, are a bit cryptic: 1 to 1 is square, 2 to 3 is the same as 35mm, 3 to 4 is approximately television size, 4 to 5 is perfect for making an 8 × 10, and 5 to 7 is the same as 5 × 7 or 10 × 14.

NIGHT NOISE

The bear and fountain scene was shot with a relatively low ISO setting of 100. I often use such settings because of the lower noise it offers, especially when I can support the camera with a tripod or other support (a small beanbag was used here). This can be especially important with night photos, as longer exposures tend to increase noise. In addition, because this shot was done with a small digital camera, noise also increases. So keeping noise lower by using a lower ISO setting helps.

There is noise in this photo, so the Detail tab is the next step:

1. How to reduce color noise is one of the first things to look for in a night photo, and there will almost always be chromatic or color noise in a photo like this. However, setting this control too high adversely affects some of the small features of the trees. A little reduction of color noise helps the fountains, so setting the slider to 5 helps without hurting the trees (see figure 10-41).

2. There is enough noise that increasing the Luminance Smoothing slider setting helps. A setting of about 25 works without hurting the trees or the grain texture of the granite used for the statue (see figure 10-42).

FINAL CHECK

Again, it is important to do a final check of the photo in full size in the preview. All of the adjustments made to a photo can affect each other. You can't expect that one adjustment will remain the same as others are made.

In this photo, the overall photo looks good (see figure 10-43). Is it perfect? Absolutely... for me. You may feel it needs more of this or that, less of something else. That's fine. A photo like this is open for a lot of interpretation — that's one thing that makes night photography fun!

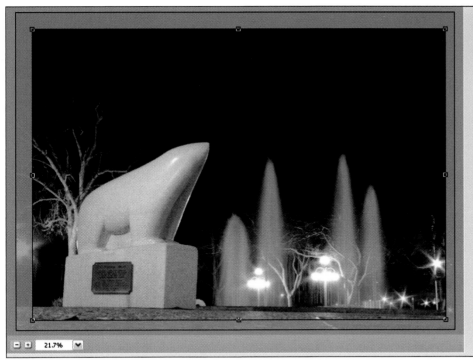

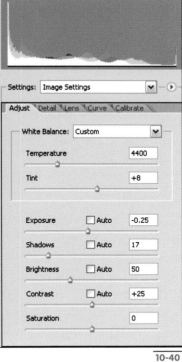

10-40

10-41

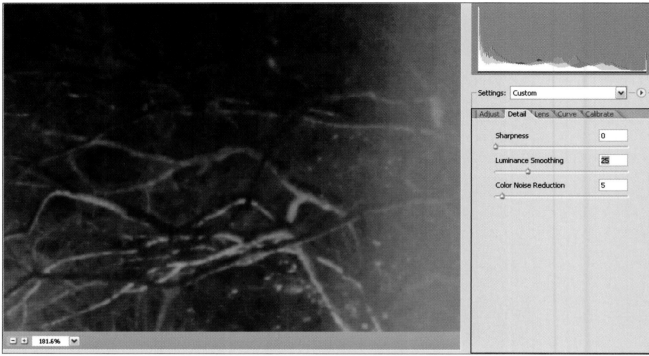

10-42

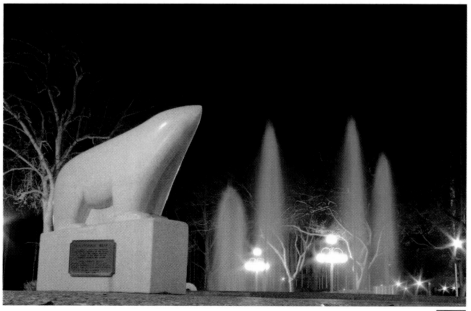

10-43

Q & A

What if I really do want to adjust colors in different ways in the same photo? If I want to get the best tonalities possible for those colors, I know I need to use Camera Raw, but it won't allow separate adjustments.

That is absolutely correct. Camera Raw is an overall or global adjustment tool. It is not designed to adjust parts of a photo differently. However, you can actually gain the same effect by doing a special technique that is explained fully in Chapter 13 on double processing for exposure.

Briefly, this is what you do: First, process the photo the best you can for the color of one area, then open that image in Photoshop. Save it as a Photoshop file. Then reopen the image in Camera Raw again and process for the color of the area that needs a different adjustment. Open that into Photoshop and save it as another Photoshop file. Now, drag one image onto the other (use the Move tool and press and hold Shift to align both photos). Next, hide the top image with a black-filled layer mask and paint in its color with a white paintbrush.

A photo with harsh contrast sometimes seems like it needs two completely opposed ways of processing in Camera Raw, but that isn't possible. How can I cope with such differences?

This can be a real challenge, especially with backlit conditions. To start, it is best to carefully choose your Exposure and Shadows slider points. Be sure you are keeping the detail you want in the highlights and shadows. Then almost always, you want to use the Tone Curve for further adjustment. Set the curve to the Linear setting, and then start clicking on different points in the curve to adjust the image. Typically, you want to anchor the very brightest and darkest tones first. Then, you brighten the dark areas and darken the bright areas.

You have to really watch your tonalities as you do this. It is too easy to get a technically adjusted photo (meaning you have pulled in the highlights and shadows as best as possible) but an aesthetically dull shot because the midtones are just too flat. If this starts to be a problem, you need to do the two-image adjustment process as described above and in Chapter 13. This allows you to carefully adjust your photo to get the most from both the bright and dark areas.

If all else fails, you may have to process the image twice as described in the previous question's answer.

Chapter 11

COMPACT DIGITAL CAMERA RAW PROCESSING

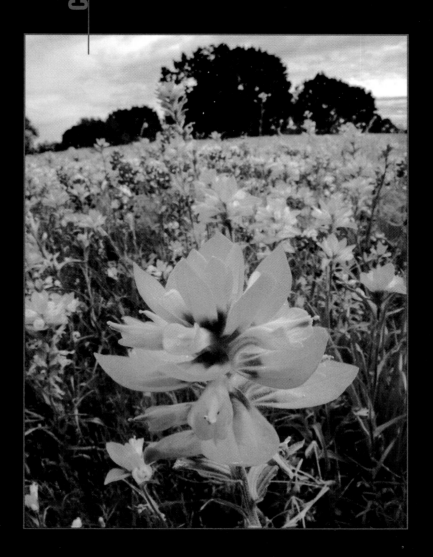

The advanced compact digital camera or advanced digital zoom camera is an amazing piece of technology. These little cameras are like point-and-shoot cameras in the sense that the lens is not interchangeable and you can shoot them totally automatically. But they are no more point-and-shoots than a Nikon D2x professional digital SLR. The advanced compact has totally adjustable controls from full automatic to aperture- and shutter-priority automation to total manual control. In addition, most of them have RAW capture capabilities. The combination of control and RAW sets these cameras apart from other small digital cameras and can achieve professional results.

These cameras are compact, yet they typically have excellent lenses and offer superb portability in a quality camera as seen in figure 11-1. They are important cameras for both the advanced amateur and the pro because of the features contained in such a compact package. In addition, you gain capabilities from these cameras that cannot be met by an inexpensive digital SLR without investing in more lenses.

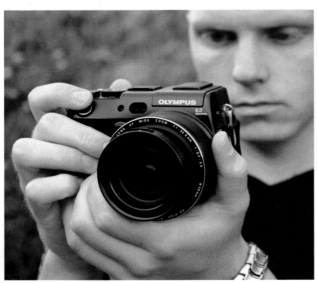

There are some important differences between the advanced digital compacts and digital SLRs that affect how to work with them and how you might process them in Camera Raw. To better understand the approach needed in Camera Raw, it is helpful to quickly take a look at these small cameras and how they take pictures.

WHY BOTHER?

If you can get great Raw files from a digital SLR, why bother with what some consider a less-than-serious camera. The answer is very photographic — these little digital cameras offer a lot of potential in small packages. Here's what you can expect and why even pros consider them for their unique attributes:

> **Size.** Even the largest compact digital camera is smaller than a digital SLR, and when you include matching lens capabilities, much smaller as seen in figure 11-2.

> **Sensor dust.** Because the lenses on a compact digital camera cannot be removed from the body, there is little problem with sensor dust (it isn't eliminated completely as a windy, dusty condition can cause dust to penetrate).

> **Complete.** A compact digital camera offers a complete package: it includes a range of focal lengths from wide-angle to telephoto, built-in flash, close-focus capabilities, full auto and manual controls, and more. This makes the camera an ideal travel companion; you need nothing else to shoot great photos.

> **Live LCD.** Live LCD shows exactly what the sensor sees all the time. Digital SLRs have a mirror to direct the light to the viewfinder, blocking light to the sensor (the mirror flips out of the way during exposure), so the sensor cannot be live. Compact digital cameras

offer a live LCD. This can be a great advantage in some shooting situations, such as close-ups, watching light and color, unusual angle shots where you cannot see a viewfinder, and more.

> **Swivel LCD.** This is a huge resource for the photographer on cameras that include it. The LCD monitor swings out from the body allowing you to see it from many angles as seen in figure 11-3. Combined with a live monitor, this lets you position the camera in many places that you could never place a camera without this feature, such as on the ground, high overhead, into tight spaces, and so forth.

> **High-quality optics.** Camera manufacturers have made these advanced digital cameras the flagships of this part of their compact camera line. Because of that, they have made excellent lenses for them, using low-dispersion glass usually seen in pro lenses. There are some design limitations due to the size of the lenses that can affect barrel distortion at wide-angle settings.

> **Low-cost quality.** High capabilities in a low-cost camera means you can afford to put these cameras into dangerous situations (for a camera) when you have to get the shot.

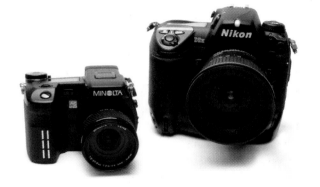

11-2

PRO TIP

Advanced compact digital cameras typically have their main close-up settings at only part of the focal length range. However, all of these cameras accept accessory lenses that can be attached in front of the camera's zoom lens. To turn the camera into a zoom macro-focusing unit, look into a high-quality achromatic close-up lens such as that from Hoya or Century Optics. These lenses are not cheap, but offer outstanding quality and will allow a full zoom capability for close-ups.

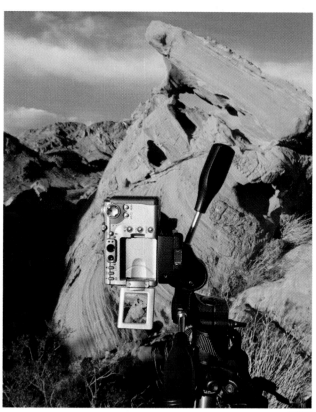

11-3

X-REF

For more information about noise, see Chapter 2.

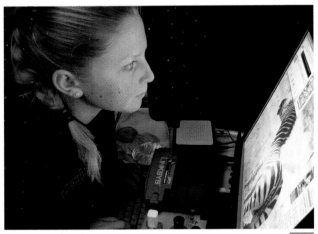

11-4

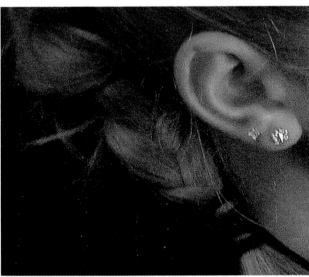

11-5

CHALLENGES OF THE SMALL SENSOR

Advanced compact digital cameras have very small sensors. You could easily fit one on a fingernail. They are a fraction of the size of even the smallest sensors used in digital SLRs. This does create some challenges in shooting and working the Raw files in Camera Raw:

> **Noise.** Noise is a distinct issue for small sensors. All advanced compact digital cameras have sophisticated noise reduction circuits built into the cameras, but you will see a lot of noise in the images from them when the ISO setting is above 100 and in very long exposures (which is why most of these cameras do not have ISO settings above 400 or allow shutter speeds longer than 15 seconds). Figure 11-4 shows a candid shot using the existing low light of an interior that required a high ISO setting with one of these little cameras. The detail (see figure 11-5) shows the noise. If these cameras are shot with ISO settings of 50 or 100 and kept to shutter speeds no longer than a few seconds, they do a very respectable job with noise as seen in figure 11-6 and its detail in figure 11-7.

> **Tonal range.** Digital SLR sensors are not simply physically larger than sensors in an advanced compact digital camera, but they also have larger individual photo sites (the actual pixels of the sensor that react to light). Larger photo sites means more light is recorded by each pixel, which allows better capture of tonalities, even when the advanced compact digital camera is shot using RAW.

PRO TIP

There is a tendency among many photographers to treat these little cameras very casually. They have outstanding capabilities if treated with respect. One thing you really have to watch is exposure. The small sensors make these cameras particularly sensitive to underexposure. Check your histogram at least occasionally as all of the little cameras that offer Raw files also have histograms.

> **Color.** The larger pixels of digital SLR sensors also deal with colors better for the same reasons that tonal range is better.

> **sRGB.** Nearly all of the advanced compact digital cameras use sRGB and do not allow any choice of another color space. This is, then, a great advantage of Raw because you can make that choice in Camera Raw as desired.

The result of these challenges is that care must be taken when shooting to capture tonalities properly and avoid noise problems. In addition, while you don't have any different workflow with the file in Camera Raw, you must look carefully at color, tonalities, and noise.

IMAGE LOWDOWN

The photo used in figure 11-8 (processed version), a Texas paintbrush from the Hill Country west of Austin, is an excellent representative of the possibilities and challenges of working with a compact digital SLR. This shot would not be easily done with a digital SLR. The camera, a Canon PowerShot G6, allows accessory lenses, and a wide-angle lens attachment was used giving the 35mm equivalent of approximately a 25mm lens.

Because of the way these little cameras are set up, you can focus from infinity down to inches in front of the lens without any accessories. With a wide-angle focal length, this offers an incredible perspective that shows off a subject up close and personal yet still allows the eye to go deep into the scene behind it. Few wide-angle lenses for digital SLRs allow that.

In addition, the flip-out, swiveling, live LCD monitor of the camera allows you to get the camera into tight, low positions without having to lay down on the ground yourself. For this shot, I only had to kneel next to my tripod; no body contortions were needed to frame the composition. It is true that in bright light the LCD can be hard to see, but with practice, it is useable and you can get little hoods to go over it, letting you better see the image.

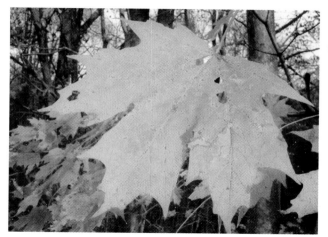

11-6

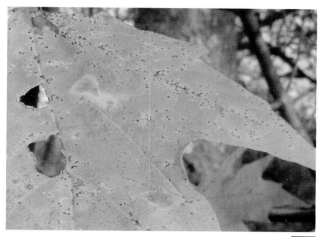

11-7

NOTE

The Texas Hill Country bloom is unpredictable. I shot this photo during a workshop I was doing near Burnet one April (a peak time). I had some local assistants and they told me that one year they helped on a class and had to search to find any flowers. The whole group had to mass around small clumps of color. Luckily, this time there were fields and fields of flowers. When the Hill Country flowers are in an "on" year, the photo experience is incredible. The Lady Bird Johnson Wildflower Center in Austin is a good resource to find out more about the bloom (www.wildflower.org).

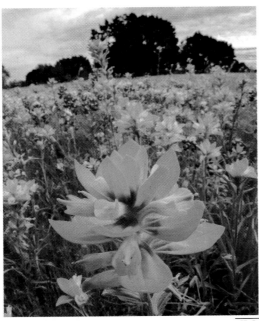

11-8

START WITH THE BASICS

Once you learn a basic workflow with Camera Raw, it makes processing so much easier. You go through the same basic steps (though interpreted differently) with every photo. This photo is no different. You always want to check for problems first and deal with them immediately. There are two problems with this image: a vertical shot sitting on its side and a blank sky.

Unless you have rotated a Raw file in Photoshop Bridge, it comes into Camera Raw on its side, making it hard to read as seen in figure 11-9. This photo needs to be rotated to vertical to make it visually correct, otherwise the viewer is easily distracted by its orientation while making other adjustments. This is very easy to fix — simply click the counterclockwise rotation tool button at the top of the image area. The photo gets smaller as the interface is really not designed to make verticals look their best, as seen in figure 11-10, but it is better than trying to adjust a sideways photo.

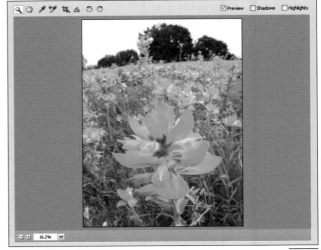

11-9

11-10

The sky is a different situation and one worth thinking a bit about. You could see the sky as a visual element, a shape, and leave it white. In that case, it acts as a frame for the trees in the background, as seen in figure 11-11 (which has been processed). It is always a good idea to keep such skies as small as possible in the image frame because such white areas can be distracting from the main composition. Bright areas and parts of a photo with high contrast (such as the trees and sky here) always attract the eye of the viewer.

I felt there might be some interesting detail in the sky that could be brought out in Camera Raw. That might also tone down the sky so that it would be less distracting. Of course, you can simply crop the sky out, but that changes the composition by flattening the image considerably, as seen in figure 11-12. I did not want to do that.

This is a situation where Raw files really shine. This photo recorded to JPEG would likely have a slight amount of detail in the sky (because of in-camera processing), but you would never be able to bring out a real-looking sky from it because there just isn't enough data there. Raw often holds detail in very bright and very dark areas as long as exposure doesn't put those tonalities beyond the capabilities of the sensor.

Going to Camera Raw then, click and drag the Exposure slider to deal with highlights. Press and hold Alt/Option to show a sky with little detail, as seen in figure 11-13. It is now worth a try to bring some detail into the shot by moving the Exposure slider to the left. Actually, it's quite amazing to see how much detail can be revealed, as seen in the highlight threshold in figure 11-14 and the image opened at this point in 11-14 (a little bit of clouds appears on the right side that is exposed beyond the capability of the sensor and cannot be anything but pure white).

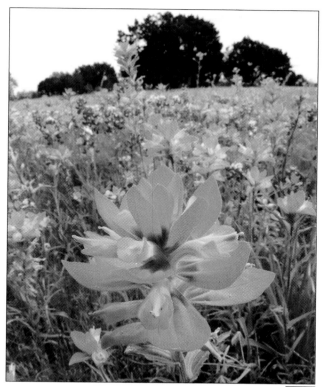

11-11

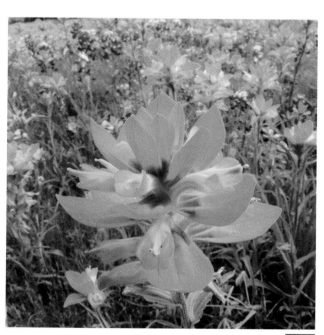

11-12

217

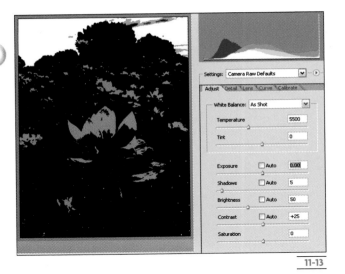

11-13

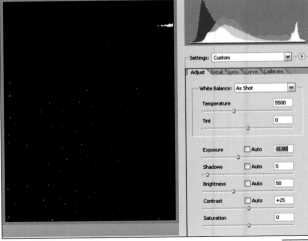

11-14

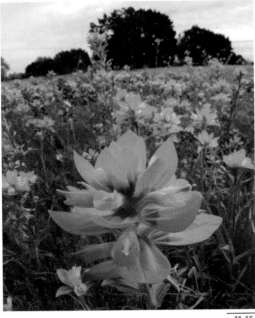

11-15

It is easy to overdo this. I backed off from making the clouds too dark because it muddied up the rest of the photo (figure 11-15 looks a little low in contrast because the blacks have not been set yet). If you have a photo that needs an extreme adjustment, you are better off doing it in stages, creating two images and bringing them together in Photoshop as described in Chapter 13. That isn't necessary in this photo, although if the setting is too high or low at this point, it can be readjusted later with no problems.

PRO TIP

An astute photographer might wonder why a graduated neutral density filter is not used when such an image is shot in order to bring the sky down in tone. If the sky was in a solid band, that would be a good idea. However, in this photo, the graduated neutral density filter darkens both the sky and the trees. So the best idea when objects move into the sky is often to NOT use a graduated filter and rely on Camera Raw for adjusting bright skies down in tone.

CORE ADJUSTMENTS

Continuing work on this photo goes back to the standard adjustments of checking blacks and correcting midtones. On this photo you would start with the following:

1. **Shadows.** Because Exposure is already set, so are highlights. So now blacks need to be set. The shadow slider is moved until the black threshold starts to appear as black in small areas, as seen in figure 11-16. The photo is a little dark, but it has good contrast at this point, as seen in figure 11-17.

2. **Midtones.** Now the image needs to be brought up in tone to better show off the colors of the flowers. Brightness works to a degree, but the overall image colors look a little flat with it and the sky gets lighter in a way that doesn't help, as seen in figure 11-18. That can be corrected in Photoshop later, but the Tone Curve settings of Camera Raw in Photoshop CS2 are a great benefit here.

3. **Tone Curve.** The Strong Contrast curve gives a good look to the image so it is a place to start. Remember that the top of the curve represents the lighter parts of the photo; the bottom, darker tones. Because the light areas, such as the sky, should be kept strong in tone, do not brighten them very much. It is worth pulling the top part of the curve back down toward the centerline.

This makes the photo look flat, however, so now the midpoint of the curve can go up, which lightens the flowers, and the bottom of the curve can go down to

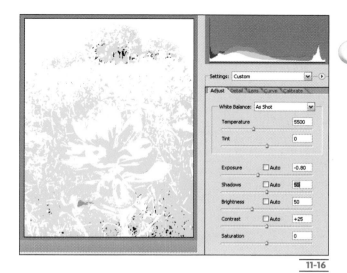

11-16

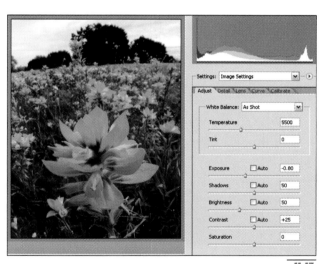

11-17

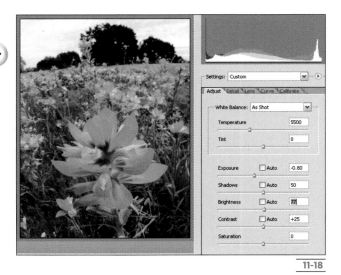

11-18

11-19

darken the darkest areas. I found that I needed to play around with several points near the center of the curve, as shown in figure 11-19. As I brought them up and balanced them against each other, the colors of the flowers started to glow. But if I went too high with certain points, the colors would go garish and lose detail.

There is no right or wrong to this. You just have to move and tweak points until the photo looks right. In part, when using a file from an advanced compact digital camera, you are compensating for its slightly limited color capabilities compared to a digital SLR. You may be surprised, however, at how much color and detail you can bring out from these cameras.

4. **Check highlights.** Adjusting the Tone Curve may move the highlights too high. You can check Exposure to see if readjusting its slider helps. However — and this is very important to keep in mind — you may not be able to do all of your adjusting in Camera Raw. Sure, you can keep playing with all of the settings from Exposure to Shadows to Tone Curve, but that quickly becomes a time-waster rather than a real benefit to the photo.

It is possible to do a lot with a curve in Photoshop (which theoretically is then possible in Camera Raw), but after a certain point, you have to ask, "Why?" Other than dazing dazzling people with curve technique, this is more of an exercise to impress than a really useful workflow. Typically — and the photo used here is a good example — you get the photo as good as you can within reason using Camera Raw, then go to Photoshop where you can use adjustment layers and their accompanying layer masks for better and faster control of local, defined areas (such as the sky).

5. **Overall tonal adjustment.** At this point, the photo is a little too dark. However, any lightening, even with the Tone Curve, adversely affects the sky. I will typically reserve further tonal adjustment to Photoshop by using a Curves Adjustment Layer to lighten the mid-tones of the flowers, and then removing the adjustment over the clouds by painting it out in the layer mask. An example is shown in figure 11-20, to simply illustrate the use of an adjustment layer in Photoshop, though at this point, color still needs to be tweaked in Camera Raw.

PRO TIP

Photoshop and Camera Raw offer a way of precisely finding where a tone in the image falls on the Tone Curve. First, if you press and hold Ctrl/⌘ as you move your cursor over the image, a little circle moves up and down the Tone Curve showing you the important areas of the curve that you may want to adjust. Second, if you then click the mouse button as you move the cursor over the photo in the preview (still holding the Ctrl/⌘), a black dot is anchored to the curve at that color or tone. That will also help guide you in moving the curve to adjust the image.

Camera Raw Workflow

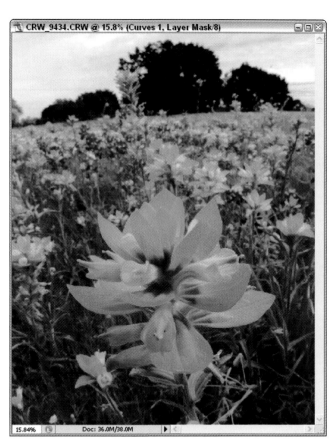
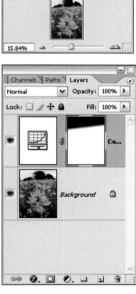

11-20

221

Color

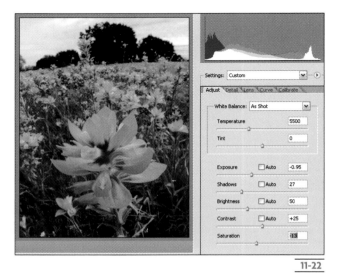

As you do tonal adjustments, you will also see color changes, especially with an image this colorful shot with an advanced compact digital camera. You may need to make compromises at times with tonal adjustments to be sure your color comes out its best. To continue on in this photo, you would check Saturation levels.

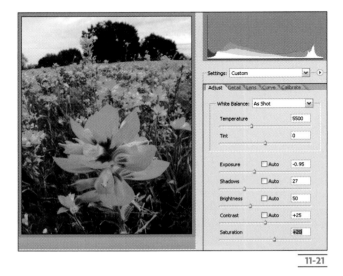

11-21

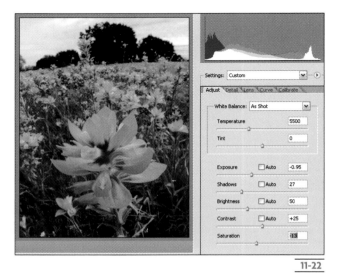

11-22

The colors of the flowers are quite saturated. Colors related to red, from orange to magenta, have a tendency to lose important tonal detail if the saturation is too high. You really have to be careful when adjusting such colors. It is possible to increase saturation and still have details appear on your screen, yet when the image is printed, the details are gone. As you work with images, you will be able to judge how well your printer or other output device handles such colors (the color gamut warnings in Photoshop may help, but they are really designed to warn about colors printing on a printing press).

In this photo, increasing Saturation brightens the flowers, but it also quickly blows out detail in the color of the flowers behind the foreground subject as demonstrated in figure 11-21. Decreasing Saturation actually increases detail in the flowers, but it does dull the colors as seen in figure 11-22. I decided to leave it at zero.

However, the flowers do seem a little magenta compared to how they are in real life. White Balance can help here. In this image, the Auto setting looks terrible, as shown by figure 11-23. The Photoshop algorithms see so much warmth (from the paintbrush flowers) that the program wants to take it out, making the photo look way too cold.

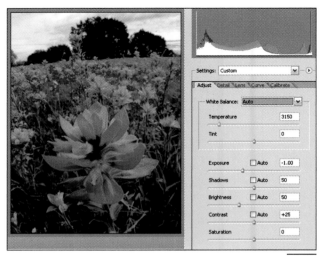

11-23

The Camera Raw Daylight interpretation of the data is similar to the As Shot selection — the image was actually shot using the Electronic Flash setting, which does, in this case, give an identical result to As Shot (remember that Camera Raw is an interpretation of the actual camera white balance settings and won't always give identical results in such a situation).

Cloudy isn't bad as seen in figure 11-24, but a bit too yellow for my tastes, as well as still too magenta (Shade is more so for both colors), but some photographers may prefer it. I think something in-between at about a Temperature of 6000 helps, which is shown in figure 11-25. I found that direction from clicking on the White Balance settings and noting how the sliders changed. This also lightens the photo slightly, making the overall tonalities look better as well.

DETAIL CHECKING

Because this photo comes from a camera with a very small sensor, it is critical to check and adjust noise in the Detail tab while still in Camera Raw. This particular shot does very well with noise because it was made with a low ISO setting in bright light and has good exposure.

There is no color noise, so the Color Noise Reduction slider needs to go to 0. Moving it off 0 at all adversely affects some of the fine color tonalities in the photo.

There is slight luminance noise, so the Luminance Smoothing slider can be used to reduce it. Again, it is important to note that this affects more than just luminance noise. While there are some hairs, pollen, and other small details on the foreground flower that are important, overall, the photo does not have large amounts of critical, tiny details. The photo is more about color than fine detail, so the Luminance Smoothing slider can easily go up to 30 or so without any problems, as seen in figure 11-26.

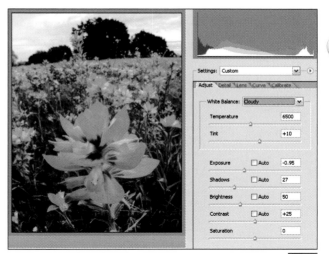

11-24

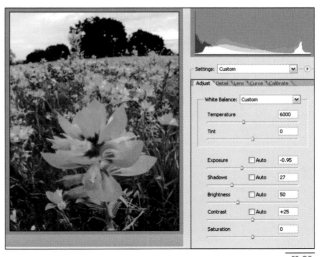

11-25

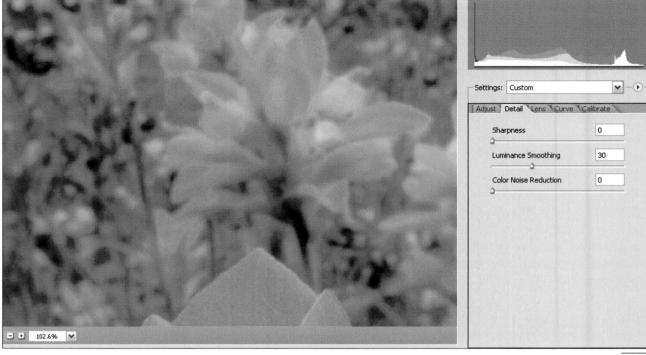

11-26

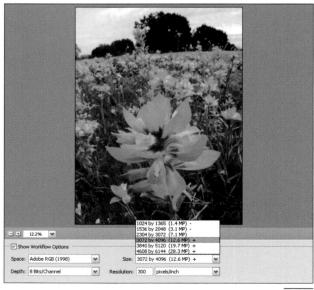

11-27

Sizing

On most of the photos in the book, the choices at the bottom left of the Camera Raw interface have been left to a standard way of dealing with them. You will find a set of choices for your workflow (which is why this area is called Workflow Options) that work best for you and keep them. There is rarely any reason to constantly change these settings.

This photo, however, is one with potentially very dramatic impact when enlarged. When you choose a new Size larger than the original file, you use the power of Camera Raw's algorithms and the benefits of dealing with a Raw file to get the highest quality enlarged file. This image easily enlarges to the equivalent of a 12-megapixel camera, so that choice was made, as shown in figure 11-27. At this point, this is as far as I go in Camera Raw.

COMPLETING THE ADJUSTMENTS

When this photo is opened into Photoshop, it needs a few adjustments to compensate for things that cannot be done in Camera Raw. The biggest thing is changing the sky and flower tones. They can both be affected in controlled local adjustments that don't do an overall effect.

> **Sky.** The sky can stand to be darkened slightly. The best way to do this is with an adjustment layer. Add a

Levels or Curves Adjustment Layer, then click OK before doing any adjustments. Now go to the layer modes at the top of the Layer Palette. Click Multiply. Instantly, the tone of sky gets deeper. And so does the rest of the photo (see figure 11-28). The layer mask is filled with black (choose Edit⇨Fill⇨Black) to turn off the effect. Then the sky area is painted with white, using a big, soft brush (the brush allows a nice blending along the edge). The result is seen in figure 11-29.

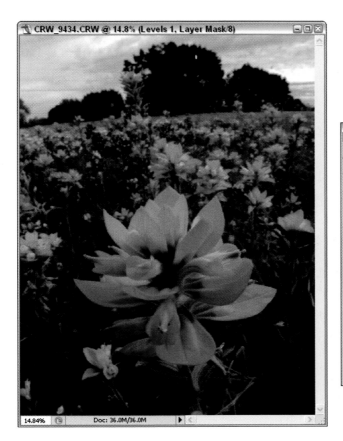

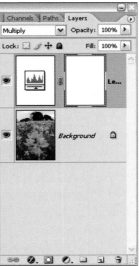

11-28

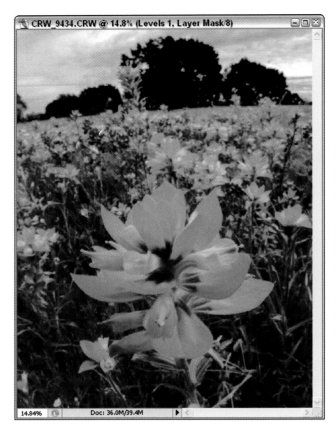

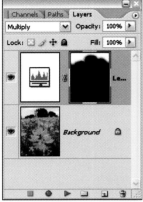

11-29

> **Flowers.** They can use a slight brightening. This sort of final adjustment is highly subjective, but to me, bright flowers on a bright day in real life look best if they are kept bright in the photo as well. So I lightened them slightly with a Curves Adjustment Layer while keeping the darkest tones dark, as demonstrated in figure 11-30. This lightens the sky slightly. I could have left it, but I decided to take out the adjustment over the sky. This is very easy to do in this photo. Ctrl/⌘-click the layer mask of the sky layer to create a selection based on the white parts of the mask. Now be sure the layer mask of the flowers adjustment layer is active (click on it to be sure), and then fill the selection with black (Edit⇨Fill⇨Black). That will turn off the adjustment for the sky, which can be seen in figure 11-31.

The completed final image is seen in figure 11-32. This image has been sharpened and some out-of-focus wires in the background removed from the sky.

PRO TIP

Layer masks are a tremendous help to the photographer, but they can be confusing to use if you don't use them regularly. To help photographers with them, I like to use the analogy of a light switch and room light. If you switch the light off, the room is dark. This is like adding black to the layer mask. It is then switched off wherever there is black, so the effect cannot be seen (just as a dark room keeps you from seeing things in it). If you switch a light on, the room is light. This is like adding white to the layer mask. It is then switched on wherever there is white, so the effect now shows up (just as a lit room lets you see things in it).

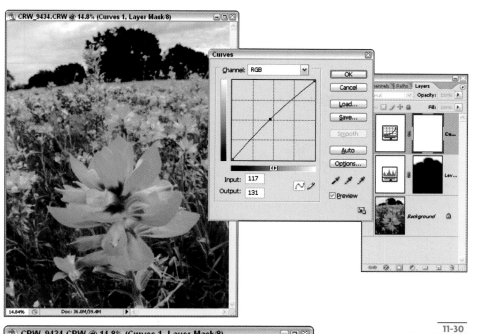

11-30

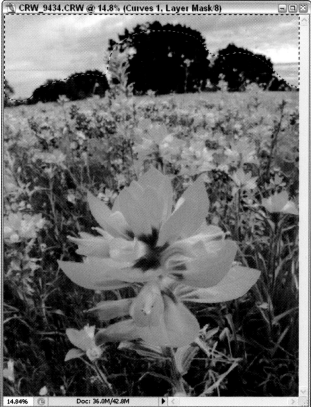

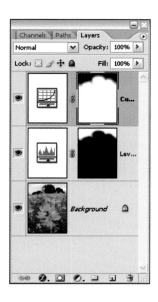

11-31

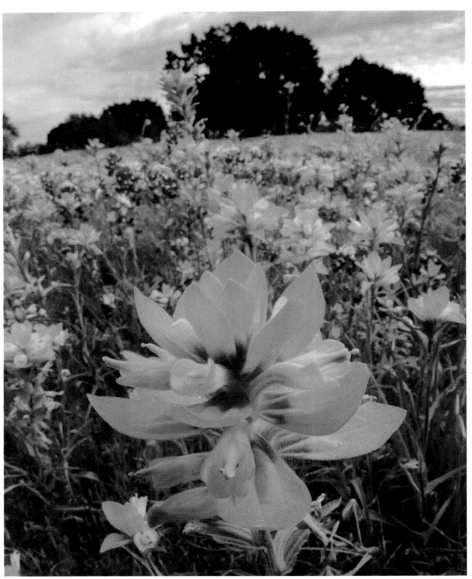

11-32

Q & A

What should I do if I have to shoot with a high ISO setting on a compact camera?

Sometimes it is necessary to be able to shoot at a certain shutter speed, for example, to minimize problems with camera movement when handholding. That may require you to use a higher ISO setting, which results in more noise. Still, that is probably better than a fuzzy photo.

You know you get a relatively high amount of noise when this is done with a compact digital camera. When you open this image into Camera Raw, it is a good idea, to deal with problems first. Go immediately to the Detail tab and use the Luminance Smoothing slider. You may have to use a fairly high setting to affect the noise. But you need to watch your details. On some photos, a high setting may be just fine. On others, you may find that too high a setting affects the appearance of important small details that should not be compromised. Depending on the exposure of the image, you may need to check the color noise, too, and make some adjustments to the Color Noise Reduction slider.

In many photos, however, you may find that you cannot bring the noise down as much as you would like just by using Camera Raw. This is why a noise reduction program can be very helpful. Open the photo in Photoshop and do final noise reduction there. Noise reduction programs like Noise Ninja, Dfine, and Digital GEM, offer more controls for dealing with noise and do a better job of finding noise versus hurting detail sharpness. Photoshop CS2 has a noise reduction filter that does help, but I find it less useful than the others mentioned.

I know that underexposure causes problems with Raw files. Is this further affected by a smaller digital camera?

Absolutely. Every problem that underexposure causes gets worse with these cameras. A slight bit of underexposure is not an issue. That can be easily adjusted to compensate. It may even help in certain shooting conditions where you are concerned about highlights.

But exposure drops of a full f-stop or more can be a problem. This is most common when a very bright area in a scene you are shooting causes the rest of the photo to go dark. Noise definitely increases as you bring up the dark areas, forcing you to use higher amounts of noise control in the Detail tab. Color noise, especially, can become a distinct concern.

In addition, you may have weaker colors. Remember that a small sensor has small photosites, which physically capture less light to begin with. Reduce the light further and they struggle to find tonal and color definition in the darkest areas of the subject. The result is when you bring the image into Camera Raw that you will not have adequate color to work with in those areas. Adjustment then becomes a real challenge. You may be forced to add saturation that then adversely affects colors in brighter parts of the photo. You might not be able to complete overall adjustments in Camera Raw, so you may need to open the image in 16-bit mode, and then make further adjustments in Photoshop.

Chapter 12

SPECIAL FEATURES OF CAMERA RAW

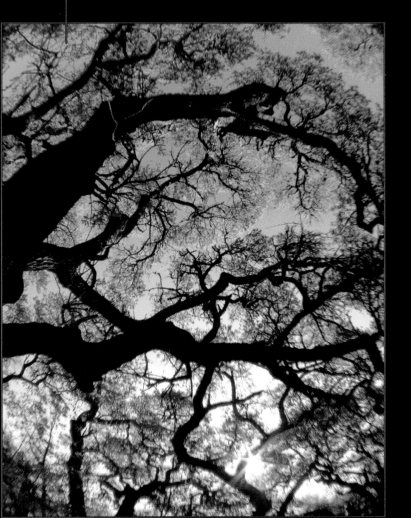

By now you have a good idea of both how Camera Raw works and how to use it to process and interpret a variety of images shot under different conditions. The program also offers some special features that can be useful when needed, but most photographers will use them on a limited basis. Anyone can take advantage of these controls at any time, with any photo, but for most images shot by most photographers, they are not a common need.

In addition, Camera Raw and Photoshop allow for some batch processing, which means adjustments can be made to multiple files at the same time, such as seen in figure 12-1. This, again, is not something every photographer will use, but it is important to understand what tools are available so they can be used when you do need them.

One thing that everyone can agree on about Photoshop is that it is a very powerful program with lots of features. This thought also carries into Camera Raw, though to a lesser degree. If you try to learn and remember everything in Photoshop, it will drive you crazy. Anyway, unless you are trying to be a master teacher, why bother?

Your photos will never need everything in the program. Master what you need. After all, Ansel Adams did all his great work with a limited repertoire of controls compared to what is available in Photoshop (even if you restrict them to black and white). Then use a reference such as this book to help you with features you don't use as often.

SPECIAL FEATURES REVEALED

So far in this book, two tabs of the adjustment window of Camera Raw have not been used: Lens and Calibrate (see figure 12-2). You learn how to use them now.

Lens is a special tool that you can use to deal with some optical problems that a certain lens may have. Its very sophisticated processing capabilities allow you to remove color fringing (for example, in a magnified part of an image as seen in figure 12-3) that sometimes occurs along the outside of an image due to a lower-quality lens or other optical issues (color aberrations). This both increases the apparent sharpness of the lens and gains better color, especially in the outer regions of the photo.

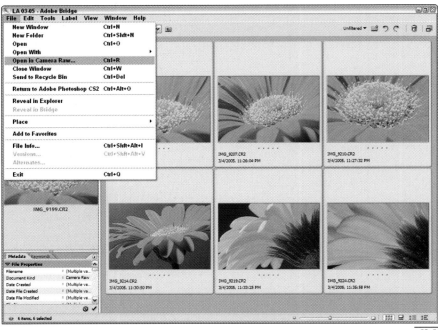

12-1

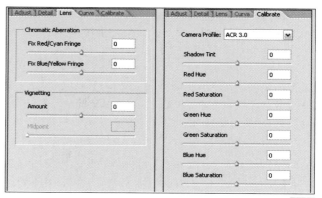

12-2

In addition, Lens has the Vignetting tool. Some lenses do not give an even illumination of the image area and the outer parts of the composition are usually darkened as illustrated by figure 12-4 (which has been artificially exaggerated so you can see the effect). It is possible, with certain lenses, to find the center of the image darkened. Darkening of the outer edges can be a problem with very wide-angle lenses and with lenses with extreme zoom ranges. It was also quite common with the old mirror telephoto lenses that are still around, but much less popular than they used to be. The Vignetting tool removes that darkening when the slider is moved to the right.

Calibrate can be a useful tool when you need it. Calibrate is misleading because what it really does for photographers is selectively affect colors. It is a little hard to control compared to other selective controls in Photoshop itself, but it does offer additional flexibility in color work inside Camera Raw that can be helpful when colors don't record as expected in relation to each other.

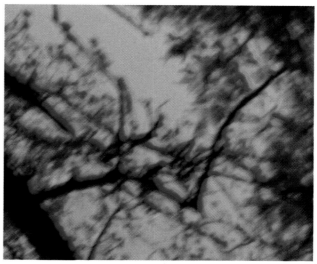

12-3

FIXING LENS PROBLEMS

The example photo used here is one that will quickly show problems with lens aberrations. Figure 12-5 is a shot of a live oak in Texas in the spring. It is shot from within the tree with an extreme wide-angle, full-frame fisheye lens. This produces a fascinating look at the inner parts of a tree's canopy. Color fringing, color that is not part of the subject, shows up on all the fine tree branch detail in a hurry.

This photo has no fringing in the center (see figure 12-6) and quite a lot toward the outer edges (see figure 12-7). I happen to really like this lens, the Century Optics Ultra

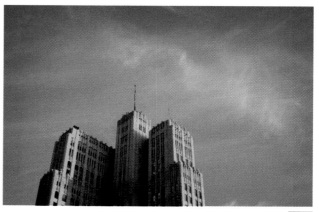

12-4

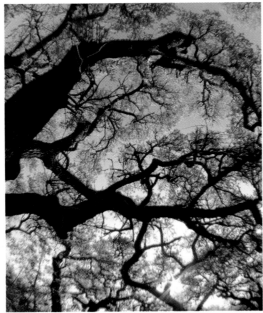

12-5

Fisheye Adapter, and its overall effect, even though it does have a limitation of creating fringing along the outer edges of the frame when used with certain lenses. It is a wide-angle conversion lens that attaches to my small-format, advanced digital compact camera and modifies the angle of view of the original, attached zoom (a quirk of this lens is that your camera must focus down to within about 1 inch of the subject for this adapter lens to focus properly; I add a small, achromatic close-up lens to help). It gives a 0.3x conversion factor to the original lens, offering a 35mm equivalent on my Canon PowerShot G6 of approximately 10-11mm.

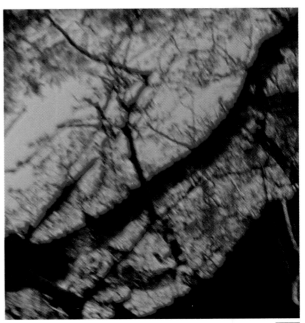

12-7

12-6

Because it is so wide and was not designed to precisely match with the camera lens, this lens faces some challenges of physics in focusing all colors when the edges of the frame are reached. So to use this lens, I always shoot in Raw because I can make corrections in Camera Raw and get a very useable image.

Some programs that have claimed to "fix" lens aberrations just mask them by changing the color fringing to a neutral color. Camera Raw goes beyond that and actually shifts pixels for the correction, shrinking the aberration while also fixing its color. It does quite a good job.

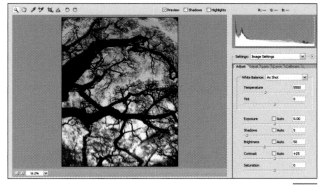

12-8

WORKING THE IMAGE

Like all the other examples in this book, this photo follows the standard workflow. While the color fringing is strong, it really doesn't affect the overall adjustment of the photo, so it would not be considered a problem that was strong enough to make you want to fix it first. The exposure is good, so the core first steps are fairly straightforward:

1. Rotate the photo with the Counterclockwise button at the top (see figure 12-8) because the photo comes into Camera Raw on its side (see figure 12-9).

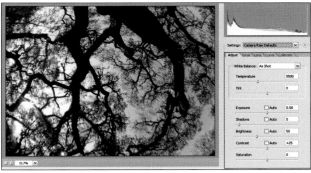

12-9

2. Check the exposure. The lower part of the photo is, perhaps, a little bright, which isn't necessarily bad as it strengthens the contrast between the branch and the sky. On the other hand, reducing the bright areas a little (press Alt/Option to see the threshold screen as shown in figure 12-10) makes the sunburst show up a little better.

3. Blacks come into this image as a default showing up as small areas beside the tree branches. That is a good interpretation of the image, but I felt making the branches have darker tones would help strengthen the pattern of the branches, so I increased the Shadow slider while pressing and holding Alt/Option to watch where the dark tones appear (see figure 12-11).

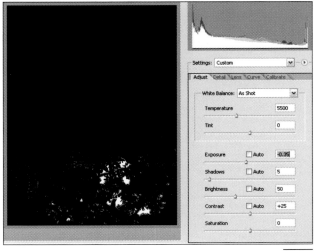

12-10

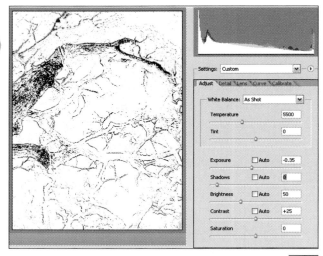

12-11

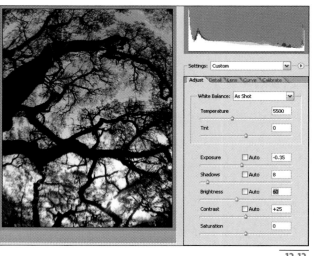

12-12

4. For Midtones, this photo works fine with the Brightness slider alone. Increasing it brings out the leaves of the tree better and lightens the dark sky at the top (see figure 12-12).

5. The As Shot setting for White Balance looks good. Other presets make the image look either too warm or add unwanted magenta. Yet, as I went through the presets, I liked what I saw in added warmth, so I increased the Temperature slider slightly. This gives the photo a stronger early-morning feel, which is when it was shot (see figure 12-13).

6. I like the look of the image after 10 to 12 points of saturation, much more change and the colors start looking unnatural. This amount of change makes the new leaves at the top gain more richness (see figure 12-13).

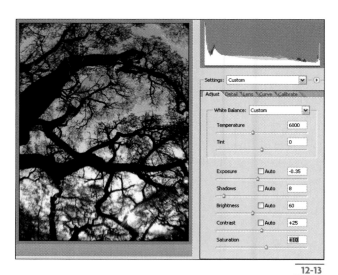

12-13

7. Because Color Noise Reduction is in the Detail tab and that is affected by the color fringe reduction to be done in the Lens tab, this is one adjustment area to use after the Lens corrections are made. Be sure this is set to zero because Color Noise Reduction affects the colors in lens aberrations; but at this point, you want the Lens tab controls to do that.

CORRECTING ABERRATIONS

The next step is to enter the Lens tab for some lens aberration correction. At this point, you must enlarge the image along some edge so you can see the aberrations as shown by figure 12-14. This control is worthless if you don't do that. You must see what is there. How much to enlarge depends entirely on the size of the image file and the amount of aberration. You need to enlarge enough to see the color fringing from the lens aberrations.

Once you size the preview and find a good sample of color fringing, you are ready to go to work. Color fringing appears most strongly along contrasting edges, such as the small branches of the tree seen here. With this lens it is quite strong and needs correction to make the photo look sharper as well as removing odd colors along the sides of the subject.

In the Chromatic Aberration area of the Lens tab, you have two sliders: Fix Red/Cyan Fringe and Fix Blue/Yellow Fringe. Both fringe types are present in this live oak photo, so both need to be adjusted. You may find that lenses you work with have only one type or the other. This photo is perfect for illustrating how the Lens adjustments work because it has both.

As you move the sliders, the color fringing lessens and the image actually shifts slightly to compensate for the colors. This shifting is quite a remarkable achievement by

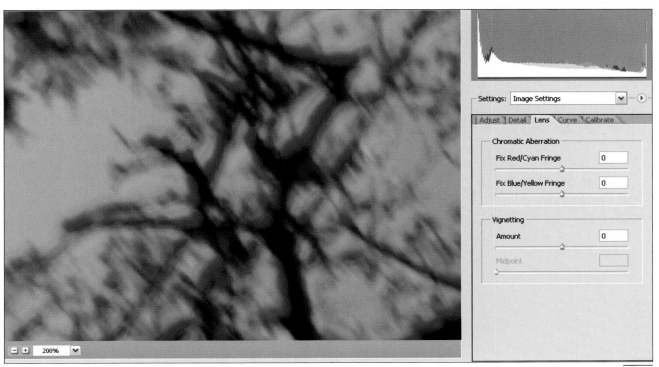

12-14

the computer engineers at Adobe because it does not affect everything in the photo. That said, it is a little like the Color Noise Reduction tool in the Detail tab. You can affect small color details in the photo that are not part of the color-fringing problem, so only use as much as you need.

In this photo, however, the aberration is so strong that the entire range of adjustment is needed, as seen in figure 12-15. This may affect some small color details, but that loss is well worth the results of removing so much of the color fringing, which makes the photo sharper and with better colors along the edges. The before and after versions (click the Preview on and off) show an amazing change. The bark of the tree, for example, now really looks like bark instead of some psychedelic texture.

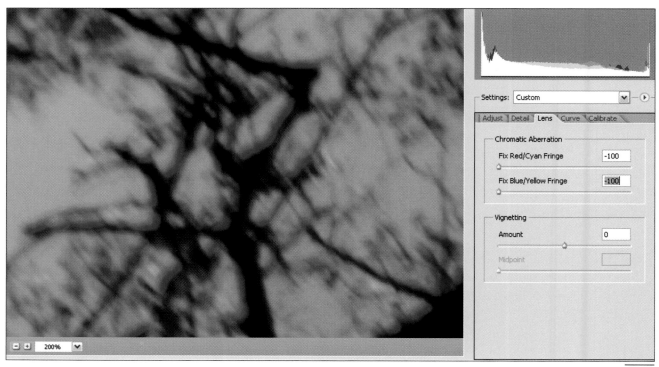

12-15

Vignetting Adjustments

Vignetting, or darkening of the image toward the edges and corners, often exists in many lenses. Whether it is a problem or not depends entirely on the subject and your preferences. In figure 12-16, for example, there is definite darkening toward the edges of the frame, but most of that is due to the change in sky tone as the scene goes farther from the very bright sky around the sun.

The photo could be evened out ... or not. I happen to like the more dramatic look as is, but a little bit of lightening (moving the Vignetting Amount slider to the right) brightens the tree green at the bottom and top of the photo. Moving the slider to the left darkens the edges and dulls the greens, so I would not go below 0.

Once you move the Amount slider to either the plus or minus side of 0, a new adjustment becomes available below it, Midpoint, which may not be the most intuitive of names. It sort of implies that you can change the midpoint of the Vignetting adjustment. You can't. What it does do is affect the spread of the change. Moving it to the right makes the circle of vignetting larger and more diffuse. Moving it to the left makes that circle smaller and more defined. This adjustment allows you to better match how a lens deals with vignetting problems. It also allows you to creatively adjust vignetting for a specific effect.

Back to Noise Fixes

Now that the Lens tab adjustments are done, it is time to go back to the Detail tab and deal with noise issues. This image is actually very clean, showing relatively little noise for an image from a small-sensor advanced compact digital camera. There is no significant

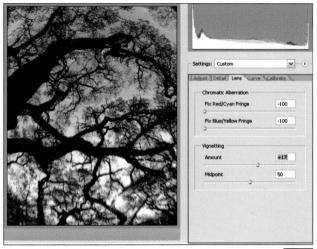

12-16

color noise and minimal luminance noise, so adjustment is fairly straightforward. Remember that to adjust these controls, you need to greatly enlarge the image so you can see what noise is there.

> **Luminance Smoothing.** This photo can use some smoothing. Some noise appears in the smooth areas, like the sky, so smoothing them now makes them less visible when the photo is sharpened later. A setting of about 30 cleans up the noise enough without causing detail problems as shown in figure 12-17.

> **Color Noise Reduction.** While there is no real color noise in this photo, you can use color noise reduction to help further refine the color fringing that was hopefully contained by the Lens tab. Bringing it up to a moderate amount of 20 (also in figure 12-17) or so helps, but without also causing detail color problems.

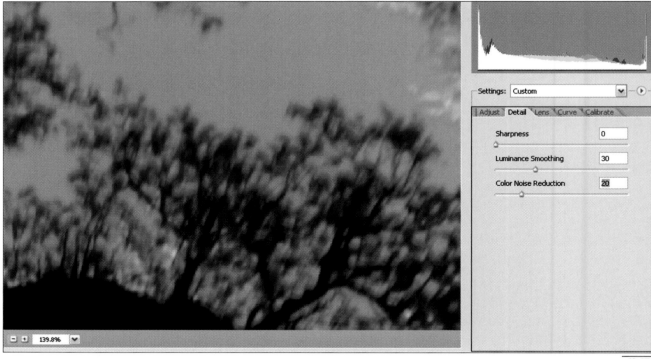

12-17

INFLUENCING COLOR CHANGES

The Calibrate tab is another name that isn't too intuitive for photographers. It is accurate in that this tab can be used to calibrate adjustments for certain color biases or preferences (it is even possible to have camera profiles; the default is Camera Raw or ACR). But frankly, few photographers will really use it that way. There just isn't the need except in special circumstances. It can, however, be very helpful in fixing problem color relationships in an image or for cleaning up color contamination in a color.

This set of adjustment controls changes how the basic RGB (red/green/blue) color scheme of the computer is mixed (the tab is shown in figure 12-18), almost like the Color Channel Mixer in Photoshop (they really are different things, so the comparison is more for a point of reference than any true correlation between these two controls). You can affect both the hue of each color as

well as its saturation, but as you affect those things, the whole color mix changes, meaning that you can rarely adjust just one slider without making some counter adjustment elsewhere. One additional control, Shadow Tint, is also available, which adjusts along the green/magenta line, but mainly in the dark areas.

12-18

While this sort of mixing of colors is easy to do with the sliders available, the actual use of that mixing is not so easy to deal with. This is not an adjustment area most photographers typically use. If you have some very precise color issues that must be controlled, however, this can be one place you can try so that the adjustments are done to the RAW file rather than later to the adjusted file in Photoshop. This is especially critical with product photography where certain colors can be absolutely critical to a pro photographer's assignment.

USING THE CALIBRATE TAB

The easiest way to really explain this adjustment section of Camera Raw is to adjust a photo. The photo used to illustrate Calibrate is a controlled, studio shot close-up of a gerbera daisy flower. Electronic flash illuminates the flower, with the light source placed high and to the left of the flower to add to the stamens and some texture to the petals.

The colors are fairly accurate overall, but the strong red petal color is reflected onto the stamens and is contaminating the yellow (see figure 12-19). The photo was first adjusted using all the tools you've seen throughout this book and following that basic workflow. You can see the Exposure, Shadows, and Brightness were adjusted slightly; White Balance is left As Shot; and a bit of a tonal curve was used to bring out contrasts in the image as demonstrated in figure 12-20. No Detail or Lens adjustments were made (or needed).

Calibrate now offers a chance to tweak the colors and bring out the yellow in the stamens. Starting from the top:

1. Adjust the Shadow Tint back and forth to change the overall color slightly (especially in the dark areas), but neither more green (to the left, see figure 12-21) nor more magenta (to the right, see figure 12-22) really adds anything to the photo.

2. The Hue and Saturation controls are intuitive. They do exactly what they say: change the hue and saturation of the image with the emphasis on a particular color. First, you usually adjust the hue to control what the color is, then the saturation to affect the intensity.

3. When the Red Hue control is used, you gain a huge amount of influence over anything with a red component. Other than changing the redness of the petals, this is, at this point, not of much use until other colors are altered, because even if you adjust the controls so the yellows are better, the red petals get way off. If the red of the subject is off for whatever reason, this group of controls helps correct that. They can also be used creatively to change colors.

PRO TIP

Something that I call the Extreme Technique can be very helpful in making any adjustment when you aren't quite sure of how the tool works. To me, it is the best way to use the Calibrate controls as most photographers won't be using them often. Move a slider to its extreme positions very quickly. This shows you instantly what the control will do to your image; that is, it tells you the direction to go and what the range of the adjustment offers you. Then you move the slider to the right spot based on how the image looks from that information.

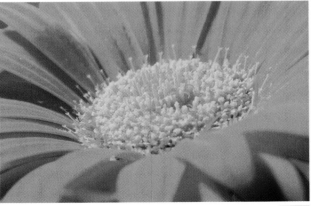

12-19

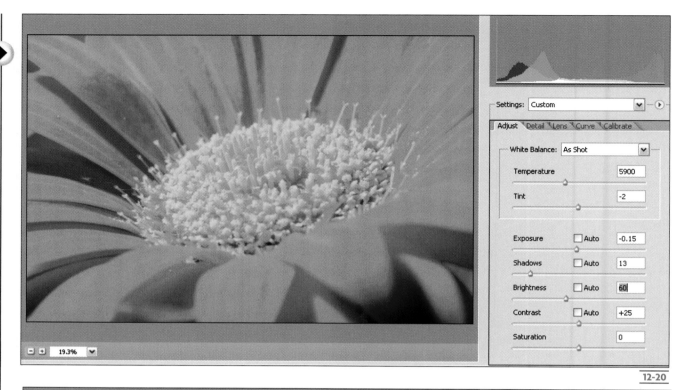

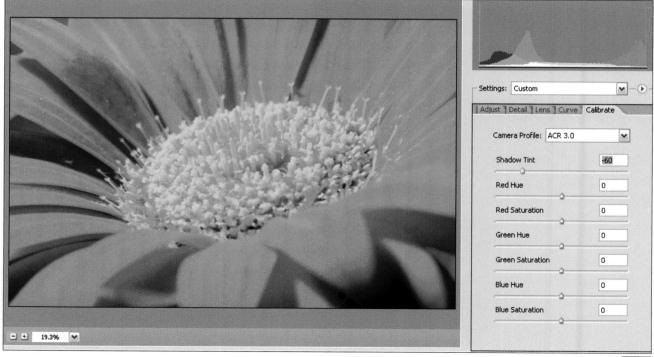

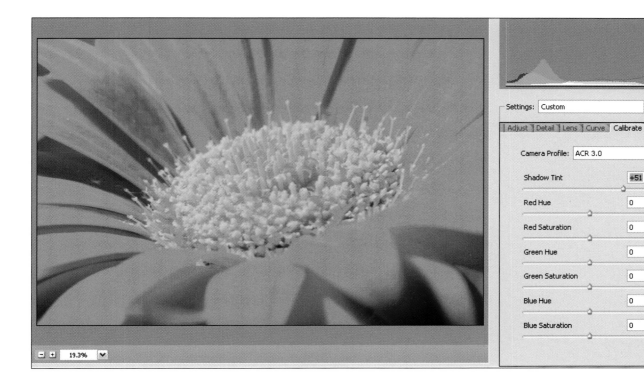

12-22

4. The yellow of the stamens starts getting a boost as the Green Hue slider is moved to the left, as seen in figure 12-23. This also warms up the overall image, so this is worth doing. The reds of the petals are slightly affected, but not a lot. It is easy to tell how all the colors are doing by clicking the Preview on and off. Saturation is not needed.

5. By moving the Blue Hue slider to the right, the yellow stamens really start to pop (see figure 12-24). However, the red of the petals has changed. Saturation is not needed.

6. Go back to the Red Hue adjustment to bring the red colors back to where they started. The Calibrate group of adjustments often requires you to do multiple adjustments with the sliders. By moving the slider to the left, the reds go back closer to where

they were before (see figure 12-25), but the intensity isn't quite there.

7. Saturation controls, including Red Saturation, allow you to move a color from gray to garish in a hurry. For the flower petals, adding intensity by moving the slider to the right helps bring the colors back to their original hue (see figure 12-26).

Now compare the before (figure 12-27) and after (figure 12-28). The yellow of the stamens on the flower is now no longer contaminated and really pops. You can use this technique any time a color needs to be cleaned up, but the effort requires a lot of trial-and-error experimenting. I know of no simple way of using this tool.

It is interesting to note a pleasant side effect: all this adjustment has not only affected the stamens, but has also brought out better detail in the petals.

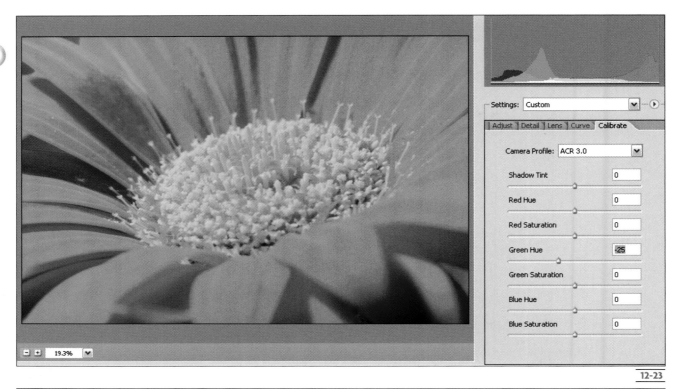

12-23

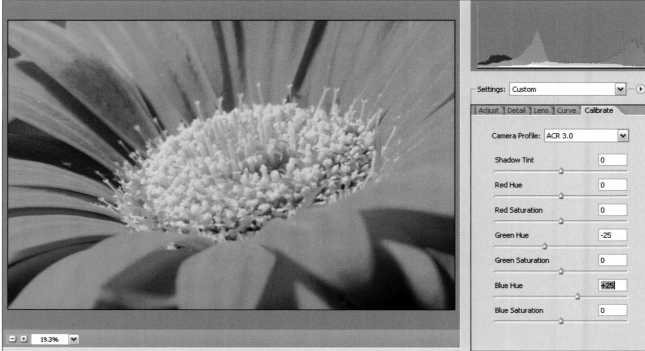

12-24

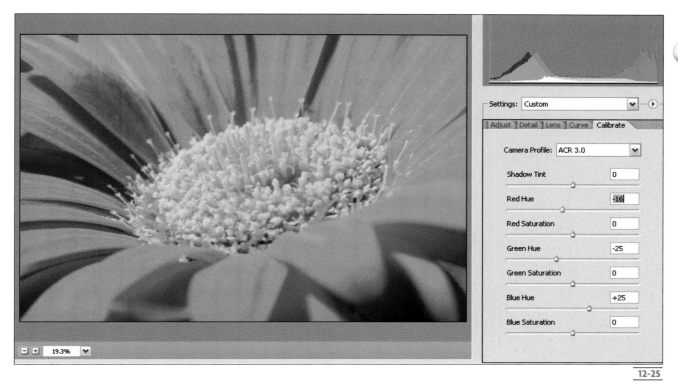

12-25

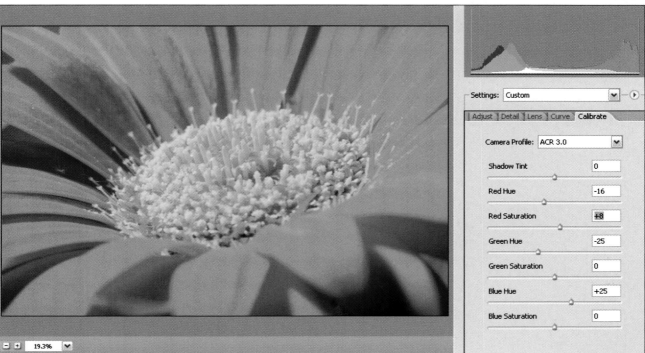

12-26

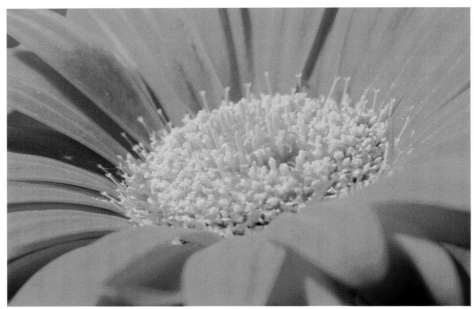

12-27

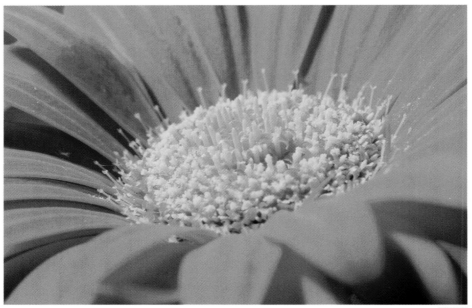

12-28

BATCH PROCESSING

Batch processing is a way of applying the same changes to a group of image files. This is one of those features that some photographers will never use and others will use all the time. Batch renaming is the most common type of batch processing that nearly every photographer can benefit from. However, if you are a location shooter with lots of different subjects and light, you will not find the batch processing that adjusts images as useful to your workflow because you mostly need to deal with each image in a unique way. The one-size-fits-all approach of batch processing won't work for those images (see figure 12-29). However, it is still worth

learning how batch processing works because sooner or later, you will have a group of similar images that, when the first one is processed, all the others can be processed in the same way to save time and effort (see figure 12-30).

For studio photographers who have a distinctive look that covers many images and for any situations where the exposure and light is consistent, batch processing can be a real help to speed up the whole workflow process. You learn a number of techniques here that allow you to deal with multiple images. Some are not technically batch processing, but they still give you the ability to make adjustments that affect multiple images.

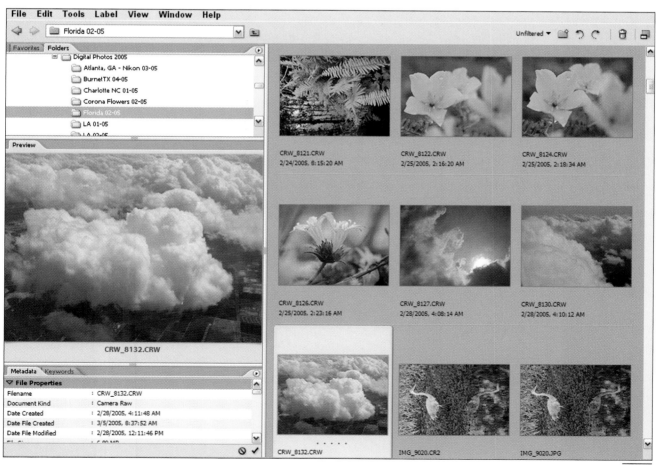

12-29

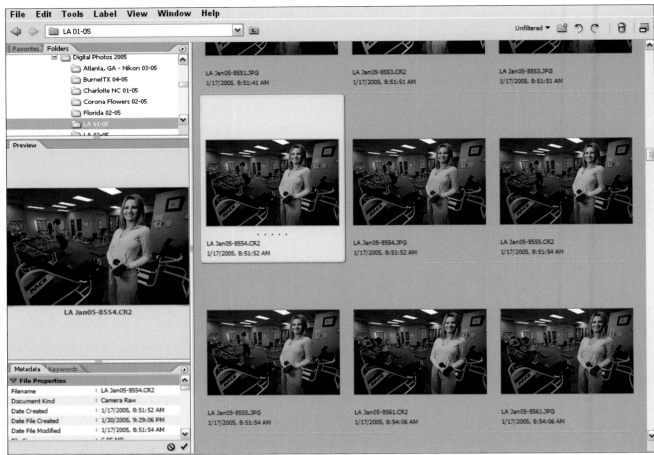

12-30

SIMPLE BATCHING — RENAMING

An easy and simple way to understand batch processing is to use Adobe Bridge controls to rename a set of Raw photos (it also will rename any other image file). It is a fairly simple process (the process is similar in the old Photoshop browser):

1. Select the files. Open the Bridge associated with Photoshop CS2 (either in the File menu under Browse or by using the Bridge icon at the upper right of the Photoshop interface by the palette well).

Select the files you want to name by going to the desired folder then selecting them all or a specific group of them. Select All is in the Edit menu. You can label images in the Bridge, too, and use Select Labeled, or you can Ctrl/⌘ click individual images to add them to the group (see figure 12-31).

2. Open Batch Rename. This dialog box is found in the Tools menu (see figure 12-32) or you can press Ctrl/⌘+Shift+R.

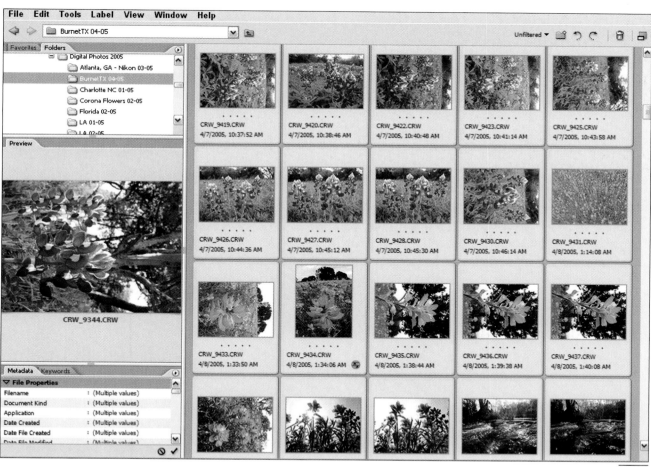

12-31

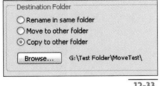

Batch Rename

Destination Folder
- ○ Rename in same folder
- ○ Move to other folder
- ⦿ Copy to other folder
- [Browse...]   G:\Test Folder\MoveTest\

New Filenames
[Current Filename ▾] [Name + Extension ▾] [Original Case ▾] [−] [+]

☐ Preserve current filename in XMP Metadata
☑ Windows ☐ Mac OS ☐ Unix

Preview
First selected filename
CRW_9344.CRW
First new filename
CRW_9344.CRW
448 files will be renamed

[Rename]
[Cancel]

12-32

3. Select a Destination Folder. This part of the process offers you three options: Rename in same folder, Move to other folder, and Copy to other folder (see figure 12-33). Each option is important. If you select Rename in same folder, your chosen images get a new name and stay put. If you select Move to other folder, your images get a new name and are moved to an entirely different folder of your choice (chosen by clicking Browse). If you select Copy to other folder, your photos gain the new name as they move to a new folder; the original files remain unchanged.

Destination Folder
- ○ Rename in same folder
- ○ Move to other folder
- ⦿ Copy to other folder
- [Browse...]   G:\Test Folder\MoveTest\

12-33

Most photographers find the Rename in same folder options a simple and easy way to use this; that usage is typical of changing names of a folder of images to reflect a specific shoot or location, for example. The Move to other folder option is useful when you select a group of images with a unique subject, for example, and you want to put them with a special name into their own folder. The Copy to other folder option is for obsessive photographers who never want to touch their original files ... just kidding. It is useful when you need separate and duplicate files with their own names for special uses; this is common for stock photography.

4. The New Filenames section, highlighted in figure 12-34, is a little confusing at first, but once you understand the structure and how you want your photos named, it has its own logic. First, you do need to decide how you want your files named. You can be as

complex as you want. This batch tool lets you choose as many as ten separate naming boxes. Once you start using these boxes, a preview of your name choice appears in a preview at the bottom of the dialog box.

5. In the Current Filename box, click the down arrow to open the drop-down menu (see figure 12-35). Several choices are available, but most photographers are going to select Text at first. Choose that and type a name for the photos based on subject, shoot, location, and so on — whatever helps you know what the images are. A preview of the changed names appears below these boxes.

6. Create a new box by clicking on the plus button to the right of the first box. If you shoot all Raw files (or if you did a shoot with all JPEG files), you can pretty much name your files however you want, so a simple choice would be Sequence Number, which numbers your files consecutively starting with the number you want and uses the number of digits you select (see figure 12-36). However, if you shoot Raw + JPEG, you get two identical images for each format, so the camera will create numbers that match for the those photos while using the different file formats extensions. It is important to retain those numbers so you can match the two images. This renaming tool will keep those numbers if you select Current Filename, as seen in figure 12-37. This simply attaches that name to your text from the first box.

7. In the additional boxes, you can add as much information in the text as you like. This can get unwieldy, but if you are shooting on assignment, this is a way to get a lot of information into the file name.

8. Select the Preserve current filename option if you change the file names and you want a way to get back to the original.

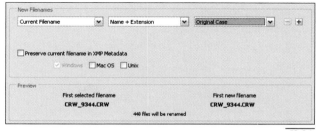

12-34

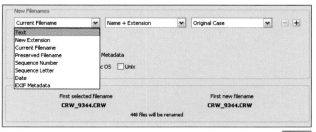

12-35

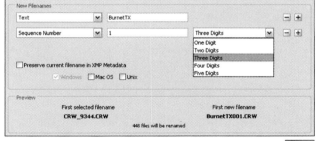

12-36

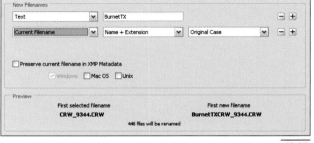

12-37

9. Select a compatibility option when your photos need to go across platforms and you want to ensure the name is compatible.

10. Click Rename. All the files selected are renamed with the text specified.

GROUP PROCESSING

When Camera Raw was redesigned for Photoshop CS2, a totally new function was added: the ability to process multiple Raw files at once as a group. In addition, Adobe engineers did a remarkable feat in allowing you to then

process all of these images in the background while you work on a single image in Photoshop, something that was not possible before.

You start by selecting a group of images and opening them to Camera Raw (see figure 12-38). This gives you a different look to Camera Raw — there is now a strip of images on the left of the image preview as shown in figure 12-39. All of these images are not actually opened in Camera Raw. That would bog down your computer in a hurry. The image in the Preview is fully opened, the others are simply active in the sense that Camera Raw now

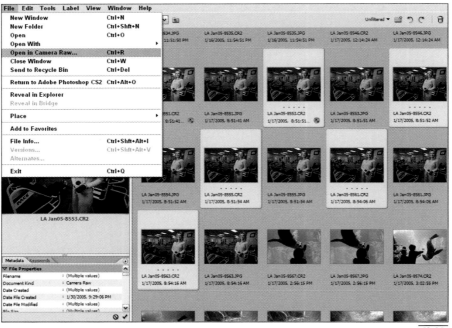

12-38

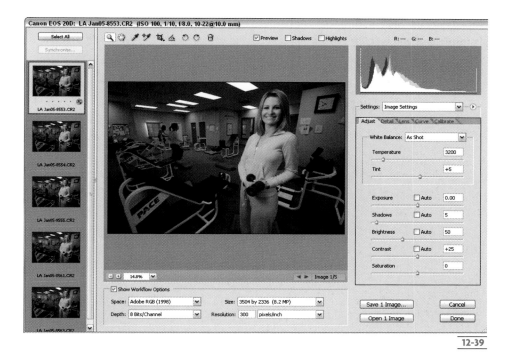

Canon EOS 20D: LA Jan05-8553.CR2 (ISO 100, 1/10, f 8.0, 10-22@10.0 mm)

Select All

Synchronize...

LA Jan05-8553.CR2

LA Jan05-8554.CR2

LA Jan05-8555.CR2

LA Jan05-8561.CR2

LA Jan05-8563.CR2

☑ Preview   ☐ Shadows   ☐ Highlights   R: --- G: --- B: ---

Settings: Image Settings

Adjust Detail Lens Curve Calibrate

White Balance: As Shot

Temperature   3200

Tint   +5

Exposure   ☐ Auto   0.00

Shadows   ☐ Auto   5

Brightness   ☐ Auto   50

Contrast   ☐ Auto   +25

Saturation   0

14.8%   ◀ ▶ Image 1/5

☑ Show Workflow Options

Space: Adobe RGB (1998)   Size: 3504 by 2336 (8.2 MP)

Depth: 8 Bits/Channel   Resolution: 300 pixels/inch

Save 1 Image...   Cancel

Open 1 Image   Done

12-39

recognizes them and can communicate with the files for processing information.

As you process the image shown in the Preview (and highlighted on the strip of images), you can apply that processing to all of the photos on the strip in several ways:

> You can click on any one of the photos in the strip to bring it into the Preview so that it is the key photo to process.

> You can select multiple photos in the strip by Ctrl/⌘-clicking (including all by clicking Select All) so that any processing done to one image is then applied to all of them at the same time. The first photo you select appears in the Preview.

> You can also process one image separately however you like without selecting any others, then select other unprocessed, multiple images as shown in figure 12-40. Nothing will happen at this point. Click Synchronize and you can apply any adjustments done to the first photo to all of them.

PRO TIP

If you want to process multiple Raw files in the background while working in Photoshop as described, you are going to need RAM and lots of it. Photoshop is a real RAM hog. If it can't get enough, it goes back and forth to your hard drive, so you will hear that drive grinding away, but working much slower than what the computer is capable of. Having a faster processor without a lot of RAM is meaningless because it will sit and wait idly while the image is moved back and forth to the hard drive as it is processed. One or more gigabytes of RAM has now become the minimum standard for Photoshop computers.

> Synchronize is a very useful tool. Once you click Synchronize, a dialog box appears asking what you want to synchronize. Often you want to only adjust a certain parameter or group of parameters consistently across a group of photos. You start by adjusting one photo as best you can, then select a group of similar images and click Synchronize. You then get a whole list of things that can be synchronized among the

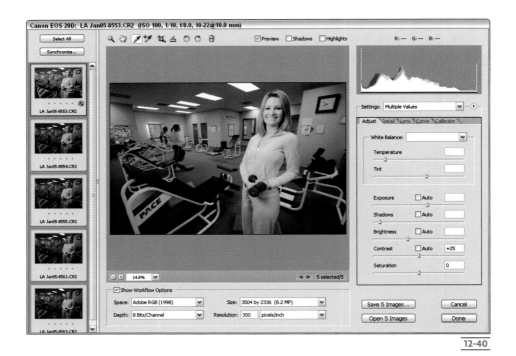

Canon EOS 20D: LA Jan05-8553.CR2 (ISO 100, 1/10, f/8.0, 10-22@10.0 mm)

12-40

Synchronize

Synchronize: Everything

- ☑ White Balance
- ☑ Exposure
- ☑ Shadows
- ☑ Brightness
- ☑ Contrast
- ☑ Saturation

- ☑ Sharpness
- ☑ Luminance Smoothing
- ☑ Color Noise Reduction

- ☑ Chromatic Aberration
- ☑ Vignetting

- ☑ Tone Curve

- ☑ Calibration

- ☑ Crop

OK
Cancel

12-41

photos as seen in figure 12-41. Select whatever you need; deselect those you don't need. All of the selected photos will update appropriately. Click the down arrow to the right of the Synchronize box to access a drop-down menu that simplifies these choices.

> White Balance is a good example. It is not unusual to have a group of images that have unique Exposure or Shadow needs, but the light color conditions are consistent, so correcting the white balance for one applies to all. You fix the color with the White Balance adjustments for your preview image (and anything else needed), and then select the photos you need to also adjust for white balance. Click Synchronize, then the drop-down menu, and choose White Balance. All of the photos selected will now be updated appropriately.

> When your photos have been processed, a little symbol appears below the right corner of images in the strip. The symbol is a little circle with adjustment sliders in it as seen in figure 12-42.

> Once you have allowed processing over multiple files or synchronized a group of images, you can then open that group (Open 5 Images) or save them to a desired file format (Save 5 Images) as shown in figure 12-43. I processed 5 images. The number on the buttons will change depending on the number of images you process together.

> If you open them into Photoshop, you have to wait for the processing to finish. Selecting Save processes the images and saves them to wherever you want (and allows you to rename the files, too). This processing and saving goes on in the background and you are free to work in Photoshop (although your computer may slow down considerably).

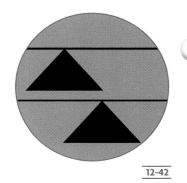

12-42

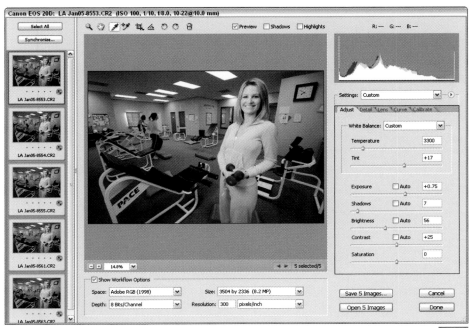

12-43

255

Another way of processing similar files in identical ways is to duplicate the processing of one file for use on others later. This is technically not batch processing in the sense that you are processing a batch of photo files at the same time. However, it is still a way of processing one photo in Camera Raw then applying that work to others in a consistent way.

To do this you use Camera Raw's ability to save its processing instructions. First, open an image file that you can use as a master. A good example of this is for studio work. You may have a consistent setup, for example, that is used for portraits. Or you might have a big shoot, such as a wedding, that has similar conditions and you don't want or need to process everything at once, so you process one typical photo as a master.

Here's how to do this:

1. Open an image file that you can use as a master. It should be something typical of the conditions that appear in the group of images.

2. Adjust the master image as needed, as seen in figure 12-44.

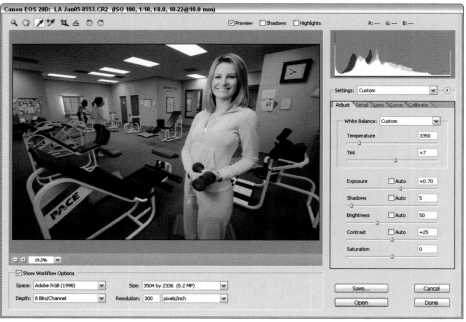

12-44

3. Click the triangle to the right of the Settings box. In the drop-down menu that appears, select Save Settings (see figure 12-45). The Save Raw Conversion Settings dialog box opens, enabling you to save the settings of your adjustments to this photo (see figure 12-46). Use a name that is appropriate to the subject type (for example, FlashSet1), the shoot (Rezults-Owner), or whatever else makes sense to you as a label. Normally, you would save to the Settings folder of Camera Raw, but you can save settings to another location so you can transport them to a different computer.

4. The Save Settings Subset choice in the drop down menu is a variation of Save Settings. Save Settings saves all settings, while Save Settings Subset lets you choose what settings to save for reapplying later (see figure 12-47). This is like the Synchronize setting described in the section on multiple file processing. You could, for example, just save the settings for the Lens tab so you could reapply them every time you use a certain lens.

Whenever you open a new photo that can use the same settings used with your master photo, simply open the drop-down menu to the right of Settings and select Load Settings. You can then choose which settings you need and Camera Raw instantly updates its corrections based on it. Of course, you can make further adjustments to that image to refine it, but that is the beauty of this system that allows you to reuse the basic adjustment settings of a master photo.

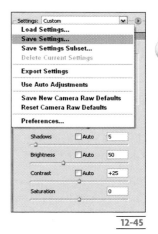

12-45

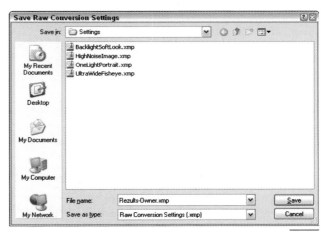

12-46

BATCH WORK

Photoshop has a wonderful tool in its Actions palette that allows you to record adjustments to a photo as an Action then you can replay that Action on any new photo. You can even batch process a whole group of image files using that Action by choosing Automate⇨Batch Processing in Photoshop, including setting up something called a Droplet on your desktop to allow you to drag and drop image files onto it for processing with that Action. The whole range of possibilities for Actions and Batch Processing is beyond the context of this book.

If you think you are going to need a lot of images processed quickly, I strongly recommend shooting JPEG so you gain the internal processing powers of your camera. I guarantee that JPEGs coming straight from the camera will almost always look better than automated batch processing of Raw files straight to a saved JPEG (or TIFF or PSD file). Those camera files have each been processed very smartly by extremely sophisticated algorithms created by the camera manufacturer to make sure its camera's images look great. If you need both fast processing and Raw capabilities, shoot RAW + JPEG.

I have seen descriptions of automated processing of Raw files with Droplets that were basically of vacation photos. What is the purpose of that? Why on earth would you want to take the time to deal with processing Raw files if you have simple vacation photos? The internal camera processing of JPEG files will save you a lot of time.

I will describe a simple way of using Droplets to open multiple similar Raw files and processing, converting, and saving them. First, I strongly recommend creating a new, working file folder for your images before you start. This is easily done in the Bridge (choose File⇨New Folder) as seen in figure 12-48. Use a name specific to your series of photos. I use working folders all the time to keep my files separated. The Bridge helps you organize them, although image browsers like iView Media Pro, ACDSee, or Extensis Portfolio can be faster and more versatile.

In this case, I would create a working folder for the similar Raw files that need to be batch processed and another folder where the actual processed files end up. This way I can move the similar files into one place for easy access and their converted versions end up in another defined location that can also be found easily.

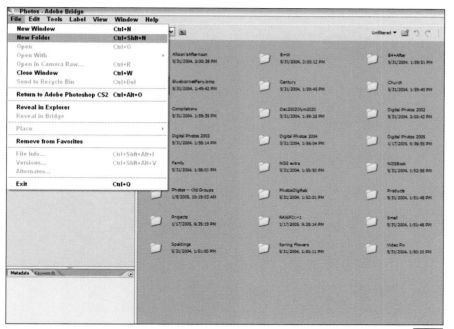

12-48

Next, set up the action for the Droplet to work with. Here's how to do that:

1. Go to the Actions palette in Photoshop and use the drop-down menu to create an action set (this is a folder that can be used for multiple actions if desired) such as Raw Conversions, as seen in figure 12-49.

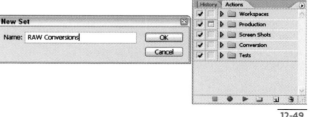

12-49

2. In that same drop-down menu create a new action based on the group on which you are working, such as HV SUV Shoot. Once you click OK, Photoshop begins recording your actions (see figure 12-50).

3. Open one Raw image file from your group of similar images.

4. Make the needed adjustments to correct that photo as seen in figure 12-51, and click Open.

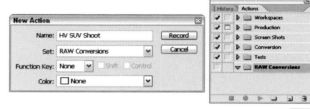

12-50

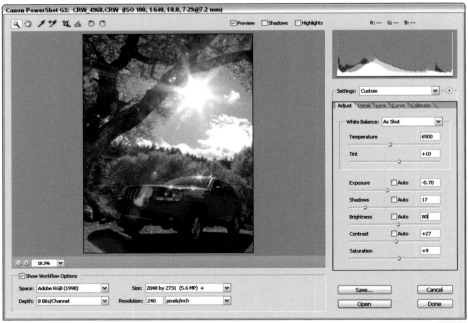

12-51

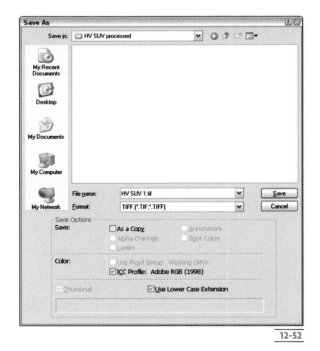

12-52

5. Sharpen the photo if you feel your adjustments will be complete at this point.

6. Save the photo as a new TIFF, JPEG or PSD file, as shown in figure 12-52.

7. Close the file.

8. Stop the Action recording (click the square at the bottom of the Actions palette). Now you create the Droplet.

9. Select the beginning of the Action (this just helps make the droplet process simpler), as seen in figure 12-53.

10. Choose File⇨Automate⇨Create Droplet. The Create Droplet dialog box opens.

11. Fill in the information in the Create Droplet dialog box as shown in figure 12-54. From the top:

> Click Choose to choose a location for the Droplet (your computer desktop is usually used, but you can use any file folder you can readily find); this command also allows you to give your Droplet a short, easily recognized name.

> Select the Override Action "Open" Commands option.

> In the Destination section, choose Folder, and then select the folder you set up earlier for your processed images.

> Select the Override Action "Save As" Commands option.

> In the File Naming section, use whatever file naming conventions work for you, choosing the appropriate boxes and their choices. Be sure to include how many digits you want for the serial number and what number to start with.

> Leave everything else the same.

> Click OK.

Check to see that your Droplet is on your desktop or in the location you selected (see figure 12-55). If so, you can drag and drop your similar Raw files from the group folder (even if you select all of them at once) onto this Droplet and they will all be processed and saved to the new folder automatically. To be sure you have this right, you may want to run a test of at least one of the files first. After that, you can literally walk away from your computer as Photoshop automatically converts your files in Camera Raw, adds any other adjustments, and saves and closes them.

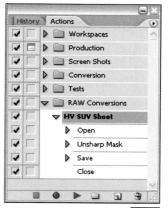

12-53

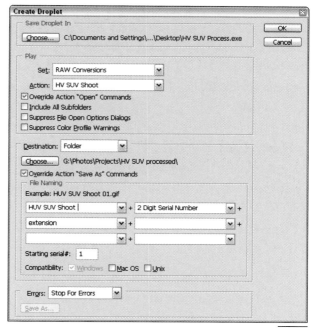

12-54

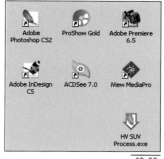

12-55

What if I overcorrect in the Calibrate tab and everything looks out of balance?

On one level, that's not necessarily a bad thing as you are learning how you might use it. This can be valuable experience. I am a firm believer that learning in Photoshop often proceeds fastest when the user is willing to play and experiment a bit — and willing to make mistakes and fail.

Remember that you cannot hurt anything in Camera Raw. You never actually change any pixels in the RAW file. You are only giving the program instructions on how to process and convert the file to something that can be used, adjusted, and saved outside of Camera Raw. So things can never truly be overcorrected, because you can always go back to the original Camera Raw defaults for the photo at the minimum. In addition, you can press and hold Alt/Option to change the Cancel button to Reset and then click Reset to reset the tools.

How can I know if and when a lens has problems that need correcting?

This is a very good question because you don't want to arbitrarily make lens corrections to a file that doesn't need it. That, as noted earlier, can cause problems with color details. There are some things to look for to help you decide what to do:

> **Lens quality.** While modern lenses are very, very good, there is no question that a low-priced, budget lens just will not match a high-end pro lens. The budget lens is more likely to have lens aberrations, so it can be worth looking for them, especially when the lens is shot wide open.

> **Zoom lenses.** These are also excellent today. However, many manufacturers have pushed the limits with them, and you can often find lens aberrations with the extreme-focal-length-range zooms, especially at the extremes of the range (for example, the widest and most telephoto focal lengths). Wide-angle ends of extreme zooms also tend to vignette, especially at wider apertures. Budget zooms can also have lens aberrations.

> **Contrasts at edges.** Magnify the image and examine strong contrasts of dark and light along the edges of the image. This is where you will typically see color fringing.

> **Skies.** Watch skies and other flat areas of tone where vignetting will appear in a hurry.

If you are concerned about any lens, it is worth doing some tests. Try different f-stops; with zooms, try different focal lengths, especially maximums. Then look at details along the edges of the image.

I know that once I process a Raw file, Camera Raw keeps processing information with that file so that it will be opened the same way each time. Can I move that processing information with the Raw file if I put it into a new folder or to a new location?

Absolutely. If you've spent some time processing images, and particularly if you have worked a whole group, you will want to be sure that work is kept with them. To do that, you need to keep the XMP file with its parent. On your hard drive (or wherever you keep your images), you will discover that a new little file appears next to your image file in its folder (this assumes you have told Camera Raw that it should not keep these files (called sidecar XMP files in Preferences) whenever you adjust an image file for the first time (after that, the XMP files will just be updated).

When you move or copy your images to a new place, make sure you move or copy the XMP files as well.

MAKING CAMERA RAW WORK HARDER FOR YOU

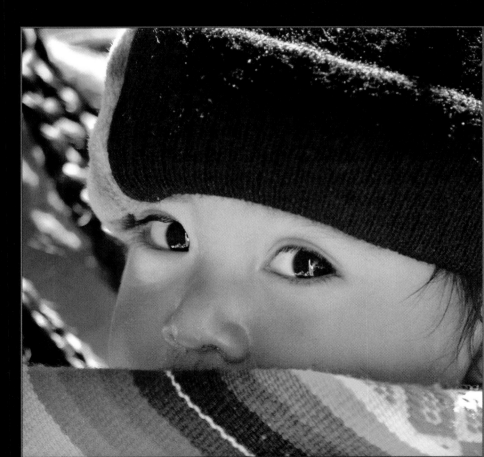

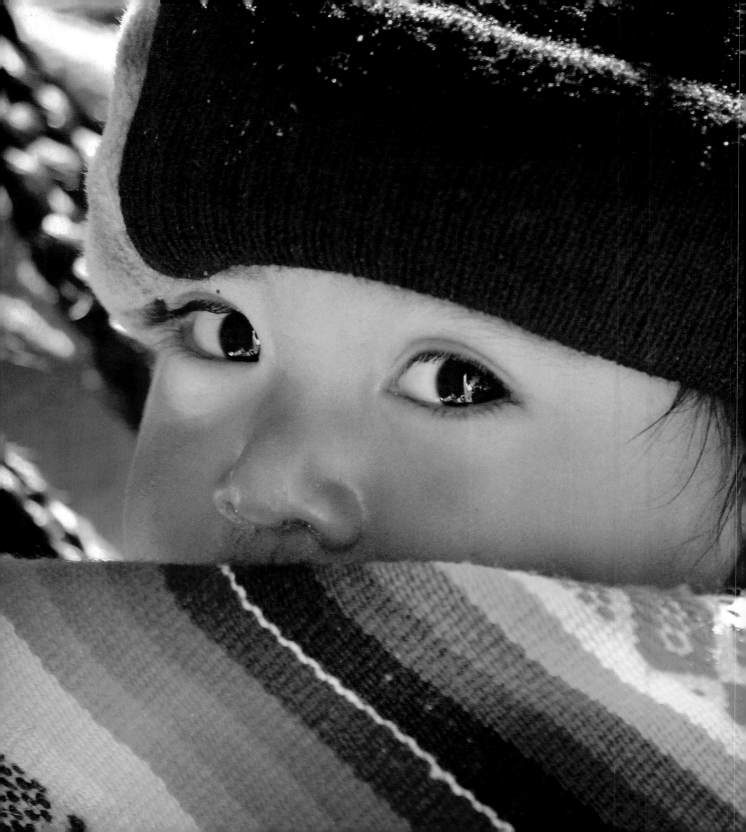

Chapter 13

DOUBLE PROCESSING FOR EXPOSURE

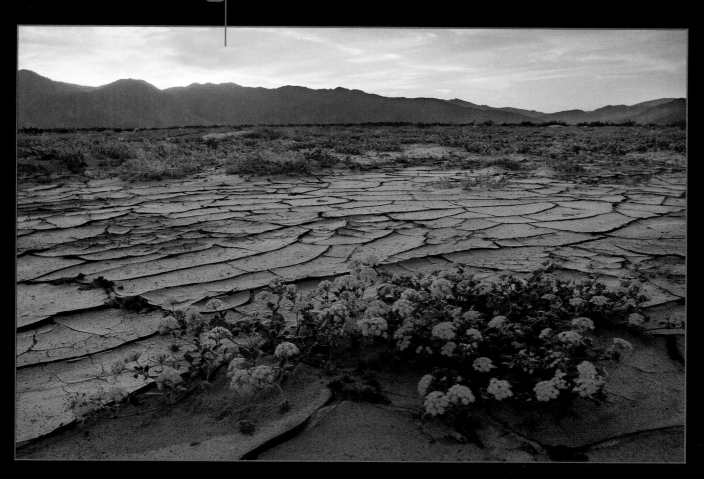

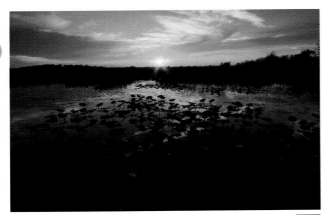
13-1

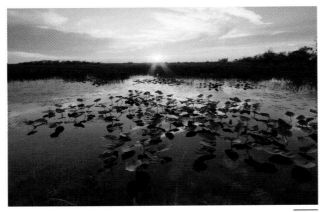
13-2

You have now learned the secrets of Camera Raw. Using its power is not so much about knowing all the controls as it is being able to interpret their use for a particular photo. After all, Camera Raw has a fraction of the controls that Photoshop itself has. Using Camera Raw takes practice and work on many varied photos, sometimes even trying different processing techniques on the same image file just to see how it can be affected.

In this chapter, you learn a technique that requires you to process the same image file in two different ways to achieve a very specific effect. You may have noticed when working on photos in Camera Raw that as you work on one set of tones that optimum adjustment of those tonalities is not optimum for something else. This is especially true when you try to make the most of dark parts of certain photos compared to the highlights.

Yet, Raw files hold a great deal of very useable detail in those dark areas, as seen in the example in figures 13-1 and 13-2, where 13-2 is an opened-up version of 13-1. One very real advantage of shooting Raw is that you can capture better shadows and highlights than you can when shooting JPEG. You need a way of getting the most from both. That can be difficult when you have a scene with a big tonal range of important details. With film, you have to be satisfied with a specific and unique result from the exposure used for a single frame. With slide film, for example, you expose for the highlights and hope for the best in the shadows. In bright light, that often results in a dramatic photo to be sure, but one with good highlights and no shadow detail.

But now you don't have to accept that. You can go beyond the limitations of standard exposure and JPEG processing to gain images with tonal ranges truer to what you saw in the first place. It is interesting to me that some so-called purists claim the processing described in this chapter is false, that it somehow distorts reality. That is truly a lot of nonsense. The great black-and-white photographers would frequently process their images differently because of different subject conditions. Just like their darkroom work, the processing you learn here actually reveals real-

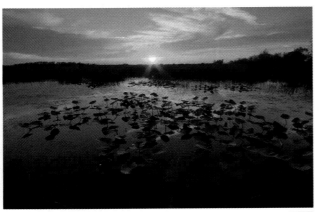
13-3

ity. In some cases, such processing might be required of photographers who are after "truth" because it really does allow you to come closer to what was really seen rather than what was arbitrarily revealed by the technology.

ONE SIZE MAY NOT FIT ALL

Standard processing of Raw files works most of the time. Double processing an image, as described in this chapter, increases the work involved for a photo and therefore changes your workflow. That may simply not be acceptable for many photographers. No wedding photographer, for example, is going to double process all of the shots from a wedding.

However, there is no question that trying to force every image into the mold of doing everything once with the controls that Camera Raw offers compromises some images. One-size processing won't fit every photo. Even that wedding photographer will find it helpful at times to process that one key photo from the wedding specially, bringing out details in both the bride's white dress and the groom's dark tux that cannot be revealed in any other way.

Camera Raw offers no ability to control one part of a photo differently than another. As you adjust dark areas, light areas are affected. The best adjustment of the bright parts of a photo may give the ability to only make a mediocre adjustment of mid- to dark tones. figure 13-3 demonstrates how much you can get from an image in different tonal areas by using all the features of Camera Raw. While the image isn't bad, it could be better as you will soon see. I also have to ask, "Why bother?" It is so much easier to focus on really important parts of the photo and process for them independently so they look their best compared to doing a lot of work trying to beat the system and process the image only once. And when bright areas and dark areas really do require different thought, rarely will you find that both look their best when forced into being adjusted simultaneously.

PRO TIP

Exposure is still important, even when doing a double-processed image. If a photo is much overexposed, then adjusting the bright areas is a challenge requiring more work at the least, and a bad compromise at worst. If a photo is much underexposed, adjusting the dark areas may also add work, but even worse, noise becomes much more prominent and colors will be weak.

So what to do? Process the image twice: once to optimize the highlights, once to get the most from shadows. Then put the two photos together in Photoshop. You learn to do all of this in this chapter.

BRIGHT SKY, DARK GROUND

One major type of shot that cries out for double processing is a scene with a bright sky and dark ground. In the photo of sunset in the upper reaches of the Everglades drainage in Loxahatchee National Wildlife Refuge, the color in the sky and clouds looks great. As I stood by the water, I knew I wanted the water and the plants with their reflections in the composition, but I also knew that the camera sensor could not handle the full range of brightness that my eye was seeing.

A 3x graduated neutral density filter helped with the exposure by knocking down the brightness of the sky considerably. At this point, the sky and ground at least recorded with detail that could be used. This gave an unprocessed result that looked a lot like what you would have achieved with slide film (see figure 13-4). Most people actually expect a scene like this to look similar in a photograph, even though that is not really how it looks to the eye. But to get an image with a range of tonalities more representative of what was seen demands Raw be used to better dig the darkest and brightest tones out of the recorded image file.

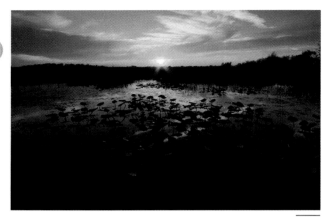

13-4

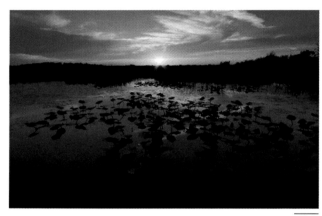

13-5

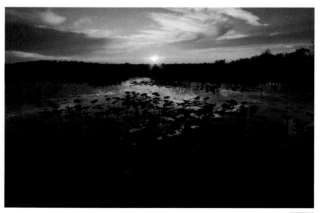

13-6

This photo presents a significant challenge facing digital photographers working today. Most people expect certain images to appear a certain way regardless of what the original scene looked like. The predominance of Fujichrome Velvia film, which has been used by professional nature photographers for the past 20 years, has created a look that now defines expectations of what a nature photograph should look like.

An easily understood example of this is a sunset. Sunset light is not anywhere near balanced to the daylight film with which it has been traditionally shot. Velvia records a far warmer, much richer color than is seen in reality. When shot with a digital camera, a sunset all depends on what white balance is used. You can actually remove the color by using a tungsten balance which will neutralize much of the color altogether (see figure 13-5). Auto white balance usually gives sunset a warm, but weaker coloration. It usually looks more like what people expect if it is shot with daylight or cloudy white balance.

With digital and with the double-processing technique, you can get a sunset with colors that people expect and more tonality than most viewers think such a scene has, based on what they have seen in photographs before. This is in spite of the fact that the film simply was not able to capture the range of detail that the eye saw. So sometimes you can adjust an image correctly for what was in the scene, yet the viewer will find it unnatural, not because it is really unnatural, but because it doesn't look like they think a photo of such a scene should look like.

BRINGING OUT THE SCENE

Double processing works on the principle of creating two image files from Camera Raw. The files have different colors and tonality based on processing for specific parts of the images, which are then combined in Photoshop. The result is that you don't have to try to make the whole image perfect by using all of the adjustments possible in a single processing. This is a way to get around the limitation that Camera Raw only allows overall, global adjustment of an image and cannot only do selected areas.

For this photo, it is possible to adjust the image once for the sky (see figure 13-6), and then open that into Photoshop. The Raw file is opened a second time and readjusted for the plants and water at the bottom (see figure 13-7), then that photo is opened into Photoshop, too. Of course, you can try to make adjustments for both by using the Tonal Curve (along with the other adjustments), but I guarantee the results on this type of image. You gain the desired tonal range but at the cost of more work, frustration with tones and colors not working together, and a flatter look to the image.

Double processing is a little tricky at first. You have to force yourself to only look at the specific parts of the photo you are adjusting for each processing and not be distracted by another part of the photo that might begin to look really bad from this adjustment. In this photo, for example, when adjusting the sky, you have to ignore the lower part of the photo. Then when the photo is adjusted a second time for the lower part of the image, the sky must be ignored. Sometimes photographers have trouble doing that until they have tried a few double-processed photos.

PROCESSING THE BRIGHT AREAS

In the double-processing technique, it is usually best to start with the most straightforward adjustments. In other words, look at the photo and see what part of it you can adjust quickly and easily. On this photo, it is the sky because it has good exposure and color. This is really a critical part of the image, too, as color and contrast in the sunset itself always influence the rest of the photo.

The sky then needs to be adjusted for itself only, ignoring what happens in the rest of the photo. You'll still need to follow a standard Camera Raw workflow, this time focusing on the sky.

1. The area around the sun is still a bit bright from the original exposure, so by using the Alt/Option threshold command and looking at the Preview, I brought the brightest areas of the sky down a bit in value (see figure 13-8).

2. Most of the photo has more than enough black from the bottom of the image, so the Shadows adjustment does not need to be stronger (go to the right). There is no reason for a pure black in the sky, so minimal change of shadows is needed. Having a little of the Shadows adjustment (in other words, not all the way to the left) will give more strength to the darkest parts of the sky, as seen in figure 13-9.

3. Brightness adjustments on the sky make it too flat (see figure 13-10). Skies with a lot of variation in tonality like this one do quite well with the Tone Curve. This allows some tweaking of contrast so certain parts of the sky brighten, while others darken for more drama. At this point, you can see immediately that while the sky is looking great, the rest of the image looks less than optimum (see figure 13-11).

PRO TIP

It can help to enlarge the image in the preview so you can mainly see the part of the image you are focusing on for a specific adjustment. For landscape photos, for example, you could enlarge the photo until the sky disappears from view, moving the preview image around as needed. This way, you only look at the part of the image being adjusted, and you won't be distracted by another area that looks bad because of that adjustment.

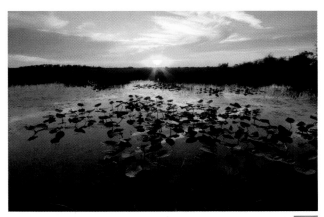

13-7

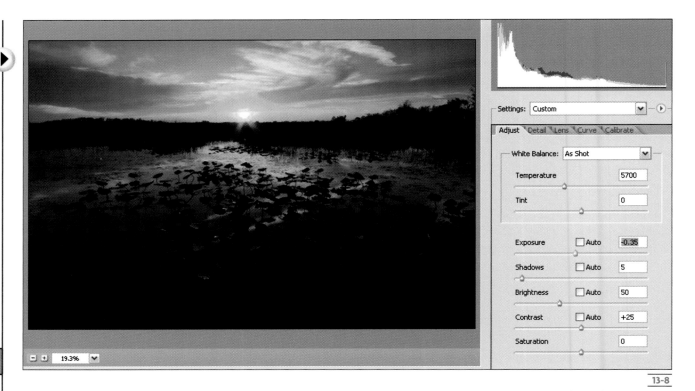

13-8

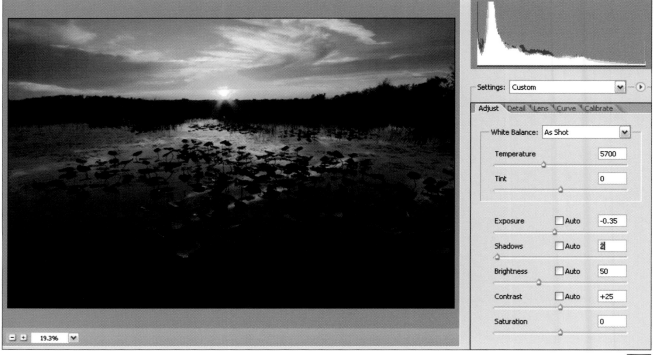

13-9

This is the point that photographers can panic and try to adjust the rest of the photo. Don't! This is exactly as the photo should look at this point.

4. A little Saturation helps the color, but adding too much can cause problems with the richest color around the sun. A better way of adding some color to the sunset is to increase the Temperature slider of the White Balance settings (in figure 13-12 a slight bit of Saturation has been added along with changing the Temperature slider). This can make for a very richly colored sunset, but if you go too far, it can be hard to balance this part of the image with the rest of the photo when the lower part is processed.

5. This photo is very clean in the sky and needs no adjustment in the Detail tab (figure 13-13).

6. Now open this processed sky image into Photoshop and save it (see figure 13-14) with a name that relates to the processing.

PRO TIP

When you open a photo from Camera Raw into Photoshop for the double-processing technique, it really helps to immediately save this image with a name related to the processing, such as LoxahatcheeSunset-Sky. This is not a necessity; Photoshop will do fine with the image if it is not saved or renamed at all. But I find this helps in three ways: the file is backed up in case you have problems with Photoshop or the computer, it makes sure there is no confusion (which can come as the photos are combined), and your photo is saved and can be used again if needed. In versions of Camera Raw before Photoshop CS2, you have to do this as you cannot open the same image twice in them.

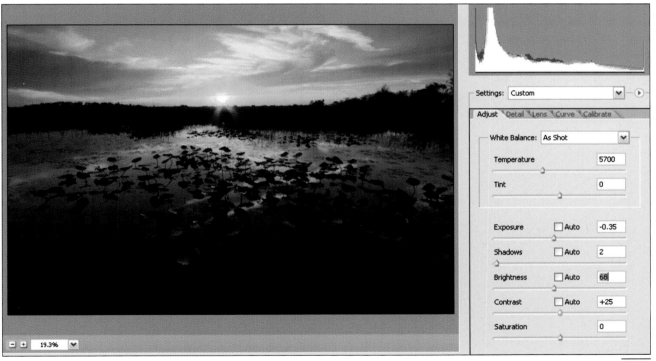

13-10

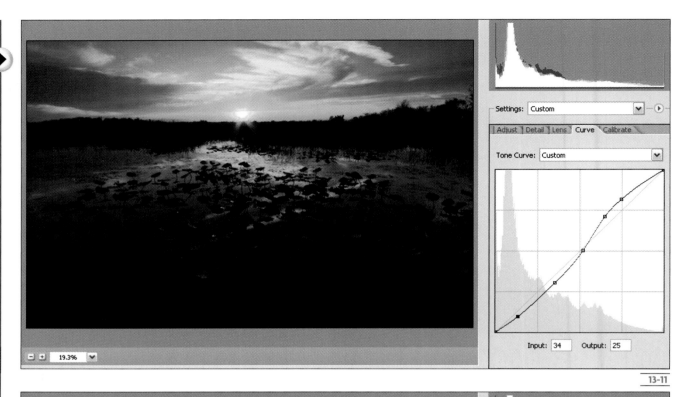

13-11

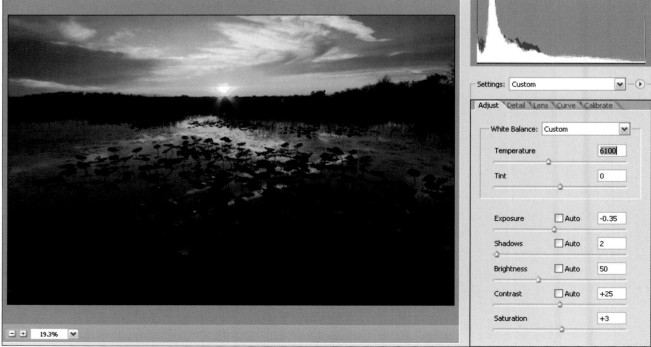

13-12

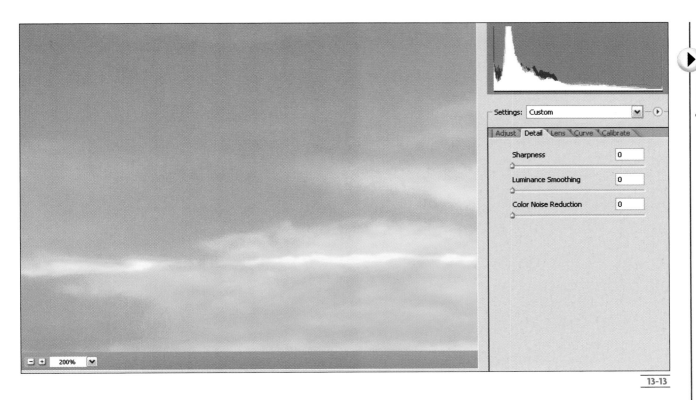

Settings: Custom

Adjust | Detail | Lens | Curve | Calibrate

Sharpness — 0

Luminance Smoothing — 0

Color Noise Reduction — 0

200%

13-13

PROCESSING THE DARK AREAS

The lower portion of this photo is dark, it has a lot of detail that can be brought out. When double processing, I like to go back to what the image looked like before the sky was processed. You do this by using the drop-down menu associated with Settings and choosing Camera Raw Defaults, as shown in figure 13-15. You can just pick up adjustments where you left off with the first processing of the image, but I find that confusing. In that case, you are adjusting your adjustments, rather than starting fresh.

This particular photo allowed me to use the Preview area to only look at the lower part of the photo and hide the sky. That can be helpful because you are not distracted by what might get ugly in that sky. By magnifying the photo slightly, then moving it up within the Preview space, the sky disappears from view as demonstrated by figure 13-16. Not all photos will work this way as this magnification hides details on the sides of the image, too. If those details are important to the adjustment, then you have a problem. But many times this magnification can help.

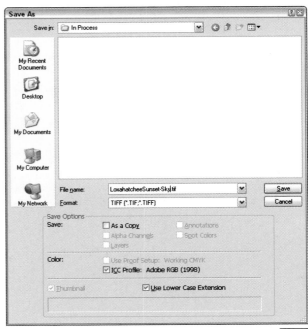

Save As

Save in: In Process

My Recent Documents

Desktop

My Documents

My Computer

My Network

File name: LoxahatcheeSunset-Sky.tif — Save

Format: TIFF (*.TIF;*.TIFF) — Cancel

Save Options
Save: ☐ As a Copy   ☐ Annotations
☐ Alpha Channels   ☐ Spot Colors
☐ Layers

Color: ☐ Use Proof Setup: Working CMYK
☑ ICC Profile: Adobe RGB (1998)

☑ Thumbnail   ☑ Use Lower Case Extension

13-14

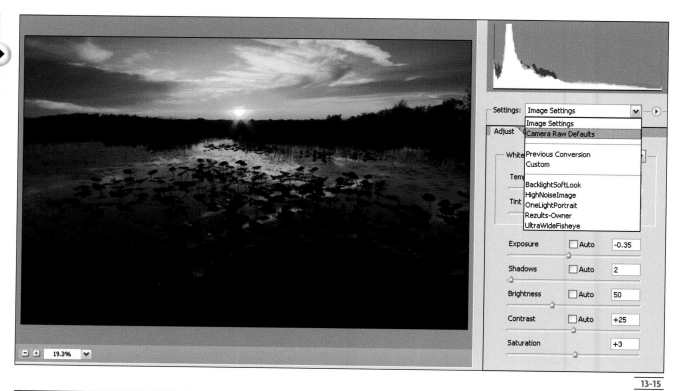

13-15

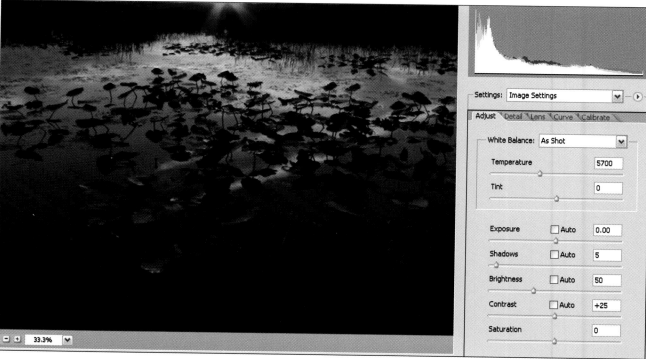

13-16

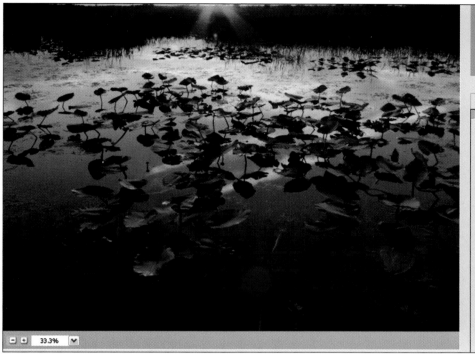
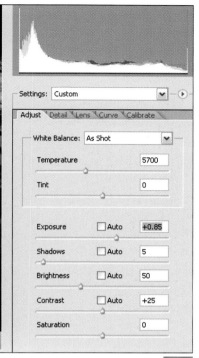

13-17

1. Freed from the demands of the bright sky, the watery landscape can be lifted in brightness quite a bit as seen in figure 13-17. I would avoid trying to go too far with the Exposure setting because this is, in fact, the dark part of the photo. You want to make it brighter, but not so much that it competes with the sky.

2. Because this part of the photo already is in the shadows and has lots of black areas, you could leave it as is. I decided to increase the blacks slightly to give this dark area more strength and, perhaps, more mystery (see figure 13-18). I did not want to open up this lower part of the image so much that it looked like a daylight photo. This would never look right against the sunset.

3. While Brightness does an acceptable job with the midtones in this photo, it really doesn't give the best tonalities possible. I really thank Adobe for adding the Curve tab to Camera Raw. It really helps with double processing as seen in figure 13-19. Most

double-processed photos deal with limited tonal ranges in each adjusted version of the image (because you usually are working with mainly the dark or mainly the light tones for each version). The Tone Curve lets you work that tonal range with more control. This often requires multiple points on the curve. You do have to be careful, however, that one area of the curve is not so over processed that it makes the image look odd, even posterized. Watch how tones blend into each other. Very steep changes to the Tone Curve can result in such problems.

Another problem that can occur as you process a part of the image with limited tonal range is that the gradations of tone can begin to tear, leaving you with odd tonal transitions as seen in the over processed figure 13-20 (noise that is revealed from strong processing can also affect this). Be aware of this possibility — you may have to temper some of your processing.

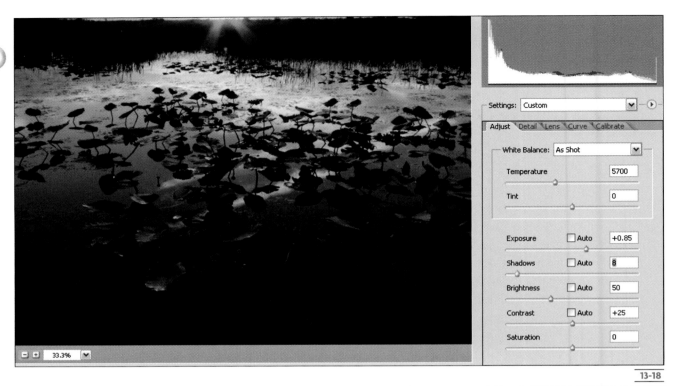

13-18

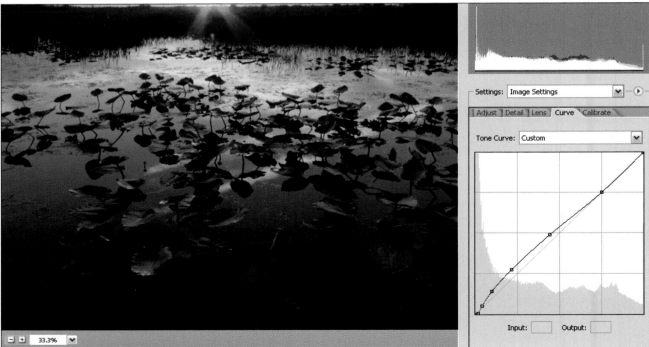

13-19

4. Saturation can often be boosted a lot in dark parts of an image because the color was originally captured weaker than it was. In this photo, the water and plant leaves look better with more saturation (figure 13-21), but there is flare from the sun cutting into the lower part of the photo, which also gets more saturation, but can get garish in a hurry. There are some things that can be done to compensate for that later in Photoshop, but for this photo, the Saturation control will be applied so that the flare color does not get out of hand.

I decided to leave the White Balance section as is. I liked the color of the water reflecting the blue sky. It gives the color in the photo a cold and warm contrast. Increasing the Temperature setting gives the photo more sunset atmosphere, but then you lose the cool blues at the bottom of the image.

5. All this adjustment of dark parts of a photo begins to show noise that is normally not seen, but is evident in figure 13-22. Both color and luminance noise appear so that some adjustment of the Detail tab is needed. There really aren't a lot of fine details in this watery part of the photo, so both the Luminance Smoothing and Color Noise Reduction sliders can be used fairly aggressively. Most of the noise is cleaned up quite well with Luminance Smoothing set at about 40 and Color Noise Reduction at about 30, as demonstrated in figure 13-23.

6. Open this processed sky image into Photoshop and save it (see figure 13-24).

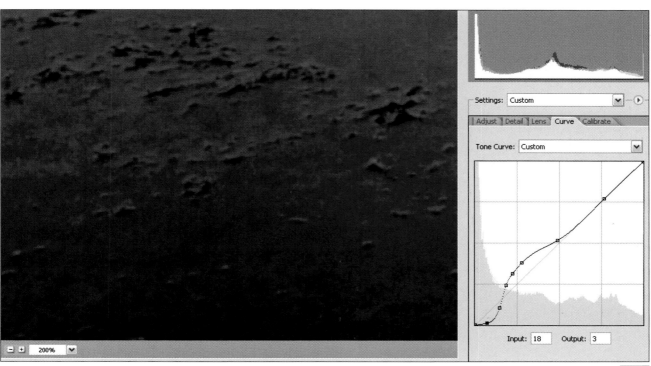

13-20

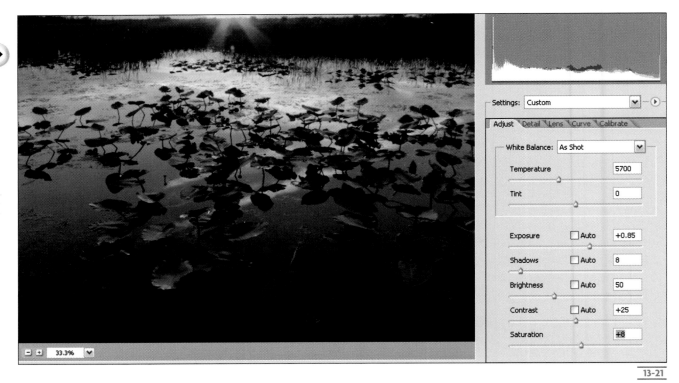

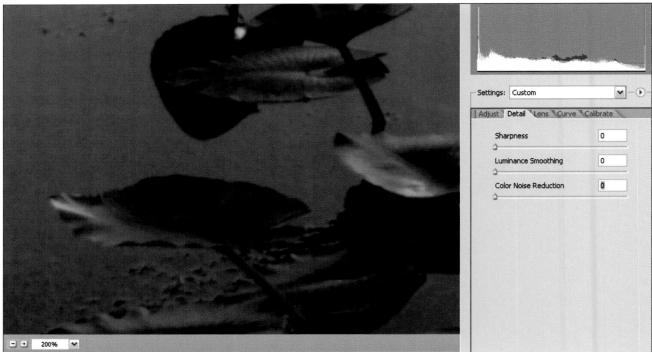

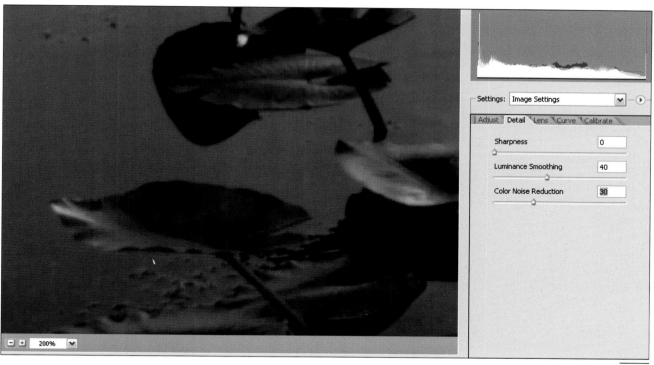

13-23

THE MERGING PROCESS

At this point there are two distinctly different images open in Photoshop, a dark one that was processed for the sky and a light one that was processed for the water and plants as noted in figure13-25. Neither one looks great overall. There are even some areas of the images that look awful. But the important thing is that there are now two images optimally processed for specific parts of the photos. Any overall processing, as you have seen, leads to a compromise that doesn't truly make the most of the scene.

Now the two versions have to be brought together into one final image, which is truly a magical moment to me. It's magic to me because now I can see in the photo something much closer to what I originally saw when I made the photograph. It is like seeing the image become real in the developing tray in the traditional darkroom. And it truly reveals the power of digital and shooting Raw.

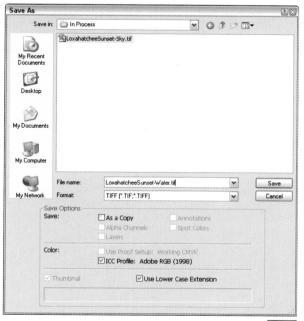

13-24

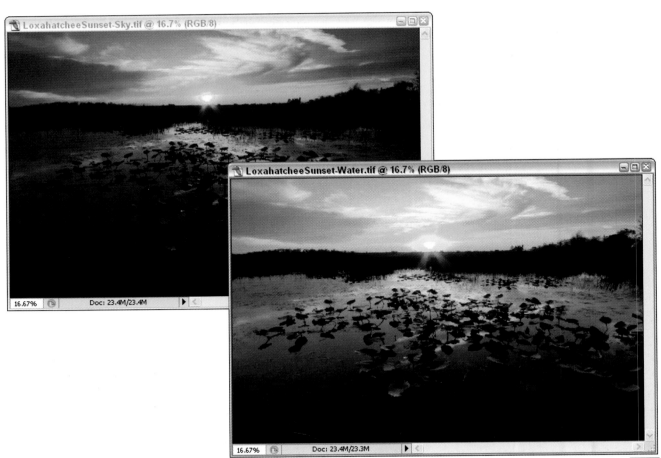

The process is simple in concept: You move one photo on top of the other (coming into Photoshop automatically as a layer), and then remove the bad parts of the top photo to reveal the better processing of those parts in the bottom image. Because both images came from the same file, they will line up exactly. But which photo goes on top? There is no right or wrong way to do that. It depends heavily on the photo. And sometimes you guess wrong, which is really no big deal; you have your two images processed and saved, so you just move the other one on top.

As you gain experience using this technique, you learn to judge which photo should be on top. Here are two things to consider:

> You will be removing parts of the top layer to reveal better-adjusted areas from the bottom layer. The photo that needs the least amount of area removal often is best on top.

> Because the top photo is on its own layer and the bottom image is on the background, the top photo can be further tweaked by adjusting the Opacity of the layer. That implies that the photo with the overall best adjustment goes on the bottom.

PUTTING TWO IMAGES INTO ONE

In this scene, the sunset-adjusted photo has an excellent sky. It's hard to say if the water-and-plant-adjusted image will balance the sky as is when it is added to the sky photo, meaning that the darker image may need some Opacity adjustment to its layer in order to balance it. This thought process is useful for any image as it will help you decide which image needs to be on top in a layer. This won't be obvious when you first start using this way of working an image, but you'll learn it as you go. Here's how to put these two images together:

1. Line up images. Move the two photos enough apart on your Photoshop workspace that you can easily see both the top photo and much of the image under it. You may need to reduce the viewing sizes of the photos to do this. Make the photo you think should be on top the active image (which makes it on top visually on the workspace) as in figure 13-26.

2. Select the Move tool in the tool palette. Click anywhere on the active photo, press and hold Shift without moving anything else, then drag the active photo on top of the bottom image. Holding Shift during this movement will make the two images line up exactly.

It is very important that you move your cursor completely onto the bottom image so that the cursor icon changes to a white cursor with a little box and a plus sign (figure 13-27). Then release your mouse button and Shift in that order. If you do not move your cursor far enough, an error message indicating Photoshop "Could not complete your request because the layer is locked." That only means you did not drag the image far enough.

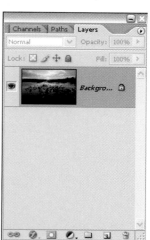

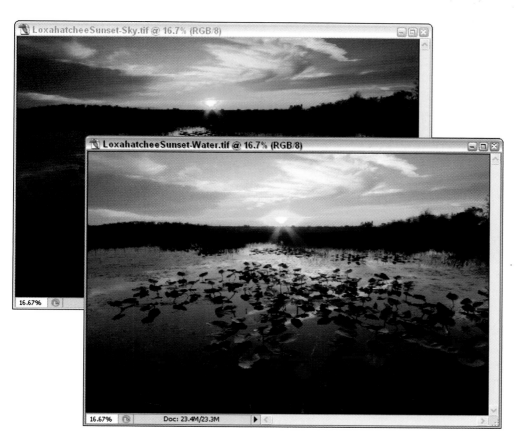

13-26

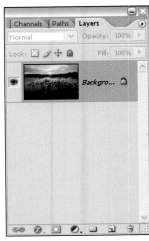

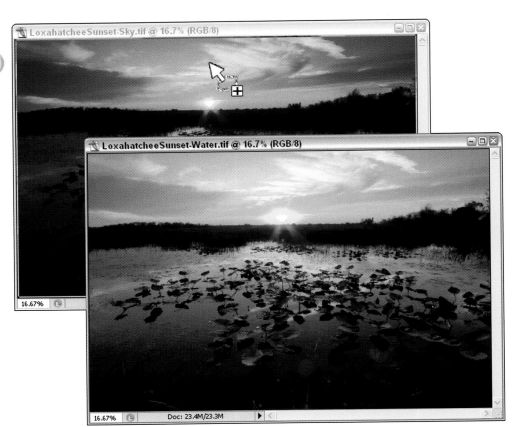

13-27

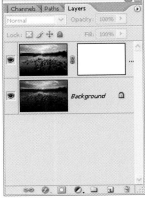

13-28

If you release Shift before you release your mouse button, the top photo's position will move, and it will not line up with the bottom photo. You can check to see if the two photos are lined up correctly by turning on and off the top layer (check the eye icon); they should change in brightness, not in position.

3. Add a layer mask to the top layer as demonstrated in figure 13-28, the photo you just dragged. You can do this through the Layer Mask icon at the bottom left of the Layers palette or through the Layer menu.

4. Remove the bad parts of the top photo. In a layer mask, black hides the layer and white reveals it, so as long as you are in the layer mask (the Layer palette shows which is active), you can paint the top photo out (black) or in (white). Use a big, soft brush to make this painting in or out blend well, as shown in figure 13-29.

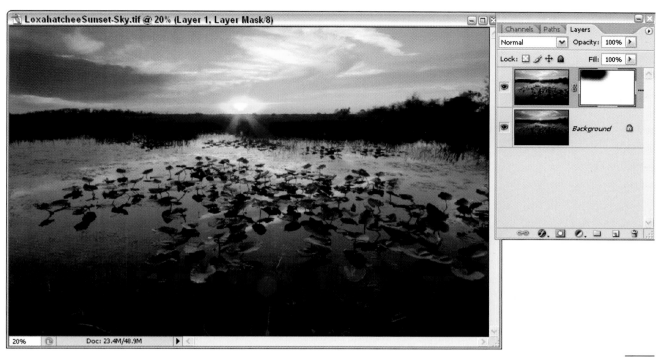

13-29

This photo offers another possibility for removing the bad parts of the photo, a gradient in the layer mask (be sure the Linear Gradient is chosen in the tool options bar as well as the first blend of foreground to background colors). By setting the foreground/background colors on the Tools palette to black on top, white below, you can use the Gradient tool to start with black (to remove that part of the photo) and gradate to white (to keep another part of the top image) wherever you click again. A gradient blend occurs between those two click points. On this photo, clicking near the sun and pulling down the blending line to just below the plants horizon, creates a blend that works well right along the horizon, as seen in figure 13-30.

You may have to try this gradient multiple times. Where the blend occurs and how big the blend is will have a huge effect on the photo, and every photo is different as to what is best. Some need a very narrow

blend, while some demand a blend halfway across the photo.

5. Refine the differences. Use a smaller brush, still soft, to paint around smaller areas that did not blend properly in the overall changes. In this photo, for example, I did some extra work through the trees to bring them out a little.

6. Tune the top layer. Often the top photo can be made to balance the bottom better by turning down the top photo somewhat by using the Opacity control of the top layer, as seen in figure 13-31.

7. Tweak as needed. At this point, you can do further work to the image by controlling and isolating changes to the layers. You might add an Adjustment Layer for the bottom photo and another one grouped with the top layer alone. You use these to make the top and bottom layers blend better.

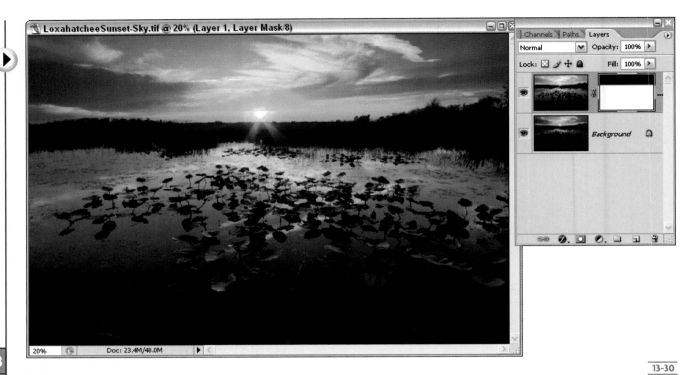

13-30

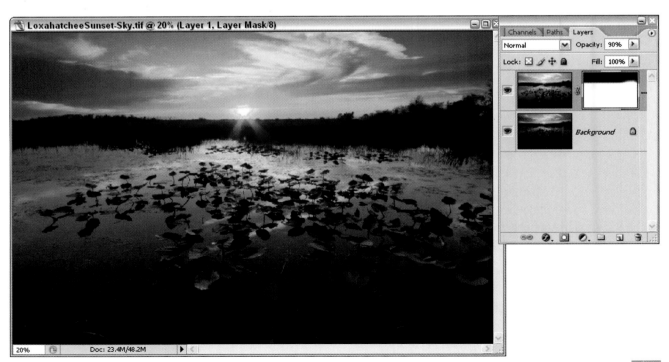

13-31

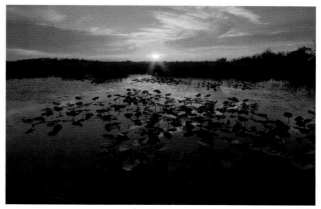

13-32

8. Save the file. I typically flatten the photo now, then sharpen and save it as a new file. Because I have already saved the two processed photos, I feel little need to save a Photoshop layered file for the whole image. If you have to make a lot of small changes, for example, painting in and out lots of isolated areas across the photo, then it is a good idea to save a whole layered file that you can go back to and readjust if needed.

Compare again the single-processed and double-processed files in figures 13-32 and 13-33, respectively. There is quite a difference! Figure 13-33 is considerably livelier and, I believe, closer to the real-world experience of that sunset. You may also notice that I removed a little bit of orange flare at the bottom of the image using a layer to copy the area, adjust its color to match, then use the Clone tool to blend.

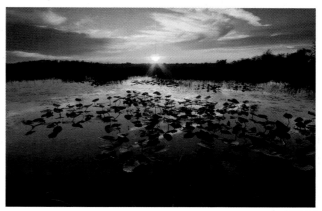

13-33

SMALL AREA CHANGES

Not all photos needing double processing will have the areas of difference so clearly defined as in this landscape example. The little jumping spider in figure 13-34 shows off the power of double processing in an image that needs the work, but only for small areas.

The backlight in the image direct from Raw without processing makes for some interesting sparkle in the sand around the critter, plus it offers nice three-dimensional modeling of the animal and a good shadow for an interesting compositional element. However, that backlight also severely underlights the front of the spider so it is difficult to see the interesting features of its head.

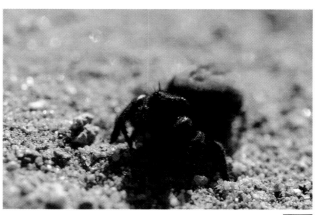

13-34

PRO TIP

Brilliant Photoshop expert Jack Davis likes to blend image layers together using Layer Styles Blending Options. This allows you to blend the two versions of your processed photo in a different way. You can experiment with this by choosing Layer⇒Layer Style⇒Blending Options. Then you use the sliders at the bottom (Blend If). Choose Gray and move the top sliders back and forth to see how the two versions blend together. You can split the sliders for more control by pressing and holding Alt/Option and dragging a slider apart. I tend to favor the layer mask and painting parts of the image in or out as needed because I like the control this offers as to where my changes appear in the photo.

Shadow/Highlight

Shadows

Amount: 30 %

Tonal Width: 20 %

Radius: 30 px

OK
Reset
Load...
Save...
☑ Preview

Highlights

Amount: 0 %

Tonal Width: 50 %

Radius: 30 px

Adjustments

Color Correction: +20

Midtone Contrast: 0

Black Clip: 0.01 % White Clip: 0.01 %

Save As Defaults
☑ Show More Options

13-35

This is a real problem with shooting existing light on many subjects. The light is great overall, but causes problems with details that need to be revealed. Flash might help, but it can also overpower the scene when this close, and it means you have to carry along a big flash. A reflector can help, but sometimes subjects, such as this little guy, have no reason to wait around while you set a reflector. The result in the past would have most likely been one of two things: tolerance of the lighting conditions so the subject could be captured on film or an image tossed to the round file when it got back from the lab.

This shot was made with Raw so that would not be necessary. I knew double processing was a real possibility that would allow both the drama and life of the backlight as well as detail in the shadowed face of the spider.

You might ask, why not use the Shadow/Highlight adjustment tool in Photoshop (see figure 13-35)? Simple — control. With the double-processing technique I don't simply brighten the shadows or darken the highlights, as in Shadow/Highlight (though it does those things well). With this technique I can specifically process an image version that absolutely favors the highlights, even to the extent of ignoring shadows, then I can process a second version that does the opposite and totally favors the shadows. Then, on top of that, I can selectively decide where to emphasize the highlights and shadows in the final image because of the way I blend the two photos together.

PROCESS FOR THE MAIN PHOTO

The spider photo is an excellent example of how to deal with processing a shot that needs a small area adjusted totally differently than most of the image. First, it is always best to do the easiest adjustments first, and that would be making the main photo look its best.

1. Do both a visual check of the image and using Alt/Option to see the threshold show a well-exposed image. There is no point to making the highlights brighter.

2. Because the dark areas of the subject will be adjusted again just for those tonalities, the overall image can afford a slight increase in the Shadows slider to deepen some of the sand shadows, as seen in the threshold screen (Alt/Option) in figure 13-36.

3. Brightness doesn't really help the midtones much on this photo. The Medium Contrast Tone Curve looks good, but the photo looks a little dark. I used it but raised the two top points slightly. As you can see in figure 13-37 the overall photo looks better, but the spider face looks worse.

4. Color doesn't look too bad using the As Shot setting, so it can be left as is at first. A little added Saturation helps, but it affects the overall look, so a little more Temperature and a little more green (minus Tint) benefit the shot, as seen in figure 13-38.

5. Detail in the image is very clean and needs no noise correction.

6. Open the processed image into Photoshop and save it.

PROCESS FOR THE DETAIL

Now the dark side of the spider has to be developed (apologies to George Lucas). Once again the image is put back to the Camera Raw Defaults, then processed for the dark face. Enlarging and moving the photo in the Preview doesn't help much to minimize distractions in this image. You just have to accept that most of the photo will look bad as the dark detail is adjusted.

1. Using the Alt/Option technique doesn't help the exposure much for processing the dark part of this photo. I just used it a little to lighten the dark areas a bit. You could actually skip the Exposure step, but I like to use it because it strengthens the bright areas of the dark part of the image.

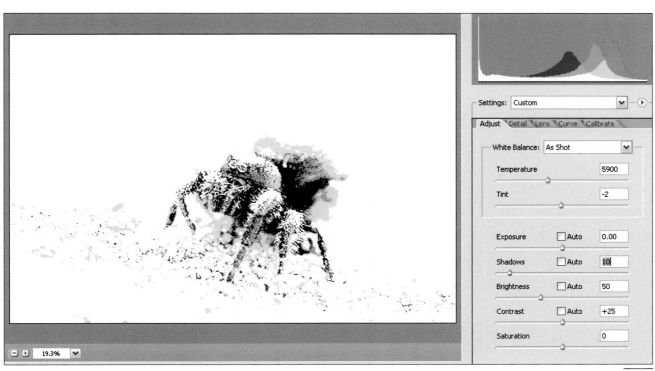

13-36

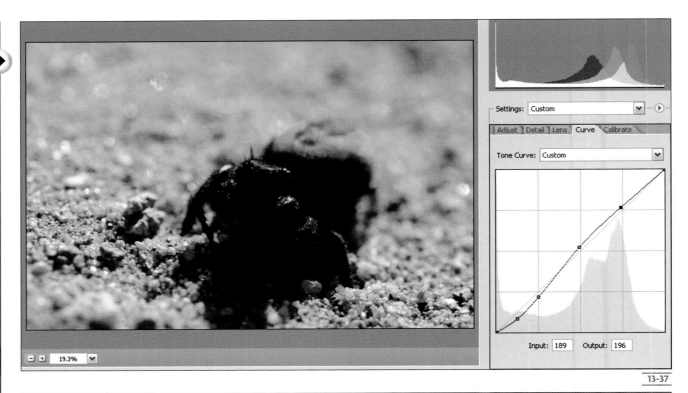

13-37

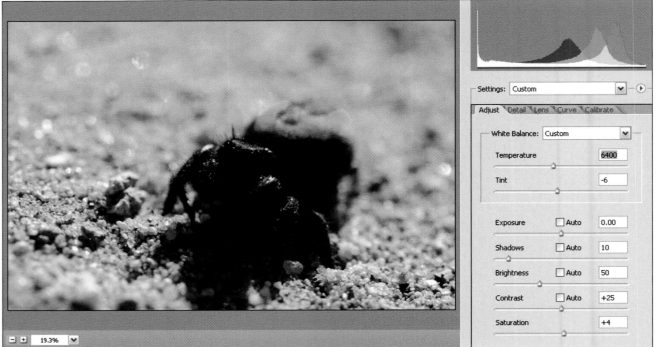

13-38

2. The Shadows control could be moved to the left slightly to make the blacks lighter, as shown in figure 13-39.

3. For the midtones, the Tone Curve is a huge help for dark areas like this. By clicking on the lowest parts of the curve and bringing those points up, the dark face of the spider really starts to light up (see figure 13-40). I also brought in the black corner point slightly from the left so that the blacks didn't turn gray. The rest of the photo gets way too bright, but that doesn't matter.

4. Color looks fine with the As Shot setting, as is Saturation. There isn't much color here to worry about except shades of dark gray.

5. All of this major dark area processing has once again made both color and luminance noise appear. There is some fine hair detail on the spider that affects how much noise adjustment can be made. Still, the photo can definitely use some noise suppression. A setting of about 20 seems to work for Luminance Smoothing and doesn't kill the hairs. Color Noise Reduction does not need a lot, maybe 7 or so (see figure 13-41).

6. Open the processed image into Photoshop and save it.

PUT THEM TOGETHER AGAIN

When doing photos like this, it is often most helpful to put the main photo, the one that has the best overall processing, on the bottom. This allows the detail photo to be blended in more easily because you can use Opacity controls to adjust how much of it is used.

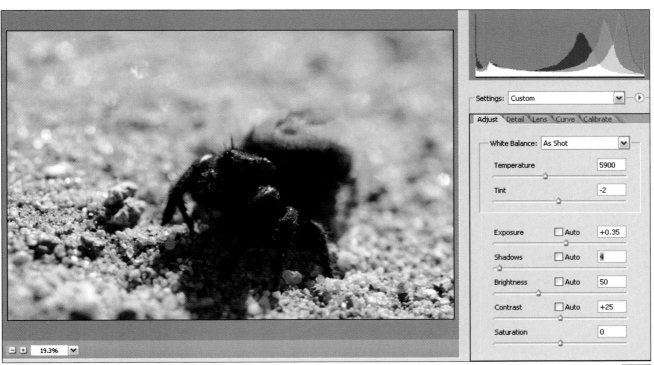

13-39

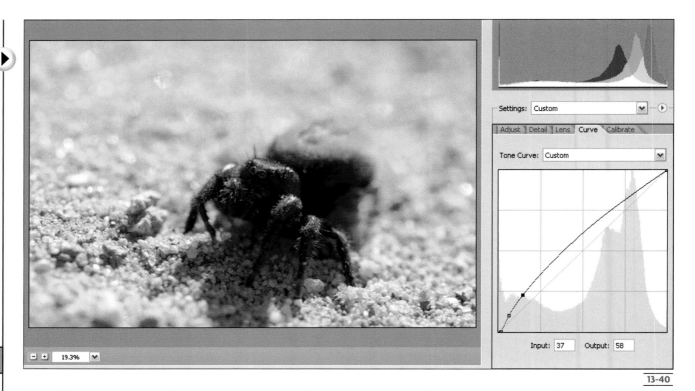

13-40

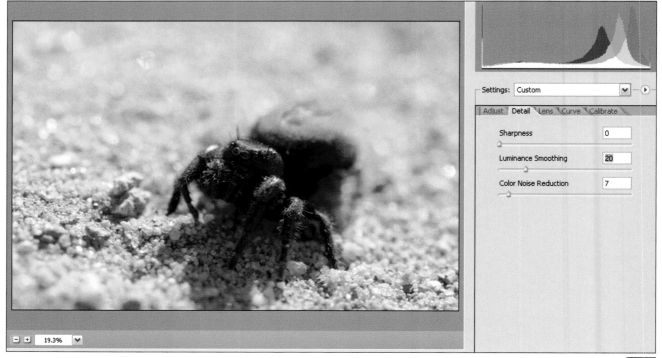

13-41

This presents a challenge, however, because the two processed images have the important details in a variety of areas. Here's how to deal with this:

1. As in the previous example, drag and drop the lighter, detail image onto the main photo (see figure 13-42) by using the Move tool and pressing and holding Shift as you move the photo from one file to the other.

2. Add a layer mask to the top layer, then hide it (in essence, removing it all) by filling the layer mask with black (choose Edit⇨Fill). You can actually add a black layer mask through the Layer menu (choose Layer⇨Layer Mask⇨Hide All) or by Alt/Option-clicking the layer mask icon at the bottom of the Layer palette. Figure 13-43 shows the black layer mask.

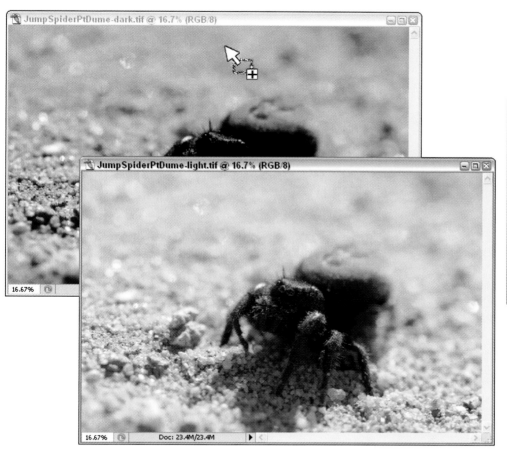

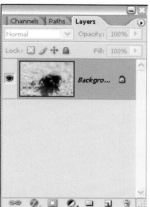

13-42

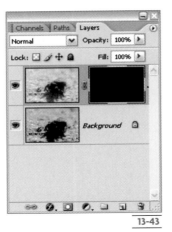

13-43

3. Paint in the detail. Here's where you can have a lot of fun. How much do you want to see of the specially processed detail? You paint that in with white on the layer mask wherever you want it. Use a soft-edged brush in a variety of sizes to bring in the details. If it starts to look overdone, change the brush to black and paint it back. You can even vary the opacity of the brush to help blend the two layers even more. This takes a bit of playing to make everything look right, as seen in figure 13-44. I pushed the lighting a bit under the spider so that the shadow is now technically uneven, but that was the only way to make the legs show up. I used as large a soft brush as I could there to make it blend.

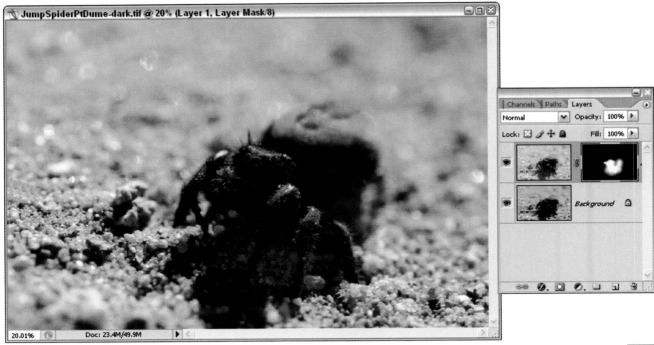

13-44

You can actually select the darkest areas of the bottom photo with the Color Range tool in the Select menu then fill that selection in the layer mask with white to reveal the dark details. This sometimes works, but usually it gives me too little control. I prefer to paint in and out the details I need. There is now a lot more detail in the dark part of the spider, yet the overall photo has not been compromised in tonality or color.

4. More detail in the dark areas can be pulled out of this spider. Duplicate the detail layer with its layer mask. Change the blending mode of the layer to Screen (modes are at the top left of the Layer palette), as

shown in figure 13-45. This immediately lightens the details even more. They get too bright, but are easily toned down with the Opacity control.

5. Flatten, sharpen, and save. You can now merge the two layers, sharpen the photo, and save it. You may also want to save an unsharpened version that can be later resized as needed, then sharpened to that specific size.

Compare again the single-processed (see figure 13-46) and double-processed (see figure 13-47) files. They are definitely different. The double-processed file allows the shadow area to have its own, more snappy adjustment so the face is more visible.

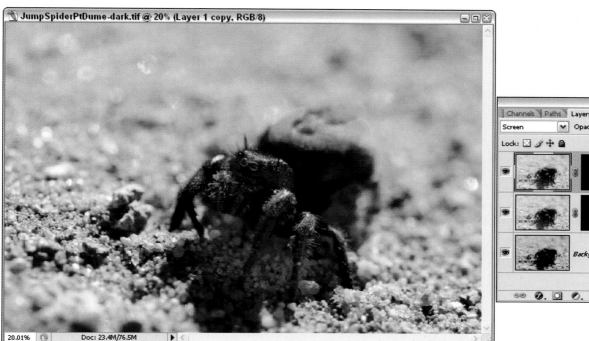

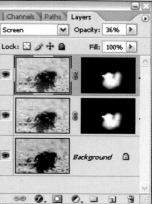

13-45

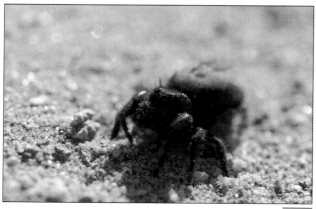

13-46

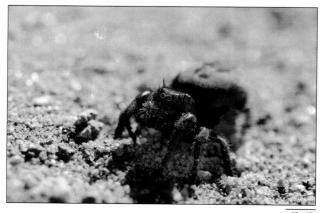

13-47

PRO TIP

Screen and Multiply are two layer modes that every photographer should know. Screen lightens the image in a very smart and attractive way depending on what is active in the Screen layer. Multiply darkens the image, also in a smart and attractive way depending on what is active in it. Screen is often used selectively to just lighten an overly dark part of a photo. Multiply is great to bring in detail in skies where it might not otherwise be seen.

DOUBLE-PROCESSING FOR COLOR

This double-processing technique works on more than tonal range challenges. It can be used with color problems. For example, you might have a scene with two different lights on it, and they are distracting. This might be an indoor scene with fluorescent lights in the center of the room and incandescent lights along the outer edges. The two colors do not look right together and cannot be adjusted in one pass through Camera Raw.

The answer is two passes. Process the image once the best you can and balance one color, ignoring the other. Then do the second processing to balance the other color. Now put the two images together just as you would do with exposure differences. This may take a little more work in painting in and out the different colors using a layer mask, but it works.

All of this is well and good if you have photographed a scene that fits within the dynamic range of the sensor. The world holds subjects that have tonal ranges from dark to white that go beyond what the sensor can handle. The human eye can see that range, but the sensor cannot. If you wanted to photograph that scene in the past, you had severe limitations as to what you could do:

> You could have created an image that favored the highlights and let the shadows go to impenetrable black (see figure 13-48).

> You could have created an image that favored the shadows and let the highlights go to blinding white (see figure 13-49).

> You could have tried some dramatic filtration if the filters fit the scene.

> You could have tried a flash if the dark area was small enough.

> You could have said, "Just forget it," and moved on to more profitable images.

With digital, you have another option. Take more than one exposure of the scene, one for the highlights and one for the shadows, for example, and then process them separately in Camera Raw to get the most from each. Bring the two images together in Photoshop for a new image that better represents the original scene than any single shot ever could. In addition, you almost never have problems with noise because each shot is exposed to optimally capture highlights and shadows.

It is interesting that Photoshop CS2 introduced a new feature, Merge to HDR (high dynamic range), which mathematically merges multiple exposures into one image with a huge dynamic range. This offers some new and interesting possibilities for the photographer, but it has a serious limitation. It merges everything into the whole image area. You have no ability to separately control how a dark area is processed compared to a bright area. The techniques described in this chapter give you more ability to make the photo communicate better as well as give you more creative capabilities. But HDR is new and may prove to be very valuable as everyone learns more how to get the most from it.

TWO-SHOT PROCESSING

Two-shot processing is exactly that: you take two shots of a scene with two different exposures. Next, you process each separately to get the most from each file (see figures 13-50 and 13-51). Then you bring them together to merge the best of both (see figure 13-52).

You can do this technique with multiple shots and bring them all together into one image, but most of the time, that is more an exercise in technique than any real benefit to the average photographer. I always try to balance workflow needs with technique. I am less interested in something that is going to take more time without a commensurate benefit.

While I have done this without a tripod, it is much easier with a tripod. A solid tripod allows you to shoot two consecutive images without the camera moving in between

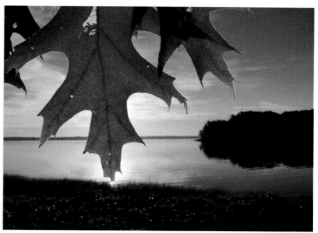

13-48

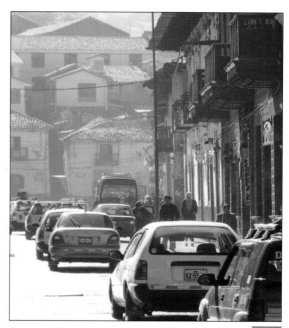

13-49

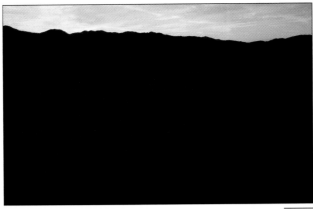

13-50

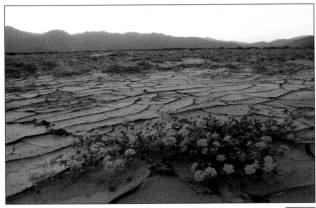

13-51

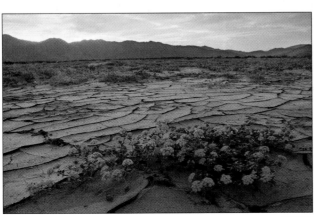

13-52

shots. That results in two images that line up perfectly in the computer, or at least they line up with minimal work. The procedure is fairly simple:

1. Lock down your camera on the correct composition.

2. Make one photograph that favors the highlights in exposure.

3. Make a second photograph that favors the dark parts of the exposure (or an important color or any other critical element of the image).

In the scene used in the next processing example, I came over some rocks near Point Dume in Malibu, California, to find this intense green algae on the big boulders at the ocean's edge (figure 13-53 is the final, processed shot). It

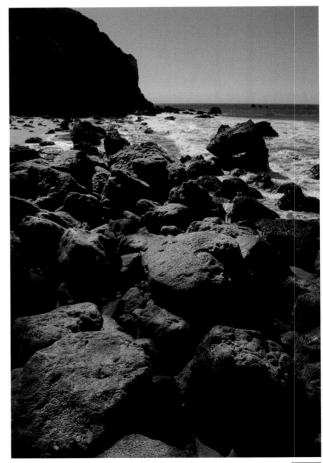

13-53

really was intense and overpowered any other impression. But in looking at the scene, I knew there was no way that an optimum exposure for the green of the algae would also give me anything but overexposed junk in the bright water above it. I wanted both, as that seemed to make the scene complete. The only way to accomplish this was with the two-exposure technique.

INTO CAMERA RAW

When you have two images of the same scene of different exposures (see figures 13-54 and 13-55), Camera Raw gives you the advantage of the best in processing so that

PRO TIP

One way of doing this technique quickly and easily is to use the auto bracketing function of your camera. Set it to do an auto bracket of at least half a stop between shots. That way, you set the camera to continuous shooting, press the shutter release, and the camera automatically takes three exposures. There will then be two shots that will be a full f-stop apart; you can discard the middle exposure. If the scene needs a greater range, set the auto bracket for a greater difference. You may also find you need to do some exposure compensation before auto bracketing, too. The advantage of using auto bracket is that you don't have to move anything on the camera between shots.

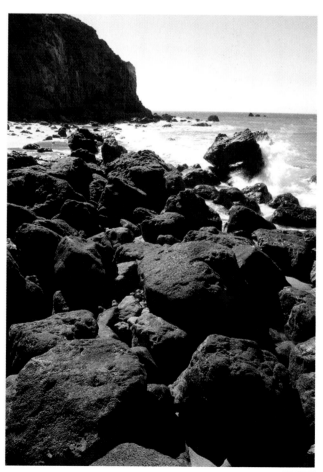

13-54

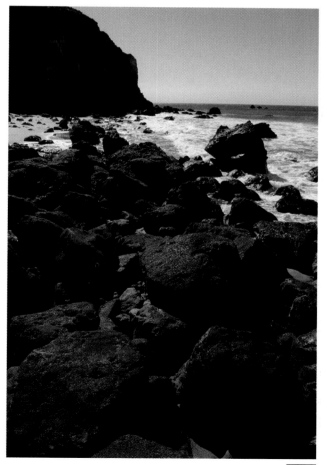

13-55

you can really get the most from each exposure. I'll quickly go through this to optimize both images. The lighter image needs to be processed to get the most from the green rocks:

1. Ignore the overexposed water and sky at the top of the image to get a good highlight brightness in the green. It does not have to have any pure white, but Exposure is used to lift the brightest spots.

2. This is a bright, sunny day with dark shadows. The shadows can be made richer and blacker, which actually make the green show up more strongly (see figure 13-56).

3. Brightness is okay to brighten the color slightly, but the Tone Curve works much better to give some definition and richness to the color (see figure 13-57).

4. There is no question that the color saturation needs to be kicked up. This color was really intense when seen in real life. You have to be careful with the Saturation slider, however, because you can block up details if it is moved too far to the right. In addition, moving the Temperature slider a bit to the right (warming up the

green) and the Tint slider to the left (adding green) also helps enrich the color. All color adjustments are seen in figure 13-58.

5. The image is very clean. There is no reason to do anything with the Detail tab.

6. Open the processed image into Photoshop and save it.

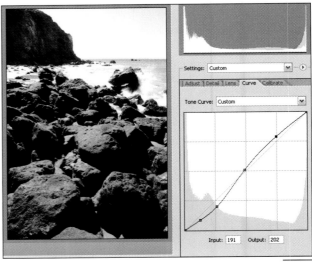

13-57

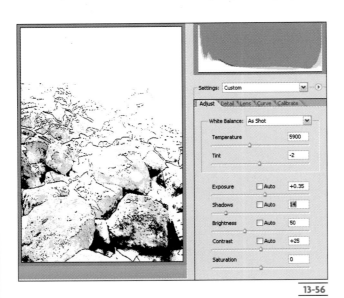

13-56

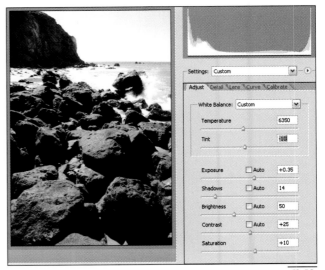

13-58

This processed-light exposure really looks terrible in the water and sky areas as shown in figure 13-59. Even if you tried, you would not be able to get good surf detail out of this Raw file.

But that is why the second exposure was taken. Adjust the darker photo to favor the water and sky:

1. The Exposure slider was slightly to the left to darken the highlights even more (see figure 13-60). I did not want the bright water to overpower the green of the rocks in any way. A by-the-rules processing of this file makes the water too bright for the scene. When I was there, the green truly visually overpowered the water, so to make the water overpower the green would do a disservice to the real landscape.

2. I like the effect of moving the Shadows slider to the right a bit to make the rocks dark and dramatic in the upper part of the photo (see figure 13-61).

3. The Brightness slider works fine for this image. I moved it to the left to darken the midtones in the water a bit. Remember, I am working this image for the highlights, but these highlights must balance with the green algae.

4. Adding some Saturation boosts the color of the sky and the sand in the small beach area. I felt that gave some color richness that would balance the green rocks. I debated about the White Balance settings a little. I like the cold feeling of the sky in the As Shot setting, but eventually decided that increasing the Temperature a little made the scene look more like a warm, sunny day (see figure 13-62).

5. Because each exposure is shot to optimize a certain part of the scene, noise should always be minimal. None was needed here.

6. Open the processed image into Photoshop and save it.

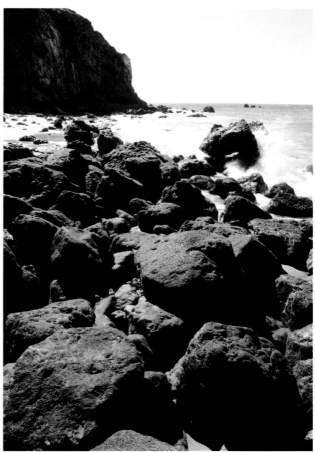

13-59

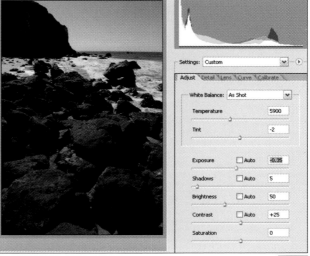

13-60

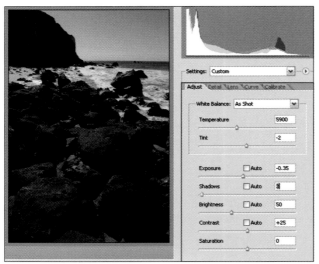

13-61

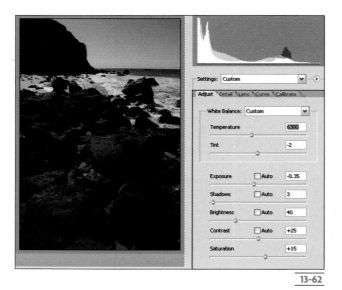

13-62

This processed dark exposure now looks terrible in the rock and algae areas, as shown in figure 13-63. Even if you tried, you would not be able to get the best green color out of this Raw file.

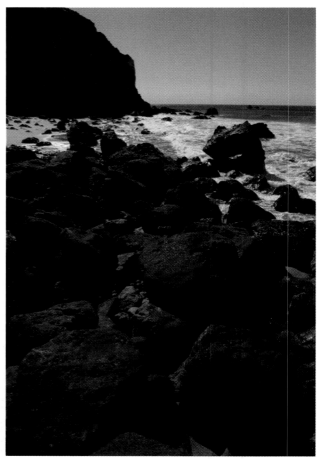

13-63

MAKING THE PHOTO WORK

The rest of the process is based on the same technique used in the combinations of two photos described earlier in this chapter. It is very important to note, however, that this is not an arbitrary, absolute process. It is totally flexible and should always be adapted to both the images you are working with and the interpretation of those images.

Any processing you do of a photo is always an interpretation of the original image. It can be an interpretation based on reality or something entirely different. Ansel Adams used to compare this to music. The negative was

the score, the unrealized notations of sound, while the print was the performance of that score. This definitely applies to a Raw file; it can also be compared to the score, while the finished image coming from Camera Raw and Photoshop is the performance.

Here's how these two rocky shoreline images could be interpreted:

1. First, the images have to be put together. It seems appropriate to reveal the green into the darker image. This is done by dragging the brighter image onto the dark version, as shown in figure 13-64.

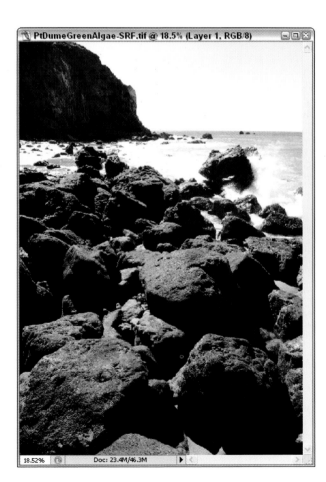

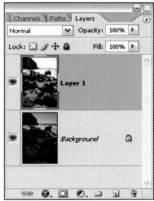

13-64

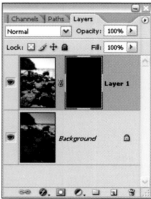
2. Add layer mask to the light layer, but use a black-filled mask to hide the layer's effects (choose Layer⇨Layer Mask⇨Hide All), as shown in figure 13-65.

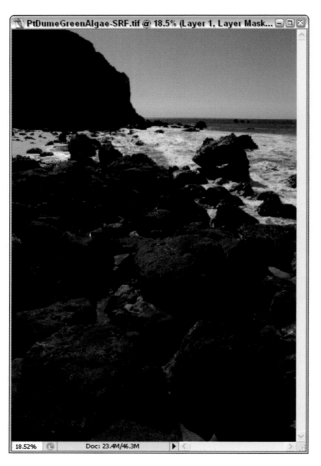

13-65

3. Paint in the areas needed. Use a large, soft brush to paint in white onto the layer mask. This gradually blends in the green from the top layer. You can paint in whatever you want. I tried to be fairly selective and limit my painting to the green parts of the rocks, as seen in progress in figure 13-66.

PRO TIP

It might seem like a dark image should go on top (it would if you were only erasing parts of it to reveal the color underneath). But with the bright color as a layer on top, that layer can always be reduced in intensity by using the Opacity slider. You can then reveal a layer gradually by adding a layer mask filled with black and painting white to gradually show it.

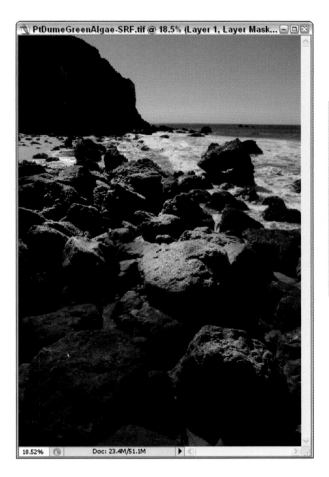

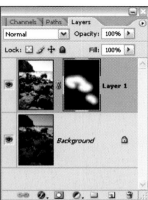

13-66

4. Refine the layer mask. Change your brush size and go back and forth between white and black to refine what is seen and not seen in the top layer. This is where the interpretation of the scene gains strong importance. Work quickly; don't think too much about it, but enlarge the image as needed to deal with smaller details as shown in figure 13-67. You can quickly change your brush back and forth from black to white by pressing X. You can also change the intensity of the painting by altering the opacity setting of the brush. For example, I found the green in the center of the rocks to be a bit bright, so I toned it down with a 10 percent setting of a black brush.

5. Check the overall relationship between the layers. In this case, I felt the green algae layer was a little out of balance compared to the darker, surf layer, so I brought down the opacity to 90 percent. Another

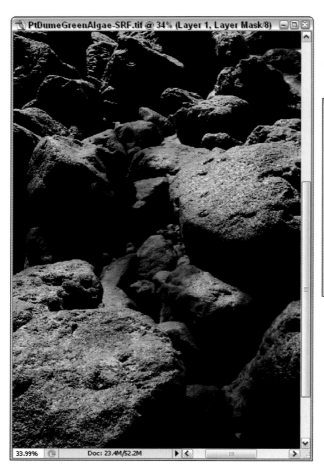

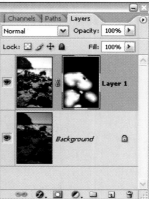

13-67

possibility would be to put a Curves layer in between these layers to adjust the bottom layer without affecting the top.

6. Flatten, sharpen, and save. You can now merge the two layers, sharpen the photo, and save it. You may also want to save an unsharpened version that can be later resized as needed, then sharpened to that specific size.

This photo now looks like the green algae is spotlighted as demonstrated by figure 13-68, but truly, this is exactly how it appeared to me. The water has excellent detail, as does the green algae on the rocks. The background cliff looked good to me dark, so I left it. However, it could have been lightened with the rocks by painting it in from the light layer.

There is no way that you can get the richness of color in the green as well as the dark, dramatic rocks and detailed surf by shooting only one exposure of this scene. Shooting two, both in Raw, offers the possibility of really showing off this scene as it appears, not reduced in intensity due to the limitations of the medium.

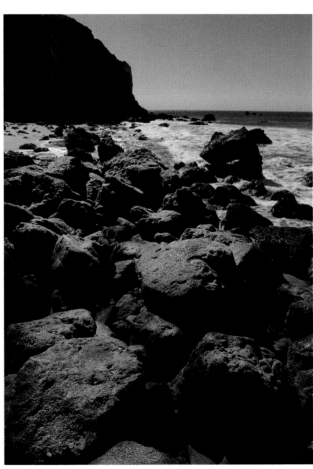

13-68

What if the two image versions I process for the double-processing technique have some parts that aren't quite their best, even though most of the image works right?

This can happen. Camera Raw can only deal with the overall image. Even when you are processing an image twice, you can find that such processing still doesn't make everything look right. You have a few choices:

> Process the image again for a third version and combine that with the other two in Photoshop.

> Process only two versions, but keep both in 16-bit and do some selective tweaking of the layers in Photoshop. This is easy to do by using an adjustment layer and a layer mask to control where the small adjustments occur.

> Process only two versions, but use 8-bit and do some selective tweaking of the layers in Photoshop. This offers a little less control, but 16-bit can have a severe memory penalty (it uses RAM in a hurry). For many images, 8-bit is fine, and still offers excellent control with an adjustment layer, but doesn't cause memory problems.

You mention processing the image for a third version. I believe that works for exposures, too, that you can get an even greater tonal range with three exposures. What do you have to watch out for when putting more layers together?

You are absolutely right; three exposures of a scene can be used. Even more if you are so inclined to deal with very large brightness ranges. This is essentially what is automated in the new HDR tool, but that tool gives you none of the control that you have seen in this chapter.

You do put your three (or more) versions of your scene together into one image with layers (dragging and dropping just as with two images). Now it becomes a little like the 3D chess they played on Star Trek — as you paint in and out one layer, then another, they start interacting with each other. It can be done, but it can also be a lot of work.

It seems that as you adjust an image one way in Camera Raw to be used with another adjusted version of the same image, it would be good to see both. Can you do that?

At this time, not really. You can do a work-around with the two-exposure technique by bringing the two different exposures into Camera Raw at the same time as described in Chapter 12. You can then click back and forth between them as they are adjusted. That will reveal the images in the Preview and show how they are different.

But you cannot do the same with double processing of the same image, though there is also a work-around, but it is a little awkward. It so happens that once you open Photoshop and go to Camera Raw, Photoshop sits in the background, unusable by you, but still there. If you process your first adjusted version and open it into Photoshop, it will also sit there. Now when you have Camera Raw opened, you can grab the top of its interface and move the whole thing, even until you reveal the first version now in Photoshop. You can make needed comparisons, then move the Camera Raw interface back into place so you can access all of its controls.

Chapter 14

POST CAMERA RAW PROCESSING

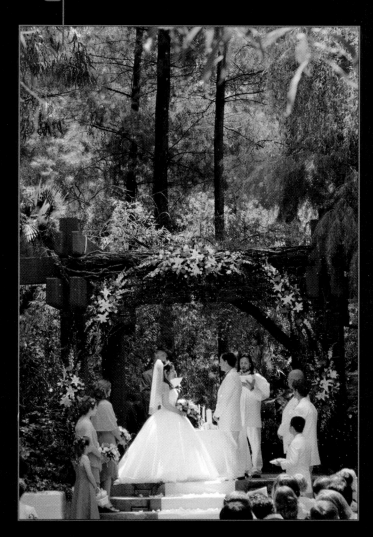

Once you process a photo in Camera Raw, you are not done. Camera Raw is a step on the route to a final image, though admittedly an important step. You may be very close to done, requiring but a few moments to finish the image, or you may have much work to do. But you will always have something more to do for a number of reasons.

> Camera Raw cannot selectively process areas of an image as you have seen throughout this book.

> Because you will always resize and sharpen an image for the best quality when the photo is needed for different purposes, you will do this in Photoshop, not Camera Raw.

> There are some things better done in Photoshop (or even other programs), such as strong noise reduction.

> Some of the strongest adjustments for tonal balancing, eye-control (how an image is adjusted to affect how a viewer sees it), composition enhancement, and more are best done in Photoshop. The image seen in figure 14-1 is processed overall in Camera Raw; 14-2 has been adjusted for specific or local areas in Photoshop.

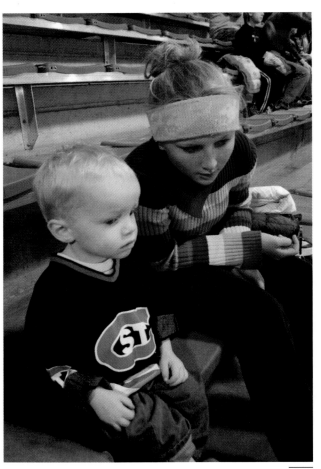

14-1

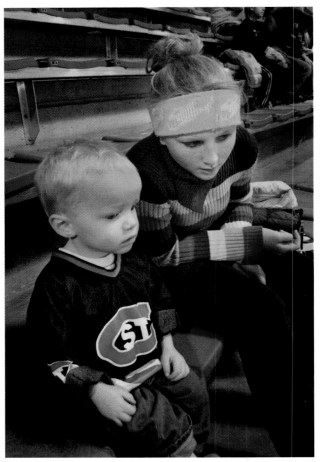

14-2

You can find many excellent books on every nook and cranny of the inner workings of Photoshop, so this chapter on post-Camera Raw processing is not meant to compete with any of them. But finishing a book on Camera Raw without a discussion of the interpretation of that file in Photoshop seems a serious omission. That is part of the process, especially for me, and to leave it out would leave the whole workflow discussion incomplete.

I have no intention of offering every possibility for post Camera Raw processing. I want to leave you with some ideas and ways of thinking about that stage of image work. I have found them very useful and helpful to me and offer them to you in the hope that you may also find them helpful and useful.

ANSEL ADAMS AND IMAGE PROCESSING

I consider Ansel Adams and his classic books, The Negative and The Print, to be very important for the digital photographer. As a Camera Raw and Photoshop user, you are not going to need to read these books from cover to cover for great tips. Much of the books cover such things as darkroom chemicals and how to process film and prints differently — not much use for the digital darkroom.

However, what Adams offers is his analysis of his photographs — why he shot something a certain way, how he printed it in the darkroom, what was dodged, what was burned, how contrast was used, and so on. All of these things can be applied to the photograph in Camera Raw and Photoshop.

Adams, as you probably know, would spend days on a photograph in his darkroom getting it right. A lot of that time was used for experimenting, processing the prints, drying them, examining them carefully, then making changes, and starting the process over. In Photoshop, you can do in minutes much of what would have taken him hours.

His books bring up a very interesting approach to Photoshop, too, believe it or not. Consider all that work in the darkroom was based on a very limited set of actions: Adams could make an image lighter or darker, give it more or less contrast, and then he could control local or limited parts of the image in those ways as well. Yet with that limited set of actions, Adams created wonderful images.

The point is that you don't have to know everything about Photoshop in order to use it well. Thinking how to interpret your photo plus using a core set of tools to do that interpretation is far more important. It is the application of Photoshop tools rather than the number of tools you know that will make your image better. Knowing certain Photoshop tools can be useful when you have specific needs, and many of the tools make the work easier, but few photographers need to know everything about Photoshop in order to use it well.

WHAT'S A GOOD IMAGE, ANYWAY?

As you may guess from what I've said in earlier chapters, I am not one for absolute answers about photography. One thing I certainly don't believe is that a good image can be contained by arbitrary definitions. As soon as someone says a photo should be this or that, be wary — even if it comes from an author telling you about Camera Raw! Some of the interpretations you have seen in this book might indeed be differently interpreted by you and would result in perfectly good images.

One thing I will particularly warn you about is what I call the tyranny of matching the monitor. I have seen a lot of photographers work too hard at matching what they saw on the monitor in a print, getting the print close, and then being very proud of how good that print was. There are several things wrong with that idea:

> Monitor calibration is to make your image processing consistent and predictable, which will make your prints better, but is not designed to make them match the monitor.

> Monitors and prints have different color gamuts — one holds glowing colors, the other pigmented reflective colors.

> Monitors and prints are designed for entirely different viewing experiences. So far, few people hang their computer monitors on the wall the way a print is hung!

> People respond very differently to monitors and prints.

> A print should stand on its own. No one is going to ask you to turn on your monitor to see if it matches it.

An image that looks good on the computer and is matched well in the print might not be the best print because of all of these reasons. The brilliant black-and-white photographer and master printer John Sexton once told me that one problem he saw with a lot of digital prints is that the photographer tried to do it all in one print and didn't make prints that could be evaluated as prints early enough in the process. He felt the printing process, even from a computer, demanded making prints, looking at them as prints, then making changes to make them better prints, not simply getting the best image on the monitor then making a print.

So what is a good print or image of any type? I believe a good image is a photograph that you like, that does what you expect of it in terms of color and composition, that communicates your intent, that does not get in the way of

why you took the photo and has some impact on the viewer. A good photograph is not necessarily something that everyone likes as people have different tastes. I can guarantee you that even though I like the spider photograph in Chapter 13, there are a lot of people who will never like it, no matter how much I work on it.

EXPRESSING WHAT YOU WANT

Back to Ansel Adams for a moment. In his book, The Print, he says, "Exposure and development of the negative follow technical patterns selected to achieve the qualities desired in the final print..." — in other words, paying attention to exposure and key technical aspects of the image (such as blacks in the shadows and details in the highlights) comes first as you've seen throughout this book. He continues, "...and the print itself is somewhat of an interpretation, a performance of the photographic idea." In other words, you the photographer take that exposure and technique to create or "perform" an image that interprets or expresses something important to you. Figures 14-3, 14-4, and 14-5 show three different expressions of the same image, different versions that cannot be made from Camera Raw alone.

How do you evaluate an image for interpretation? That is certainly up to the individual, but here are some things to consider:

> **Balance.** How are tones balanced in the image? This was a basic consideration of the black-and-white darkroom worker. You would never see a composition that favored the subject graphically but emphasized something else based on tonalities in the past. Yet, that is all too common, even among news photography that should balance tones so the news is communicated clearly.

> **Composition.** Can you adjust colors or tones to emphasize your composition?

> **Mood.** What kind of a mood do you think your scene expresses? Can you use darker or lighter tonalities to emphasize that?

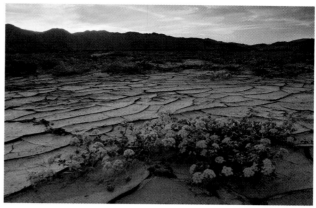

14-3

> **Color interactions.** While it is true that you can totally change colors in Photoshop, for most photographers, that is an exercise, not something they really need. I am talking more about how the subject and scene colors react with each other. For example, for a sunset-lit scene, the shadows might be intensified in their blue component and the highlights in their yellow/red component so the scene's colors look richer. In another example, a brightly colored background might be desaturated slightly so that it doesn't compete with the subject.

> **Eye-control.** Adams talked a lot about this. Photographs are always visually flatter than the scene because they are two-dimensional compared to three-dimensional reality. This results in two things: the eye tends to go off the edges of the photo, and the eye wanders the imaged scene more than in real life. In the first case, the answer is the traditional darkening of the edges (especially brighter edges) of a black-and-white print (this can easily be applied to images in Photoshop). In the second, the answer is selective lightening and darkening of photo elements to better express the scene to the viewer.

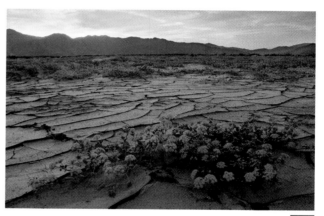

14-4

INTERPRETING AN IMAGE

The photo seen in figure 14-6 is from some friends' beautiful outdoor wedding and is processed as far as possible in Camera Raw. You've seen all the steps throughout the book, so I won't show all that again as there is nothing

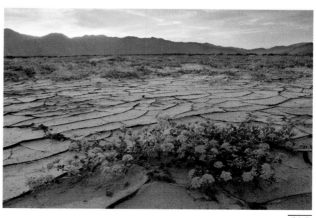

14-5

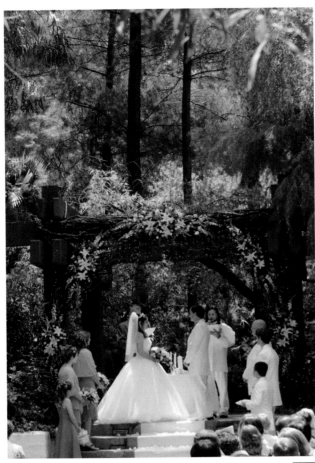

14-6

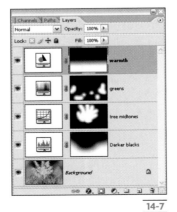

14-7

unique about processing this particular image. As it stands, it looks good as seen in figure 14-6, and it is perfectly usable in many applications. It has good tonalities from dark to light, and the color looks right. But now you'll see how this can be made a more expressive and richer image.

My process is simple in its use, but requires thought in its application to specific images. I use mainly adjustment layers to control specific tonalities and colors in the image, keeping each specific change to the image isolated to its own adjustment layer as demonstrated by the illustration in figure 14-7. This allows a huge amount of control. Consider this: As one part of the photo is changed, that change often affects another part of the image, so to bring them back in balance, a compensating adjustment is needed. If that compensation is just a resetting of an adjustment layer, you have no image quality loss, and you can always go back to original pixels (adjustment layers do not change the original pixels).

Also, the process is always an evolving one because one change will affect another. As you work one part of an image, you'll realize that another part needs some work, too. This does not have to be a chore. Adjustment layers with their layer masks and settable opacity levels let you do this very quickly. You can quickly control where the adjustment appears in the image by painting black or white in or out of the layer mask (as was done in Chapter 13). This is far, far faster and easier than using a selection tool to carefully isolate parts of a photo and adjusting each selection separately (whether on a layer or not). Selection tools can help in using layer masks, but whenever I can avoid using them, I do, because they can take so much time to deal with.

For the wedding image, I noted several things right away. The top of the photo is brighter than the bottom. While the white clothes of the wedding party attract the eye, the composition is not served by that tonal difference. The eye definitely wants to wander up into the trees. Not a bad thing, necessarily, if you wanted a photo that emphasized the setting over the wedding party, but I wanted to interpret this image so as to emphasize the wedding party as part of the setting.

Sometimes I add a Levels adjustment layer just to check to be sure where my blacks and whites appear in the photo. Checking black and white areas of a photo is part of the process of using Camera Raw, but once you go beyond that initial work, you may decide you want another interpretation of the photo's blacks, for example, when you see it open in Photoshop (that may seem odd, but the interfaces are very different and can influence how you see a photo). I didn't feel this was needed here.

This is how I proceeded:

1. Tone down the top. The first thing is to add a Brightness/Contrast layer (if you stopped reading in shock, check the previous Pro Tip) as shown in figure 14-8. The top of the image needs to be darkened, so you make a guess at how much to darken by moving the Brightness slider to the left (this is easily and quickly readjusted if the guess is wrong). The whole photo goes dark.

2. Next, the bottom of the photo needs to have that adjustment removed by use of the layer mask. The gradient tool is ideal for this. By having the tool go black to white (foreground/background colors), the cursor can be clicked at the top of the arbor and dragged up into the trees above. A longer drag blends the tones more and is often needed. This immediately helps balance the photo better (see figure 14-9).

PRO TIP

There is a Brightness/Contrast adjustment layer being used for good reason. I know that you have probably heard that you should never, never use the Brightness/Contrast control. And for overall adjustment of an image, I totally agree. It is a rather blunt instrument that does not allow for subtleties. It is perfect to use as a way of darkening parts of an image exactly because it is so blunt. When Adams and other darkroom workers darkened a part of a photo, they darkened it all by burning in that area and didn't try to affect varied tonalities differently. That's exactly what the Brightness/Contrast adjustment layer does and it does it simply and easily.

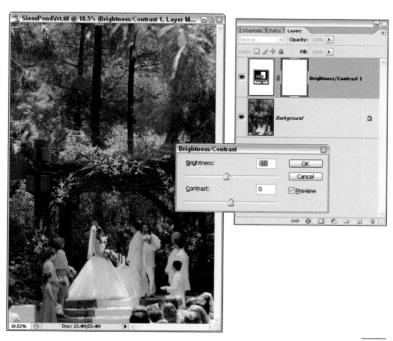

14-8

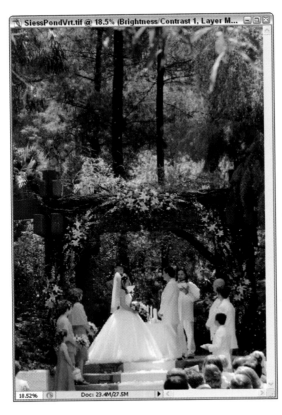

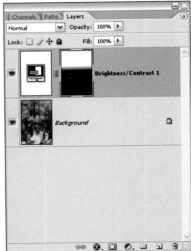

14-9

3. Tone down bright areas. There are some bright areas that need additional toning down as they stand out too much from the first adjustment. These are in the top of the image such as the backlit leaves above the arbor, but also include hot spots of brightness throughout the image. Again, a Brightness/Contrast layer is added and used to darken the image. The best way to deal with small areas of adjustment like this is to fill the layer mask with black (choose Edit⇨Fill⇨Black; this hides its effect) then paint in the effect with white only where needed. I vary the Opacity of the brush to vary the strength of the effect. For example, the leaves above the arbor get 100 percent but the light area of trees a little above it gets a much reduced amount. The layer mask is really getting a workout and starts to look like a star field as seen in figure 14-10.

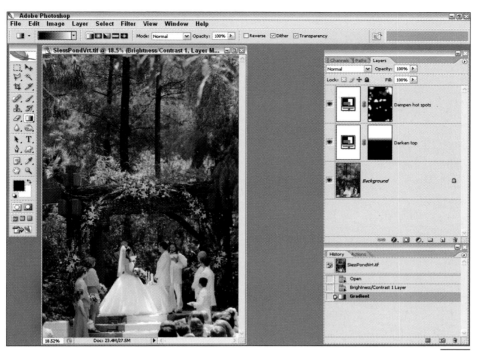

14-10

4. Make readjustments. Being able to readjust on the fly makes this so much easier than the process Ansel Adams had to follow. He would make a change to his image during the exposure of the print, then have to process the whole thing for many minutes to evaluate the results. You can make a change and instantly see the effect. The toning down of bright areas in Steps 1, 2, and 3 helped those areas and balanced the photo better. But it seems that the whole photo lost a little of its feeling of brightness. This is not something that is easy to predict when processing an image in Camera Raw. You have to see how the various changes interact with each other. So I added a Curves adjustment layer and opened up the image until it looked better, as seen in figure 14-11.

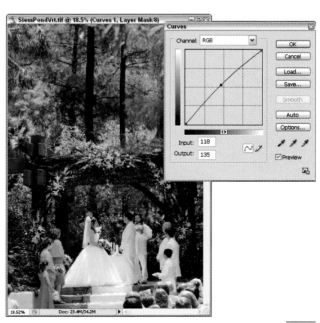

14-11

5. Brighten the arbor flowers. The arbor flowers are quite nice and deserve some more attention. First, a Curves adjustment layer is added to brighten the area. I find Curves works better for lightening an area because Brightness/Contrast-lightened areas often appear to have weak-looking contrast. The layer mask is filled with black and the effect painted in only where desired along the route of the flowers, shown in figure 14-12. You will need to constantly change the size of your brush as you do this type of work. I use the bracket keys to the right

of the P on the keyboard. Press [to make the brush smaller; press] to make it bigger. In addition, it is helpful to go back and forth between white and black to paint affected areas in and out. Press X to change the foreground or background colors instantly.

Next, a Hue/Saturation adjustment layer is added to brighten the colors of the flowers (see figure 14-13). After boosting Saturation about 10 points, the layer mask is filled with black, and once again, the effect painted in with white.

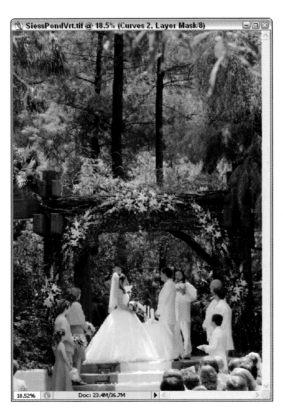

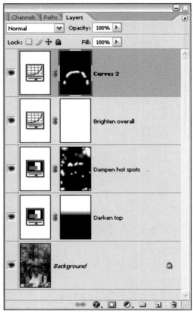

14-12

6. I was still not completely satisfied with the flowers on the arbor. I felt the top blended too much with the background, so I felt a little traditional Ansel Adams-style burning in or darkening of the leaves above would help. In this case, I needed to drop the brightness without hurting the feeling of bright leaves. I added a Levels adjustment layer and clicked okay without changing anything (I could have used any adjustment layer for this effect). The mode for the layer is changed to Multiply, which darkens everything, so the layer mask is filled with black, and once

again, the effect painted in with white over the top flowers, as seen in figure 14-14.

7. Readjust. At this point, the arbor below the flowers looks too light. Go back to the first darkening adjustment layer to paint in that darkness in the arbor so that it is balanced with the latest adjustments (figure 14-15). You can see this way of working an image in Photoshop is a continually balancing process. It takes much longer to describe here than to actually do it. With a little practice, you will find this goes very fast.

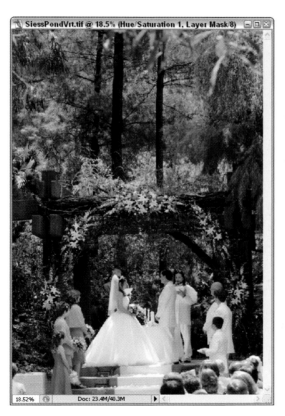

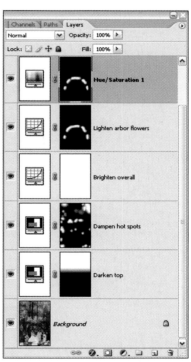

14-13

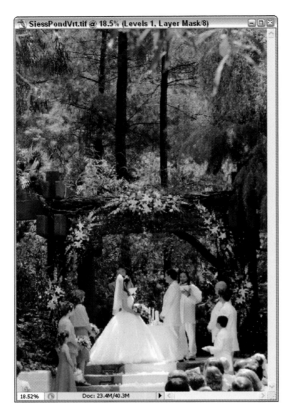

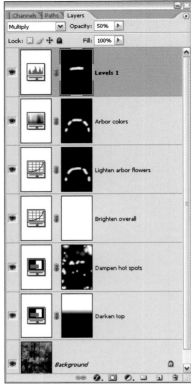

14-14

8. Highlight the subject. Be sure the subject — the bride and groom — stand out from the crowd, so to speak. Lightening this subject is the wrong thing to do. To make them stand out, other areas must be toned down, such as the bridal party around them. This time, I use a Curves adjustment layer rather than Brightness/Contrast. I did this because I wanted more control. I wanted to be sure the colors of the bridesmaids' dresses did not get muddy, for example, which Brightness/Contrast can do. The layer mask is once again filled with black to turn off its effect, and then white painted in to add darkness only to those areas

that need it (see figure 14-16). The brush is a large one (as seen by the circle) — a large, soft brush gives a nice blended edge to the brush strokes. You might ask why not go back to the first darkening Brightness/Contrast layer to do this darkening? My answer, as you may have guessed from most of this book, is control. I want to control these areas totally separately and be able to make adjustments to the layer independently of any other layer, as well as being able to use exactly the right type of layer for each adjustment.

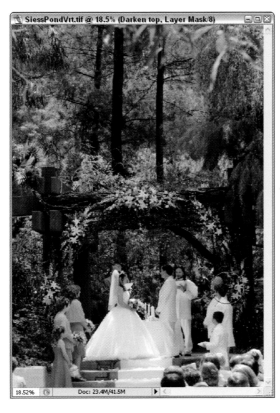
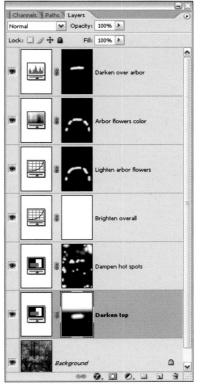

14-15

9. Darken the bottom corners of the photo, which are still a little bright; they are important to the composition because they show there were people at this wedding. Again, the Brightness/Contrast adjustment layer comes out for a little darkening work. This time, the Brightness slider is moved to the left to darken the photo and the Contrast slider is also moved to the left to lower the contrast (darkening an area and reducing its contrast is a common painter's technique to reduce emphasis on an area). The astute Photoshop user will note that something similar to this is also possible with Curves, but the amount of work needed for the same effect is increased, and I am never in favor of more work for the same results. Once again, the layer mask is filled with black and the darkened corners painted in with white (see figure 14-17).

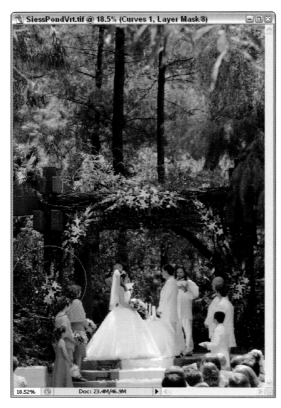

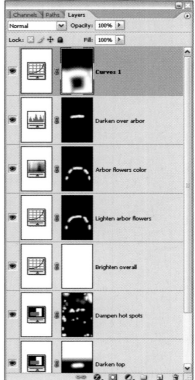

14-16

10. Brighten the faces. Overall, the image has come much closer to the photograph I saw when I made it. However, in looking closely, I noticed the bride, groom, and the man speaking had darker faces than needed. There are a lot of ways to fix that. Selecting the faces, however, is not a workflow I would recommend. Using a layer of gray set to overlay and painting dark or light to dodge and burn is an option, but it is too heavy handed for good face tones in this photo, in my opinion. So I went with a Curves adjustment layer. I found the actual point on the curve where the faces were by pressing and holding Ctrl/⌘ and

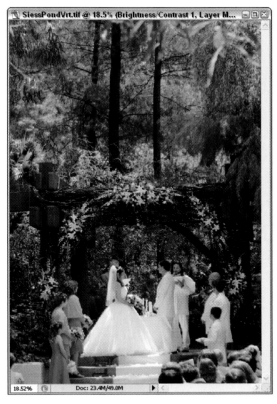
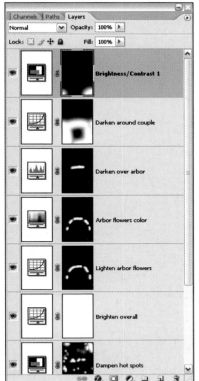

14-17

clicking on the face as seen in figure 14-18. This sets a control point on the curve that corresponds exactly to the point. I lifted that point to brighten the faces and brought down the lower part of the curve to keep contrast strong. The whole photo looks ugly with that adjustment, but a quick fill of black turns it off, and then a small white paintbrush brings it in on the faces, as seen in figure 14-19. The cool thing about this technique is that you don't need to spend a lot of time outlining the faces as long as the brush is soft. You just paint, and if it is off a little, change the brush to black, reduce its size, and fix it.

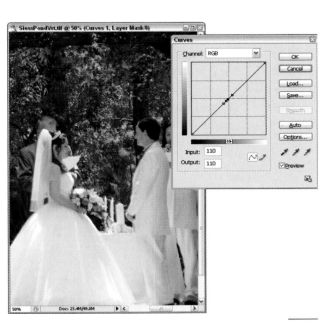

14-18

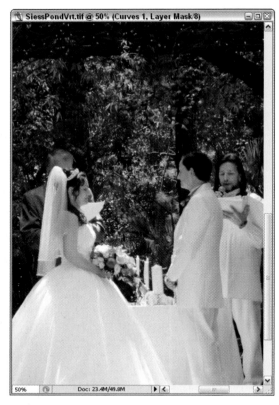

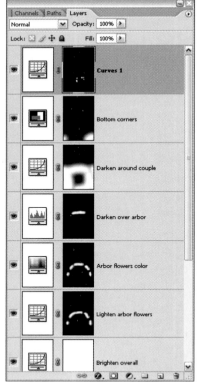

14-19

Compare the photos now in the before, figure 14-20, and the after, figure 14-21, and you see a distinctive change in emphasis. Nothing has changed in the original scene. No truths were manipulated, no falsities added. In fact, I would argue that the image is now truer to the original scene as perceived by the participants as the final shot

truly gives emphasis within the frame to how one would really view such a scene. Notice how the eye goes quickly to the bride and groom in that shot compared to the before image. The camera's interpretation is a rather artificial and flat version that is its own way of capturing the world, but not necessarily more real than what we see.

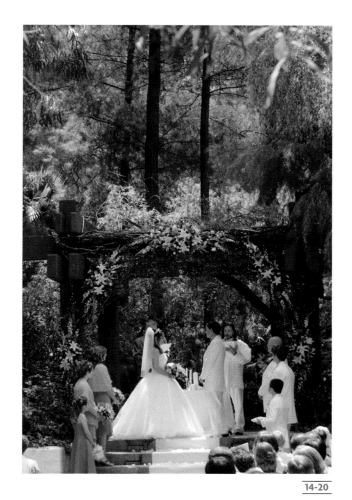

14-20

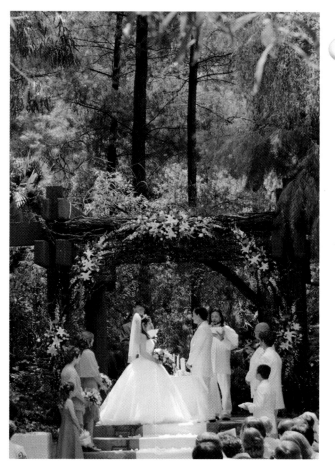

14-21

SHARPENING

Again, this is not a complete guide to Photoshop book, but because I told you early on not to use the sharpening in Camera Raw, I need to at least wrap up the sharpening discussion here so the process is complete. If you want a more detailed discussion of sharpening, you can find that in most Photoshop books. The bottom line is that you need to do some sharpening of your digital images. You may already know this, but because it is still a big misconception by many photographers, sharpening the processed photo is not about making an unsharp photo sharp but only about bringing out the inherent sharpness of the original image as captured by your camera and lens. The name of the key sharpening tool, Unsharp Mask, confuses the issue (although the name actually comes from a true process for sharpening that was commonly used by the printing industry).

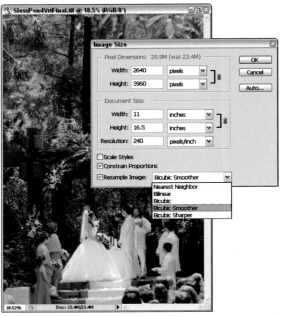

14-22

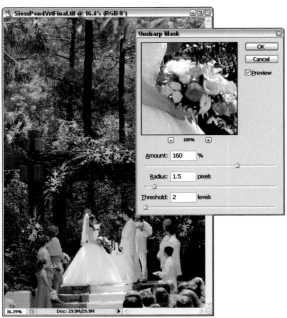

14-23

There are two key parts to sharpening:

> Size your image to its usage (see figure 14-22).

> Use Unsharp Mask as your sharpening tool (see figure 14-23).

Unsharp Mask has three controls for sharpening: Amount, Radius, and Threshold, as seen in figure 14-24. You will find a huge range of ways that photographers use these controls, and you will also discover that some folks are quite passionate about their particular recipe. I have found that all of them usually work great for those photographers' work, and may or may not work equally well for others. I will give you some numbers that work for me, and you can try them to see how they perform for your images.

Unsharp Mask looks for contrasting edges in an image and adjusts them to increase the appearance of sharpness. Amount is the intensity of the sharpening on that edge; Radius is how far Photoshop will look for edge differences; and Threshold tells Photoshop at what point to start changing those edges. Any recipe for these controls is always based on numbers for all three because you can't adjust one without affecting the others.

I tend to prefer an Amount typically between 130 and 180 percent depending on the detail in the image (which is also affected by the size of the photo — small photos will get even less). Except for very small photos, I usually choose a Radius between 1 and 2 pixels. Radius is strongly affected by the file size of the image. For file sizes (opened in Photoshop; the flattened size, not the layer size) of approximately 10 to 20 megabytes, I commonly use something between 1 and 1.5 pixels. For larger files, I will go up to 2, but rarely higher.

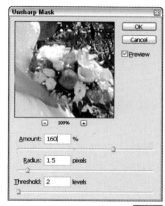

14-24

You can consider the Threshold the noise sharpening control. With more noise, more Threshold is needed up to about 10 to 12 (more than that and you will have some real sharpening challenges). As Threshold increases, you will usually need to increase the Amount, too. For most digital camera shots with low noise, I typically choose a Threshold between 0 and 3. The best way to see this is to click your cursor on an area without much detail, such as the sky, and see what noise shows up in the Unsharp Mask preview image. With moderate noise, a Threshold from 4 to 6 or so often works. For high noise, you may need to go as high as 12. If that is still a problem, then you may want to consider some noise-reduction software.

One easy way of getting great sharpening results without having to deal with all of these choices is to use the plugin from nik multimedia called nik Sharpener Pro (see figure 14-25). This is a very intuitive sharpening tool that allows you to choose how large the image will be, how it will be used, on what type of paper, and so forth, as well as how strong you like to sharpen. In the latest version, it even lets you control how sharpening affects different tones and colors in the image, which can be a great benefit for dealing with noise.

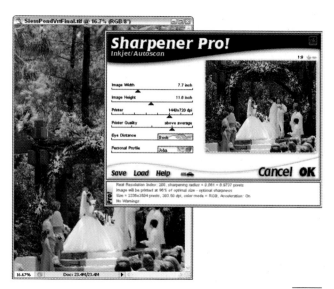

14-25

■ **I like lighter images, it seems, more so than many people. What if I always process an image to make it lighter? What problems will I have?**

Photography is such a great way to express how you relate to the world, which includes how you relate to photos. There is no arbitrary rule that photos have to be processed a certain way. It is true that some types of processing will affect an image in such a way as to change its meaning or how it might be used, but if it works for you, go for it.

The one thing I would recommend, however, is that you do these adjustments to layers and save an image as a layered Photoshop file (.psd) for a master file that you can always go back to. This way if you decide your lighter interpretation of the image is not exactly as you want, you can easily reopen that master file and readjust it.

Some photographers use the original Raw file as this master. I think the original Raw file should be kept as the ultimate, revisable original, but I like to keep the Photoshop file with layers that represents my last interpretation of the image as a master. That is a lot easier and faster to open and just tweak an adjustment layer for a specific purpose.

I notice that Photoshop CS2 has a Smart Sharpen tool. Why don't you use that instead of Unsharp Mask?

I could, I suppose, say you can't teach old dogs new tricks, and once you learn Unsharp Mask, you never want to go back, but that wouldn't be true. I was really rooting for Smart Sharpen when I first saw it, and it may eventually prove very useful to the photographer. This tool does an excellent job of sharpening. It does some very nice things to edges without causing sharpening halos as easily as Unsharp Mask and makes images gain more sharpness quite easily.

I would love it except for one thing: the engineers left off the Threshold control. Smart Sharpen sharpens noise too much for my taste. Because of that, I don't find it as useful for sharpening digital camera images as I do Unsharp Mask. The Threshold control, in my experience, is a key control in affecting how noise appears in the image.

What if I sharpened the image in Camera Raw? Do I still use Unsharp Mask in Photoshop?

In most cases, if you do any sharpening early in the process, whether that is in Camera Raw or in the camera, you will do less or no sharpening in Photoshop with Unsharp Mask. This is dependent on how much sharpening was done before. The more sharpening done early, the less likely you will want to sharpen later. While how much sharpening you need and like is definitely a very personal thing, sharpening on top of sharpening can cause problems with image artifacts such as noise and edge haloing.

Most nonpro digital cameras, both SLR and non-SLR, tend to apply some sharpening to the image by default that shows up in JPEG files (many cameras will allow you to turn that off or down). That sharpening is not applied by Camera Raw, although it may be applied by the camera manufacturer's RAW processing software (you can turn it off if it does). This is a real advantage to shooting RAW because you can always control when and how you sharpen an image.

ALTERNATIVES TO CAMERA RAW

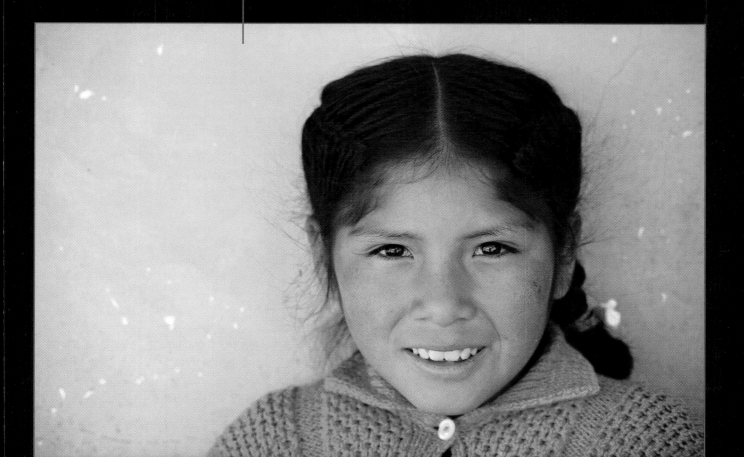

Adobe Camera Raw is the most popular way of converting and processing RAW files because of its connection to Photoshop. It simply is the easiest and most convenient way of adding Raw files to a photographer's digital workflow. Most other Raw conversions and adjustments must be made in separate, stand-alone programs whose interfaces are not the same as Photoshop. Although many features are similar, there is not that congruence of programs.

There are certain purposes, however, when other methods of converting and processing Raw files can be very useful. It is worth knowing a little about them. While I have seen all of the programs described below demonstrated and I have had hands-on experience with many, I simply don't use all of the cameras that would be needed in order to use all of these programs. Most are specific to one camera manufacturer; if you don't use a camera from that company, you cannot use a program specific to it. This group does not include every little program that can convert a Raw file, but all of those listed are available in both Windows and Mac versions and include the major programs available today.

I have spoken to all of the manufacturers so that I can fairly report on all of them. Obviously, I can't give you in-depth instruction on them, but then, that's not the purpose of this book. Because the photographer may have use for some of the unique characteristics of these Raw programs, it is worth presenting an overview about them.

WHY USE OTHER PROGRAMS?

Why would you even consider using another Raw conversion and adjustment program if Camera Raw does such a good job? It is entirely possible that you never will need to consider any other program than Camera Raw, but here are some reasons why you might:

> **Image quality.** The engineers at Adobe do a great job of putting together algorithms to get the most from a RAW file in Camera Raw. Yet, it is true that the very, very best in quality comes from the manufacturer's

own RAW program (though not necessarily the best in software interfaces — Japanese camera companies are not known for software design expertise). This makes sense because the manufacturer built the RAW file in the first place, so who else should be better able to process it? The difference, however, is generally not great and requires a lot of file magnification to see it. Is it worth it? This is really up to the photographer.

> **Color.** Camera Raw does a great job of building a color image from the RAW file data, but it is still Adobe's interpretation of what the color palette of the image should be. There is no such thing as color management when you're looking at translating a RAW file into a color file simply because the manufacturer has its own proprietary standards. Some photographers like the color better that results from the manufacturer's RAW converter or independent converter.

> **More controls.** Camera Raw has a fairly simple interface. While I appreciate this simplicity, there are some photographers who want more controls than Camera Raw offers. There are even some unique looks to color controls that offer more possibilities in a more intuitive interface than Camera Raw.

> **Unique features.** Almost all manufacturers build certain information into the metadata of the Raw file that tells their converter how to deal with that file, information that Camera Raw has to interpret in its own way (and sometimes can't even read). This may be as simple as certain white-balance information to unique tone curve interpretations built into the camera. In fact, Nikon encrypts the white balance information in their Raw files, which means that Camera Raw can only do an approximation of the white balance set by the camera (auto or preset).

> **More and easier batch processing capabilities.** Many Raw converters allow batch processing to be done more completely and more easily than in Camera Raw.

This appendix summarizes the key features of the main Raw converters on the market at the time the book was written. Each has its advantages and every one of them will have its champions. They all include basic functions such as exposure and color adjustments, as well as browser capabilities. This appendix starts with the camera manufacturers' Raw programs, in alphabetical order, then goes to the independent software, also in alphabetical order.

CAMERA SPECIFIC RAW CONVERTERS

CANON ZOOMBROWSER EX AND DIGITAL PHOTO PROFESSIONAL

Canon upgraded its Raw file format and came out with a new Raw software program when it introduced its Mark II series of cameras. Frankly, it really needed to do that. Even Canon admitted its EOS File Utility program left a lot to be desired (for a time this was the only Canon software that opened and converted Canon Raw files). Digital Photo Professional (DPP) was developed to bring Canon Raw file processing up to speed with the rest of the digital world and was introduced with the EOS-1D Mark II camera.

Today, Canon includes basic Raw conversion features in its ZoomBrowser EX as well as the advanced controls in DPP. While ZoomBrowser EX is a good browser program for Raw and JPEG files and offers Raw conversion capabilities that use Canon's own proprietary algorithms, in reality, that is about it. The program acts like simple point-and-shoot camera software with very little control. For serious processing of RAW files, it really doesn't offer the photographer a lot.

With the Mark II .CR2 Raw files and DPP, new capabilities and flexibility in processing Canon Raw images arrived, but more important, they could be processed in DPP with totally new algorithms. DPP was developed totally in response to photographers who wanted a better Raw processor from the manufacturer. It was built totally from scratch and even allows processing of JPEG files.

DPP is designed for more speed, and it is faster than Camera Raw. The program is designed for the pro and its interface shows that. It includes a whole range of valuable controls, including tone curves, exposure compensation, white balance, dynamic range, brightness, contrast, color saturation, ICC Profile embedding, and more. The program can even save adjustments to a file (like Camera Raw) that can then be loaded and applied to other RAW files. DPP also has a great feature that might be something worth considering by Adobe: a comparison mode that allows original and edited images to be seen side by side or in a split image.

Another feature that I like is the use of a very intuitive and flexible color wheel for color balance adjustments. DPP also offers a cropping tool like Camera Raw, CMYK printer simulation, batch conversion, and much more. Its batch conversion allows continuous work on images while other files are rendered and saved in the background, similar to Camera Raw.

FUJIFILM HS-V2 SOFTWARE

HS-V2 is Fujifilm's oddly named software designed for its S-series digital cameras. It includes the Raw File Converter EX as well as shooting software for more control over the camera itself (such as remote control of the camera from a laptop). To understand the importance of Raw File Converter EX to the S-series of cameras, it is worth understanding that Fujifilm cameras use a unique honeycomb pattern to the photo sites on their sensors. No other sensor manufacturer uses such a pattern. This requires an entirely different interpretation of the pixels than any other Raw file.

Consequently, many Fujifilm S-series camera owners have found the only way to get the best conversion of their Raw files is to use the Fujifilm software. Early versions of Camera Raw simply could not do the job. I have been told that the latest version of Camera Raw has corrected that problem. You would have to try both to see.

The Raw File Converter EX includes tonal curve adjustments, white balance controls (including a color wheel of sorts), a gray picker, saturation settings, something called Sensitization (a sort of +/- exposure compensation control), and more. In addition, it includes a very good interpolation algorithm tuned specifically to the honeycomb sensor that essentially doubles the effective megapixels of the camera.

NIKON CAPTURE

Nikon Capture is a well-thought-out Raw conversion program that offers added benefits to Nikon users and for use of the NEF file, Nikon's type of Raw file. This program was developed from the start to help pros make the most of a Raw file's capabilities and has continually evolved over the many years it has been on the market. Nikon has managed to keep Capture current with all versions of NEF files, and even offers a plug-in for Photoshop to make its use more convenient by loading directly into Photoshop. For a long time, however, Capture had a reputation of being very slow, especially with Mac computers, but that seems to be past history now.

Like most Raw converters, Capture lets you crop the image, adjust its size and resolution, change exposure and color, and batch process. It offers a different interpretation of colors than Camera Raw, but both are certainly good. It includes a Histogram tool that allows you to click on an image and capture that point's brightness value on the histogram display for further adjustment. Other unique features include the Noise Reduction filter that works well on images shot with higher ISO settings, image straightening (to adjust for a crooked horizon), the highly distinctive D-Lighting feature (a semi-automated way of getting more from poorly exposed images), an LCH editor (luminance/chroma/hue including curves for luminance and chroma), a Color Booster palette, and Image Dust Off (to remove problems from sensor dust). In addition, Capture allows you to add nik Color Efex filters for even more control at the RAW stage.

Nikon makes a big deal about its NEF files being able to store several things: the Raw data, a thumbnail version of the photo, and an Instruction Set. That really isn't that different than most modern RAW files, but according to Nikon, its Instruction Set has more information and is more easily used for better workflow than competitors. Capture does have an excellent feature set to access NEF file capabilities. You can also save multiple Instruction Sets and apply them to more than one file.

KODAK PROFESSIONAL DCS PHOTO DESK

Kodak has long been an important part of the digital camera landscape, though its importance to the pro and photo-enthusiast has varied considerably. Its present digital SLRs use either Canon or Nikon lenses, but the body and files are all Kodak. With the Kodak Raw file, these cameras are capable of producing very large image files from their 14-megapixel sensors.

Professional DCS Photo Desk provides all the basic tools for adjustment of Raw images. It includes a tone curve with histogram, color balance sliders, and more. However, the most interesting part of this program is geared toward a big market for the Kodak digital SLRs, — wedding and event photographers. This is called DCS Custom Looks, and with the appropriate camera, offers DCS Wedding and Event Looks. These offer higher image quality for the unique needs of these situations and provide better shadow detail and rendering.

KONICA MINOLTA DiMAGE MASTER

Konica Minolta came late to the digital SLR party, but has brought a great package to it in the Maxxum 7D. With that camera, the company also introduced DiMAGE Master for image management and Raw file conversion. Their engineers developed something called their 3D Lookup Table for Raw processing that they claim enables more accurate color reproduction. There is likely some truth in that as typically the camera manufacturer can do excellent color translation with its own Raw files.

Like most other Raw programs, this one includes browser capabilities, but what sets that apart from the rest is an interesting Examiner window. This allows you to make comparisons among several images at once, allowing them to be compared visually as well as through analysis of exposure, histogram, and white balance.

For image processing, DiMAGE Master features a Photofinisher window that includes basic adjustment choices such as white balance and tone-curve, but it also has a variation palette to allow you to compare an image with slightly corrected versions around it. There is also a nice feature, a "focus checker," that enlarges just a selected portion of a photo to check its sharpness. Batch processing is also available.

OLYMPUS STUDIO

Olympus Studio is a multipurpose, digital processing software that can be used for managing and viewing Olympus digital images as well as high-speed processing of Olympus Raw files. It also includes the ability to remotely control Olympus E-series digital SLRs. It includes some standard browsing features, but adds a unique Light Box Mode. This allows some interesting capabilities for working with multiple images, including a two or four group of magnified photos for comparison and a Collection Area to make sorting of images easier.

The Raw conversion part of Studio includes the adjustment of exposure compensation (+/- 2 stops in increments of 0.1 steps), overall white-balance control, white-balance fine adjustments in up to +/- 10 steps (including gray point selection), +/- five steps of contrast adjustment, +/- five steps of sharpness adjustment, five steps of saturation change, a very interesting memory color emphasis selection (lets you choose presets like red emphasis or body warmth emphasis), 10 steps of false color suppression control (makes better color interpretations from a RAW file), and 10 steps of noise reduction. Batch processing is possible.

PENTAX PHOTO BROWSER/LABORATORY

Pentax offers its browser and Raw converter in two different programs, Photo Browser and Laboratory. Photo Laboratory is a standard sort of Raw converter designed specifically for the Pentax Raw files. It includes multiple white-balance controls as well as simple contrast and tonal range adjustments. There doesn't seem to be anything particularly unusual about it except that it is optimized for the Pentax files.

SIGMA PHOTO PRO

Sigma's digital cameras offer an unusual approach to digital photo files. You can only shoot Raw files. At first, the software was the only software that even recognized, let alone processed, the files. That is not true today. Sigma's foray into the digital SLR world is quite unique in that it is the only company to use the once-hyped Foveon sensor. This sensor promised improved color rendition but never really proved to be any better than the advanced sensors all the other camera companies used.

Photo Pro works in several ways to adjust white balance, exposure, color, and contrast. The X3F mode uses auto settings and manual adjustments to convert RAW data much like Camera Raw does. X3 Fill Light is an alternate mode that increases the dark values of images with high contrast or for backlit photos. The underexposed areas of the photo are increased in brightness without changing the highlights. In addition, the processing can be reversed, in a sense, allowing you to bring out highlight detail without changing dark areas.

INDEPENDENT RAW CONVERTERS

DxO RAW ENGINE

DxO Labs is a very unique company that offers software unlike anything else on the market. It doesn't simply offer programs for converting Raw or adjusting digital files: It goes in and analyzes specific cameras and lenses, then creates software that compensates for the weaknesses and limitations of those exact products, such as lens distortions (from astigmatism to barrel distortion to chromatic aberrations to vignetting) and image noise, all at the pixel level. The software won't work if you try to use it for lenses or cameras that aren't included; it is that specific in its correction of lens and camera problems.

DxO Optics Pro is the main software. Because it is based specifically on defined and recognized issues in image files, it is not adjustable; you just tell it which photos to work on and it just works. The company now includes its proprietary Raw converter, DxO Raw Engine, with Optics Pro. Based on its specialized research on specific cameras and lenses, the company developed Raw Engine with unique algorithms that it claims does a better job of putting together the Raw pixels for images that are sharper and more detailed. It also says its software creates images with less ghosting, false colors, or misaligned pixels. You might consider that the standard hype of software companies, but I have used DxO Optics Pro and found it quite remarkable in its capabilities. I have also met and talked with the key engineering types who run DxO labs, and to them, none of this is marketing hype. They can demonstrate very credible support for all of their claims. DxO Raw Engine includes all of the standard RAW conversion adjustments.

PHASE ONE CAPTURE ONE

Capture One was one of the first of the independent Raw converters and has been among the leading and most respected of the independents since it first came on the market. Phase One is a company that started with the sole purpose of marketing high-end digital imaging products, so no one thought it unusual that it would come out with Raw software geared to the professional. Right from the start, Capture One software has offered high image quality and speed. Speed was not always a key part of other Raw conversion programs, including the manufacturers'.

Capture One comes in several versions, which have changed over the years, but at the time this book was published included Capture One Pro (the top-of-the-line version with the most features), Capture One DB (purely for photographers using Phase One digital backs), and Capture One LE (lower priced, lighter version of Pro). All are designed for meeting the workflow needs of the professional, including little touches like automatically optimizing the interface for horizontal and vertical images.

The software includes a useful browser function and keeps all of its adjustments on tabs like Camera Raw. It includes, as they say, a full range of advanced features, including full color management, multiple tone response curves, unlimited batch capabilities, and a useful multiple output feature to allow you to immediately get multiple files from a single conversion. It includes camera profiles, plus the ability to edit those profiles; a color editor; and IPTC (metadata captioning) support.

PHOTOSHOP ELEMENTS

Photoshop Elements is a popular sibling of Photoshop. It is not a dumbed-down or excerpted version of Photoshop like the old Photoshop LE was (Photoshop LE was never a very good alternative to Photoshop). This program is specifically designed to enhance the average photographer's digital processing of photographs while using some of the core elements of Photoshop's processing engine. There are actually some very useful features in Photoshop Elements that are not included in Photoshop, such as the Selection Brush (you can do something similar in Photoshop, but there is no specific tool like this one).

Before Photoshop Elements 3.0, Raw files could not be processed in this program. You would have to use the camera manufacturer's Raw converter or an independent program, then reopen the files into Elements. With Photoshop Elements 3.0 and 4.0, Adobe adds Raw conversion capabilities based on Camera Raw to this easy-to-use program.

When you open a Raw file into Photoshop Elements 3.0 or 4.0, you see an interface that looks much like Camera Raw. For all practical purposes, it is simply a variant of Camera Raw. Nearly all of the key controls discussed in this book are there. Some of the advanced capabilities are not here, however; there is no tone curve, you can't do batch processing, you can't select an image size, and you can't choose a color space. The interface is definitely simpler and does not include multiple tabs for different adjustments. Still, with core Raw adjustments, you can do just about everything that is described in this book. It certainly does bring Raw capabilities to more casual photographers.

PIXMATIC RAWSHOOTER

Pixmatic RawShooter is a relatively new arrival on the Raw conversion scene and wouldn't be grouped with the major players except for one thing: Corel has thrown its support behind it. That suddenly gives this software a much bigger presence in the marketplace. At the time of this writing it is a free download, so there is no cost but time for anyone who wants to try it.

RawShooter offers all the standard Raw conversion controls: color and exposure correction, noise suppression, and so on, and some special tools, including Detail Extraction and Fill Light to make exposure and contrast adjustments faster and more intuitive. It also includes strong batch processing capabilities and a Raw browser feature. The browser feature is actually quite interesting and makes sorting and editing Raw files quite easy (which may make the program worth considering even if you do all of your processing in Camera Raw). What it does is create a slide show of sorts that allows you to quickly go through all of the images in a folder, seeing them sized as large as possible on your monitor. Then you prioritize each one when seen as to how you want to deal with it.

The company claims this Raw converter is the fastest on the market, which is especially important for batch conversions. From what I have seen, I would say it easily matches or beats any other program in that area.

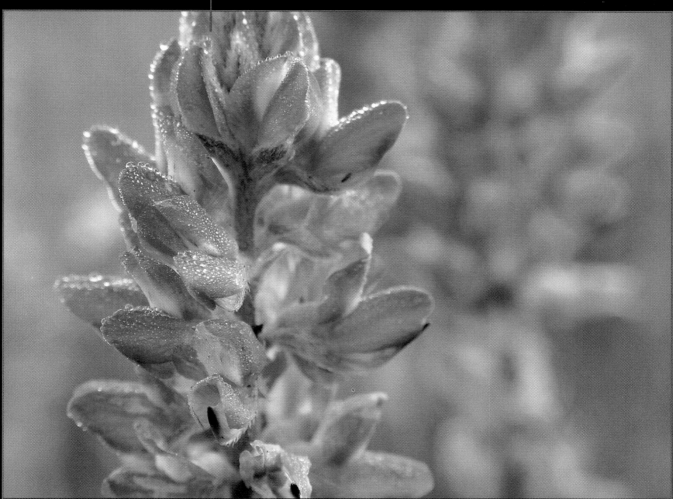

Adobe RGB: a working color space based on the standard computer RGB colors created by Adobe Systems. It includes a wide gamut of colors that makes it a very flexible color space for using in Photoshop.

Algorithm: the computations, formulas and procedures used in digital devices and programs to process data.

Anti-Aliasing: using software to soften and blend rough edges (called aliased).

Archival Storage: using external, non-magnetic media such as CDs to store information long-term.

Artifact: defects in an image or other recorded data created by the tool used to record or output; something in an image that did not exist in the original scene but was inadvertently added to the photo by the technology.

Batch processing: a way of making one or more changes, such as new file type or image size, to a group or "batch" of image files all at once.

Bit: the smallest unit of data in a computer.

Bit-depth: this refers to the number of bits required to represent the color in a pixel. With more bit-depth, more colors are available. This increases exponentially. True photo color starts at 8-bit.

Browser: 1. a program that's used for examining sites on the World Wide Web; 2. a software program designed to show small, thumbnail images of digital files.

CCD (charge-coupled device): a common type of image sensor used in digital cameras. The CCD actually only sees black-and-white images and must have red, green, and blue filters built into it in order to capture color.

CD-ROM (CD-Read-Only Memory): a compact disc that contains information that can only be read, not updated or recorded over.

Chip: common term for a computer-integrated circuit; the "brains" of a computer.

Chroma: noise in a digital image that has a strong color component to it; commonly found in dark areas in long exposures. Also called color noise.

CMOS (complementary metal oxide semiconductor): this is a chip used as a sensor in digital cameras. CMOS sensors use less energy than CCD chips.

CMYK (cyan, magenta, yellow, black): these are the subtractive primary colors and the basis for the CMYK color space. They're used in so-called four-color printing processes used in books and magazines because they produce the most photo-like look for publications.

Color noise: noise in a digital image that has a strong color component to it; commonly found in dark areas in long exposures. Also known as chroma.

Color space: colors in the computer are described by a set of numbers and these numbers can be interpreted differently by different devices. Models of color are based on a range of color that can be described by a particular digital device. This is its color space. There are many color spaces, though the two main ones used for photography are RGB and CMYK. Within those spaces are subsets of spaces such as Adobe RGB 1998 (larger) and sRGB (smaller).

Continuous tone: the appearance of smooth color or black-and-white gradations as in a photograph.

Copyright: a legal term that denotes rights of ownership and, thus, control over usage of written or other creative material. Unless otherwise noted, assume all images are copyrighted and can't be used by anyone without permission of the photographer.

Data compression: the use of algorithms to reduce the amount of data needed to reconstruct a file.

DPI (dots per inch): resolution of a peripheral as a measurement of the number of horizontal or vertical dots it's able to resolve in input or output. This is confusing because dpi for a scanner is the same as ppi of an image, yet both are different than the dpi of a printer. Dpi for a printer refers to the way ink droplets are laid down on paper.

Dye-sublimation: printing technology that results in continuous-tone images by passing gaseous color dyes through a semi-permeable membrane on the media surface.

Pro Glossary

Dynamic range: the difference between the highest and the lowest values, as in the brightest highlights and the darkest shadows in an image.

EVF: electronic viewfinder.

Exposure: 1. the combination of shutter speed and f-stop used in a camera to control the light hitting the sensor or film; 2. a specific control in Camera Raw that affects highlights.

File Format: how the data that makes up an image is defined and organized for storage on a disk or other media. Standard image formats include JPEG, RAW and TIFF.

FireWire: a very fast connection (meaning lots of data transmitted quickly) for linking peripherals to the computer; also called IEEE 1394 and i.Link.

Graphics tablet and pen: a way of controlling your cursor's movement and actions by using an electronic tablet that senses where its graphic pen is moving; an alternative to the mouse.

Gray Scale or (Grayscale): a black-and-white image composed of a range of gray levels from black to white.

Histogram: a very important tool for adjusting a photo that is a graph of pixels at different brightness levels in the photo, with black represented at the left, white at the right and gray in-between.

Hue: the actual color of a color.

Inkjet: a digital printing technology where tiny droplets of ink are placed on the paper to form characters or images.

Interpolation: a way of increasing the apparent resolution of an image by increasing the number of pixels in an image by filling in the gaps between the original pixels.

JPEG (Joint Photographic Experts Group): a file format that smartly compresses image information to create smaller files; the files are reconstructed later. JPEG files do lose quality as compression increases.

JPEG Artifacts: image defects due to file size compression that look like tiny rectangles or squarish grain.

Lens aberration: a defect in the optical path of a lens that creates optical artifacts such as color fringing that can affect color and sharpness of a lens.

LCD (liquid crystal display): a display technology used for small monitors that act as viewfinders and playback display for digital cameras.

Lossless compression: any form of file compression technique where no loss of data occurs.

Lossy compression: any form of file compression technique where some loss of data occurs.

Luminance noise: noise in a digital image that looks like a dark/light pattern without colors in it (other than the original subject colors).

Mouse: a piece of hardware for controlling your cursor's movement and actions by using a handheld electronic device that senses movement.

Noise: an artifact of the digital technologies, largely the sensor, that shows up in the photograph as a fine pattern that looks like grain or sand texture.

Photosite: the individual, actual photosensitive site on a sensor that captures the brightness for a single pixel in the image. There is one photosite for every pixel in the image.

Pixel: short for picture element (pix/picture, el/element). The smallest element of a picture that can be controlled by the computer.

PPI (pixels per inch): a way of measuring linear resolution of an image and refers to how the pixels are spaced, meaning the number of pixels per inch in an image, often used interchangeably with dpi.

PSD file: the native file format for Photoshop and Photoshop Elements. It allows the saving of layers, layer masks and more.

RAM (Random Access Memory): the computer's memory that's actually active for use in programs; comes on special chips.

Raw file: an image file that is minimally processed after it comes from the sensor in a camera. Data comes from the sensor and is translated to digital in the A/D converter; that data is then packaged for the Raw file. A Raw file is not generic; there are actually proprietary files made by each camera manufacturer.

Resolution: the density of pixels in an image or the number of pixels or dots per inch in an image or that a device, such as a scanner, can capture.

RGB: the primary color system of a computer based on red, green and blue, the additive primary colors. Computer monitors (CRT and LCD) display RGB-based screen images.

Ringing: white, ring-like border at distinct edges in a photo when that photo has been oversharpened.

Saturation: the amount of brilliance or intensity of a color; how colorful or dull a color is.

Sensor: the light-sensing part of a digital camera, usually a CCD or CMOS chip.

sRGB: a common color space in the RGB color system that is more restricted than others.

Thumbnail: a small, low-resolution version of an image.

TIFF (Tagged Image File Format): an important, high-quality image format common to most image-processing programs.

Tone Curve: an adjustment for tonal values in an image that offers a great deal of flexibility. It appears first as a 45° angle line running up to the right in a graph. When that line is clicked on and moved, it changes tones in the image. The upper part of the curve is light, the bottom dark. Moving the curve up lightens tones, down darkens tones. It is possible to move parts of the curve in different directions.

Tonal range: the difference in brightness from the brightest to the darkest tones in an image.

USB: a standard computer connection for linking peripherals to the computer; high-speed USB 2.0 is very fast, comparable to FireWire.

Unsharp Masking (USM): the name is misleading because it is based on an old commercial printing term; it is a highly controllable adjustment used for sharpening an image and includes three settings: amount, radius, and threshold.

Vignetting: the darkening or lightening of the outer part of an image due to the way the photograph was shot (either the lens used or special vignetting techniques employed).

White Balance: a special digital control that tells digital still and video cameras how to correctly represent color based on the color temperatures of different light sources. All cameras have automatic white balance; most also let photographers adjust it manually.

index

continued

Index

345